THE STORY OF ALL OF US

MANKIND™

BY PAMELA D. TOLER

HISTORY

RUNNING PRESS
PHILADELPHIA · LONDON

Published by Running Press,
A Member of the Perseus Books Group

Books published by Running Press are available at special discounts for bulk purchases
in the United States by corporations, institutions, and other organizations. For more
information, please contact the Special Markets Department at the Perseus Books Group,
2300 Chestnut Street, Suite 200, Philadelphia, PA 19103, or call (800) 810-4145, ext. 5000,
or e-mail special.markets@perseusbooks.com.

All the first-person narratives are fictionalized accounts based on historical evidence.

ISBN 978-0-7624-4703-9
Library of Congress Control Number: 2012946700

E-book ISBN 978-0-7624-4717-6

9 8 7 6 5 4 3 2
Digit on the right indicates the number of this printing.

Edited by Geoffrey Stone

Running Press Book Publishers
2300 Chestnut Street
Philadelphia, PA 19103-4371

Visit us on the web!
www.runningpress.com | www.history.com

CONTENTS

FOREWORD

From our very first days on earth, we humans have confronted enormous challenges. Erupting volcanoes that blotted out the sun. Cruel ice ages that lasted for centuries. Deadly plagues that invaded our bodies and ruptured our cells. Ferocious weapons of mass destruction.

Time after time, unforeseen dangers have threatened to bring our story to an abrupt end.

But *Mankind* is also a story of triumph, because through it all, humanity has risen to meet every challenge. What does not kill us makes us stronger, and in learning to overcome adversity, we have made one great leap forward after another.

Across the last ten thousand years, these leaps have taken us from tiny bands of hunters following flocks of animals across empty landscapes to our great modern cities, crowded with tens of millions of people and crackling with energy.

Mankind is an ambitious and entertaining account of this journey. It tells our story in a new, exciting way, in vivid images and in the words of the people who lived through the events.

Unlike history books you may have read before, *Mankind* looks in the most surprising places for keys to explain how we got here.

Some keys lie in the planet itself—in the tides of the oceans, the contours of mountains, the minerals we mine from the ground.

Others are in our own bodies—how we see, in our blood, in the antibodies that protect us against infection.

Many are hidden in things we use everyday—humble goods like pepper, salt, sugar, and ice, all of which have played their part in the story.

Others still come from the mysterious remains of the past that dot the earth—the pyramids, Stonehenge, the Great Wall of China.

At times, we even have looked far beyond our own world—at the formation of stars or solar flares or the way the sun's gravity causes our planet to wobble and tilt on its axis as we spin through space.

And often the answers are found in how things work—in the spin on a bullet as it leaves a rifle, in the perfect balance of an arch, or in the flow of water along a Roman aqueduct.

Mankind pulls the latest findings of historians and scientists together into a single gripping narrative, and shows how the lives of billions of individuals have come together to build the world we live in today.

Some of these individuals are famous names—Julius Caesar, Genghis Khan, George Washington, Abraham Lincoln—whose decisions changed the direction of history.

But others were just ordinary people caught up in extraordinary events—like Agnolo di Tura, who had to bury his own wife and children when the Black Death killed half the people in his hometown. Or like Alice Harris, a missionary in the Congo whose photographs exposed one of the most horrifying crimes ever committed against humanity.

From the taming of fire to the invention of iron, from the birth of Buddhism to the crucifixion of Jesus, from the fall of Rome to the Industrial Revolution, from the earliest formation of democracy to the triumph of the civil rights movement, from the printing press to the computer—this book shows us history from the inside. It is alive, immediate, and always surprising.

Since the Stone Age, the pace of change has been speeding up, and one of the greatest lessons we learn from history is that the world will change more in the 21st century than in all previous times combined. It will present mankind with new challenges, which will take forms that we cannot yet even imagine.

History shows us who we are and where we have come from; and it also teaches us that the possibilities before us are endless. The human spirit has shown itself capable of meeting any challenge.

But history also shows that nothing is ever guaranteed.

If we are to go on succeeding in our struggle, triumphing over adversity as we have done so often in the past, we all need to understand our own story.

And for this, there is no better place to start than *Mankind.*

— IAN MORRIS
STANFORD UNIVERSITY

INTRODUCTION

We call it the *big bang*:

13.7 billion years ago, when time and space collided to produce the pure energy that ultimately formed matter and every species that ever lived, including us. Our human bodies are made, as are the skies, oceans, and mountains of planet Earth, from this same swirling mass of elements, later named *carbon*, *oxygen*, and *hydrogen*.

AFTER THE EARTH COOLED ENOUGH TO FORM ITS

SPHERE, IT TOOK ANOTHER HALF BILLION YEARS FOR

IN ITS DEEP OCEANIC VENTS, AND TWO BILLION MORE

From specks of star dust to single-cell life-forms, the evolution of the human race into a form recognizable as the species we are today began some 150,000 years ago.

Mankind has existed for a fraction of time in the history of the universe, and most of it spent in a life-and-death struggle for survival—with no guarantees of success at any point, not even the present.

Mankind: The Story of All of Us retraces the path of learning that made us masters of fire and iron, gave us the comforts of food and shelter, and remade us into inventors, builders, and space travelers. Perhaps the most unlikely accomplishment of all on our zigzag learning curve as a species is our survival. Surprise has been the only constant in human history.

If there is one key to our longevity, it has been our ability to adapt to frequent, often violent change. We have turned our most vulnerable weaknesses into strengths, beginning with our relatively small size and lack of speed compared to other mammals. Such an extreme physical disadvantage forced us to develop and employ bigger brains to outwit our foes, whether man, beast, or vast swings of temperature and climate.

A fair amount of luck was involved in humanity's triumph over the astonishing odds wrought by

ice ages. Mankind has faced predators five or ten times our size and strength. Also, unlike other species, we are born relatively fragile and unformed, requiring a long period of parental care that left our earliest ancestors vulnerable to violence, illness, and sudden death.

Physicist Paul Davis attributes our ability to persevere against these overwhelming odds to a chain of "Goldilocks moments" in which everything needed to help us adapt occurred exactly the way it needed to—or close enough to get us through another ten or twenty thousand years until a continent thawed or migration brought us closer to a vibrant river, the perfect prey, or a stretch of fertile soil.

Planetary and human history is traditionally presented in time lines lacking any visceral sense of the huge obstacles and near misses that pushed the human species to become smarter, more adept creatures. In third grade social studies, high school world history, or college surveys of Western civilization, a typical textbook follows an illusory linear progression. And while a time line can be a useful tool, it generally starts too late, since, in the context of the universe, we've been here barely long enough to catch our breath. Not only is the textbook time line too short; it is also too narrow, focusing with a few exceptions

UNIQUE CONFIGURATION OF ELEMENTS AND ATMO-
THE FIRST SINGLE-CELLED ORGANISMS TO BLOSSOM
FOR THEM TO BEGIN TO DIVIDE AND DIVERSIFY.

on humanity itself, with no reference to the world around us.

In fact, our history was shaped not just by our own actions, collective and individual, but also by incidents as large as a tilt in the earth's orbit and as small as a genetic mutation in a grain of wheat. Human evolution has never been a forward march of progress consisting of evenly divided positive steps from archaic humans to their modern counterparts, each change in our appearance and behavior an improvement on the last. Several new hominid species coexisted in Africa between 2.5 million BCE and the arrival of modern man in 150,000 BCE. Which one would triumph and become our direct ancestor was far from settled as recently as fifty thousand years ago.

The majority of evolutionary changes have been relatively minor things—the refinement of an opposable thumb, a fractional increase in cranium size, the ability to stay upright long enough and stretch an arm far enough to grab a fruit from a low-hanging branch—the consequences of which play out incrementally over thousands of generations. This change in perspective does not detract from the significance of each Goldilocks moment. On the contrary, it underscores the precarious nature of the human drama: depended on the right behavioral adaptation meeting a hospitable setting.

In the chapters ahead we tell the story of pivotal points when natural forces intersected with human ingenuity and a bit of luck to make (or break) us as a species. In these times and places, the human race faced mysteries and obstacles so

> Our history was shaped not just by our own actions, collective and individual, but also by incidents as large as a tilt in the earth's orbit and as small as a genetic mutation in a grain of wheat.

formidable that if they had not been solved and surmounted, chances are we would not be here today. By reliving these transitional events, we can better understand what our predecessors were up against when they made the huge leaps forward that ultimately ensured their survival—and set the stage for ours.

So we begin at mankind's beginning, when staying alive translated into an unrelenting, often dangerous search for the day's food.

1

SEEDS *of* CHANGE

THE HUMAN RACE WAS BORN ON THE GRASSLANDS AND FORESTS OF AFRICA'S GREAT RIFT VALLEY, A FRACTURE IN THE AFRICAN CONTINENTAL PLATE WHERE DIVERSE ECOLOGICAL SYSTEMS AND

human-friendly temperature ranges made it the perfect laboratory for the development of a hairless, toolmaking ape. It is here that we join human evolution reached its first critical pivot: the transition from ape to human.

We have no precise dates for such monumental advances in the human condition as hunting and fire making, but scientists have amassed substantial evidence about what life was like before and after these breakthroughs. These traces of early human history come to us as artifacts: tools, abandoned campsites, ruined villages, hidden art, and skeleton fragments.

In recent years, we've learned to read ancient artifacts more closely than we could in the past. Geologists study climate changes using drill cores from lake sediment. Paleobotanists trace the evolution of foodstuffs using fossilized pollen DNA testing and sequencing. Techniques such as biomechanical modeling of teeth and bone scanning give paleontologists and paleoanthropologists a window through which to view the relationships between humans and animals, and between humans and other humans, across time and space. With the help of these new technologies and methods, we are finding more and more that we are all part of the same whole.

On the most basic level of survival, we know that our earliest human ancestors were scavengers who foraged for fruit, nuts, and seeds. They ate birds' eggs, termites and ants, and dead birds or animals, at least when they were lucky enough to find them. Even after someone picked up a rock, threw it at a rabbit, and invented hunting, most of the diet consumed by these small human bands—men, women with children, and extended family members—still came from their collective efforts at foraging for wild grains, berries, and roots.

But how long ago did mankind make its appearance? That depends on how you define being human. If you don't stand up and walk on your own two feet, you're an ape, not a human. And while there is no clear moment at which we can draw a line between apes and humans, the Human Genome Project repeatedly brings us one step closer. Historians and scientists now believe that the first protohumans appeared in East Africa as early as 5.5 million years ago, but they weren't direct ancestors of early humans. Like modern apes, they could walk upright for a brief time if circumstances required it, but for the most part they were tree climbers and knuckle walkers.

The first true hominid—a member of the family Hominidae, which includes modern humans—showed up 2 million years later, around 3.5 million years ago. Paleoanthropologists call her Australopithecus, or the southern ape; we'll keep it simple and call her Lucy.

LEFT: *Our early ancestors made the first tools more than 2 million years ago by striking one stone against another. Simple choppers evolved over the centuries into cleavers, hand axes and finely worked stone blades.*

MEET LUCY

Australopithecus made headlines in 1974 when an expedition
under the leadership of American paleoanthropologist Donald
Johanson discovered a substan-
tially complete female skeleton
in the Afar region of Ethiopia.
Members of the expedition
named her "Lucy" after the Bea-
tles song "Lucy in the Sky with
Diamonds," which they played
over and over on the evening
they celebrated the find. Members of the international press
quickly labeled her the "missing
link"; she helped all of us understand the origins of humanity.

Finding Lucy was more than
just a human-interest story in
the evening news. Her skeleton
was the oldest specimen of the
genus *Australopithecus* found
to date. ("Earliest" can always
change when you're talking
about prehistory. The new earliest is always just one dig site
away.) More important, enough
of Lucy's skeleton remained to
establish that *Australopithecus*
did indeed walk upright, like a
human.

In 1975, Johanson's team
found more specimens of what
is now termed *Australopithecus
afarensis* at a single site in the
same region, which they called
"the First Family."

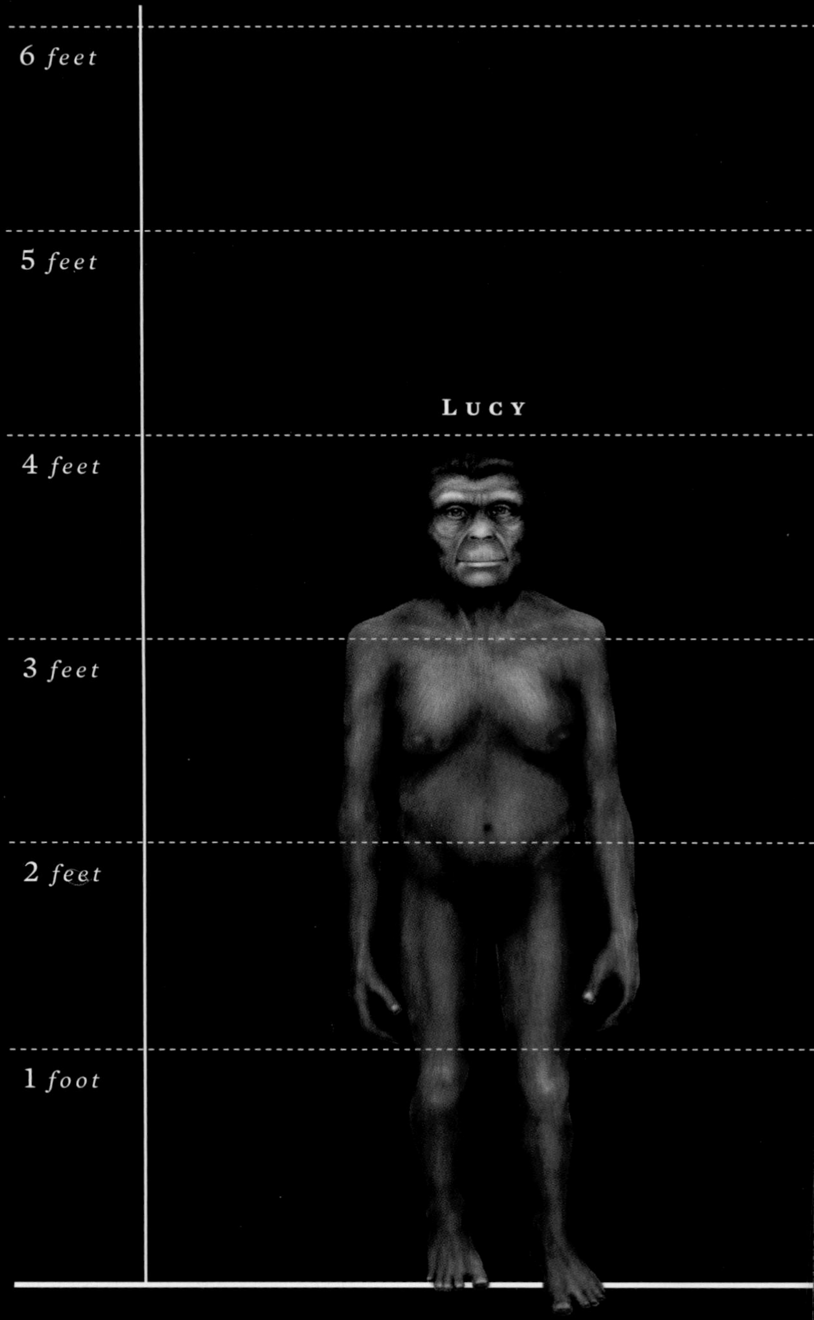

6 *feet*

5 *feet*

L U C Y

4 *feet*

3 *feet*

2 *feet*

1 *foot*

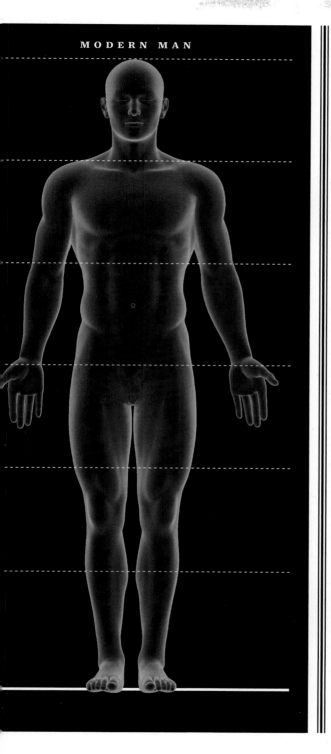

LUCY WAS CLOSER TO AN APE than an early human. She stood only three or four feet tall and had a brain about the size of an orange. Her face was more like an ape's than a human's, her arms were longer than ours, and her fingers curled like those of a chimpanzee. She may have chosen to use those long arms to climb a tree, like an ape, but she had all the physical equipment she needed to walk upright on two feet. In fact, she was probably better designed for walking upright than we are. The human pelvis is a compromise between standing upright and giving birth to babies with large skulls and sizable brains.

Being bipedal has a major advantage: it leaves your hands free. Combine that with the opposable thumbs that small primates developed fifty million years earlier and you're ready to pick up a tool. Lucy did. She probably didn't make tools, but she used rocks and sticks to help her hunt for food and fend off predators.

After Lucy, our story gets more complicated. There may have been up to one hundred hominid species that coexisted in Africa between Lucy's time and the arrival of modern humans around 150,000 BCE. We don't know how they relate to each other, or which species we can call our direct ancestors, but after much controversy, anthropologists are in general agreement about two groups of proto-humans with whom they think we have more direct familial connections.

Homo habilis, literally the "handy man," is considered the first protohuman, and he carries the distinction of being an adept toolmaker. He appeared in East Africa around 2.5 million BCE, making him a contemporary of some of Lucy's descendants. *Homo habilis* was still much smaller than a modern man, but his brain was twice the size of a chimpanzee's. He learned to hunt and to make crude stone tools by using one piece of flint to chip flakes off another. One of the great chicken-and-egg questions of human development is whether *Homo habilis* learned to make tools because he had a larger brain or whether the exercise of creating tools developed a larger brain. Chances are it will remain a mystery.

With *Homo erectus*, who lived around 1.5 million years ago, hominid life begins to look more familiar to us. *Homo erectus* probably had only rudimentary language ability, but he made more refined stone tools, most notably the hand ax; began to cook his food; established semipermanent camps; and perhaps formed long-term male-female bonds.

Homo erectus, like his fellow hominids, could raise a sharpened stick and bring down a small animal. But he was the first to go the next step and cook raw meat over an open flame. With the domestication of fire, *Homo erectus* changed everything for the *Homo sapiens* who came after, making the intentional use of fire the first Goldilocks moment in human evolution.

FIRE

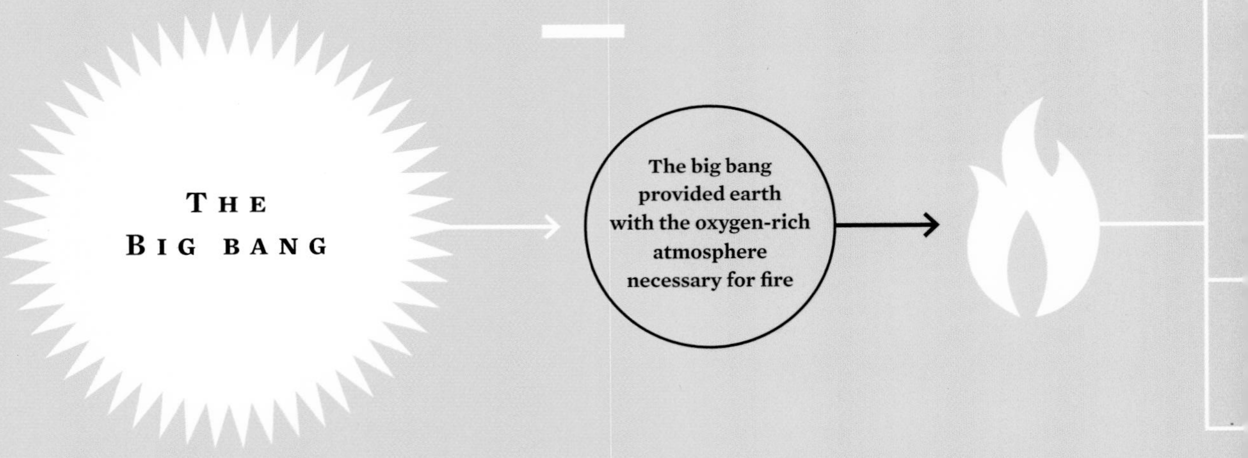

THE BIG BANG

The big bang provided earth with the oxygen-rich atmosphere necessary for fire

Mastery of fire was the first step toward civilization, and it could only happen on Earth. Fire requires three elements: fuel, heat, and oxygen. It's the oxygen that's the tricky part.

Oxygen is the third most abundant element in the sun after hydrogen and helium. It is the most abundant element not only in the rocks, meteorites, and asteroids that litter space, but also in the terrestrial planets. But most of that wonderful oxygen isn't available in a form that either human lungs or hungry flames can use. Gaseous oxygen is one of the

Today, sealed in our twenty-first-century man-made environments, it is hard to fathom the competition for survival that occupied our early human ancestors from sunup to sundown. It is even more difficult to imagine living without the benefit of millennia of human know-how, and without language, history, science—or fire.

BASED ON ANCIENT MYTHS and primitive art we can speculate that the earliest hominids learned the fine points of hunting by watching and imitating the actions of the nonhuman hunters with whom they shared the Great Rift Valley, and later, Eurasia and the Americas. Unlike the animal-teachers with whom they often competed for the same prey—rabbits, small cats, and warthogs—early humans had no sharp teeth or claws. To compete with other predators, our ancient relatives employed stone-tipped spears fashioned with their more dexterous limbs and fingers, and applied their superior problem-solving skills to outthink their prey and work in cooperation with other human hunters. With these assets in place, the prehistoric hunt was finally on.

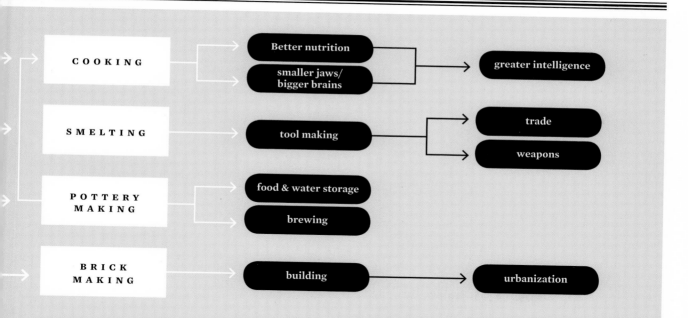

first by-products of life, produced by the blue-green bacteria that covered the earth's oceans three billions years ago as they photosynthesized sunlight and carbon dioxide into food. From the viewpoint of those early bacteria, oxygen was toxic pollution, pure and simple. Over time, life developed in such a way that some creatures produced oxygen and others consumed it, creating an atmosphere with a stable oxygen level of 21 percent. (Mars comes in second among the terrestrial planets, at 9 percent.) That abundant supply of oxygen makes fire possible.

Chapter 1: SEEDS OF CHANGE

HUNT TO SURVIVE

TWO STRONG YOUNG MEN IN THEIR TWENTIES RUN with muscular legs through the brush, holding spears. One man signals to the other. Both stop and crouch down, using binocular vision to scan the horizon for signs of motion in the grass. The first man has seen something, and indicates it to the other, his brother. There ahead, an antelope is grazing.

A hundred feet behind, a woman stands, holding her spear, watching her men conduct the hunt. By her side, holding her free hand, is her toddler son. The mother leans down and puts her mouth next to the child's ear, urging the boy to keep quiet, and watch. He is learning his own future and the survival of his species. Concerned only with the present, mother and son watch as the men chase the warthog, their actions urgent and swift as they slip stealthily through the bush, out of the woman's sight.

The hunters sprint ahead, and again they stop. Crouching, the first man reaches into the dirt at his feet and pours some out of his hand to check the wind direction. They are upwind from their prey. They turn and reverse direction, stalking, low, and far enough away to remain out of the animal's sight and hearing range. The man in the lead stops and raises a hand, his other hand gripping his spear firmly. Suddenly the antelope bolts. Instantly the men are on their feet and running, chasing and encircling the animal. The first man releases his spear, landing it in the antelope's flank. The hunt ends in blood and victory.

Chapter 1: SEEDS OF CHANGE

Hours later, against a darkening sky, the two men are reunited with the woman and child. The group sits around a fire, with a skinned hog flank suspended above the fire pit, pierced by a stick. Juices drip from the carcass, causing flames to spike and tickle the meat as it turns shades of brown and charcoal black. While the family waits, there is time to savor the hunt, and to enjoy a rare opportunity to socialize and rest.

Once the meat is cooked and pulled from the flames, the men use their teeth and hands to strip it from the bone, chewing each piece thoroughly. The woman shreds hers into smaller bits, placing them one at a time in her child's open mouth.

EARLY HUMANS PROBABLY LEARNED to use naturally occurring fire before they learned how to create a spark with a flint stone, tending the embers to create their own fires. But fire under those conditions was a force of nature, both boon and bane. Things changed when *Homo erectus* learned to use flint stones to start their own fires. With fire at their call, if not completely under their control, humans could do more than cook their food, and share it around a hearth as a family or tribe. They could keep animals away at night, including the cave bears and giant wild cats that had previously made life in a cave exciting, if not impossible. They could bake clay to make a waterpot, an image of a fertility goddess, or bricks to build a shelter or even a temple. Fire was the tool that made other tools possible, from the first copper blade to the propulsion tanks for a communications satellite. Fire didn't just shape tools; it may also have contributed to the evolutionary movement from *Homo erectus* to *Homo sapiens sapiens*.

Cooking meat doesn't just make an animal taste better; it breaks down proteins, making the meat easier to chew and digest. With fire, humans no longer needed massive jaws to chew their raw food. Smaller jaws left room for a larger brain, taking hominids one step closer to modern humans.

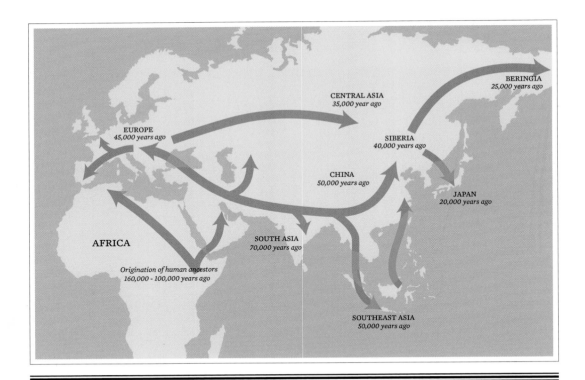

OUT OF AFRICA

AFTER ABOUT ONE HUNDRED thousand years, bands of *Homo erectus*, now armed with fire to keep them warm and probably driven by increased population and competition for resources, began to travel farther from the warmth of the Great Rift Valley in search of food, eventually crossing the land bridge where Africa joins Asia. By about 400,000 BCE, small tribes of *Homo erectus* lived throughout Eurasia, reaching as far east as China.

When they arrived, they found they weren't the only hominids on the planet.

Hominids in Africa and Eurasia took different evolutionary paths in the half million years after *Homo erectus* left Africa. When bands of *Homo sapiens* reached the Near East, they found that Europe and the Middle East were already populated by

another bipedal, big-brained species, *Homo neanderthalensis*, popularly known as "Neanderthal man."

Today, the word Neanderthal is often used as shorthand for an uncivilized or unintelligent brute. Cartoons show Neanderthals as hulks whose knuckles scrape the ground. It's true that Neanderthals were stockily built, with heavy bones and signs of powerful muscle attachments that suggest they were extraordinarily strong by modern standards. Their faces looked more like those of *Homo erectus* than of modern humans, with a protruding jaw, a receding forehead, a weak chin, and a large nose. Nonetheless, Neanderthals walked upright, and their brains were larger than ours.

Comparing evidence from archaeological sites in Africa and Europe suggests that *Homo sapiens* and Neanderthal man were at a comparable cultural level when they met. They made similar stone tools. They hunted small, easy-to-kill animals.

Chapter 1: SEEDS OF CHANGE

Though they created no art that we know of, you could argue that Neanderthals were one step closer to civilization than our ancestors, since they were the first hominids to bury their dead in a way that suggests ritual behavior.

Neanderthal man and *Homo sapiens* were close neighbors in the Middle East and Europe for about seventy thousand years; then the Neanderthals seem to disappear from the fossil record. For many years, the standard theory about their disappearance was that Neanderthal man was slowly pushed out of his habitats and into extinction by *Homo sapiens*, who was assumed to have been better adapted for the fight for survival. The latest science provides a more complex picture.

Beginning around 70,000 BCE—for Neanderthals and *Homo sapiens* alike—survival meant confronting a time of subfreezing temperatures and massive glaciers known as the Great Ice Age. It was not the first time ice had covered Earth. It might not be the last.

Born in fire, the earth is gradually cooling off. For roughly two million years, glaciers have expanded and contracted more than twenty times,

MODERN NEANDERTHALS

Until recently, scholars have assumed that interaction between the two species of human stopped short of mating, or, as one author puts it, hybridizing. DNA sequencing has destroyed that theory.

About ten years ago, scientists at the University of Montreal identified a set of DNA variations in the human X chromosome that didn't seem to fit. These variations formed a haplotype, meaning they are normally inherited together. The Montreal researchers were not able to identify the origin of the haplotype. It remained unexplained until 2010, when researchers from Harvard and MIT sequenced more than 60 percent of the Neanderthal genome, using more than one billion DNA fragments taken from Neanderthal bones. Researchers then compared the Neanderthal genome with both the unusual haplotype and the DNA of living humans from around the world. The haplotype matches a sequence of the Neanderthal genome. It also makes up between 1 and 4 percent of the DNA of modern humans who are not from sub-Saharan Africa or Australia. Evidently the rumors of Neanderthal man's extinction are exaggerated. He lives on in us.

at intervals of roughly a hundred thousand years. Brief periods of interglacial warming lasting about ten thousand years are followed by long periods of cold. ("Brief" is relative. The entire recorded history of mankind has occurred during the most recent warm spell.)

At the height of the Great Ice Age, around 20,000 BCE, glaciers covered one-third of the planet, including all of Greenland and much of Europe, northern Asia, and the Americas. As water froze, sea levels dropped hundreds of feet, exposing land bridges in the shallow waters of the Bering Strait, the English Channel, and the South China Sea. The temperature dropped to roughly minus 60 degrees Celsius (minus 74 degrees Fahrenheit). Glacial expansion seems to be caused by a combination of tiny changes in three different ways the earth moves: the tilt of the earth on its axis, the earth's orbit around the sun, and the wobble of the earth on its axis (picture what happens when a top slows down).

Each of these movement patterns operates on a different cycle; each affects the relationship between the earth's poles and the heat of the sun in a different way. The wobble, in particular, is erratic, affected by earthquakes, tidal waves, typhoons, and, ironically, the melting ice at the end of an ice age. Over time, the patterns interweave, pulling together and apart, sometimes increasing their effects, sometimes canceling them out.

Humans had evolved in the warmth of Africa's Great Rift Valley in an interglacial period. They had grown accustomed to the harsher climate of the Middle East and Europe in the thirty thousand years since they moved out of Africa. But with the advent of the Ice Age, survival required much greater resourcefulness. It was a make-or-break moment in time.

HOW COLD IS AN ICE AGE?

———

Can't imagine what 60 below feels like? The average temperature in Fairbanks, Alaska, in January is minus 23 degrees Celsius (or minus 9 degrees Fahrenheit). For our Ice Age ancestors, 23 below would have been a heat wave.

SOME OTHER COLD SPOTS

SOUTH POLE
Average winter temperature: -58°C

THE TOP OF MOUNT EVEREST
Average January temperature,
before wind chill: -18°C

Average January temperature,
with wind chill: -100°C

THE COLDEST TEMPERATURE RECORDED ON EARTH?
Vostok Station, Antarctica, July 21, 1983
-89°C

Outside the space shuttle, facing deep space
-156°C

Cryonic freezer
-195.85°C

STICKS AND STONES AND ANTELOPE BONES

In the years before the Ice Age, humans supplemented their diet of foraged vegetation by hunting animals that were easy to kill and not particularly dangerous. With the arrival of the glaciers, foraging provided less food, and humans looked with hungry eyes at the herds of large herbivores that roamed the tundra. It was the age of what paleontologists call megafauna: aurouchs, Irish elk, cave bears, woolly mammoths and rhinoceroses, and forest elephants. Humans learned to work as a group to hunt animals that were too big for one man to hunt alone: a woolly mammoth could easily weigh six tons. Individual animals were isolated and driven off cliffs or into ravines.

Hunting megafauna required more than just working as a group. Early Stone Age knives and spears required hunters to get close to their prey. In the Ice Age, hunters developed new weapons that allowed them to attack their prey from a distance. The first and most important of these improvements was the *atlatl*—a wood or bone rod with a hook at one end that fit into a socket at the base of a spear. The hunter held the end of the atlatl in his palm and threw the spear with his arm and wrist. The atlatl effectively increased the length of the spear thrower's arm,

adding both range and impact: the principle is similar to that of a catapult. From the hunter's point of view, it was as revolutionary as gunpowder.

The atlatl gave the Ice Age hunter's arm extra power; new techniques and materials for creating blades gave it a sharper point. Blade flakes—long, thin flakes cut off a central core of flint or obsidian—allowed Ice Age weapon makers to maximize their production of points, producing 300 to 1,200 percent more cutting edge from the same amount of stone. The blades were mankind's first interchangeable parts, used to make knives, hide scrapers, spear points, and drills. At the same time, bone and antler, more durable than wood and more flexible than stone, allowed the creation of new tools with more complicated shapes: fish hooks; long, thin knives; sewing needles; clothing fasteners; and harpoon barbs.

RIGHT TOP: *replicas of artifacts found in Gough's Cave, first explored in 1890* • RIGHT BOTTOM: *Stone Age sharpened bone fragments found during excavations at the Blombos cave site in South Africa.*

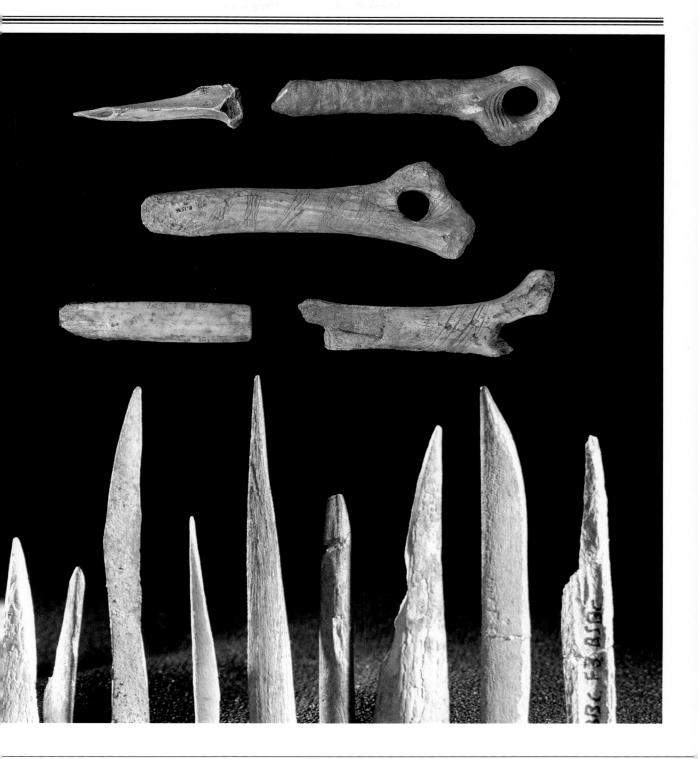

AN ICE AGE FAMILY FINDS SHELTER IN A SHALLOW cave in Southern France around eighteen thousand years ago. Mile-thick glaciers covered northern Asia, Europe and America, locking up so much water that the sea level was more than three hundred feet lower than it is today. With average temperatures similar to those at the modern South Pole, and little buffer against the elements, these humans lived a precarious existence.

These Ice age humans make spears from antlers and sticks, tipped with blades chipped from stones. Theirs is a life and death contest for survival with other beasts, requiring ingenuity and dexterity. Foraging no longer provides enough food to sustain them. Instead they must hunt the herds of large mammals: dangerous work for many men.

Today, they are after smaller game. At midday, when the outside temperature is warmest, the family leaves the protection of the cave to check on a trap set the day before. They are clothed in the furs and hides of different animals, sewn together with needles fashioned from small animal bones. Each type of animal skin offers a different level of insulation from the elements—making fur an unnecessary adaptation for mankind.

The group walks silently over snow-crusted ground until they reach patches of exposed dirt and wet ground where ice has melted. They walk in single file, always watchful for danger that may lurk ahead from a larger predator, or the appearance of opportunity in the form of a carcass left behind. Along the way the woman forages: today she is lucky enough to find berries and gathers them into her basket. At the trap, they rejoice to see that they've successfully snared a rabbit. They bring the animal back to their camp at the mouth of the cave, where they skin it and place the raw flesh over a fire.

While the rabbit cooks, a particularly bold wolf approaches the young boy who has finished his skinning chore and is now wandering outside the cave. The boy's mother rises, shouts, and throws something at the wolf—a bone. The wolf runs to the place where it landed, crouches down and chews. The boy returns to the fire with his mother, leaving the half-tamed animal to enjoy its share of the day's bounty. This wolf and these humans have been in each other's midst for years now, evolving from competitors to friends.

The family has managed to survive another day.

Chapter 1: SEEDS OF CHANGE

Chapter 1: SEEDS OF CHANGE

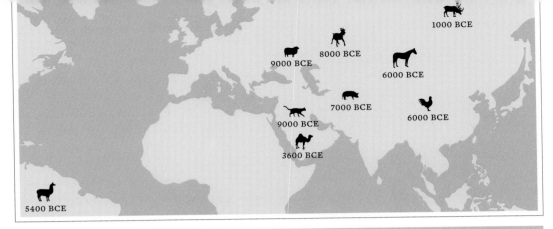

WHAT WAS DOMESTICATED WHEN					
CAT	ca. 9000 BCE	Mesopotamia	CHICKENS	ca. 6000 BCE	China
SHEEP	ca. 9000 BCE	Western Asia	LLAMA	ca. 5400 BCE	The Andes
GOATS	ca. 8000 BCE	Western Asia	CAMEL	ca. 3600 BCE	Southern Russia and the Arabian Peninsula
PIGS	ca. 7000 BCE	Western Asia			
CATTLE	ca. 7000 BCE	Eastern Sahara	REINDEER	ca. 1000 BCE	Siberia
HORSES	ca. 6000 BCE	Central Asia			

EVERY DOG ALIVE TODAY IS descended from Eurasian wolves. Dogs were the first animal that humans domesticated, possibly up to thirty thousand years ago. There's a difference between taming and domesticating an animal. Individual wild animals can be tamed to live, and even work, with humans. Domestication implies that over time an animal changes into a form that is biologically and behaviorally different from its wild ancestors, a form that is presumably more useful to humans. At various times, white deer, elephants, and cheetahs have been tamed by humans, but they have never been domesticated.

The relationship between man and dog may have begun when earlier canines followed nomadic humans as scavengers. The relationship continued because wolves are "preadapted" for domestication, thanks to their well-defined pack hierarchies, high degree of sociality, and pack hunting behaviors. At first, dogs served humans as sentinels, hunting companions, and a food source when times were tough. (Some dogs were bred specifically as food animals in ancient China, Aztec Mexico, and Polynesia.) As humans domesticated other species, dogs learned to herd animals they had previously hunted.

Domesticated animals have provided humans with food, clothing, and friendship. They've pulled plows, carts, and barges. They've caught rats, treed possums, and retrieved waterfowl. We've ridden them, raced them, and taught them silly tricks. But we've also caught diseases from them. Most of the serious epidemics of modern history, from the plague to AIDS, began life as relatively mild animal diseases. When these germs were transferred to humans, they evolved into deadly killers.

IN THE ICE AGE, HUMANS PAUSED in their struggle for survival and created the first known art. Some of their art was small and portable, the kind you would expect nomadic peoples to create. They carved three-dimensional images of their prey on their atlatl handles. They made necklaces and bracelets from bones, teeth, and shells. They made small carvings out of limestone, soapstone, bone, antlers, and horns, as well as baked clay figurines. Some Ice Age figurines depict animals, similar to the soapstone carvings made by modern Inuit. The most common human figures are the so-called Venus figures: small statuettes of the female form that are all breasts and buttocks, with unformed facial features and stubby legs.

The best-known examples of Ice Age art are neither small nor portable. They are the massive and visually powerful cave paintings that can still be found from France to Siberia. These works were painted by firelight on the walls of hard-to-reach caves. Their primary subject is the game Ice Age man hunted—deer, wild cattle, buffalo, and mammoths. The animals are portrayed with the power of a Picasso print: a combination of closely observed detail, rounded form, and powerful abstraction. They are always in profile, always in motion. The rare human figures who appear beside them are generally no more than stick figures.

The techniques used to create these works were surprisingly sophisticated. Ice Age artists painted with the tips of their fingers, well-chewed twigs, and possibly even brushes made with animal hair. They made paint in shades of red, yellow, and brown by dissolving iron ochres in water, mixed with egg whites, fats, plant juices, and blood. Animal charcoal provided black tones and the strong lines that outline many of the figures.

Side by side with paintings of game animals are handprints, painted on the walls using techniques familiar to any modern parent or kindergarten teacher. In some cases, the artist's hand was coated with paint and pressed against the wall. In other cases, the hand was outlined with paint blown through a pipe, creating a negative handprint.

Art, religion, or ancient graffiti? Painted between 25,000 and 40,000 years ago, prehistoric cave paintings represent our only direct look at what our Ice-Age ancestors thought about, what was important to them.

Chapter 1: SEEDS OF CHANGE

FROM PICTOGRAPHS TO PARAGRAPHS

It's a short step from a painting that represents a deer to an abstract picture that means deer. Such pictures, called pictographs, were the earliest form of writing. The problem with pictographs is that they require a character for every object and make it difficult to write abstract ideas. Pictographs evolved into writing systems based on syllables. In a syllabic language, the abstract picture of a deer can represent both the object deer and the sound deer ('dir). The symbol for deer could mean either deer or dear or could be combined with other symbols to create the words reindeer, dearth, or commandeer. True alphabets move the concept one step further, linking a symbol to a sound.

The universal symbols now in use for such things as toilets, telephones, public libraries, and stairs are a return to the pictograph: mankind's oldest and newest form of written communication.

LEFT: *Egyptian hieroglyphics, a pictographic writing style* • ABOVE: *pictograph of bull and symbols from Mohenjo-daro in Pakistan*

Paintings and carvings created by Ice Age humans give us our only clues about how these ancestors of ours thought. They are also the first examples we have of humans thinking symbolically. Symbolism is the basis of language and every other form of culture. Working backward from what we know about later cultures, scholars guess that these cave paintings were intended as hunting magic, the handprints were part of a ritual, and the plump little female figures were related to fertility. But we don't really know all the answers—historians and scientists continue to search for the clues that link us all to early humans.

became less certain. Large game animals were dying out: at least fifty types of megafauna became extinct in the last five thousand years of the Ice Age, from climate change, increased hunting, or both. As hunting became less reliable, gathering became more important. Some nomadic tribes began to methodically harvest wild grains, roots, and berries, becoming a little less nomadic in the process.

Harvesting wild grains differs from planting seeds with the aim to grow more plants and thereby yield large volumes of grain. The latter is called agriculture, and its discovery was another Gold-

The person who first noticed the power of wheat to reproduce by burying fertile seeds in the soil was probably female.

AROUND 10,000 BCE, THE EARTH began to warm again. The glaciers retreated, leaving behind moraines, kettles, drumlins, and grooves gouged out of the bedrock. Sea levels rose, once more covering the land bridges that linked the Americas to Eurasia. The weather became warmer and wetter.

New adaptations were required of post–Ice Age *Homo sapiens*, who now dwelled on every continent except Antarctica. The specialized big game hunting that humans depended on during the Ice Age

ilocks moment for man. The person who first noticed the power of wheat to reproduce by burying fertile seeds in the soil was probably female, not male, since it was the women who primarily harvested wild seeds, while their men continued to hunt. The woman credited with the human innovation of agriculture was probably a member of the Natufian tribe—seminomadic farmers who lived in the area that is now Palestine and southern Syria around 9000 BCE.

THE MIRACLE OF SEEDS

A YOUNG WOMAN WALKS THROUGH A GROUP OF HUTS, carrying some bones from a meal to discard at the communal garbage dump. She passes two men working beside a hut, threshing grain with forks, repeatedly lifting it to allow the fine, wispy materials to blow away in the breeze.

At the dump, the young woman throws away the bones. As she turns to leave, something protruding up through the discarded bones catches her eye. When she bends down, she notices wheat sprouting there. It looks just like the kind that grows in the high meadow where she goes to harvest grains. Curious, she removes some seeds from these plants.

Instead of walking home, she goes immediately to the high meadow. At the edge of the field, she kneels down and uses her fingers to push the seeds from the garbage dump plants into the ground.

Weeks later, when she returns, the young woman notices that seeds from the garbage pit plants are more robust than those produced by wild plants growing in the meadow. She has discovered one of the gritty facts of wild plant propagation: some seeds need time in a digestive tract before they can perform their miracle.

Chapter 1: SEEDS OF CHANGE

Chapter 1: SEEDS OF CHANGE

WHY WHEAT?

The grain in wild grasses, like wheat, barley, and the wild-grass relative of maize, grows at the top of the stalk. As it matures, the stalk "shatters," dropping its seeds to the ground, where they germinate and produce more stalks of the wild grass.

In wheat and barley, a relatively common single-gene mutation creates a stalk that does not shatter, and the seeds remain on the stalk. In the wild, the stalks that don't shatter are an evolutionary dead end. Seeds that remain on the stalk do not reproduce. From the hunter-gather's point of view, seeds that remain on the stalk are a bonanza. From a farming point of view, seeds that remain on the stalk were to be desired.

IT PROBABLY TOOK MANY STEPS between this one discovery of the ability of wheat seeds to reproduce themselves to planting annual crops, but over time the Natufians learned to set aside a portion of each harvest for seed and tended their fields with sharpened digging sticks and simple wooden hoes.

Seeds are a near-perfect food source, rich in proteins and carbohydrates. They don't spoil quickly, and they can be easily stored and transported. One seed contains all the genetic information to create an entirely new plant, which in turn will bear dozens more seeds the following year. Over just a few seasons, replanting the best seeds produces new plants with bigger seeds. Wild grasses are domesticated, and transformed into wheat, barley, and rye.

IN ITS EARLY STAGES, FARMING didn't necessarily tie nomadic tribes down. A tribe cleared a piece of ground, planted a crop, stayed in one place long enough to harvest it, and moved on. Over time, people created permanent settlements, which led to changing gender roles, new social structures, and the concept of property.

New technologies developed to fill new needs: fired pottery containers for storage, grindstones and mortars for processing foodstuffs, and clay bricks for building houses.

By 7000 BCE, farmers cultivated wheat and barley in a continuous zone that stretched from western Turkey to modern Pakistan. Farming then spread west from Anatolia through the Balkans, along the Mediterranean shore, and slowly into Central Europe, where the first farming villages appeared around 5400 BCE.

In 5000 BCE, settled agriculture was a primary way of life in four regions of the world: the Middle East, Egypt, northern India, and the Yangtze and Yellow River basins in China.

AN A-MAIZE-ING TRANSFORMATION

THE MIDDLE EAST WASN'T THE only region of the world to discover farming. The ancient peoples of Central America domesticated what Americans call corn and the rest of the world calls maize sometime between 7000 and 10,000 BCE. Unlike the domestication of wheat, where the evolutionary path is relatively clear, with corn, we don't know how they did it.

Corn's closest wild relative that we know of is a grass called teosinte. Unlike wild wheat, it is not an obvious food source. Botanically, teosinte is two or three important genetic changes away from corn, processes that would take millennia to occur in nature and would leave a trail of maize missing links behind it. The grain head, the equivalent of an ear of corn, is not more than an inch long and made up of seven to twelve woody seeds. Like wheat, it spreads its seeds by "shattering." Unlike wheat, it has no known variant that does not shatter.

Botanists are divided into two passionate camps on the subject of how ancient Americans created maize. One group theorizes that maize is descended from a now-extinct wild ancestor and a different wild grass with more obvious traits for domestication. The other group argues that ancient Americans bred maize from teosinte in spite of the difficulties.

One way or the other, by 6000 BCE, the ancient peoples of Central America had created a system of farming that later Native Americans would call the "three sisters"; beans and squash were planted in the same field with maize, creating a symbiotic relationship in which bean and squash vines use the maize stalk as a trellis, while beans' nitrogen-fixing roots provide the nutrients the maize needs. The symbiotic relationship between the "three sisters" continues in the cook pot as well. Beans and maize together make a nutritionally complete meal.

By the time Europeans arrived, "three sisters" agriculture had spread north and south through the Americas.

THE DOWNSIDE OF FARMING

Eventually, successful farming offers a society a more stable food supply and a wider variety of food than hunting and foraging. Over the short run, farming was no more secure than life as a hunter-gatherer, and it was a lot more work.

Hunter-gatherer cultures cannot afford for a woman to bear a child until her previous child is able to walk on its own. Without that limitation, permanent farm settlements allowed families to raise more children. Population growth created a demand for more fields, which in turn created a demand for more children to work them. When fields wore out after several years of intensive gardening or a season of bad weather damaged crops, famine struck.

The result? Archaeological studies comparing early farmers with similar hunter-gatherer populations show that the farmers were often smaller, had less diverse diets, suffered from more diseases, and died at a younger age.

THROUGHOUT THE WORLD, agriculture led to the creation of permanent settlements. Increasing crop yields created food surpluses that supported larger settled communities. For the first time, not everyone needed to be part of the effort to create food. A few people were able to specialize in creating other things that the community needed. Potters were probably the first craft specialists, but they were soon followed by weavers, tanners, brick makers, builders, metalworkers, and others who played specialized roles.

The first towns, known as the tel cultures, from the Arabic word for "hill," appeared in western Asia around 9000 BCE. True to their name, they were often built on hills and were surrounded by defensive stone walls, suggesting that towns felt a need to protect themselves against nomadic peoples who coveted their food surpluses. The most well-known of the Natufian towns is the multilayered site of Jericho, also known as Tel es-Sultan, located in Palestine's West Bank.

Jericho and the other cities of the tel cultures weren't the only neolithic towns to appear and disappear in the agricultural regions of Eurasia. Others followed as agriculture spread: Çatal Hüyük in western Turkey around 7000 BCE, Karanovo in Bulgaria in 6200 BCE, Kot Diji in Pakistan in 3000

JERICHO

Jericho is possibly the oldest continuously occupied place in the world. The first town dates from 8300 to 7300 BCE, but the oldest remains at the site suggest that it was a campsite for the Natufian tribes long before a permanent settlement was built.

The earliest town builders of Jericho constructed a defensive exterior wall around a freshwater spring and beehive-shaped stone houses that were built halfway underground. The find that makes Jericho stand out from other neolithic towns are the human skulls covered with individually modeled plaster faces and seashell eyes. Apparently the townspeople of Jericho buried the decapitated bodies under the floor of their houses and displayed the decorated heads in their homes.

Jericho dwindled back down to a farm settlement around 5000 BCE. The town was rebuilt two thousand years later into what has been identified as the Jericho of the Old Testament, complete with ten-foot-high stone walls with twenty-five-foot watchtowers.

LEFT: *Jericho palace*

BCE, and Chengziya in China in 2500 BCE. The cultures were different from region to region, but the towns shared common concerns. They struggled with irrigation and flooding. They built temples and granaries. They buried their dead with ritual and sacrificed to their gods. They created distinctive pottery. They traded over amazingly long distances. (Archaeologists have found obsidian from Turkey, turquoise from the Sinai, and seashells from the Mediterranean and the Red Sea in the ruins at Jericho.) They went to war.

It isn't a coincidence that the great civilizations of the ancient world were all tied to major river systems. Neolithic agricultural techniques could not support a large settled population. After a period of intense cultivation, the fertility of the fields decreased and the towns they supported failed. The only exceptions were those river valleys where flooding fertilized the land year after year. In the areas where settled agriculture was a primary way of life, three river systems provided the conditions under which cities could flourish: the fertile land between the Tigris and Euphrates rivers in modern Iraq, the Nile River valley in Egypt, and the Indus River valley in modern Pakistan and northern India.

Located between the Tigris and Euphrates rivers, Mesopotamia was literally "the land between the rivers." Also known as the Fertile Crescent, Mesopotamia was home to the world's first civilization: the Sumerian city-states, which were founded between 4500 and 4000 BCE.

The city-states were politically independent and culturally linked. They shared a common language, culture, and religion. Built almost entirely from mud bricks, the cities were small by modern standards: with roughly the same population as Duluth or Asheville. Ur, best known from the Hebrew Bible as the city from which Abraham fled, was the dominant city for most of Sumer's history.

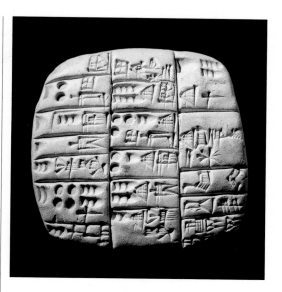

Sumerian clay tablet in cuneiform script

BASE TWELVE

The city-states of Sumer are long gone, but they affect our daily lives in one very basic way.

The Sumerian counting system was based on twelve rather than ten. It survives today in our sixty-second minute, sixty-minute hour, twenty-four-hour day, and 360-degree circle.

We know more about the city-states of Sumer than we do about their predecessors at Jericho and Çatal Hüyük because the Sumerians were the first people to develop a written language. Cuneiform is a syllabic script with about three thousand characters, halfway between a true alphabet and pictographs. It was written by incising a soft clay tablet with a wedge-shaped stylus. If someone needed a permanent copy of a document, he baked the tablet. The earliest surviving tablets date from 3100 BCE. Many of them are financial records, detailing the complicated economic life of the culture. Each city

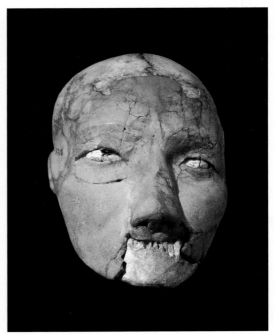

CLOCKWISE FROM RIGHT:
bust of a priest king, terracotta toy, terracotta figurine all from the Mohenjo-daro dig in Pakistan. • ABOVE: *one of the skulls of Jericho discovered in the mid-1950s.*

had a major temple that owned property, collected tribute, and bought supplies for a household of priests and scribes. Merchants traveled by donkey caravan across the desert to trade with Turkey, Iran, Syria, and the Indus Valley.

Financial records weren't the only things recorded on clay tablets. Sumerians wrote religious works, historical accounts, lists of kings, and the earliest surviving epic poem, the *Epic of Gilgamesh*. We can read their hymns, their law code, and a magical spell for protecting an infant from blood-sucking demons.

In 2004 BCE, Sumer was conquered by invaders from Iran, the first of several waves of conquerors who overran Mesopotamia and built on the accomplish-

> More than thirty-five thousand people worked on a pyramid site—all at the same time, in synchronized, constant motion. This was organization on a scale never seen before.

ments of the first civilization. The Sumerian language died out, but cuneiform remained in use in international diplomacy and trade until the first century CE.

BY 3000 BCE, MANKIND WAS ready to add a new skill set to its résumé: complex engineering. The result was construction on a massive scale, both in the great civilizations of Mesopotamia, Egypt, and India and in the relatively undeveloped Bronze Age cultures of Western Europe. Armies of workers were organized to build temples, tombs, palaces, and great walls. Many of these constructions have fallen. Others, like Stonehenge in England and the Great Pyramid of Giza still stand—sources of wonder five thousand years later.

We know very little about the purpose and construction methods of Stonehenge. The proximity of its massive stone monoliths to farming villages and the scientific precision of its alignment with the sun suggest the purposeful creation of a celestial calendar to mark the seasons. It is also thought to have been a ceremonial ground for burying the dead—but these are only informed guesses.

We know much more about how the Great Pyramid of Giza was built, thanks to written records left behind by an ancient Egyptian civilization that lasted from around 3100 BCE until Cleopatra was vanquished by the Romans in 31 BCE. Egypt was born on the fertile strip of land created by the Nile in the North African desert. Egyptian culture was driven by two fundamental beliefs: the divinity of the pharaoh and the need to provide for life after death. These two beliefs were combined in the creation of Egypt's most notable monuments, the pyramids, and were celebrated in ancient Egypt's most well-known literary work, the Book of the Dead.

The pyramids were the largest, and most expensive, attempts to provide comfort for an individual's immortal soul. Influential officials and priests also built tombs that were meant to last and decorated the walls with hieroglyphic inscriptions and scenes of everyday life. Even a common man could hope for immortality if he could save the price of having his body properly treated for preservation. Much of what we know about daily life in Egypt comes from these tombs and their contents, providing the residents with a type of immortality after all.

More than thirty-five thousand people worked on a pyramid site—all at the same time, in synchronized, constant motion. This was organization on a scale never seen before. All of these workers had to be fed, sheltered, given water, provided with tools, and managed down to the smallest details.

TWO TEAMS OF TEN WORKERS EACH ARE HAULING large stones over log tracks. The stone pullers are helped by people pouring oil on the logs for lubrication. To the workers with the logs and stones, the pyramid off in the distance seems impossibly far away.

High up on a segment of the pyramid, a ramp goes around a tight 90-degree corner. From the perspective of a team member on the ramp, the view of the drop-off is breathtaking. But there's not time for gawking. He turns back to focus his attention on his hands, one of twelve pairs hauling a giant stone up the ramp. The men work together unified in purpose.

The top workmen building the pyramid belong to a professional class of men that split themselves into teams. This team consists of specialists in carving, moving, and placing stones. The pressure on them is intense; they need to place one giant stone after another on the structure according to a strict timetable. To do this they depend on the entire engineering project being orchestrated with military precision.

Behind the stone handlers stands their leader, barking orders and writing down calculations. Around him workers are busy measuring, watering, chipping, and hauling. These Egyptian builders are capable of great accuracy in measuring large horizontal distances. Key to this ability is an important new tool in the story of all of us: a precise basis of calculation.

BUILDING BLOCKS

The Great Pyramid of Giza and Stonehenge were built at roughly the same time. Both are miracles of ancient engineering. Both have been the subject of what can only be called "imaginative speculation." How do they add up?

THE GREAT PYRAMID

WHERE: Giza, Egypt

WHEN: Between 2550 and 2530 BCE

WHY: Final resting place of the pharaoh Khufu

WHAT: The pyramid covers 13 acres. It is 481 feet high, and measures 756 feet on each side. It is made of roughly 2.3 million blocks of granite, weighing 2.5 tons each, with a facade of 144,000 white limestone blocks.

HOW: As many as 100,000 workers, skilled and unskilled, free and slave, worked on the pyramid over a period of twenty years.

WHO ORDERED THE WORK: Khufu

STONEHENGE

WHERE: Wiltshire, England

WHEN: Between 3000 and 1500 BCE

WHY: We don't really know. The most popular theory is that it served as a ritual calendar, a speculation fueled by the alignment of its stones with sunrise and sunset at the summer and winter.

WHAT: The first phase of Stonehenge is a large earthwork, some 300 feet in diameter. The outer stone circle measures 108 feet across. It is made up of thirty standing stones, with a ring of lintel stones resting on top of the standing stones. The standing stones weigh between 25 and 50 tons each.

The inner stone circle is made up of eight standing stones, weighing up to 4 tons each.

HOW: Built over hundreds of years, it was reworked at least four times.

WHO ORDERED THE WORK: We have no idea.

Chapter 1: SEEDS OF CHANGE

MEASURING AND LEVELING

The basic unit of length for the Egyptians was the mH, which is referred to in English as the cubit. There were two types of cubit, with the longer cubit divided into seven palms and the shorter one divided into six palms. The palm was in turn divided into four fingers.

The smaller of the cubits, around 45 centimeters in length, was based on the length from a man's elbow to his fingertip. The larger of the two cubits, often called the "royal cubit," was most widely used. The exact length of the royal cubit varied (very slightly) over time. When the great Pyramid was built, the cubit measured approximately 52.3 centimeters. The device the Egyptians created and used for this purpose was the cubit measuring rod, made of wood or stone. They also used rope of set cubit lengths, for longer measurements.

Egyptian stonemasons were able to create very large, flat plane surfaces. It is not known exactly how the Egyptians established their base plain. It has been suggested that such accuracy was achieved by establishing an approximately flat surface, and then obtaining a very precise finish by flooding the surface with water.

To test whether a stone surface was horizontal, the Egyptians used an "A frame." This consisted of a small wooden frame in the shape of the letter A. A plumb line was suspended from the peak of the A, and the level was known to be horizontal when the string coincided with a vertical line drawn on the horizontal bar of the A.

Proof of the Egyptians' amazing accuracy is still there for all to see. The base pavement of the Great Pyramid deviates just fifteen millimeters (less than two centimeters!) between the northwest and southeast corners.

AT THE SAME TIME THAT HUMANS began to build monumental structures in stone, we also discovered the use of a new material that would transform our lives, from agriculture to industry to warfare—metal. Copper was the first metal that humans used for utilitarian purposes. It was soft and simple to work with, but it was expensive and better suited for ornaments than for implements. Even hammered copper blades bent easily and couldn't keep an edge.

Metal didn't really come into its own as a material for tools until around 3000 BCE when metalworkers in Western Asia discovered that copper is much stronger when it is mixed with tin. The resulting alloy, bronze, was not only stronger than either copper or tin alone; it kept an edge. Copper knives were pretty toys. Bronze knives were weapons. Suddenly new tools and weapons appeared, including chisels, punches, swords, battle-axes and primitive body armor.

Any aspiring chieftain could easily see the value of having more effective weapons. It took thousands of years for the agricultural revolution to spread from its birthplace in the Middle East; the new technology of bronze spread in a fraction of the time. By 2000 BCE, Shang dynasty artisans were producing extraordinary bronze vessels in China. Thriving mining, metalworking, and trade centers had developed in Central Europe by 1800 BCE and in Scandinavia by the middle of the second millennium.

Because copper and tin seldom appear in the same locations, the demand for bronze helped develop interlocking circles of regional trade networks that moved goods from the Baltic through the Mediterranean to northern India and back. Because tin was rare, it was the primary commodity in an international market that handled amber, furs, fine textiles, gold, faience beads, graphite, worked bronze, and salt. New cities and cultures rose along the trade routes. Those places where both copper and tin were easily available, such as the Unetice culture settlements near modern Prague, became centers for producing tools and weapons.

The Bronze Age was a period of increasing wealth—and increasing insecurity. Bronze weapons were more lethal than those of stone or copper. They were also more expensive. A farmer could pick up a stone sickle and do battle against a man armed with a copper-tipped spear. He had no chance against a man armed with a bronze sword, wearing bronze body armor. A new class of military

elites emerged. For the first time in history, weapons were specifically designed to kill humans instead of animals.

By 1500 BCE, the Bronze Age of the Old World was at its glittering height. Bronze had made its way from Shang China to the wilds of Britain, where local chieftains were buried in stone chambers with elaborately worked bronze axes and helmets. Only a few thousand years after the first towns appeared in the Middle East, it looked as if civilization was here to stay.

Early bronze axe head and spear point

Chapter 1: SEEDS OF CHANGE

THE AGE *of* IRON

BILLIONS OF YEARS AGO, THE BIG BANG PLANTED SEEDS FOR THE BIRTH OF THE HUMAN RACE. THAT SAME COSMIC EXPLOSION CREATED ELEMENTS THAT HUMANS WILL LEARN TO USE FOR MANY PURPOSES, CHANGING OUR ENVIRONMENT AND SHAPING OUR HISTORY.

Now, in the twelfth century BCE, humans enter a new era of history, shaped by the first alphabet, the new idea of democracy, and a new metal that gives the era its—Iron Age. Smelting iron will allow ordinary men to plow more fields, make new tools, and take arms against the military elite of mighty empires.

But first, they must face down the forces of darkness set loose in the Iron Age.

IN 1250 BCE THE HITTITES, Egyptians, Assyrians, and Mycenaeans were at the center of Bronze Age power and culture. With vast wealth derived from the fertile lands of Mesopotamia and the Nile Delta and robust trade throughout the Mediterranean and beyond, kings and pharaohs ruled as theocracies protected by military elites. But this social hierarchy proved fragile. The

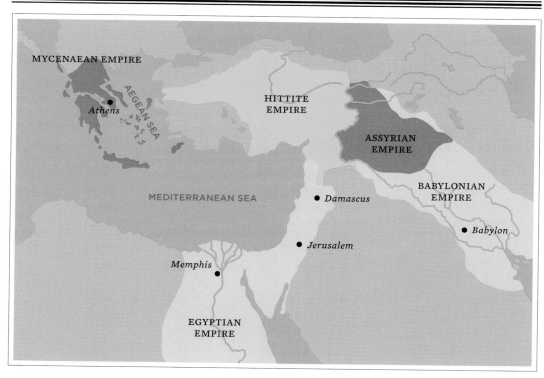

LEFT: *Mount Hekla, Iceland* • ABOVE: *map of Mycenaean, Hittite, Assyrian, Babylonian, and Egyptian empires*

Chapter 2: THE AGE OF IRON

ATLANTIS?

———

Sometime between 1610 and 1550 BCE, Mount Thera, on the island of Santorini in the Aegean Sea, blew with a force that geologists estimate was equivalent to several hundred atomic bombs going off in a fraction of a second. The eruption sent more than sixteen cubic miles of debris into the air, and up to forty times the volume of magma than the twentieth-century eruption of Mount St. Helens (see image), throwing a large portion of the island into the sea.

The aftermath of tsunamis and underwater earthquakes throughout the region killed thousands of people. Some scientists believe the volcano may have caused the climate changes and crop failures that plagued the Mediterranean in the thirteenth and twelfth centuries BCE. Could this geologic event be the basis for the legend of the lost continent of Atlantis?

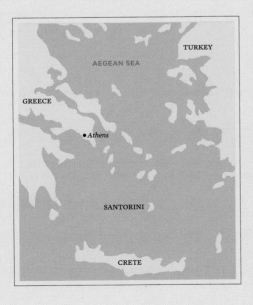

discovery of how to create weapons from iron made possible the violence of the period known as the Ancient Dark Age, extending from 1200 to 500 BCE.

In the fifty years between 1200 and 1150 BCE, calamities both natural and man-made brought down these empires. Geologic records suggest that earthquakes and a large volcanic eruption on Iceland wreaked havoc on northern and western Mediterranean settlements. Assyrian and Egyptian state documents tell of "scanty rains" and rising wheat prices, indicating that widespread drought and failed crops led to famine and mass migrations. Known to us only as the Sea People, desperate refugees, probably driven from their homelands by famine or invasion, donned wrought iron helmets and shields and armed themselves with foundry-formed iron javelins and swords. Population growth dropped. With trade routes disrupted, merchants stopped recording transactions; writing faded from civilization.

Declining resources, natural disasters, and the breakdown of order contributed to the advent of the Ancient Dark Age. When nature acted as an enemy, humans also turned against one another, fighting tooth and nail to conquer and survive. However, it was man's ingenuity in discovering a way to extract, smelt, and weaponize a new metal that led to the mayhem for which this period is better known. Iron ore transformed the "who" and "how" of warfare, taking armed conquest out of the exclusive domain of the rich and powerful and giving it to the hungry masses. And so we arrive at the point in human history when our taming of the earth's most common metal merged with our need to prevail against threats from nature and other humans, setting loose violence on an unprecedented scale.

Chapter 2: THE AGE OF IRON

IRON BREEDS CIVILIZATION

Humans have used iron in one form or another since the beginning. Our prehistoric ancestors employed iron ochres to color their cave paintings and later as glazes on clay pottery. They placed chunks of meteoric iron in amulets. Still, it's a long way from grinding ochre for paint to smelting iron for metal. Like many of mankind's discoveries, the move from expensive bronze to cheap iron as the eleventh-century metal of choice was the result of an inventiveness born of desperation. When the tin required to make bronze was no longer available, the famed bronze smiths of Cyprus turned to the red and black iron ore found all over the Mediterranean. Iron cut better than bronze, so it was used in axes and swords. Iron nails built better ships. Within a century iron democratized agriculture and warfare.

The most abundant of all Earth's elements, iron makes up 90 percent of Earth's core. As the planet spins on its axis, this iron generates Earth's magnetic field, forming a protective layer that extends thousands of miles above our heads and keeps us safe from dangerous solar winds and sun spots. Without the earth's iron core continuing to spin, life could not exist on this planet. Iron is so fundamental to our planet's makeup that it can be found not only in vast deposits in the earth's crust, but virtually everywhere beneath our feet.

Africans in central Niger developed ironworking independently of Mediterranean smelters. Working with special high-temperature furnaces with tall "reverse chimneys," they used the wind as a natural bellows to increase the heat of the fire. The remains of these furnaces still stand today throughout the grasslands south of the Sahara Desert. The earliest examples date from about 1500 BCE, well before iron smelting technology reached Egypt and Cyprus. Not only did African smiths discover the secrets of iron smelting earlier than their Mediterranean brethren, but archaeological evidence also suggests that their furnaces operated at a temperature hot enough to bond carbon atoms to the iron—allowing them to create the modern world's preferred iron derivative: steel.

Since 1000 BCE, when iron first challenged bronze for the role of the world's dominant metal, the use of iron increased exponentially. We've used iron for swords and plowshares; for wagon wheels, railroad tracks, and automobile parts; for two-penny nails and the framework for skyscrapers. In some ways, we're still in the Iron Age. Iron and steel account for 90 percent of the metal used in the world today, from cast iron skillets to nuclear reactors.

ANNUAL IRON PRODUCTION

7 BCE..........150,000 metric tons a year
1700 CE......300,000 metric tons a year
1800 CE .....500,000 metric tons a year
1970 CE......More than 1 billion metric tons a year
2010 CE......More than 2 billion metric tons a year

ABOVE: *early humans smelting and working iron* • RIGHT: *iron tools and objects from the Byci skala Cave, Moravia, Czech Republic, circa fifth century BCE*

Chapter 2: THE AGE OF IRON

IRON IN WAR AND FARMING

O N T H E I S L A N D O F C Y P R U S , C I R C A 1 2 0 0 B C E ,
metal craftsmen toil in a foundry. These men, like their forefathers, are famed for their bronze-making skills. But now,
with diminished supplies of copper and tin, they smelt a new metal.

Instead of using the wood and dung that traditionally fueled the
fires for smelting copper for bronze, these workers have adapted. They
now use charcoal to heat chunks of iron ore to temperatures hotter
than 1150 degrees Celsius. Without exposure to the carbon in charcoal,
iron is not strong enough to be an acceptable substitute for bronze.
This discovery has transformed the two most important areas of their
twelfth-century life: war and farming.

As work goes on in this Cypriot foundry, one iron maker uses a bellows to pump air into a furnace filled with red-hot charcoal. Another
man, his face dripping with sweat, repeatedly raises a muscular arm
and brings down a hammer onto a molten piece of iron set at waist
height on an anvil. With each strike of metal against metal, sparks fly,
and the iron slowly bends to take its intended shape. When the hammer pauses, a third man uses a long fork to lift the hot iron from the
anvil and place it into a vat of water, filling the workshop with steam.
The brawny laborers repeat this firing, hammering, and cooling process several times until a glowing iron sword is fully formed. It will go
to a member of the Cypriot king's army to defend the island against the
recurring threat of seaborne marauders.

Iron is the hardest metal man has yet produced with his own hands.
Eventually, every village throughout the Near East and the Far East
will have its own iron foundry, and iron will become the metal of the
people. Farmers will use iron tools, including scythes, hammers, axes,
hoes, and plows to work heavy clay soils.

Iron farm and wood implements from around the first BCE

But given these violent times, iron will have its most immediate impact on warfare. Iron weapons will transform the "who" and "how" of warfare, taking armed conquest out of the exclusive domain of the rich and powerful and giving it to small farmers, shopowners and craftsman for the first time.

Chapter 2: THE AGE OF IRON

Ancient Egyptian inscriptions depict the feared invaders of the Iron Age as a cross between pirates and refugees. Coming from places as far away as the Balkans, southern Italy, Sicily, Greece, or Palestine, many carried their women and children in tow, suggesting a forced mass migration more than an arbitrary bid to conquer. Wherever they came from, whoever they were, whatever drove them from their homes, these "Sea Peoples" left devastation in their wake. Over the course of a decade, they would demolish every important city in Macedonia and the Hittite Empire, modern Syria.

Four hundred years before they faced the invasion of the Sea Peoples, the Hittites had been on the other end of the invaders' sword. Around 1600 BCE, tribes of Indo-Europeans, including the Hittites,

migrated from the Eurasian steppes, first into Persia and then into Egypt, Mesopotamia, and India. The Indo-Europeans had two major advantages against the civilized peoples of the ancient world: horses and war chariots. By the fourth century BCE, the Hittite empire was Egypt's major rival in the Near East.

The thriving Hittite city of Ugarit on the southern coastline of modern Syria was among the first and hardest hit by the Sea Peoples. Around 1190 BCE, the marauders utterly destroyed this ancient cosmopolitan city. Surviving clay tablets, known as "letters from the oven"—because they were written by scribes (and left not fully baked) on the eve and days after Ugarit's destruction—allow us to visualize the city's final hours through the eyes and unheard pleas of those living through its horror.

THE DESTRUCTION OF UGARIT

K ING AMMURAPI OF UGARIT, SURROUNDED BY HIS wife, advisers and scribes, is in the House of the Evens, an inner chamber of his fortressed palace. Pacing the stone floor, Ammurapi repeats a message read to him off a clay tablet received from his overlord, Hittite king Suppiluliuma of Anatolia: "The enemy advances against us, and there is no number. . . . Our number is . . . Whatever is available, look for it, and send it to me."

Ammurapi is stunned by this desperate appeal for help from the most powerful king of the southeastern Mediterranean. Suddenly, he is all too aware of the imminent threat he, too, faces from this new enemy of whom he has heard scarcely believable reports over the past few years.

His chief military adviser begs him not to send their ships and armies away at such a dangerous time. What if the marauders come to Ugarit first? Ammurapi shakes his head, saying he must respond to his overlord—or risk his wrath later. Surely King Suppiluliuma will defeat the Sea Peoples with Ugarit's ships and men—and make their own defense unnecessary.

Another clay tablet, bearing a letter Ammurapi wrote subsequently to his father-in-law, the ruler of Alashiya (modern Cyprus), indicates that the Ugarit King acquiesced to his neighbor's request, sending most of his fleet to aid in Anatolia's defense. Unfortunately for Ammurapi, the Sea People promptly conquered Alashiya and then turned their flotilla in his direction. As his adviser had warned, the city of Ugarit had virtually no military defenses left to fend them off. This letter offers the king's sober assessment of the brutal attack that left his city in ruin.

Chapter 2: THE AGE OF IRON

My father, behold, the enemy's ships came; my cities were burned, and they did evil things to my country. Does not my father know that all my troops and chariots are in the Hittite country.... Thus the country is abandoned. May my father know it; the seven ships of the enemy that came here inflicted much damage on us.

By the time they had finished their conquests, the seafaring invaders had demolished all the major population centers of Cyprus and Hattusas, the Hittite capital. The fact that these once formidable Bronze Age cities could be taken down by marauders whose total force, according to Ammurapi, traveled on just seven ships, shows both the vulnerability of these kingdoms and the aggressive capabilities of the Sea Peoples.

In another undelivered tablet addressed to someone named Zrdn, Ammurapi provided more gruesome details of the city's demise. "Our food on the threshing floor is burned and also the vineyards are destroyed," he wrote. "Our city is destroyed and may you know it."

The city of Ugarit was never rebuilt.

AFTER ITS FALL, THE SEA PEOPLES set sail for Egypt. Their first Egyptian target was Medinet Habu, near Luxor, the site of the mortuary temple of Pharaoh Ramses III, ruler from 1198 to 1166 BCE. In Transcriptions still visible on the temple walls provide an after-the-fact record of the enemy invasion—celebrating the successful defense of the city by the Pharaoh's army. Ramses' account of the battle shows a great civilization routing a barbarian force, but Egypt's victory over the invaders was by no means assured. In fact, the Egyptian state would never fully recover from the assault their elite army waged against a grossly underestimated upstart force known as the Sea Peoples in 1175 BCE.

ATTACK OF THE SEA PEOPLE

IT IS DAWN IN A COASTAL VILLAGE ON THE MOUTH of Egypt's Nile Delta. A boy of around ten and his grandfather are crouched next to their fishing boat, inspecting nets before they set off. The aged man holds a sharp stick with a large eye threaded with string in one hand, a net in the other.

In the distance, residents of the village and its surrounding farms are starting their chores—crushing grain, feeding farm animals—unaware that their lives are about to be savagely disrupted.

The boy finishes his inspection and tosses the net into the boat. His grandfather is still hunched over his net, repairing a large hole, so the boy leans against the side of the boat to rest, closing his eyes for a brief return to dreamland before he must put all his attention on the day's work. When he opens his eyes a moment later, he is startled by a strange sight. There, just off the coast, a line of unfamiliar boats approaches. Confused, the boy turns to his grandfather to ask who they might be. He fails to notice that one of the boats has already reached land—and its occupants have disembarked.

Making their way up the beach, occasionally dropping back to hide behind other moored boats and equipment, a dozen heavily armed warriors, some wearing face paint and horned helmets, advance. By the time the boy and his grandfather see them, it is too late.

One of the brutes grabs the boy by the back of his neck and holds a machete against his throat. The old man jumps to his feet and waves his netting tool in the air, railing at the invader to let go of his grandson and to come after him instead. Seeing that he has become the brute's new target, he yells at the boy, telling him to run to the village and warn the others. The child obeys and darts away, a look of terror on his face; his last image is of his beloved grandfather falling to the sand in a pool of his own blood.

Chapter 2: THE AGE OF IRON

As the boy flees down the beach, he gets a closer look at his attacker's grounded boat. He's surprised to see women and children on board. Thinking of his mother and sisters still at home, he runs as fast as his legs can carry him from the beach through the outlying streets, hoping to reach his home in time. He shouts out warnings to the few people he encounters, pointing behind him.

Reaching the center of the village, the boy stops and looks quickly in every direction, dismayed to see more men resembling those on the beach. They fan out ahead of him, carrying torches and leaving homes ablaze in their wake. One marauder grabs a young Egyptian woman and forces her, screaming, into a house, pulling the door shut behind him. A wave of nausea comes over the boy when he sees two more brutes use their blades to slash down two men attempting to defend their home and families. He thinks of his grandfather and fights back tears.

From where he stands, the boy looks to the northeast and sees that his own neighborhood is engulfed in flames. Black smoke pours up above the rooftops into the sky. He steels himself against the thought of his family's fate.

Remembering a small shed used for storing surplus grain, not far away, he turns and speeds in the opposite direction. He is relieved to find the shed unlocked and half full of grain sacks. The boy crouches behind a pile, but still feels exposed, so he lies down in a fetal position, pulling several sacks of wheat down on top of him.

With his hands over his ears to block out the screams and cries that are getting louder and more desperate from the street, the boy doesn't hear the heavy footsteps outside. By the time he smells the smoke and pushes the sacks off, the shed is already engulfed in flames, and he is trapped.

He prays to Isis for his safe journey into the afterlife.

Ultimately, the pharaoh of the time, Ramses III, rallied a strong defense and triumphed over the invaders, but Egypt never recovered. Economic problems created social unrest, including the first documented labor strike in history. The king's successors lost control of the country. In 1069 BCE, the central government collapsed.

While the Sea Peoples savaged the civilizations of the Near East, foreigners called Dorians invaded and destroyed the Bronze Age Mycenaean civilization of Greece. Their arrival marked a step backward from civilization. Major cities were destroyed or suffered a substantial decline in population. Greek society reverted to small-scale farming and animal herding. Trade withered. The art of writing vanished for roughly five hundred years.

Who were these Dorians? They were thought to be another branch of the Sea People. According to their own mythology, the Dorians were descendants of the mythical hero Hercules, and had returned to southern Greece to reclaim their rightful inheritance. Unlike the raiders who attacked the Hittites, the Dorians stayed, settling first in central Greece and then moving into the Peloponnesus and along the coast of Asia Minor. They soon divided into smaller groups, including the Spartans, who would develop some of the most advanced military tactics the world had ever known.

FOR THE POPULATIONS RIMMING the Mediterranean Sea, recovery from the catastrophes of 1200 BCE was slow. If the invasions of the Sea Peoples in the Near East and the Dorians in the Aegean marked the end of the ancient world, they also provided the opportunity for something new to grow. Beginning around 1000 BCE, new, smaller states proliferated along the Mediterranean coast, created by survivors, refugees, and rebels at the edges of the empires; thus were born the city-states of Israel, Rome, Phoenicia, and Greece.

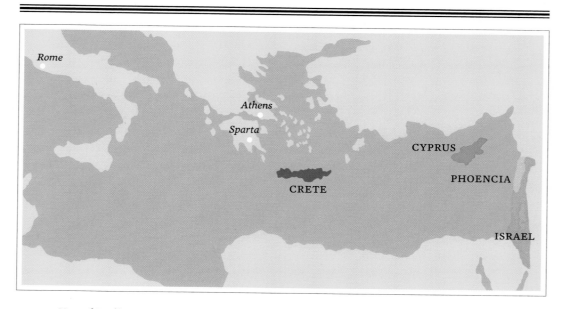

Map of Mediterranean, showing city states: Rome, Athens, Sparta, Phoenicia, and Israel

Chapter 2: THE AGE OF IRON

In a demonstration of how geography influences culture, the mountainous landscape and scattered islands of Greece gave birth to independent city-states. Some, like Athens, were smaller Mycenaean cities that escaped destruction by invaders because they were not particularly important. Others, like Sparta, were colonized by the Dorian invaders. For the most part, the city-states were built around an urban center on a defensible hill. This acropolis—literally, a "high city"—became the political, administrative, and religious center for the surrounding countryside.

Like the Sumerian city-states before them, the Greek city-states were politically independent and linked by a sense of common identity as Hellenes. Residents were bound together by language, religion, and a group of cultural institutions that were shared by all the city-states, most notably the oracle at Delphi and the Olympic Games.

Greek citizens considered themselves "politically free," in contrast to the "bound barbarians" of the Eastern empires—particularly Persia, ruled by a tyrannical god-king. A council of elders, elected by citizens from both the city and its surrounding territory, governed most of these states.

Who was eligible to be a citizen and participate in public life, and just what citizenship meant, differed from one city to the next. As a rule, though,

View of the Acropolis, Athens, Greece

land ownership and participation in the city's defense were the defining factors. Since landowning peasants were the backbone of the Greek city-states, most of a city's adult males were often citizens. Slaves, landless peasants, resident foreigners, and women were not. Over time, two city-states came to dominate the Hellenic world: Athens and Sparta. Yet despite their common culture, they were organized on fundamentally different principles.

Athens is best known for creating the first template for democracy out of the council structure of the Greek city-state. Like other Greek city-states, Sparta was ruled by a council elected by its male citizens. Unlike other Greek city-states, Spartan society was based on a rigid class system that divided the population into a tiny group of

"citizens" and a much larger group of "helots." Helots were owned collectively by the Spartan state. They had no political rights. Like medieval serfs, they were tied to the land and owed a portion of every harvest to their Spartan overlords. Individual helots could win their freedom or even become Spartan citizens for acts of bravery, but it didn't happen often. By the fifth century BCE, roughly two hundred thousand helots supported about ten thousand citizens. Periodic revolts by the helots were a fact of Spartan history.

The army, created to protect Sparta from attacks from without and helot uprisings from within, was the central institution of Spartan society. To ensure a strong army, weak or deformed infants were exposed to the elements and left to die by order of the state.

Male Spartans were raised by the state in common barracks from the age of seven. Their first task was to weave a mat from river reeds; it would be their mattress for the rest of their lives. They were assigned to units, subjected to harsh discipline, and educated in a curriculum designed to turn them into perfect soldiers of a warrior state. By age twenty, Spartan males had become part of a fearsome, disciplined fighting force. Those who entered the ranks of the most elite warriors wore armor made of expensive bronze.

Much like today, access to natural resources and superiority in manipulating them were key in securing power and advantage. The Spartans had a definite advantage over any army they might face: they controlled the richest iron mines in the region, and their metalworkers used them to produce a huge armory of lethal weapons. Spartan soldiers were armed with iron spears and swords capable of piercing bronze and leather armor. These arms would become critical in their next battle.

As different as they were in the fifth century, arch rivals Athens and Sparta were ultimately forced to unite against the threat of annihilation posed by a common enemy: the mighty Persian Empire to their east. Had these city-states not come together to resist this imperial invasion, thereby preserving the seed of democracy planted in Athens, we can never know whether the idea of rule "of the people, by the people" would have re-blossomed in the Roman Republic and taken hold in Colonial America.

Relatively untouched by invasions by the Sea People, the inland nation of Persia took advantage of the disruptions in the Mediterranean and expanded unchecked to engulf two million square miles from India to Greece. Its borders contained fifteen million people, making it the greatest empire the world had yet seen. When the Persian Empire began to covet lands to the west, it came in direct conflict with the "politically free" Greek city-states to whom the Persians were "bound barbarians."

Armed conflict between Persians and Greeks began during the reign of Persian king Cyrus the Great, who conquered the Greek provinces of Ionia in 546 BCE. Always accommodating to the beliefs of conquered peoples, Cyrus granted the Greeks self-government for their internal affairs. Nonetheless, the Ionian provinces gave the Persians constant trouble. In 499, the unrest in Ionia escalated into revolt, supported by a small fleet of ships from the city-state of Athens. It took the Persians five years to suppress the Ionian revolt. Then they turned their attention toward the larger Greek city-states.

The first stage of the Persian Wars, or Greco-Persian Wars, occurred in 490 BCE, when the Athenians fought the Persians alone: seventy-two hundred infantrymen from the Athenian militia against Persia's twenty-five thousand professional soldiers.

Amazingly, the Athenians won, thanks to a surprise maneuver on their part and a slow response from the Persian commanders.

The Persians tried again ten years later. King Xerxes led a huge army across Anatolia and into Greece, supported by a fleet of twelve hundred warships. The Persian army was so large that it traveled slowly, giving the Greeks time to prepare. The war began badly for the Greeks. They made their first attempt to stop the Persians at Thermopylae, a narrow pass between the mountains and the sea. The effort failed, but it was the Greeks' last major defeat.

The Persian Wars were not just a battle between empire and democracy; they were also a contest between two very different kinds of warfare. From the beginning, the Persian army had been based on elite corps of armed horsemen and accurate archers. The Greek army depended on infantry, armed with long spears and two-edged swords. Each city-state had its own militia, made up of citizen soldiers, called hoplites, after the round shields they carried. The shield was a critical element in the Greek battle tactic known as the phalanx. Heavily armed soldiers stood in long, closely packed lines several ranks deep. Each man's shield covered his own left side and the right side of the man to his left. The densely packed lines moved forward in step to the sound of a flute. The formation was difficult to turn; it was equally difficult for an opposing army to stop as long as the formation held. If the enemy penetrated the formation, it became little more than a mob.

The Greek historian Herodotus recorded for posterity the heroic deeds of a Spartan general named Pausanias in the final, decisive battle between the Greek city-states and the Persians. Through his accounts we can witness the dramatic events preceding the battle of Plataea in 479.

Chapter 2: THE AGE OF IRON

SPARTAN WARRIORS

Young Pausanias, a rising Spartan commander, is still relatively untested as he prepares his unit to do battle against the Persian superpower. For the city's elite, the impending fight is about proving their military superiority and maintaining Sparta's independence. For Pausanias, it is also a personal vendetta. The Persians killed his uncle, and he is set on revenge.

Pausanias drills several hundred of his men in formation, a sea of helmets and red cloaks spanned out against the parched foothills outside the city. Each fighter carries an iron-tipped spear in one hand and a sword in the other. Marching together, they form an impregnable hedge of spikes. Those on the front line hold interlocked shields and move as a single wall of iron and synchronized might. The phalanx requires strict military discipline. If one man breaks rank, the entire unit is threatened.

Unhappy with the performance of one young soldier, whose shield is not in alignment, Pausanias orders his men to halt and pulls the errant man out of the line to make an example of him. Pausanias proceeds to humiliate him by forcing a fellow soldier to fight him. Bloodied but chastened, the young recruit takes his position again, this time holding his shield in lockstep with the others.

At this moment, the Persians—three hundred thousand strong—are camped north of Sparta in Central Greece. Their commander, Mardonius, second in command after King Xerxes, leads an army of conscripts, fighting under the threat of the lash. They are in stark contrast to both the militant Spartans and the citizen soldiers of Athens.

To break the fragile alliance between the two Greek rivals, Mardonius attempts to isolate the Spartans by negotiating separate terms of surrender with the Athenians. He sends an emissary, Alexander I of Macedon, to Athens to offer its residents the right to maintain self-governance as long as they submit to the ultimate rule of the Persian king. Acceptance will constitute surrender in no uncertain terms.

Such a major decision requires public debate and a vote by the people in the assembly. Sophanes, an Athenian citizen, witnesses and participates in these events. He has heard news of the Persian bid for peace and is adamant that his city not accept the yoke of Persian rule under any circumstances. On the day of the assembly, Sophanes joins two thousand Athenians already standing shoulder to shoulder in oppressive summer heat. They are average citizens like him: farmers, tradesmen, vintners, along with the city's scholars, actors, and playwrights; few practiced politicians or soldiers are among them. They form an agitated crowd, shouting back and forth arguments to accept or reject Persia's terms with equally righteous passion. The war-weary make pleas for peace over more bloodshed, returned by counterpleas declaring death is better than submission to any foreign king.

A group of four Spartan nonvoting representatives watches and listens to the proceedings. Their presence reflects Athens' desire to remain united with the neighboring Greek state—despite the fact that the Spartans have already made clear their preference for war over negotiation.

From a central raised stage, a presiding Athenian leader invites Alexander of Macedon to personally deliver Mardonius's offer to the assembled crowd. Alexander reads the proposed terms for Athens' surrender from a scroll: the Athenians will be subsumed into the Persian Empire, he announces, thereby allowing its citizens the freedom to take part in all of the empire's delights and riches.

The response to Alexander of Macedon is decidedly mixed. Sophanes is among those shouting him down. He knows that if he and his brethren accept the Persian king's offer, they will lose one precious freedom they are about to exercise: a democratic vote on the decision between war and peace.

Finally, debate is exhausted, and the time for the ballot arrives. Sophanes joins the long line of men forming to mount the stage and exercise their

right to self-governance. When his turn comes, Sophanes picks up a pebble and places it in the cask for those opposed to the Persian peace offer. Then he returns to the throng and patiently awaits the outcome.

Hours later, as thousands remain in the city center to watch, the casks are emptied, their stones counted by a council of the people. When tabulation is completed, the announcement Sophanes had hoped for rings out: "Such is our love of liberty, that we will never surrender."

The Athenians opt to fight alongside their Spartan rivals to preserve their shared Greek independence. The stunned Persian envoy is sent away to deliver this decision to Mardonius. Soon, though not a trained soldier, Sophanes will don the tools of combat and distinguish himself in the most important clash of a war that will last for decades.

T HE DATE: AUGUST 749. TWO UNEVENLY MATCHED armies face off on the plains near Marathon. Three hundred thousand professional soldiers on horseback make up the Persian side. One hundred thousand Spartan and Athenian foot soldiers oppose them, making excellent use of their unity and the military prowess of the Spartans. Put to the test, the phalanx formation proves to be a capable fighting machine that will soon turn an unlikely Greek victory into an inevitability.

Rank after rank of Persian infantry crash ineffectually against the Spartans' interlocked shields, only to meet the girded spears and swords of the full Greek force. The enemy scarcely knows what has hit him, and falls en masse. Having gained the upper hand, the Greek force breaks out of formation to slay the Persians in hand-to-hand combat. To add to the Persian king's humiliation, his deputy, Mardonius, is hit by a stone thrown by a lowly Greek citizen-soldier, and knocked from his horse. Spartan general Pausanias is then given the satisfaction of finishing Mardonius off with a swift sword stroke. The frenzied Persians attempt to flee, but are cut down by the Greeks.

Chapter 2: THE AGE OF IRON

It is a glorious victory, but the fledgling idea of people power is the true victor of the battle of Plataea. Nurtured in the ancient Greek world, democracy will re-appear in the Roman Republic and later blossom in colonial North America.

The destruction caused by the Sea Peoples left a political void along the Mediterranean coast, creating an opportunity for a new age of seaborne exploration. Just north of Israel, in what is now Lebanon, autonomous Phoenician city-states appeared along the coast after 1200 BCE: most notably Byblos, Sidon, and Tyre. Over the course of a century, they grew from small settlements into a sea-based power that dominated the Mediterranean trade routes between 1100 and 800 BCE. The Greeks sneeringly called them Phoinikes, meaning "the purple land," after Phoenicia's most valued commodity, a precious purple dye produced from the murex, a type of sea snail.

Tyrian purple wasn't the Phoenicians' only trading commodity. They exported pine and cedar, linen, wine, metalwork, and glass. They traded in papyrus and ivory from Egypt, wool from Anatolia, resins from Arabia, copper from Cyprus, and silver and tin from Spain. Phoenicia was part of the amber trade that stretched from the Baltic to the Indus. In addition to long-distance trade in luxury goods, their ships carried foodstuffs, like olive oil, grain, and wine, over the short trade routes of the Aegean.

The Phoenicians sailed farther than any other ancient people, traveling through the Mediterranean and into the Atlantic, where they sailed down the coast of Africa. A trove of Phoenician coins found in the Azores suggests the Phoenicians may even have reached the mid-Atlantic. They kept tight control over their knowledge of the ocean currents and winds on the Atlantic side of the "Pillars of Hercules," the ancient name for the Straits of Gibraltar.

At the end of the ninth century BCE, the Phoenicians founded colonies in North Africa, Spain, and Sardinia, including Carthage, which later became the most important sea power in the western Mediterranean.

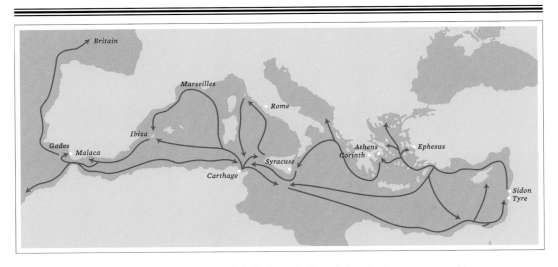

Phoenician mariners expanded the boundaries of the Mediterranean world, sailing into the Atlantic and down the coast of Africa.

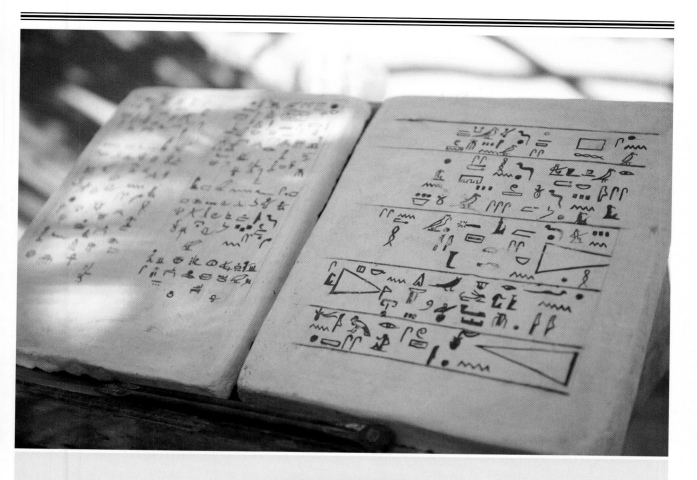

THE ALPHABET

The Phoenicians' most important contribution to modern life was their alphabet.

Like the Sumerians before them, the Phoenicians needed a way to keep records of their extensive trading. In 1100 BCE, cuneiform still dominated international correspondence. Like all syllabic scripts, it was difficult to learn and cumbersome to use. Over time, the Phoenicians replaced it with the first true alphabet, in which characters corresponded to sounds. Like later alphabets for other Semitic languages, such as Hebrew and Arabic, the twenty-two characters of the Phoenician alphabet consisted entirely of consonants. Some of our own letters are believed to take their shape from the ancient world as seen by Phoenician seamen; for example, the letter *M* represents the peaks and troughs of the ocean.

Today there are hundreds of alphabets, but the Phoenician system of letters and numerals is one of few still in use after three thousand years. It was borrowed and adapted first by the Greeks (who added vowels) and later by the Romans. The Roman adaptation of the Phoenician system is the basis for the alphabet we use in the West today.

Chapter 2: THE AGE OF IRON

AT THE SAME TIME THAT THE Phoenicians were pushing the boundaries of the Mediterranean world, a new people moved into what would become some of the world's most coveted and fought-over lands.

The Israelites were a federation of tribes when they migrated into Canaan in the mid-thirteenth century BCE, farmers and herders who terraced the inhospitable hillsides to produce level farmland and collected water in plaster-lined cisterns to irrigate it. Two centuries later, threatened by neighboring tribes, the Israelites chose their first king:

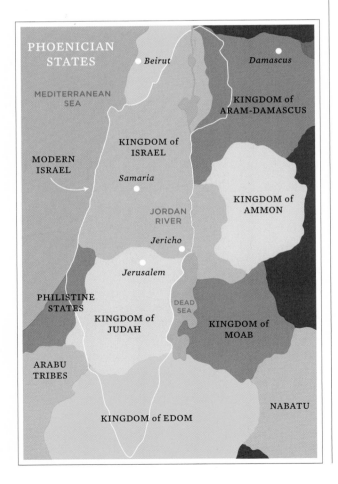

Saul. He defeated the Moabites, Edomites, and Philistines, but proved to be unsuited for rule. His successor, David, united the Israelite tribes into a single state, with Jerusalem as its religious and political center. King David expanded the kingdom's territories until they reached from the Euphrates River to the Red Sea. Under David and his son Solomon, the kingdom prospered.

Tensions mounted between the northern and southern tribes, however. After Solomon's death in 926 BCE, the kingdom split into two parts over the claims of rival successors, with Judah in the south centered on the city of Jerusalem, and Israel to its north. The more prosperous Israel became a military power, ruled by a succession of generals who seized the throne from one another in bloody coups. But the kingdoms of Judah and Israel flourished only as long the great powers of the Near East were rebuilding. When first Assyria and then Babylon were restored under new dynasties, the Israelite kingdoms, like the rest of Near East, became prizes to be conquered. Israel was first to fall. Judah and the city of Jerusalem were next.

The Babylonian king Nebuchadnezzar first conquered Judah in 597 BCE, taking the king of Jerusalem and ten thousand of his nobles captive and placing the exiled king's nephew, Zedekiah, on the throne. Zedekiah swore an oath of allegiance to the Babylonian ruler, but three years later he rebelled. The Babylonians marched on Judah again, ravaging the countryside before closing in on Jerusalem. Nebuchadnezzar took the city in 586, after a siege that reduced even the wealthy to digging in the dunghills for food. From Nebuchadnezzar's perspective, the Judean king was an oath breaker and a rebel. Nebuchadnezzar killed Zedekiah's sons before his eyes, blinded him, and took him in shackles to Babylon, along with most of the inhabitants of Judah. Solomon's Temple was destroyed, and Jerusalem was razed.

NEBUCHADNEZZAR

Most of us know Nebuchadnezzar only from the perspective of the Old Testament: the tyrant who first plundered and then razed the city of Jerusalem, destroyed King Solomon's Temple, and took the Israelites into captivity.

But from the Babylonians' point of view, Nebuchadnezzar was a great ruler. His father was the Chaldean general who joined forces with the Medes to win Babylon's freedom from their Assyrian oppressors. Nebuchadnezzar, in his turn, restored the kingdom to its former glory. He conquered Egypt, Palestine, and most of the Phoenician city-states. He turned the city of Babylon—which had been destroyed seventy-some years before by the Assyrians—into a showplace. The main gate to the inner city and the processional way that led to it were faced with blue-glazed brick and decorated with golden dragons and bulls. The king's palace was covered with glazed tile reliefs of golden lions. Nebuchadnezzar himself created the Hanging Gardens of Babylon, an enormous pyramid of vaulted terraces, to comfort a young wife who was homesick for the green hills of her Median home.

Nebuchadnezzar remembered his gods as well. He dedicated the city's main gate to the goddess Ishtar, and built an enormous seven-story ziggurat to honor the kingdom's primary god, Marduk. He named the temple Etemenanki, "the house which is the foundation of heaven and earth." It appeared in the Old Testament as the Tower of Babel, the ultimate symbol of human pride.

"Godless conqueror" is in the eye of the beholder.

Chapter 2: THE AGE OF IRON

The Hanging Gardens of Babylon, lithograph by Ferdinand Knab, 1886

With the forty-year forced exile of Judah's king and his people in Babylon, Judah's culture should have been wiped from the face of the earth. Instead, the period of Babylonian captivity defined the Judeans as a nation in a new way. It also changed the course of Western civilization by laying the foundation for the first monotheistic religion, Judaism, and the moral code laid out in its Ten Commandments.

While some Judeans were absorbed into their new culture in Babylon, others kept their commitments to their god and dreamed of return to Israel. With no temple in which to worship, they replaced their former rituals with prayers, fasts, and study of the Torah. During this period the Hebrew Bible took its shape, as scribes and priests in exile refined and collated the Five Books of Moses with the histories of their people.

Things deteriorated in Babylon after the days of King Nebuchadnezzar. In 556 CE his successors lost the throne to King Nabonidus.

Nabonidus spent much of his reign on campaign, but he was in Babylon itself long enough to alienate the powerful Babylonian priesthood. He refused to worship the city's primary god, Marduk, raising the moon goddess, Sin, above him. This created tension in the capital, so in 550 he installed his son Belshazzar as regent in Babylon and withdrew to the oasis of Tayma in the Arabian Desert.

The Persian king Cyrus II used the dissatisfaction of the Babylonians, or at least the priests of Marduk, as an excuse to invade in 539 BCE. The city fell almost without resistance, and Cyrus entered Babylon as a liberator. He shrewdly chose to worship at the temple of Marduk, the neglected

SAVING THE SCROLLS

O N A TEEMING STREET IN THE CAPITAL CITY OF BABYLON, a Judean man named Zerubbabel pushes his way through the crowd. Zerubbabel is the grandson of the last king of Jerusalem, who ruled before the capital city of Judah was destroyed and its people taken to live as exiles in Babylon.

Zerubbabel learns from another Jewish man in the crowd that Babylon will soon be under siege by the army of Persian king Cyrus. Word in Babylon has spread, the man tells him, of thousands of Persian soldiers assembling to storm the city's walls and plunder its treasures. As one of a handful of Judeans working secretly to preserve written copies of Judean history for future generations, this news greatly alarms Zerubbabel. Among the secret scrolls, kept in a small library in Babylon, is the only surviving record of the Hebrew alphabet, the Judean culture's code and lifeline. It would be disastrous for these scrolls to be lost or to land in Persian hands!

As Zerubbabel hurries to reach the library building, three Judean scribes leave their desks and rush to a small window to ascertain the reason for the commotion they hear outside. There is a loud knock at the library door. The scholars hurry to see who is there. It is Zerubbabel, and he has come to warn them: they must immediately gather up the hidden scrolls for safekeeping. The men busy themselves emptying stacks, storing scrolls in baskets, boxes, whatever they can carry. Then Zerubbabel ushers them and their treasure out of the library through a back alley.

god of Babylon. Cyrus later claimed that Marduk had chosen him to be "king of all the world." He took the title Shahanshah—King of Kings.

The Persian king had always shown mercy toward the cities he captured. In Babylon, he went one step further. He not only freed the Jews; he guaranteed their rights and laws. Zerubbabel, descendant of King David and King Solomon, was granted a wish he dared never express, a return to the city of his ancestors: Jerusalem. As a last gesture, King Cyrus gave the Judeans money to rebuild Solomon's Temple, destroyed forty years earlier by Babylonian king Nebuchadnezzar.

In time, the records and writings of this small tribe rescued from Babylon and taken back to Judea and Jerusalem will come together to construct one of the most important books in the world: the Torah.

In the centuries to come, more than six billion copies will be sold. It will become the foundation stone of Judaism, of Christianity, and of Islam.

THE JUDEAN PEOPLE RETURNED to Jerusalem in small waves, rebuilding first their city and then their temple. More conquerors followed. But no matter how many times it was conquered, Jerusalem remained the sacred city of Judaism, with the site of Solomon's Temple at its heart. Over time, it became the Holy City for Christians and Muslims as well. For Christians, Jerusalem was the center of the Holy Land, where Jesus lived, preached, and died. For Muslims, it was third only to Mecca and Medina in importance. As the home of the prophets, it played a role in one of Muhammad's visions. In it, he flew with the Archangel Gabriel on a winged

LEFT TO RIGHT: *the Church of the Holy Sepulchre, the Jewish Western Wall (a.k.a. Wailing Wall), the Dome of the Rock*

horse from Mecca to Jerusalem, where the prophets of the past, including Jesus, entertained him at a lavish feast. At the end of the night, he ascended from Jerusalem into the heavens on a celestial ladder.

Today Jerusalem is host to millions of visitors from all three traditions.

AFTER CYRUS THE GREAT BUILT the Persian Empire on those of the Medes and the Babylonians before him, his successors maintained his policy of expansion. Cyrus's son, Cambyses II, took Egypt in 525. Cambyses' successor, his cousin, Darius I, expanded the empire to its greatest extent.

Under Darius's rule, the Persian Empire spanned three thousand miles from east to west. To maintain closer control over his ever-rebellious western provinces, Darius built a paved road connecting his capital in Susa with the provincial capital of Sardis, sixteen hundred miles away on the west coast of Anatolia. It was an unprecedented project. Workers used layers of clay, sand, and gravel, to build the ancient highway, then topped it with a surface layer of large cobblestones.

When it was completed, Darius constructed 111 lodges along the road, one roughly every fifteen miles—the distance a man on foot could travel in a day. These lodges provided travelers with free food, water, and bedding. According to Greek traveler and historian Herodotus, Darius personally guaranteed the travelers' safety.

The Royal Road was an imperial administrator's dream. It made it easier to collect taxes, to send messages to provincial rulers, and to send armies when armies were needed. However, in time Darius's Royal Road would become the very route his enemies would take to defeat him, when the Persian Empire was disassembled at the hands of another, more ambitious ruler and commander, this time from the small kingdom of Macedonia.

ALEXANDER THE GREAT

In 331 BCE, Alexander III of Macedon, known as Alexander the Great, defeated Darius, and briefly ruled the largest empire then known to man—only to meet his match in 326 BCE, when he invaded northern India.

Alexander's army crossed the Hindu Kush, fought its way across the Indus River and through the Punjab, defeating an Indian army supported by war elephants. But when they reached the banks of the Hyphasis (now the Beas), Alexander's troops refused to go further. Alexander reluctantly led his army back to his new capital at Babylon, leaving garrisons behind to rule the conquered Indian provinces. He  later claimed that the only military defeat he ever suffered was at the hands of his own men.

When Alexander died unexpectedly in 323 BCE, his empire crumbled. The generals he left behind as provincial governors found themselves rulers of small states in northern India and Afghanistan.

IN ANOTHER CORNER OF THE world, far from the turmoil of the Mediterranean, a new civilization was taking hold in China. There too, man's new ability to forge iron brought rapid transformation of the social and political order.

In the late fifth century BCE, in a chaotic period known as the Era of Warring States, seven major kingdoms fought among themselves for control over China. In these fights, the use of several new weapons changed the nature of warfare, most notably the crossbow. In addition, iron swords and armor replaced bronze. Cavalry replaced war chariots. Conquerors, primarily using siege warfare, made cities their main targets.

The Qin (pronounced Chin) dynasty of northwest China was considered less cultured than its rivals, but it made up for lack of culture with a powerful army, needed to fight the mounted nomads that threatened its western border. Shortly after Ying Zheng took the Qin throne in 246 BCE at the age of thirteen, he led his armies against the other kingdoms of the "Warring States." He soon earned the nickname "the tiger of Qin" for his ferocity on the battlefield. By 221 BCE, Ying Zheng had united the Warring States and proclaimed himself Qin Shi Huang, the First Emperor Qin.

Once Huang had conquered his rivals, he set out to build a powerful centralized state. Using the same principle that governs modern efforts to remap voting districts, he divided the kingdoms of the Warring States Period into new administrative districts, changing their boundaries and moving hereditary aristocrats away from their power bases. To create a uniform culture, he banished local customs, introduced language reforms designed to diminish regional differences, standardized writing, and burned all books in private libraries. He replaced the hereditary feudal hierarchy with a centralized bureaucratic administration and gave peasants the right to buy land. He then constructed an imperial highway system, rivaling the one later built by the Romans, connecting the capital to the frontier. He built waterways and canals to facilitate transportation from the Yangtze to Canton.

At the same time, Huang was quick to kill his critics, particularly the Confucians and Taoists who questioned the legal basis of his rule. He imposed

Qin Shi Huang

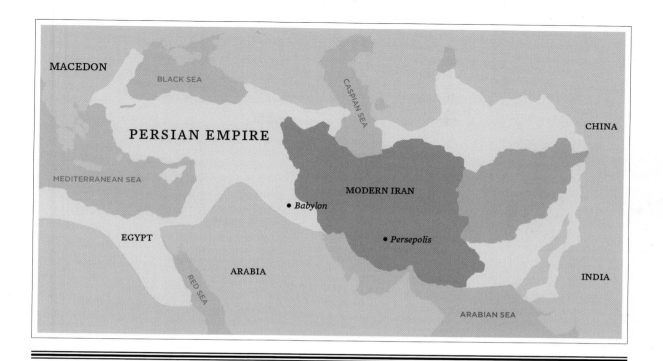

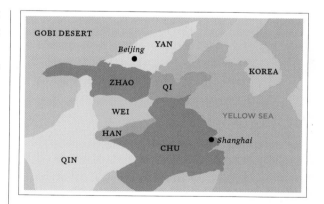

heavy taxes and drafted millions of workers to work on public projects, including the massive tomb that he built for himself.

After Huang's death in 210 BCE, outlying provinces rose in revolt. Huang's son survived him on the throne for only four years before his own prime minister forced him to commit suicide. The dynasty was overthrown by the Chinese peasant general Liu Bang, who reunited the empire and founded the Han dynasty.

WHILE THE ANCIENT DARK AGE is most often remembered for the escalation of violence and the mass production of the tools of war, at the latter end of the era, the fifth century BCE, important thinkers in many different traditions created philosophical systems that would shape human thought for centuries. In China, Lao Tse (604–531) and Confucius (551–479) were the best-known members of a flowering of philosophical thought known as "Hundred Schools," which searched for the foundation of social order during the Warring States Period. In India, the Buddha (ca 500 BCE) preached enlightenment. In Persia,

CAST IRON

———

Cast iron is made by melting iron ore in a furnace. Liquid iron is then poured or hardened into ingots, which are later remelted along with alloy elements and cast into molds. The process takes less labor than wrought iron, but requires higher temperatures.

Chinese craftsmen routinely produced cast iron by the sixth century BCE. The process did not reach Europe until the fourteenth century—two thousand years later.

CHINESE CROSSBOWS

The power of the traditional bow varies tremendously from person to person because it is dependent on an individual's physical strength. The Chinese invention of the crossbow in the sixth or fifth century BCE transformed Chinese warfare, increasing the individual archer's power and speed by fixing the bowstring on a notched trigger mechanism that allowed the soldier to draw the bowstring, load the arrow, and aim in three separate motions instead of one. The first crossbows were wooden bows mounted horizontally on a wooden stock with a metal trigger.

Combining the principle of the crossbow with the ability to produce high-quality cast bronze and iron allowed the Chinese to make the first mass-produced weapons. By 209 BCE, the Qin army—soon to rise as victors among those armies vying for control of China—fielded fifty thousand crossbowmen.

Human ingenuity allowed warfare and destruction on a scale never seen before, but the crossbow was only one step in humanity's creation of more sophisticated and deadly weapons. In retrospect, it was not such a long distance from China's first mass-produced crossbows to the twentieth-century assembly lines that turned out the modern rifles, aircraft engines, and tanks that enabled wars to be fought on a truly global scale.

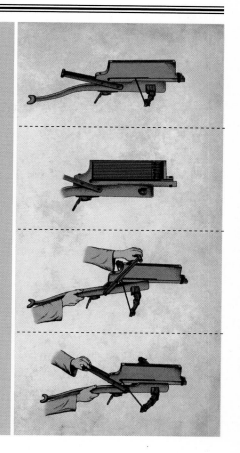

Zarathustra, known in the West as Zoroaster, was a century ahead of the rest. He taught that the world is a struggle between the forces of light and dark, good and evil. He believed that in the end the world would be consumed by fire, and good would banish evil. In Greece, Plato (429–347), Aristotle (384–321), Socrates (469–399), and other classical philosophers questioned the nature of things. Some scholars refer to this later period as the "axial age," during which basic ways of thinking were established for early civilizations. It could just as easily be called the ancient Age of Enlightenment.

By the end of the Ancient Dark Ages, mankind has reshaped the social and political landscape of the Mediterranean world. Ancient empires have fallen to common men wielding iron weapons. New city-states, built by traders, rebels, and refugees, have risen in their place. In the Far East, mass production and one man's driving ambition have created the foundations of a new empire.

Soon another great empire will rise to power on the Italian peninsula.

Within one hundred years, more than half the world's population will live under the rule of these two empires, which will find common ground in a rare commodity—silk.

Chapter 2: THE AGE OF IRON

C I T I Z E N S

TWO SUPERPOWERS RULE THE WORLD. ONE CONTROLS THE EAST, WHILE THE OTHER DOMINATES THE WEST. ONE IS A HIGHLY CENTRALIZED STATE WITH A CENTRALLY MANDATED CULTURE;

the other is a melting pot of peoples and cultures. Sound familiar? Welcome to the third century BCE.

Two great empires control more than half of the population of the ancient world from opposite ends of Eurasia. Almost five thousand miles of some of the most inhospitable terrain on the planet separates the Romans from the Han Chinese. In time, they will be linked by the trading routes collectively called the "Silk Road." As we begin, neither has more than a faint impression of the other; in fact, each believes it alone dominates the globe.

THE ROMANS AND HAN CHINESE may have been very different culturally, but in other ways they were very much the same. Both conquered vast territories and organized new ways to govern them. Both battled attacks by "barbarians" from the lands outside their control. And both practiced cultural as well as political imperialism.

Roman towns from Palestine to Britain looked the same—and offered the same benefits to local rulers prepared to make an alliance with their conquerors. The Han dynasty continued the ruthless drive to create a uniform culture, which was started

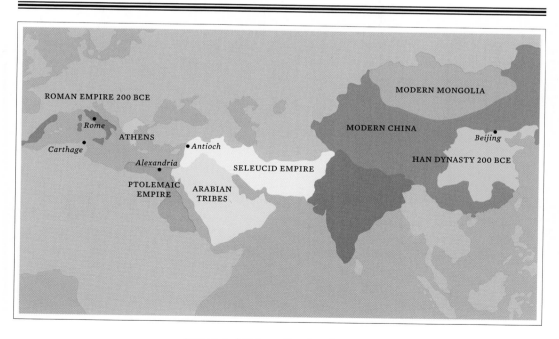

Roman and Chinese Empires 200 BCE

by Qin Shi Huang. The Romans, from Britain to Syria, spoke Latin and Greek. The Han Chinese communicated using a standardized written version of Chinese that bridged the differences between China's mutually incomprehensible dialects. Each culture at its mightiest reflected centuries of conquest and assimilation, and both empires left legacies that shaped the political ambitions of the states that followed them.

That these two superpowers existed as equals ultimately created an environment in which long-distance trade and exchange networks flourished on a scale never seen before—to the benefit of both. Two empires, separated by thousands of miles and substantial culture gaps, somehow made the world a little smaller.

Discontent was widespread in the final years of China's Qin dynasty, the last imperial regime before the Han. The nobility were enraged by the dynasty's attacks on privileges and power. At the other end of the social ladder, peasants were angered by heavy taxes, harsh laws, and the excessive burden of providing forced labor for Qin Shi Huang's public works. In 209 BCE, a group of peasant workers, delayed by rain, abandoned their involuntary assignment, choosing to become outlaws rather than face the death penalty. Thousands joined them. More rebellions broke out across the empire. Qin generals defected. Nobles raised private armies. The struggle to overthrow the Qin dynasty turned into a tussle between rival groups of insurgents, eager to seize the throne.

Liu Bang, a charismatic general of peasant origin, emerged as the victor and became the first Han emperor. He had previously served the Qin as a minor official in charge of a postal relay station. In 206 BCE, he founded the Han dynasty. Like American president Abraham Lincoln, Liu Bang demonstrated his humble origins with modest, sometimes shockingly simple manners and speech. Liu Bang would comfortably squat down on the floor to meet with his official visitors. In one popular anecdote, some scholars came to visit him dressed in ceremonial robes, including elaborate headgear. Liu Bang snatched off one of the scholars' hats and urinated in it. In another story, he commissioned a new court ceremonial to bring order to the daily life of the palace, giving him one instruction—"Make it easy."

The Han dynasty played a key role in expanding Chinese trade, beginning with its Near East neighbors in the second century BCE, when the dynasty needed to defend its borders against the Xiongnu, Han's nomadic neighbors to the north. In 138 BCE, Han emperor Wudi sent an officer of the palace, named Zhang Qian, to make alliances with the kingdoms of Central Asia that the Chinese called the "Western Territories." He was captured

Liu Bang, first emperor of the Han Dynasty

on the way by the army of one of those kingdoms and held prisoner. Only two members of the hundred-man mission survived. After thirteen years, Zhang Qian escaped and made his way back to China. He brought news of people and lands of which the Chinese had never heard: Ferghana, Parthia, Bactria, Babylonia, Syria, and India.

The central challenge for the Han dynasty as it grew from a kingdom into an empire was how to maintain the centralized state created by Qin Shi Huang without the harshness that had characterized the previous Qin rulers. The Han based their government on the ideas of Confucius. Confucianism stresses the moral basis of duties between subordinates and superiors, defined in terms of three basic relationships: ruler and subject, father and son, husband and wife. The most important duty was loyalty.

Under the Han emperor Wudi, Confucianism became the official philosophy and religion of China. Whereas Confucian books and ideas had previously been burned and banned by Qin rulers, under the Han, Confucian texts were again at the heart of political and ethical thought. Scholars wrote commentaries designed to make the texts more useful as sources of moral guidance.

In 130 BCE, Wudi established a civil service of Confucian scholars, who earned their positions by passing a standardized examination. The examinations tested candidates' understanding of the tenets of Confucian moral and ethical thought on which Han dynasty government was based. Standardized testing requires a system of training. In 124 BCE Wudi established an imperial academy in the capital city of Chang'an. Intended as a training program for imperial officials, the curriculum was based on the Confucian canon, with specialists in the five classics of Confucian thought. During Wudi's reign, the number of students in the imperial university was limited to fifty; by the mid-second century CE, thirty thousand scholars had gone through the academy.

PAPER

The Han dynasty's most lasting contribution to the story of mankind was paper.

Classical Chinese historians credit a Han official named Cai Lun, chief eunuch and director of the imperial workshops in the reign of the emperor He, with the invention of paper. In 105 CE, he created the first sheet of paper intended as a writing surface, made from bamboo fibers and the inner bark of the mulberry tree. Emperor He rewarded him for his efforts with titles and wealth.

Cai Lun's writing paper was a clever innovation, but it wasn't the first paper invented in China. Archaeologists have discovered remains of paper in northern China that predate Cai Lun by almost two hundred years.

The basic papermaking process is simple: create a slurry from fibrous material and water, spread the slurry out flat, drain off the excess water, and let it dry. The end result is a dry, light sheet of matted fibers. The trick is finding the right combination of fibers. The earliest Chinese paper was made primarily from hemp. Over the years, papermakers experimented with various barks, bamboo, and rattan.

At first the Chinese used paper for wrapping, packing, decoration—and toilet paper. It was only when paper began to be used as a writing and printing medium that its true

Paper making in early China

possibilities appeared. Paper changed civilization's relationship to knowledge. It inspired new forms of notation: building plans, written music, street maps, and paper currency (a Chinese invention from the seventh century CE).

Picture a world *without* paper. A man named Gutenberg would have had no reason to invent a printing press. Without a way to print on paper cheaply, there would be no widespread distribution of books. Only religious scholars and the wealthy would be reading and writing the expensive, hand-copied books that remain in limited circulation from long ago; the rest of us would still be illiterate. Forget newspapers, the Protestant Reformation, or modern democracy. Nearly everything that makes civilization modern is traceable to the invention of paper by a Han bureaucrat in 105 CE.

TARQUIN THE PROUD

WEALTHY ETRUSCAN TRADER'S WIFE SITS WITH a female companion of the same rank in the family's open-air living quarters in a palatial estate on a Roman hilltop. Splendidly dressed in silks and brocades, the ladies wear baubles made of copper, ivory, and amber. A slave removes the remains of their midday meal from a low stone slab, which holds a vase carved with Greek iconography, and a gleaming bronze statue depicting Adonis and Aphrodite. Through arched windows, stone walls enclose the estate, giving way to fields of grapevines reaching to the Tiber River. The man of the house is gone, off to sell lumber, furs, and slaves to his eastern and southern trading partners. It is not unusual for an Etruscan trader to be away for several months, but this absence comes at a precarious time for his wife and the three-generation household she oversees.

With her lady friend, the woman of the house gossips, but their news is not idle. A new wave of political turmoil is sweeping Rome. Their unpopular Etruscan king, Lucius Tarquinius Superbus, is being threatened. The appellation *Superbus*, meaning "proud and haughty," is indicative of the public attitude toward Tarquinius's despotic reign. However, this current crisis has nothing to do with the king's imperial manner.

Following an indiscretion by royal son Tarquinius Sextus, Romans are openly discussing possible dire consequences. Word has it that Sextus raped Lucretia, his cousin's wife, leading Lucretia to stab herself to death in shame. Before taking her own life, Lucretia told her husband, Lucius Tarquinius Collatinus, about the terrible act committed against her and elicited a promise of revenge for her dishonoring. True to his word, Lucius Junius Brutus—the king's own nephew—leads the revolt against the crown.

Upon hearing the news that her king is to be deposed and expelled from Rome, the lady of the house covers her face with her hands and begins to cry. As a trader, her husband relies on connections with King Tarquinius for patronage and protection. The two women embrace to comfort each other, agreeing that nothing good can come of this foolishness—with the already strong dissent coming from the Roman rabble who would like to do away with the monarchy once and for all. Their concerns prove well-founded. King Lucius Tarquinius Superbus—whom his subjects call "Tarquin the Proud"—is the last Etruscan king to rule Rome.

"The Rape of Lucretia" detail of a painting by Titian.

In the two millennia that have passed since her rape, Lucretia's tragic fate has been painted by Titian, immortalized in Shakespearean verse, and sung by opera companies around the world. In 510 BCE, the soap opera that began with the violation of a royally connected Roman wife by an arrogant heir to the throne toppled the entrenched Etruscan political dynasty. Lucretia was the epitome of Roman feminine virtue, making her rape a property crime against her husband, one that necessitated that his honor be restored by any means necessary—even if it meant the end of the "family business." A moment of human weakness and indiscretion paved the way for another trial run for participatory democracy and laid the seeds for the Roman Empire. It would not be the last time a powerful government toppled because of a sexual indiscretion by its leader.

THE STORY OF ROME REALLY began in 509 BCE, when the Roman people revolted against the Etruscan dynasty of kings that had ruled the city for almost two hundred years. After ousting the last Etruscan king, the Romans initially set up an aristocratic, republican form of government, ruled by a three-hundred-man senate and two consuls, who were chosen each year by the Senate. Tension between plebeians and patricians was a constant factor in Roman society. Over time, government in the republic moved closer toward democracy with the institution of a popular assembly open to any man of any social class.

In theory, from 267 BCE until the end of the Republic in 31 BCE, Rome was a democracy in which power derived from the people. In practice, the senatorial class remained firmly in control. Patricians and plebeians were linked through client relationships in which patricians looked after the economic and legal interests of individual plebeians in exchange for their political support.

Patrician power, based on wealth and influence, was further supported by patricians' willingness to allow successful plebeian leaders to join the senatorial class.

At the same time that the Romans were busy creating the most powerful state on the Italian peninsula, they faced nearly constant war with their neighbors.

Cicero, a Roman senator from the Republican period.

CARTHAGE

Founded by the Phoenicians in 814 BCE, Carthage had become a powerful maritime empire in its own right by the sixth century BCE. When the First Punic War began, Carthage was the leading power in the western Mediterranean, with colonies in North Africa and along the Mediterranean coast as far west as Spain. At the end of the Third Punic War, the Romans razed the city and sowed the ground with salt, ensuring that nothing would grow there.

Julius Caesar resettled Carthage in 29 BCE, making it the capital of Rome's North African province. In the fifth century, this North African port city became the base of operations for the Vandals' takeover of the western Mediterranean, culminating in their sack of Rome—the death knell of the Roman Empire.

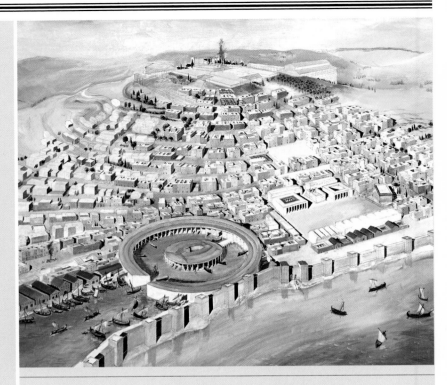

ABOVE: *artist's rendition of ancient Carthage*
RIGHT: *mosaic from ancient Carthage*

The First Punic War has been compared to World War I: a series of small incidents and alliances that dominoed into a major conflict. The war began when a group of mercenaries known as the Mamertines, or "Men of Mars," raided eastern Sicily and seized the town of Messina. Neither the Romans nor the Carthaginians had obvious reasons for intervening in the conflict, but once they became involved, the war escalated. Faced with war against the most powerful maritime power in the Mediterranean, the Romans scrambled to build a navy, capturing a Carthaginian ship to use as a model. Roman crews trained on land, learning to row their vessels on the safety of solid ground before they put to sea.

Together, the three Punic Wars lasted almost 120 years. By the end of the Punic Wars, the Romans had replaced Carthaginians as the dominant power in the Mediterranean, ruling not only the territories of defeated Carthage, but Corsica, Sardinia, Sicily, and large portions of Greece. The Roman sphere of influence reached from Spain to Rhodes.

The Romans used a system of alliances to expand their empire eastward. The Roman Senate was quick to accept alliances with smaller Aegean states that felt threatened by the power of Macedonia or the Seleucid Empire. As in the Punic Wars, alliances soon led to war. Between 200 and 189 BCE, the Romans waged a series of small wars in Greece and the Near East, defending their allies against Macedonia and the Seleucids. In the process, they slowly expanded their power over the Hellenistic states through a combination of treaty and conquest. In 146 BCE, Rome annexed Macedonia as a province. In 133 BCE, the Romans added a second eastern province to the empire when the last king of Pergamum willed his kingdom to Rome.

Only after these victories could the Romans legitimately begin to call themselves an *empire*.

The republican form of government, born in revolt during the second century BCE, did not survive Rome's rapid expansion into a global force. Wealth poured into the city of Rome, exacerbating the ever-present tension between patrician and plebeian, wealthy and poor. Political disorder became a way of life. It also led to challenges to patrician control of the state.

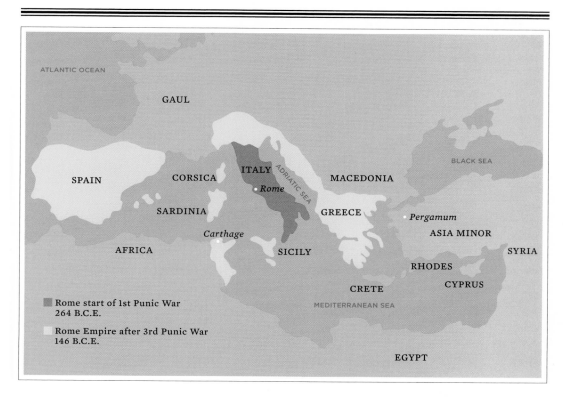

Roman territory before the Punic Wars and after the Third Punic War

THE SECRET OF ROMAN CONCRETE

From the remains of a volcano churning and spewing molten lava from the earth's crust, the Romans discovered an essential ingredient for man-made construction—at their feet.

Volcanoes occasionally knocked Roman buildings down, but the Romans' use of volcanic ash in their concrete mix is the reason so much Roman concrete is still in good repair after two thousand years.

Modern concrete is made from varying combinations of water, lime, sand, and aggregate (small rocks or gravel). Engineers call the proportions in which these ingredients are combined the "mix design"; different projects call for different mix designs. The mix design for Roman concrete didn't include sand or aggregate. Instead, Roman builders used *pozzolana*, volcanic ash from the area around Mount Pozzola.

The Roman use of volcanic ash in its design mix isn't the only difference between Roman and modern concrete. Today contractors typically pour liquid concrete into molds, and strengthen it with lengths of steel rod called *reinforcing bar*, or *rebar*.

Instead of casting concrete in molds, Roman masons built concrete in layers. Water, lime, and pozzolana were mixed together into a mortar that was too thick to pour. A layer of aggregate was covered with a layer of mortar, which was tamped down into the aggregate by hand, using a special tool called a "beetle." Reinforcing bar was an unheard-of concept, and apparently not needed. The Pantheon in Rome is holding up just fine without it.

Today, concrete is the most common building material used around the world. Houses and offices are built from it, rivers are dammed with it, and millions of cars drive over it every hour of every day. Yet few of us appreciate that the concrete first used by the Romans is more durable than that which was used in most twentieth-century buildings. These newer buildings will require regular and expensive renovations to last as long as the Roman Pantheon or Colosseum.

Amazingly, with the fall of the Roman Empire, the secrets of concrete manufacturing were lost for over a millennium. Only toward the end of the nineteenth century did concrete come back into common use around the world.

The Pantheon in Rome, completed in 126 CE, has been in continuous use since it's completion. Its dome is still the largest un-reinforced concrete dome in the world.

THE FIRST MEGACITY

Rome is most often recognized for its success as an imperial power and, though a republic, for its early experiment in democracy. Equally significant, during both periods, is the record of technological innovation and construction that made Rome the world's first megacity.

The Romans constructed aqueducts to serve their large cities as well as some small towns and industrial sites. Water for the city of Rome was supplied by eleven aqueducts constructed over a period of about five hundred years. These structures served drinking water and supplied Rome's numerous public baths and fountains. Aqueducts also emptied water into sewers, where once-used "gray water" performed its last function by removing waste matter.

The first Roman aqueduct was the Aqua Appia, built in 312 BCE during the Roman Republic. Aqueducts were ordered to be built on a larger scale by Emperor Claudius after he came to power in 41 CE. The largest, which came to be known as Aqua Claudia, presented an extraordinary engineering challenge. To begin with, the source springs for Aqua Claudia were located some thirty miles outside the city. Between the water's source and its end users, the structure had to traverse a series of hills and valleys. Trickier still, the aqueduct had to maintain a precise gradient—typically declining just a few

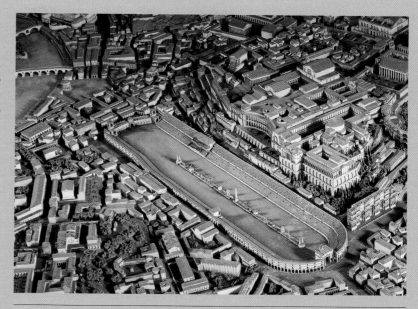

A model of ancient Rome with the Circus Maximus, a chariot-racing venue, in the foreground.

feet per mile to ensure that the water didn't overflow or dry up. Amazingly, the flow of water through a Roman aqueduct was powered by gravity alone.

Hundreds of slaves, as well as skilled laborers and freemen, worked tirelessly to complete the Aqua Claudia, a monumental task of precision engineering using only basic tools by modern standards. In addition to masonry aqueducts, the Romans built many more *leats*: channels excavated in the ground, each usually having a clay lining. Leats were much cheaper than the masonry design, but all aqueducts required good surveying to ensure a regular and smooth flow of water.

Infrastructure was a key to Rome's success as a civilization. The Romans built a vast network of roads, as well as water and sewage systems, using standardized weights, measures, and currency. From the model of engineering excellence provided by this first-century Roman aqueduct, we have continued to build our megacities outward and upward, while still copying Roman original designs in places as far-flung as California and Abu Dhabi.

The first challengers tried to work within the system. The patrician-born tribune Tiberius Gracchus passed laws designed to redistribute public lands to the poor in 133 BCE—and was murdered by a mob organized by obstructionist senators. His brother, Gaius, elected ten years later, revived Tiberius's land law and passed additional measures designed to create a political party that could challenge the strength of the Senate. He, too, died at the hands of a mob of senators and their dependents.

In the years after the Gracchus brothers, the Romans divided into two factions: the remaining supporters of the Gracchus brothers, known as the *populares*; and supporters of the Senate, called the *optimates*. Twice the people of Rome flared into civil war. Each time the rule of law slipped a little farther away.

In 59 BCE, three powerful Romans—Pompey, Crassus, and Julius Caesar—seized power together, forming the First Triumvirate. The formation of the Triumvirate did nothing to heal the constitutional wounds of Rome. Pompey, Julius Caesar, and Mark Antony each seized power in turn, plunging the Romans into another two decades of civil war.

The people of Rome finally achieved peace with the rise to power in 31 BCE of Caesar's adopted son, Octavian, who became Rome's first emperor. Like Julius Caesar before him and George Washington after him, Octavian refused to take the title of king. He claimed to be a defender of the Roman constitution. At first, the offices and titles he held were modifications of those traditional to the Republic. Over time, new words developed to describe his position. Octavian began to use the title "Imperator," traditionally a temporary honor given to a victorious general by his army. In 27 BCE, the Senate voted to give him the title *Augustus*, meaning "venerable."

Under Augustus's reign, the territory controlled by the new Roman Empire doubled in size. Roman armies, some of them led by the new emperor himself, campaigned in northern Spain, the Alps, the Danube, Germany, Ethiopia, Armenia, and Arabia. The army conquered new provinces and expanded the border of old provinces. Despite being backed by the power of the Roman Empire, the legions sometimes suffered failures, most notably in Germany, where a revolt by local tribes in 9 CE wiped out the occupying Roman army.

At its height, the Roman Empire covered an immense territory that stretched from Britain to Syria, with occasional gaps and bumps. Tin and silver from Britain, olive oil from Spain, grain from Egypt, lions from Africa, and sophists from Greece flowed into Rome. Merchants and soldiers carried Hellenistic culture and Roman engineering with them. Surveyors laid out new Roman cities on a grid plan that left room for aqueducts, bridges, public baths, and amphitheaters, built of concrete faced with brick.

The Empire was linked together by more than fifty thousand miles of hard-surfaced roads—one of Rome's most impressive and longest-lasting achievements. Roads were laid out by professional surveyors and built by specially trained army units. They were straight whenever possible and pitched for drainage. Depending on what materials were available locally, they were generally built with multilayered foundations of timber, rubble, and sand, and then paved with tight-fitting stones or gravel. Unpaved pedestrian paths flanked each road. Major roads had milestones placed at regular intervals, showing the distance to the next city. In many parts of Europe, Roman roads continued to be used well into the seventeenth century.

Emperor Augustus's rule ushered in a period of two hundred years of peace within the eastern Mediterranean, if not the whole empire, a period known as *Pax Romana*. It was a peace that depended on the strength of the Roman army, which became a permanent professional force for the first time during Augustus's rule. The army built the famous Roman roads—and then policed them. It patrolled for bandits, escorted public officials when they traveled, and collected taxes.

At this point, despite its reach from Western Europe to Mesopotamia, the Roman Empire still did not comprehend the size and cultural sophistication of its Far East counterpart, Han China. That would soon change.

Roman authorities had long heard rumors of a significant land in the Far East called "Sinae," or "Thinae." This remote power was in reality the Han Empire, the great political regime that rivaled Rome in both its territorial scale and the size of its subject populations. In 70 CE, a Roman author noted that "the land of Thinae is not easy to reach, saying few men come from there, and seldom."

Han histories describe the first Roman visitors to China in 166 CE as official ambassadors from the Roman leader. In fact, the first Romans invited to China were ambitious merchants who wangled their way into the Han court, seeking an advantage as importers of silk and other Oriental rarities.

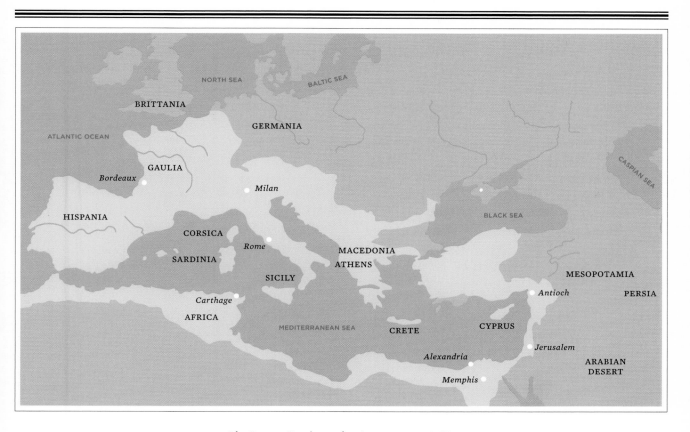

The Roman Empire under Augustus, c. 14 CE.

ROMAN TRADERS

A PARTY OF ROMAN MERCHANTS SAILS TO Vietnam by way of Malaysia. After months of waiting for word through intermediaries to China's Han regime, the traders are losing faith in their mission. Some among them argue that they should cut their losses and return to Rome with goods they've amassed at other Southeast Asian ports. When representatives of the Chinese emperor Huan finally arrive to take them to a waiting caravan for the trip to the emperor's palace in the capital of Luoyang, the Romans are pleased but less sure of themselves. They are told an audience with the emperor requires a high-value diplomatic gift. Without such a gift in hand, the Romans scramble, settling on elephant tusks, rhinoceros horn, and turtle shell—items they acquired en route.

The travel overland to the Chinese capital in the company of the emperor's escorts lasts several days. The landscape is strange and dramatic, since the Romans carry no preconceived notions of Chinese geography or the distance to be covered. Upon arriving in Luoyang, the merchants are driven in rickshaws through streets teeming with people and industry. They marvel at the distinctive Chinese architecture and goods offered by street vendors and storekeepers, including fine silks of every color and exotic produce they have never before seen or tasted.

The Roman traders are brought to the emperor at the imperial palace, and for the first time, men from the world's two greatest empires stand face-to-face in the same room. Standing within feet of the emperor, the Romans are told to bow humbly on the stone floor as they present their gifts. They do so uncomfortably. The emperor accepts the Roman tribute, giving no outward indication of his disappointment. In fact, Huan finds the traders' offering paltry, at odds with the reported wealth and power of the great empire they purport to represent. Still, he does not doubt the word of the intermediaries who have vetted these men as legitimate representatives of Rome, a state with which the emperor knows it is wise to make friendly contact. As a result, the gratitude he expresses for the trinkets laid at his feet is no less than what his guests would have received had they brought a more deserving tribute of Roman gold coins, jade, and amber—and the visiting traders are none the wiser as they leave the emperor's palace that day.

The Roman trading ships depart Han China stocked with the finest Chinese silks and spices, making the mission a historic breakthrough in global trade and diplomacy. Even so, given the inherent difficulties in traveling the five thousand miles between Rome and Han China by land or sea, the nomadic middlemen who link East-West trade will not disappear for the foreseeable future.

THE PARTHIANS

The Parthians did not fight like any other enemy the Roman legions had faced. Like their Persian forebears, the Parthian army was made up largely of cavalry forces, both heavily armored cavalrymen who wore the ancestors of the medieval suit of armor and, more important, light horse archers. The light horse archers were famed for a hit-and-run tactic that became known as the "Parthian shot": they would ride swiftly at the enemy, shoot their arrows, and then wheel around and retreat.

ABOVE: *A brick from a tomb structure with a design of a warrior executing a Parthian shot* • BELOW: *Parthian shot depicted in advertisement trade card.*

In actuality there was never a single Silk Road between China and its Near East and Western trading partners. Multiple routes took traders across the small kingdoms of Central Asia. From the oases of Central Asia, one route led through Afghanistan to Kashmir and northern India. Other routes traveled across the Caucasus Mountains to the Eurasian steppes, over the Iranian plateau or through the Syrian Desert to the Mediterranean. Darius's Royal Road from Susa to Sardis became the main trade route across Anatolia to the wealthy cities of Mesopotamia.

The Parthians, and their successors, the Sassanians and the Islamic kingdoms of Central Asia, effactually blocked direct trade between China and the West. Both the Chinese and the Romans would complain that the Parthians did not allow merchants from other kingdoms to travel the sections of the routes that were under their control.

In 53 BCE, Marcus Crassus, consul-triumvir of Rome and governor of the new province of Syria, led seven legions of Roman soldiers across the Euphrates River toward the Parthian Empire, hoping to match the military accomplishments of his fellow triumvirs, Pompey and Julius Caesar. The Parthian army attacked them outside of Carrhae. Then the Parthians unfurled their embroidered banners, described by Plutarch as "shining with gold and silk." The Romans fled in confusion by their first glimpse of silk.

Whether the Romans discovered silk at Carrhae or through the normal trade channels of the Near East, silk was an immediate hit. Within fifty years of the defeat at Carrhae, the Roman Senate passed sumptuary laws forbidding men to wear silk. The laws were ignored. The demand for silk grew.

Romans paid one pound of gold for one pound of unwoven silk thread, but the trade between the Romans and Chinese was not completely one-sided. The Romans imported silk, cinnamon, and lacquer ware from the Chinese; caravans returning east carried woolen and cotton textiles, coral, pearls, amber, and colored glass back to China.

Roman critics grumbled about the effects of silk both on Rome's morals and on its trade balance. Naturalist and philosopher Pliny the Elder estimated that Rome lost forty-five million sesterces (roughly $255 billion) to the silk trade each year.

According to Chinese legend, silk was first discovered by Xi Ling-Shi, the wife of Huangdi, a semimythical Chinese emperor who ruled China in the third millennium BCE. One day, while the empress was strolling in the palace garden, she plucked a white cocoon from the leaf of a mulberry tree. Later, as she drank her tea, she accidentally dropped the cocoon in the steaming hot liquid. When she fished it out, it unraveled into a

The Empire was linked together by more than fifty thousand miles of hard-surfaced roads—one of Rome's most impressive and longest-lasting achievements.

long, white thread. It's not a bad description of how silk is made.

The silkworm is the caterpillar of the world's only domesticated moth, *Bombyx mori*. Its preferred food is the broad leaf of the white mulberry tree. Timing is crucial in silk production. Caterpillar eggs are kept in cold storage for six to ten months until the first leaf buds appear on the mulberry trees. The newly hatched silkworms are fed finely chopped mulberry leaves for roughly thirty-five days, during which time they eat twenty times their weight per day and shed their skins four times. At the end of the process, the worms weigh ten thousand times more than they did when they were hatched.

The mature silkworms are put on a bamboo rack, where they spin their cocoons. A few moths are allowed to mature in order to produce another batch of silkworm eggs. Most of the cocoons are steamed or plunged into boiling water to kill the pupae and loosen the sticky secretions that hold the cocoon together. Once softened, the long continuous inner threads of the cocoon are unwound.

Wild silk, spun from the short broken fibers found in the cocoons of already-emerged silk moths, was produced throughout Asia. Only the Chinese knew how to domesticate the silk moth, *Bombyx mori,* and turn its long fibers into thread. They kept close control over the secrets of how to raise the domestic silkworm and create silk from the long fibers in its cocoon. Exporting silkworms, silkworm eggs, or mulberry seeds was punishable by death. It was more profitable to export the finished product than the means of production.

HOW MANY SILKWORMS DOES IT TAKE?

A single silkworm cocoon can produce almost a mile of continuous silk filament.

It takes nine silk filaments to make a 14-denier silk thread, which weighs one-half ounce per 30,000 feet.

It takes sixty mulberry trees and 2,000 to 3,000 silkworms to produce a pound of silk.

Silk may be soft and, well, silky, but it's also strong. A single silk fiber has the same tensile strength as a steel wire of the same diameter. A silk thread has greater tensile strength than steel. If stored carefully, the woven fabric lasts almost as long as metal.

THE CENTURIES IMMEDIATELY surrounding the life of Jesus Christ were a time when political empires flourished. Men seized power using unprecedented military might, new technologies, and robust trade between nation-states of the East and West. With these assets in a leader's hands, ultimate power was his for the taking.

By the time Western civilization comprehended the significance of the trial and death of Jesus Christ, the two mighty empires that had dominated during his lifetime would be in tatters. Much later, mankind would come to see that the power of a fervently held religious faith could rival that of any secular king. But none of this was clear when the actual events in the life of Jesus of Nazareth took place.

The Christian gospels that are our best source for the historical life of Jesus Christ place him in Judea during the reign of Herod the Great, who had eliminated the last of the Maccabean kings of Judea and assumed the throne in 37 BCE as a client of Rome. Rome is an active force in the story of Jesus, from Caesar Augustus's call for all citizens of the Roman Empire to be taxed, to Jesus's death by crucifixion, a Roman form of execution reserved for criminals, political agitators, and slaves.

What do official Roman records of the time tell us about the life of the man who transformed first the Empire and then the world in the centuries after his death? Absolutely nothing, though the historians Suetonius and Tacitus, writing some years later, mentioned that a man they referred to as Chrestus was responsible for disturbances among the Jewish community.

The biblical account of Jesus Christ's arrest, trial, suffering, and execution by crucifixion is called the "Passion," from the Latin word for "suffering." The story is told in the world's Christian churches on Good Friday of Easter week, in Passion plays and oratorios. The fourteen Stations of the Cross are numbered events that take place during the Passion,

beginning with the crowd's taunts of "Crucify him!" as Jesus is tried as a traitor. The Passion also reenacts Roman governor Pontius Pilate's pronouncement of Jesus's guilt, and the moment he is condemned to die on the cross. It goes on to depict the placement of a crown of thorns on Jesus's head and the wounded Jesus being forced to carry the cross on which he will die through the streets of Jerusalem, where he sees his mother, Mary, and falls to the ground.

One person mentioned in the Bible as standing in the crush, watching the fallen Jesus struggle to get back on his feet, is a young Jewish man, Simon of Cyrene.

Simon sees two women he presumes are Jesus's followers kneel down to wipe Jesus's dirt-covered and bloodied face with a cloth. Just ahead, Jesus's Roman escorts shout at the women to back away, telling Jesus he must get up and keep moving. Seeing that Jesus is too weak to get up on his own, the soldiers pull a stunned Simon from the crowd, instructing him to carry the cross. Simon is fearful but does what they say, first reaching down to pull Jesus to his feet, then using every ounce of strength to bear up under the weight of the immense wooden cross.

Slowly walking forward with Jesus at his side, Simon takes in the sharp contrast between the scorn of those mocking Jesus, and the love and anguish on the faces of those who believe this man to be their Messiah, God himself returned to Earth to help the chosen people out of their oppression.

Farther along, Jesus falls once more, and once again Simon must pull him back to his feet to continue their march up Mount Calvary. Once they reach Golgotha, Simon is pushed to the side to witness Jesus's further humiliation and suffering. First Jesus is stripped and then nailed to the same cross they'd just carried on their backs. Then, in the last moments before Jesus's cross is raised to stand next to two other crosses, bearing common criminals, the soldiers place a sign above Jesus's head reading, "King of the Jews."

After most of the spectators, except the women, have left, Simon remains, watching the Roman soldiers go to the cross to see if Jesus is dead yet. They stab him in the side to be sure and then instruct others to take the body down for burial.

Shaken and sad, Simon of Cyrene retraces the steps he took with Jesus and makes his way back down Mount Calvary.

FOR THE MODERN WORLD'S 2.1 billion Christians this scene reflects a core belief that Christ's suffering at the hands of his Roman and Judean prosecutors redeems humanity from sin, now, two thousand years later, just as it did at the moment of Jesus's death. From the perspectives of first-century Jewish leaders and their Roman provincial rulers who ordered his death, Jesus's teachings and rising popularity posed a threat to the stability of Judea.

At first, Christianity seemed to be just another Jewish sect at a time when Judaism was an evangelizing faith. The new sect spread first through the Jewish communities of the Middle East and the

Mediterranean. In 60 CE, the apostle Paul moved away from Christianity's Jewish roots and began to found new churches in the Greek cities of the Roman Empire, traveling between them on the network of Roman roads and using the imperial postal system to maintain contact with the churches he left behind. We have little information about how Christianity spread, but it is clear that it moved quickly from one enthusiastic convert to another.

By the middle of the first century, there was a growing Christian community in Rome itself. At first Christianity appealed primarily to those with little power: women, slaves, and the urban poor. By 200 CE, the new faith was beginning to attract a few wealthy adherents, and increasing amounts of unwanted official attention.

The Romans were a multiethnic people who recognized many gods and many religions. A Roman citizen, or a citizen of one of Rome's allied states, could worship any god he pleased as long as he participated in the state cult that venerated the emperors as gods. The Christians condemned the state cult as idolatry and refused to worship the emperor, a position that was seen as treason. Refusal led to their persecution as enemies of the State. Christians brought before Roman judges were given the option of lighting incense before the statue of the emperor. Those who did were set free. Those who did not were often tortured and executed.

The first official attacks against Christians occurred after the fire of 64 CE, when Nero tried to blame the unpopular minority for the destruction in Rome. Thereafter, wild rumors about Christian practices spread through the empire: they sacrificed infants, they ate human flesh at their rites, and they had incestuous group orgies. (Ironically, Christians would later spread some of these same rumors about Jews and women rumored to be witches.) Official persecution occurred in waves, reaching its height during the last years of Diocletian's rule.

IN 203 CE, CARTHAGE WAS A thriving city (located in modern-day Tunisia) under Roman rule. Romans there and throughout the Empire worshipped multiple gods and goddesses, with cults for Jupiter and Diana among the most favored. Believers in the teaching of Jesus Christ who lived in Carthage had to keep their beliefs and the rituals of their Christian worship secret lest they be arrested and face torture and death.

Among them was a married woman named Vibia Perpetua, who is described in historical accounts, including her own diary, as a "respectably born, liberally educated citizen, having a father and mother and two brothers, one of whom, like herself, was a catechumen (one receiving instruction

Triumph of Faith - Christian Martyrs in the Time of Nero, 65 AD by Eugene Romain Thirion (1839-1910)

PERPETUA AND FELICITY

IN THE AGONIZING DAYS AWAITING HER FATE, Perpetua, in the company of her slave Felicity, struggles to make sense of what is happening to her and why. In her diary she offers this account of a vision of ascending on a ladder up into heaven. Ahead of her on the ladder is her brother Saturus (who is executed before her). Upon reaching Heaven, Perpetua is greeted by a white robbed man who welcomes and feeds her. She describes the sweetness of the cake she eats as a lasting symbol of the passion of her Christian beliefs.

And he raised his head, and looked upon me, and said to me, "Thou are welcome, daughter." And he called me, and from the cheese as he was milking he gave me as it were a little cake, and I received it with folded hands; and I ate it, and all who stood around said Amen. And at the sound of their voices I was awakened, still tasting a sweetness which I cannot describe. And I immediately related this to my brother, and we understood that it was to be a passion, and we ceased henceforth to have any hope in this world.

After the vision, Perpetua continues to deny her family's pleas to renounce her faith. Perpetua learns she will face a trial when she will be given the opportunity to renounce her faith and receive her freedom. During this time her family visits her and tries to convince her to renounce her faith in order to avoid execution. Perpetua refuses, saying "No. Neither can I call myself anything else than what I am, a Christian." Several days later, Perpetua and Felicity are thrown to a wild bull, trampled, and gored to death.

from a catechist in the principles of the Christian religion with a view to baptism) and a son an infant at her breast."

Perpetua had a slave, Felicity, and her newborn baby with her when she was apprehended by soldiers while praying in a clandestine house of worship in Carthage. In her diary, Perpetua described her terror after being taken to a dungeon. She feared especially for her baby in the hot and crowded conditions of their confinement.

THE ULTIMATE FATE OF CHRISTIANS in the Roman Empire was tied to a Roman political power struggle. In 312 CE, already master of Britain, Gaul, and Spain, the future Roman emperor Constantine led his army south to battle with Maxentius for control of Italy and Africa. According to Christian legend, at some point in the journey, Constantine saw the image of the cross and the words *In hoc imago vince* ("conquer in this sign") superimposed on the sun. Advancing toward Rome and battle, he ordered his troops to mark their shields with the sign of the cross.

Constantine won his final battle with Maxentius at Milvian Bridge, just outside of Rome, although his troops were outnumbered by at least two to one. He attributed the victory to the power of the cross.

A few months later, Constantine and his co-emperor in the east, Licinius, issued the Edict of Milan, which guaranteed Christians the right to practice their religion without persecution.

Constantine did not formally convert to Christianity until he was on his deathbed, in 337. He did not make Christianity the state religion of the Roman Empire. (Often mistakenly attributed to Constantine, that step was taken by Theodosius I in 380.) He did appoint himself the public and openhanded patron of the religion that only a few years before had been literally forced underground by official persecution. During Constantine's reign, the enormous Old Saint Peter's Basilica was built in Rome. The bishopric of Rome took its first step toward the modern papacy, receiving extensive land endowments and one of the imperial palaces for use as the bishop's residence. The new capital of Constantinople was built as an explicitly Christian city. Constantine even sent his mother, Helena, to Jerusalem to restore the city to its former glory. Helena knocked down Hadrian's temple which the emperor Hadrian had built on top of the site of Solomon's temple. She also constructed shrines and churches that honored the sites of Jesus's life, creating Jerusalem as a site of Christian pilgrimage.

THE *PAX ROMANA* DIDN'T LAST. In the middle of the third century CE, the Roman Empire began to crumble from the top down. Between 235 and 284 CE, twenty-six more or less legitimate rulers and forty usurpers were crowned emperor of Rome. Most of them were incompetent. All but two died violent deaths. The shortest reign lasted less than three months. Often, competing emperors ruled at the same time. The only stable power remaining was the Roman army, which made and unmade emperors at the command of their generals.

Across the globe, the Han dynasty maintained the throne in China but never regained the power enjoyed by the earlier Han emperors. In the middle of the second century CE, a succession of child emperors took the throne. The accession of each boy-emperor led to factional disputes and court intrigues as court eunuchs and the relatives of the most recent empress or consort competed for power. In 220, the last Han was deposed and the empire was divided into three independent states, known as the Three Kingdoms.

As turmoil reigned at the top of China's power structure, the Silk Roads remained open. Over time, first Byzantium and later the kingdoms of Western Europe replaced Rome as a market for China's luxury goods.

In the thirteenth century, trade along the Silk Roads entered a golden age when Genghis Khan and the Mongols conquered an empire that included China, Central Asia, the Middle East, and much of Eastern Europe.

Today the ancient Silk Roads are in use again, part of a thriving trade corridor between China and the Central Asia states that were once part of the Soviet Union. Trucks carrying consumer electronics and ripe melons trundle down the roads where camel caravans once carried silk and amber.

In the Iron Age, mankind saw and realized the potential to tame a metal from deep inside the earth and use it to topple and build great empires. The advent of people power led not to a full blossoming of democracy, but to a few men exercising absolute power over vast lands and peoples—spreading war over land and sea.

This time in human history also showed that when men and women are willing to die for an idea or belief, history becomes more volatile. The divisions and conflicts born in the Iron Age would have staying power. For the people of the fifth century and immediately beyond, the dismantling of old empires led to even larger and fiercer dynasties with the weapons and armies to control all in their reach. The East arose and ushered in a new age of enlightenment, and with it, a titanic clash of civilizations.

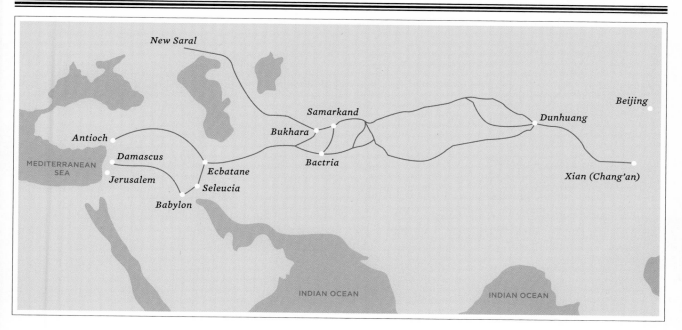

Map of the Silk Roads

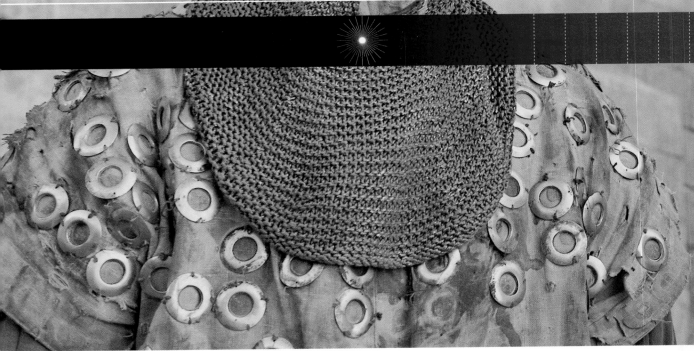

HOW THE EAST SAVED THE WEST

455 CE. AFTER CENTURIES OF DECLINE AND ATTACKS BY VISIGOTHS AND HUNS, CIVILIZATION'S GREATEST METROPOLIS, ROME, RECEIVES ITS FINAL, FATAL BLOW.

Vandals sack the city, kidnap its empress, and reduce its buildings to rubble. (The most important churches in the city only survive the invaders' worst wrath because of a deal worked out by Vandal king Gaiseric and Pope Leo I.) Philosophy, history, science, plumbing, and literacy are lost in the ruins, replaced by the promise and poetry of the early Roman church. Now, in place of an empire, dozens of small kingdoms form around large landowners and tribal chieftains who can offer defense, if not security. The vaunted Roman roads stand but are hazardous to travel. It is a time remembered as the "Dark Ages."

Though it's a Dark Age in Europe, civilization is on the rise for peoples and lands to the east.

Byzantium, capital of the eastern Roman Empire, still stands. Muhammad leads the "army of the faithful" across the Arabian Desert, spreading Islam by an inspired combination of conversion and conquest—much of it paid for by Arabia's gold mines.

Before the end of the Middle Ages in the thirteenth century, armies of Western knights wearing the cross on their breastplates will do battle with their Muslim counterparts and turn Palestine into a bloody battlefield. Their confrontation will sow seeds of learning and commerce between East and West, while setting the stage for a clash of civilizations that will continue for centuries.

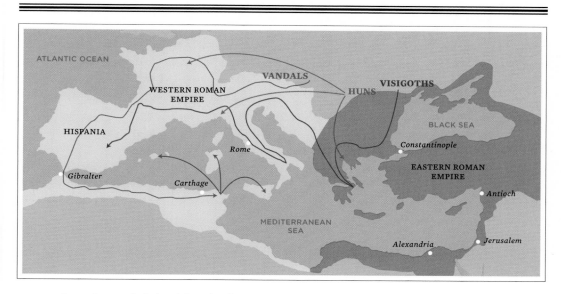

LEFT: *Crusaders sacked the cities of Palestine in search of fortune, glory, and a papal dispensation for their sins.* • ABOVE: *map of invasions by the Huns, Visigoths, and Vandals*

In 410 CE Alaric, king of the Visigoths, attacked the Romans with a force swollen beyond its original size with thousands of members of other barbarian tribes and escaped slaves.

The Visigoths were a contrast to the clean-cut Roman soldiers, with their armored breastplates and skirts of leather or fabric strips that protected the upper legs. The barbarians colored their bodies with paint. They left their hair and beards uncut, dressed them with oil, and braided them into shapes that looked outlandish to the Roman eye. They wrapped their legs in awkward garments called *braccae* (breeches). Compared to the ordered ranks of the Roman legions, there was no discipline in their ranks. They moved in chaotic clusters. They were dirty. They stank of animal grease and unwashed skin. And they were terrifying.

Alaric and his barbarian forces had besieged Rome twice before. Each time the Roman Senate had bought them off. The last time it had cost the city five thousand pounds of gold, thirty thousand pounds of silver, four thousand fine silk tunics, three thousand scarlet-dyed skins, and three thousand pounds of precious pepper from the Indies. Once again, the Senate sent a pair of envoys to deal with him, threatening the king with the Roman army's might.

Alaric shrugged. "The thicker the grass, the more easily it's scythed."

The envoys weren't surprised. They'd had to buy him off before. The only question was what the price would be this time. When the answer came, it was staggering. Alaric demanded all the gold and silver in the city, everything of value, including every barbarian slave.

The envoys gasped. "What will that leave us?"

Alaric paused, then gave a wolfish smile. "Your lives."

BARBARIANS

Who's a *barbarian*? Today, we use the term to mean an "uncultured brute"—two more words that require definition. The ancient Greeks, the imperial Chinese, and the Romans were much more specific.

The Greeks and Chinese labeled everyone a barbarian who spoke a language other than Greek or Chinese. As far as the Greeks were concerned, that included the Romans, no matter how many Greek slaves were employed as tutors by Roman patricians.

The Romans borrowed the term from the Greeks and adapted it to mean anyone who lived outside the limits of Roman rule. They pictured the world with the empire at the center, surrounded by barbarians. The farther away from Rome, the wilder the barbarian.

ROME FELL GRADUALLY.

The succession of inept rulers and military usurpers who sat on the imperial throne between 235 and 284 CE were unable to hold the empire together in the face of the threat of Germanic tribes from the north and west and the newly founded Sassanian Empire in Persia. Emperor Diocletian's division of the Roman Empire into four semi-independent regions ruled by "coemperors" stemmed the decay for a time. In the long run, it made things worse by dividing the empire into East and West. The Eastern Empire, with its capital at Constantinople, had all the wealth. Its emperors concentrated their resources on defending the eastern border against the Sassanian Persians' considerable might. In the West, Rome was left to the mercy of corrupt and inadequate administrators and barbarian tribes.

The fabled Roman army was both a protection against the barbarians and a veiled threat to the

King Alaric and Visigoths pillaging Rome (detail).

Chapter 4: HOW THE EAST SAVED THE WEST

IRELAND KEEPS
THE LAMP BURNING

Unlike England, Ireland was never part of the Roman Empire. When the first Christian missionary, Saint Patrick, arrived in Ireland from England around 432 CE, the Irish accepted Christianity, but not the institutional framework of the Roman Church. Instead of building a hierarchical structure of bishops and recognizing the primacy of the bishop of Rome, the Irish followed the example of the desert saints of the Near East, founding monasteries in wild and remote places.

Newly converted and newly literate, Irish Christians turned their monasteries into seats of learning and missionary zeal. They sent monks to convert the pagans and founded monasteries, first in northern Britain and later on the European continent.

Missionaries needed copies of the Gospels. Monasteries needed libraries. Making copies of texts became an important activity in the Irish monasteries and their sister institutions from the seventh century and onward. The first books they copied were the Gospels, but they soon copied any text they could get their hands on, including ancient Roman literature, the works of the Venerable Bede and Isidore of Seville, and their own folk literature. Today, the manuscripts copied in Irish monasteries are our primary source for the literature of ancient Rome and Britain.

With Charlemagne's rise to power around 800 CE, Europe's cultural center moved from Ireland to France, but Ireland's role did not diminish. According to Charlemagne's secretary and biographer, the emperor "loved the little wandering monks." No longer needed to convert pagan rulers to Christianity, the learned monks of the British Isles helped give birth to the "Carolingian Renaissance" and the first step out of the Dark Ages.

emperor. Since the time of Vespasian in the first century CE, new emperors had come from the army, been approved by the army—then been pulled off their thrones by the army. Like a half-tamed beast, the army had to be fed. The need to pay the troops on time became the government's driving force.

When the barbarians began to move across the Roman border, they were seen as a nuisance, not a threat. Romans viewed them as heavily armed migrating tribes rather than an organized invasion. The barbarians came in trickles, insinuating themselves into the fabric of Roman society. They were craftsmen seeking employment in Roman cities; warriors enlisting in the Roman legions; tribal chieftains who adopted Roman ways. By the middle of the fourth century CE, many Roman generals were members of Germanic tribes. Theodoric, king of the Ostrogoths, summed up the process: "An able Goth wants to be like a Roman; only a poor Roman would like to be like a Goth."

Following the Sack of Rome by the Visigoths in 410, life in the empire grew increasingly unstable. In 452, Attila led the Huns almost unopposed on a rampage through the Italian peninsula, driven back by malaria and famine rather than the Roman legions.

Three years later, the Vandals finished the destruction of Rome, causing more ruin than the Visigoths.

Following Rome's demise at the hands of the Vandals, large landowners ignored the emperor's decrees and used the great public buildings that had been Rome's pride as quarries for churches and private strongholds. Bandits infested the solidly built roads that had linked one end of the empire to another. The imperial *curiosi*, half border guard and half highway patrol, began to demand protection money from travelers. Freemen were enslaved

THE SACK OF ROME

"Plundering of Rome by the Vandals", engraving based on
an 1865 drawing by Heinrich Leutemann

WORD OF THE EXPECTED ARRIVAL OF THE Vandals' fleet at the mouth of the Tiber River has caused panic in and around the palace of Emperor Petronius Maximus. From Empress Licinia Eudoxia's point of view, her husband has displayed characteristic cowardice by attempting to escape. She is not sad to see him stoned to death by an angry mob of his own people outside the palace gates. Eudoxia watches numbly from a window as her husband's head and other body parts are severed. Then, with the roar of angry Romans still audible from the streets, she returns quickly to her living quarters.

Realizing she has few choices, the empress grows more concerned about her own safety and that of her two daughters, Eudocia and Placidia. A few months before, Eudoxia had sent a letter to Vandal king Gaiseric, asking for his help in toppling Emperor Petronius—who had murdered the last emperor and forced Eudoxia to marry him. Now she regrets the offer to ally herself with him.

The empress gathers her daughters and, after donning disguises, the three leave the imperial fortress with two palace guards in an unadorned carriage. Eudoxia hopes to reach a waiting vessel and flee Rome for the north. The disguised royal party manages to get past the Roman mob and reach the port but cannot escape the Vandal king, whose fleet has by now encircled the city. Vandal troops are already making their way through the streets, taking anyone and anything they see fit.

When she, too, is taken into Gaiseric's custody, Empress Eudoxia is forced to watch helplessly as the Vandal army plunders Rome, toppling its buildings and robbing the city of its coins and stripping the gold trim from its statuary and church altars and rooftops. When his ships can hold no more Roman treasure, Gaiseric sets sail again, taking the empress and her daughters back to Carthage, where he marries her and then gives her eldest daughter, Eudocia, to his son and heir, Huneric.

With his long-sought alliance to Roman royalty in place, Gaiseric declares himself ruler of Europe and Africa. Gaiseric's successors will rule North Africa until 534, a long reign by the standards of these tumultuous times.

in great numbers, seized by barbarians, and then reduced to serfdom on the estates of the great landlords who ransomed them. Rome itself, abandoned first by the emperors and then by anyone who could afford to leave, was looted by Roman citizens as well as by barbarians.

TO THE EAST, THE VIOLENT interruptions that nearly dismantled the foundations of the West had not slowed human progress toward modernity. Buoyed by wealth derived from the mining of gold and silver, the peoples of Arabia and Mesopotamia were building rather than destroying civilizations, creating science and mathematics to usher mankind into the future.

July 30, 762 CE. Al-Mansur, the second caliph of the Abbasid dynasty, stood on the banks of the Euphrates and watched as the architects laid out his new capital city, Baghdad.

The caliph was careful with both details and dinars. Used to the lavish spending of the recently overthrown Umayyad dynasty, al-Mansur's subjects sometimes called him "the father of pennies" because he counted them all. That was all right with him. He'd grown up in poverty and knew that the man who counted the pennies had the dinars for the projects that matter. His new capital city was a project that mattered.

Al-Mansur was determined that his new capital would be like no other city the world had seen. He had searched for almost ten years before finding the perfect site for his new capital, at the point where the Tigris and Euphrates Rivers were so close together that the city could fill the space between them.

Like Paris in the 1890s, Baghdad was a cultural magnet. Scientists, poets, scholars, and artists came from all over the civilized world to settle in the Round City of the Abbasids. Most important of all, Baghdad had libraries. Encouraged by an official policy of intellectual curiosity, Islamic scholars in Baghdad collected works of literature, philosophy, and science from all corners of the empire. (One of al-Mansur's successors reportedly negotiated for a copy of Ptolemy's *Hè Megalè Syntaxis* as part of a treaty with Byzantium.)

Collecting and translating manuscripts from around the Islamic world required room to work, clerical support, and storage space. With financial backing from the caliphs, an army of scholars manned a translation bureau, a royal library, a book depository, and an observatory—collectively known as the House of Wisdom. Academic patronage became a path for political advancement. Ambitious nobles created their own libraries, many of

> To the East, the violent interruptions that nearly dismantled the foundations of the West had not slowed human progress toward modernity.

them open to the public. By the ninth century, the Street of Stationers had more than a hundred book and paper shops.

An informal academy of scholars and their students grew up around the House of Wisdom. Working in a culture that encouraged learning, Abbasid scholars in the eighth through the tenth centuries not only transcribed and translated the classical scholarship of Greece, Persia, and India, they transformed it, pushing the boundaries of knowledge forward in mathematics, geography, astronomy, and medicine.

The disciplines at the heart of Arabic science were astronomy, geography, and mathematics, all of

THE BIRTH OF BAGHDAD

The Arab caliph al-Mansur consulted with the three best astrologers of his court—an Arab, a Persian, and a Jew—to cast a horoscope to determine when work should start on the round city he determined would be the new capital that would become Baghdad. Now they were ready to begin.

Following al-Mansur's instructions, the architects laid out the city walls in a perfect circle, drawn using the teachings of Euclid, the caliph's favorite Greek geometer. They marked the circle first with ashes and then with cotton seeds soaked in naphtha. Once lit, the cotton seeds burst into flame,

burning the outline of the Round City into the ground. "By God!" the watching caliph exclaimed. "I shall live in it my entire life, and it shall become the home of my descendants; and without doubt, it will become the most prosperous city in the world."

Nicknamed the Round City, al-Mansur's new capital took five years to build: an enormous palace complex within a circular brick wall one mile around, 95 feet high and 145 feet thick. Within twenty years of its completion, it was the biggest city in the world, with more than a million people: Muslim and Christian Arabs, non-Arab Muslims,

Jews, Zoroastrians, Sabians, and an occasional Hindu scholar visiting from India. People and goods poured in from every corner of an empire that stretched from Spain to Samarqand. A growing disorderly ring of merchants and craftsmen surrounded the perfect circle of the inner city. Every type of business had its own street: cloth merchants, fruit sellers, leather workers, perfumers, bakers, even booksellers. An Arab geographer of the time claimed that the city had six thousand streets, thirty thousand mosques, and ten thousand bathhouses.

which were tied to the ritual requirements of Islam. To accurately calculate the timing of the five daily prayers and the month of fasting at Ramadan, Muslims scholars created increasingly sophisticated ways of making astronomical observations. They used tools from the new disciplines of astronomy and mathematics to determine the direction of Mecca from any point in the caliphate.

Muslim scholars' achievements in the golden age of Islam went far beyond the practical requirements of Islamic worship. By the ninth century, scholars in Baghdad could measure the earth using astronomical readings with a degree of accuracy unsurpassed until the twentieth century. They had also begun work on the conundrum of how to represent the round surface of the earth on a two-dimensional map. Muslim alchemists developed and refined processes that were the foundation of modern chemistry, including distillation, crystallization, reduction, and filtration. Muslim doctors accurately described the mechanism of sight and the anatomy of the eye, discovered how blood circulates through the body, developed effective surgical techniques for removing cataracts, laid out rules for testing the effectiveness of new drugs that form the basis for clinical trials today, and wrote medical works that remained standard texts in Europe well into the seventeenth century.

It was a busy couple of centuries.

The golden age of Islam created new states, cities, and academic disciplines. This Islamic renaissance was built on the backs of thousands of slaves, servants, and prisoners, who worked as miners extracting gold, along with silver, copper, and lead, from vast precious metal reserves under the Middle Eastern desert. These minerals were originally brought to Earth by meteorites from outer space. In the seventh century, with no major agricultural or

AL-KHWĀRIZMĪ + ALGORITHM = ALGEBRA

———

The ancient root of the word *algorithm* is little understood today, despite its ubiquitous usage to describe the magic formula behind everything from the Google search engine to NASA spacecraft.

Mystery solved.

Muhammad ibn Māsa al-Khwārizmī is the father of modern mathematics. His name lives on in English, in mangled form, in the word *algorithm*.

We know very little about al-Khwārizmī's life. His name suggests he was born in the region of Khwarazm in what is now Uzbekistan. There are clues that he was a Zoroastrian who may have converted to Islam.

We know a lot about al-Khwārizmī's work as a scholar in al-Mansur's court in Baghdad. He introduced what were then called "Hindu numerals" to the Muslim world. He also produced an important astronomical chart that made it possible to calculate the positions of the sun, the moon, and the major planets and to tell time based on stellar and solar observations.

Al-Khwārizmī's most important contribution to science was a groundbreaking mathematical treatise: *Al-Kitab al-Mukhtasar fi hisab al-jabr wa'l-muqabala*. The title translates as *The Compendium on Calculation by Restoration and Balancing*, but the book is most often referred to as al-jabr, or algebra. His treatise was a combination of mathematical theory and practical examples related to inheritances, property division, land measurements, and canal digging. He was the inventor both of quadratic equations and mathematical word problems. Some of his word problems became classics, which meant they were still giving students grief several centuries later.

AN ARABIAN MINE

JAMAL, A SLAVE IN HIS LATE TWENTIES FROM Northern Africa, awakens at the morning call on his sleeping mat in the miners' barracks. He quickly cleans up and kneels for the morning prayer. After a brief meal, he carries a lantern and his pick and walks with his fellow miners the two hundred yards from their barracks. Near the entrance of the tunnel, the men form a line. Just as he has done every morning for the last ten years, Jamal lights his lantern and checks that it has sufficient oil as he readies himself to enter the Mahd al-Dhahab mine. He'll be underground for the remainder of the day, not returning to the surface until after sunset.

At the mouth of the mine, Jamal sees the owner-operator, a prominent man of the local Quarashi tribe, known to the men as al-Hajjaj. Jamal averts his eyes when al-Hajjaj barks orders at the men to make haste, pointing at the newer of two tunnel entrances. *As if we don't know which tunnel to enter*, thinks Jamal as a current of fear travels up his spine. New tunnels bring extra danger to miners since there is still rock to break apart and rubble to be cleared before picks can be used to extract gold nuggets from new veins—yet to be found.

Jamal leads his gang until they reach the spot where they finished yesterday fifty meters underground. He takes up his pick and begins to loosen an area of rock from the low ceiling ahead of him, working at the same crevice for several hours, handing loose rock back to the man behind him, who hands it to the next man, continuing until the rock reaches the wagon at the rear of the line used to bring rock up to ground level, where it will be inspected for traces of gold.

Suddenly Jamal hears the dreaded sound of loose rock falling behind him, followed by muffled sounds of panic. He freezes with his pick in midair. As more rocks fall from above, Jamal crouches on the ground, with his arms over his head, praying for the collapse to stop, or for his

death to come quickly. When the dust from falling rock clears and it grows quiet again in the tunnel, Jamal realizes he's alive and alone on the wrong side of a collapsed pile of debris. He calls out several times, but gets no response.

Jamal then begins the difficult work of removing the stones that separate him from the only exit from this tunnel, not sure how much rock has fallen. He has no idea whether he is the only survivor of this collapse, or its only victim. Jamal tells himself not to think, just to keep going, and be thankful for the fact that he still has a working lantern. Rock by rock, beginning with the least precarious, his work continues slowly and carefully.

When enough loose stones have been cleared, Jamal braces himself on his haunches and picks up a rock as big as a man's head, noticing it

is heavier than the others. He twists his torso to drop the rock behind him, turning it over, about to put it down, when he thinks to bring the rock up to eye level for closer inspection. Unbelieving at first, Jamal brings the lantern closer, amazed to see a shiny piece of gold nugget buried deep inside the now-split piece of ore. Jamal's excitement is immediately tempered by the thought that he may not live to celebrate this important find—the first sizable nugget to come from the new tunnel. He calls out again to the others, hoping to be heard. When he is greeted by silence again, Jamal's spirit falls; tired and hopeless, he lies down on the mine floor, just as the oil in his lantern runs out, leaving him in total darkness.

On the other side of the collapsed tunnel, other miners scramble to remove fallen rock from the legs and torsos of partially buried miners. So much rock has fallen and so many are buried; things don't look good for Jamal.

At daylight, back at the mouth of the mine, a large crowd has gathered to watch and wait for news of the trapped miners. Owner-operator al-Hajjaj directs a party of rescuers, who carry miners out of the tunnel one by one, some writhing in pain but still alive, others lying dead on stretchers.

Finally, the last man to be pulled out is placed on the ground by his rescuers. It is Jamal, covered with dirt and sweat, but smiling as he holds up the piece of ore with its nugget of gold. Shouts and cheers are heard from the other miners in the crowd.

The next day, again at daybreak, Jamal's piece of gold is stocked by another worker on a camel that is then led away for the trip to the Mahd al-Dhahab smelting operation. Jamal, proud of his find, stands again at the head of the line of miners, preparing to reenter the same tunnel from which he was rescued the day before.

industrial resources, mining and exporting gold bullion enabled the Islamic empire to trade with the rest of the world—and served as the means to mint a new Islamic currency.

Gold mining was dangerous and backbreaking work.

One Arabian mine, the Mahd al-Dhahab (Cradle of Gold), is 155 miles southeast of Medina and 170 miles northeast of Mecca, the major religious centers of the Islamic world. Still in business today, Mahd al-Dhahab produced 1.5 million ounces of gold from more than a million tons of ore in historic times.

IN 750 CE, THE ARMIES OF Abu al-Abbas defeated the last of the Umayyad caliphs in a series of bloody battles. Now a new caliph, and a new dynasty, sat on the throne of Damascus.

Some men in al-Abbas's position would have hunted down the remaining members of the old dynasty to ensure no heirs remained to lay claim to the throne. Instead, the new caliph invited the surviving Umayyads to a feast. At first, his guests perched nervously on the cushioned benches in the dining hall of the Abbasid family estate in Damascus. Servants moved around the room, offering them tidbits of spiced meat, honeyed dates, and fresh oranges. Wine flowed without regard to the Prophet's prohibition on alcohol. Skilled slaves played tambuts in the background. Slowly, the Umayyads relaxed and began to enjoy al-Abbas's hospitality. They didn't notice when someone gave an unobtrusive signal.

Suddenly, the servants stripped off their robes, displaying the armor beneath. Someone screamed. The Umayyads sprang to their feet. Some ran to the doors, which had been blocked. Others fought back as best they could, unarmed men against armored solders.

ABD AL-RAHMAN ESCAPES DAMASCUS

Abd al-Rahman and his younger brother escaped from al-Abbas's slaughter together. As al-Rahman later described it:

Joined by my freed man, Badr, we reached the bank of the Euphrates, where I met a man who promised to sell me horses and other necessities; but while I was waiting he sent a slave to find the Abbasid commander. Next we heard a noise of the troops approaching the farmhouse; we took to our heels and hid in some gardens by the Euphrates, but they were closing in on us. We managed to reach the river ahead of them and threw ourselves into the water. When they got to the bank they began shouting "Come back! You have nothing to fear." I swam and my brother swam.

Al-Rahman made it across the river. His brother was captured and killed.

One young Umayyad prince, Abd al-Rahman, not yet twenty, survived the slaughter. He fled through the North African deserts toward present-day Spain—the newest, most distant, and most neglected province of the Islamic empire. When al-Rahman finally reached his goal, five years later, he deposed the ruling governor in the name of the Umayyad dynasty.

SPAIN HAD BECOME PART OF the Islamic empire forty years earlier when a band of Muslim invaders from North Africa defeated the last of its Visigoth rulers. By 720 CE, Muslims had conquered most of the Iberian Peninsula. A cluster of small Christian kingdoms managed to hold a narrow strip of the desolate country in the northeast, an area so wild that not even the Romans had managed to subdue it completely. The conquerors named the region *al-Andalus*, the land of the Vandals, and chose the old Roman city of Córdoba as their capital. By the standards of the vast Islamic empire ruled from Damascus by the Umayyad caliphs, the new province was poor, backward, and unattractive. Just like the rest of Medieval Europe.

Abd al-Rahman and his Umayyad successors brought the technical, cultural, and commercial benefits of the Islamic world to al-Andalus. The previously impoverished country literally blossomed under their rule. Muslims brought Arab technologies for making the most of scarce desert resources to the semi-arid climate of the Iberian Peninsula. Dams and irrigation systems weren't the only change. Muslims also introduced new crops that would transform Europe's diet, including rice, sugar, oranges, lemons, spinach, melons, and eggplant. By the tenth century, the Arab agricultural revolution had transformed Spain into the wealthiest, and best-fed, region of Europe.

More productive land allowed more workers to move to the cities and work as specialized craftsmen. Soon Spanish luxury goods were traded throughout the Muslim world, including musical instruments from Seville, leather goods from Córdoba, and steel weapons from Toledo. As the prosperity of Muslim Spain grew, its cities became oases of luxury, wealth, tolerance—and learning.

Abd al-Rahman's successors consciously chose to create a city that would rival Baghdad in the pursuit of the arts and sciences. They actively recruited scholars, poets, musicians, and artists, offering them tempting incentives to leave the comfortable metropolises of the Abbasid empire for the wild west of Spain. They sent agents to the older cities of the Muslim world to purchase copies of important books. They funded libraries, hospitals, and research. The royal library alone held some 400,000 books at a

THE WORLD'S FIRST AVIATOR

875 CE. Sixty-five-year-old scientist Abbas Ibn Firnas leapt off the top of the Rusafa palace of Córdoba in a device made of feathers attached to a wooden frame. He had designed the hang glider himself after hours of watching birds in flight. For several minutes he glided on the air currents, able to adjust his altitude and steer toward his targeted landing spot. The gliding was wonderful; the landing was rough. Ibn Firnas was badly injured in the crash. After he was pulled out of the wreck, he claimed that he hadn't paid enough attention to the way birds use their tail feathers; if he'd only added a tail apparatus to the glider, he'd have been just fine.

Abbas Ibn Firnas is not well-known in the West, but he is honored as the first aviator in the Arab-speaking world. Both a moon crater and the Ibn Firnas Airport in Baghdad are named after him.

time when the largest library in Christian Europe had only 640 books in its catalog. By the reign of Abd al-Rahman III in the tenth century, the Benedictine nun, Rosita, would describe Córdoba, the region's capital, as "the ornament of the world . . . it was wealthy and famous and known for its pleasures and resplendent in all things, especially for its seven streams of wisdom."

As 1999 demonstrated again, people get very nervous when a millennium is about to end. In 999 CE, many European Christians believed the world would end in a matter of months. Signs of the apocalypse had been reported throughout Europe: eclipses, rains of blood, Viking attacks. Amid this fear, Gerbert d'Aurillac, archbishop of Ravenna, soon to be Pope Sylvester II, sat at his tilted writing desk, composing a letter in response to an urgent request from his friend, Adalbold, bishop of Utrecht: "In these geometrical figures which you have already received from us, there was a certain equilateral triangle, whose side was thirty feet, height twenty six, and according to the product of the side and the height the area is three hundred ninety."

The apocalypse could wait. The question of how to find the area of a triangle was more important—and more difficult.

By the middle of the tenth century, rumors of the *studia Arabum* began to reach curious minds in Europe.

The Dark Ages were no longer quite so dark, but education was still limited in terms of both who was educated and what they learned. Charlemagne's reforms had created monastic and cathedral schools designed to train boys for service in the Church, for running a large estate, or for running a large estate for the Church. In a time when even nobles were often illiterate, reading, writing, and the simple arithmetic possible in Roman numerals represented giddy heights of intellectual achievement. In theory, more advanced students moved on to the seven liberal arts of the classical world: the *trivium* of grammar, rhetoric, and dialectic; and the *quadrivium* of arithmetic, geometry, astronomy, and music. In practice, there was no one in France qualified to teach the quadrivium in 967 CE, when Gerbert was ready to advance. If he wanted to learn more, he would have to go to Spain, where the "seven streams of wisdom" flowed freely.

Gerbert, later known as the Scientist Pope, was the first and the most infamous of the handful of European scholars who made their way to Spain and Sicily to study the black arts of mathematics and

Pope Sylvester II

astronomy. Just as in Baghdad, the early interest was in these fields of study. Gerbert tried to introduce Arabic numbers and the art of algebra on his return. (And was accused of practicing "Saracen magic" for his pains.) Adelard of Bath, who followed him more than a hundred years later, translated Euclid's *Elements* into Latin and wrote treatises on using the astrolabe and Ibn Firnas's version of al-Khwārizmī's astronomical chart.

The Europeans' first attempts at learning the *studia Arabum* were stumbling. Gerbert and his friends struggled with the simplest problems in geometry. Adelard's translation of Euclid included more than seventy transliterations from the Arabic when there was no Latin word to describe the concept. Europe's first real access to Arabic learning came in 1085, when the Christian ruler Alfonso VI captured Toledo from the Muslims. Under the rule of "Alfonso the Wise," the city became the center of an informal school of translation, similar to that in ninth-century Baghdad. By the thirteenth century, texts translated into Latin from Greek and Arabic were finding their way to the new universities of Oxford and Paris.

Islam had set the West on the path to the Renaissance and the rise of modern science. English philosopher and mathematician Roger Bacon summed up the role of the East in keeping civilization alive during Europe's Dark Ages when he wrote, "Philosophy is drawn from the Muslims."

JUNE 8, 793 CE. FOR MORE THAN a hundred years, the monastery of Saint Cuthbert had been a sanctuary for learning. It was also a storehouse of riches. Golden crosses and crosiers gleamed in its lavishly appointed chapels. Illuminated manuscripts filled its library. Tapestries decorated its walls.

Situated on the tidal island of Lindisfarne off the east coast of England, the monastery's inhabitants had been sheltered from the fighting between local chieftains that was a regular part of life in the British Isles. When three strange ships landed directly on the beach, it excited no more than curiosity. Then bands of armed men poured out of the ships, and the violence began. Monks and villagers alike tried to defend the settlement, but the raiders beat them back. They pillaged houses and religious buildings, taking food as well as treasures. They seized cattle and took captives for ransom or sale as slaves. According to the British cleric Alcuin, the Vikings

> The Dark Ages were no longer quite so dark . . . Islam had set the West on the path to the Renaissance and the rise of modern science.

left "the church of St. Cuthbert spattered with the blood of the priests of God, despoiled of all its ornaments." The raiders left as quickly as they had come, leaving the island's remaining inhabitants in shock.

THE ATTACK ON LINDISFARNE was the beginning of the "Viking Age." Sometime in the eighth century, the Norse people of Scandinavia began to produce light, fast ships that could sail across open seas and travel inland up rivers using either oars or sails. Soon after, Viking raiders began to harry the coasts of Europe. The first targets of those who went "a-viking" were unprotected settlements on the coast or near the mouths of navigable rivers.

Most of the Norse were farmers, craftsmen, and merchants, but each spring a portion of them turned into raiders, pillaging monasteries, setting villages on fire, killing men, capturing women, and profaning the churches. The wealthy monasteries of the British Isles were a favorite target. A special prayer was added to the Christian liturgy in the British Isles: "Save us, O Lord, from the fury of the Northmen." It did no good.

Surprise was a key element in the Norse raids. Their ships' speed and maneuverability made their attacks difficult to withstand. The anonymous author of the Annals of Ulster described the raids as if they were an Atlantic storm: "The sea spewed forth floods of foreigners over Erin, so that no haven, no landing place, no stronghold, no fort, no castle might be found, but that it was submerged by waves of Vikings and pirates."

In the 830s, Viking raids changed. Instead of attacking isolated monasteries, raiders mounted larger expeditions and constructed fortified camps, known as longphorts, which could be used as bases for further raids. Fortified camps grew into settlements. Raiders contracted marriage alliances with local kings and became involved in local political struggles, gradually transforming from Vikings to Hiberno-Norse, Normans, and Rus'.

The Norwegian Vikings built harbor strongholds on the sheltered east coast of Ireland: first Dublin, then Annagassan, Wexford, Waterford, and Cork. Initially these were simply sheltered winter camps where the Norse could refit their ships for the coming year's expeditions against England and France. In time, these harbor strongholds became permanent commercial centers with craftsmen and industry. From Ireland, the Norwegians plundered the French port of Nantes, sailed up the Loire Valley between 843 and 862, reached Spain in the 850s, and made their way as far as North Africa, where they captured two women from the royal household and received a large ransom for their return.

The Danes concentrated on England. Beginning in 835, they established fortified bases along the River Thames. From these they mounted violent land attacks over a period of thirty years. By the end of the ninth century, the English were under Danish rule from the north of Yorkshire to the Thames. Like the Norwegians, the Danes also extended their raids to the other side of the English Channel, where they established themselves along the lower reaches of the Seine. In 911, the Danish leader Rollo signed a treaty with Charles the Simple, the king of the Franks. Rollo received the duchy of Neustria (modern Normandy) in exchange for becoming a vassal of Charles. Rollo converted to Christianity and was baptized as Robert. His Viking warriors became the Normans, who later defeated the Danish rulers of England at the Battle of Hastings in 1066.

The Swedes turned eastward, first as traders in the Baltic and later as conquerors in Russia. In 858, a leader named Rurik founded a new Russian state, with its capital at Kiev. Rurik's Vikings, now known as the Rus', used the River Dnieper as a trade route to Byzantium. (They also used the river to launch regular and unsuccessful attacks on Constantinople, beginning in 860.) The Volga gave them access to the Caspian Sea, where they became part of the East-West trading network, selling furs and slaves and buying Chinese silk.

One surviving account of an encounter with tenth-century "Rus'" Vikings was written by a man named Ahmad Ibn Fadlan, after his party of Islamic ambassadors chanced upon the Vikings while traveling from Baghdad to modern-day Kazan (Russia).

THE WESTERN HALF OF THE Roman Empire plunged into the Dark Ages after the fall of Rome. The eastern half of the Roman Empire lived on until the mid-fifteenth century.

A VIKING BURIAL

IBN FADLAN'S PARTY, CULTURED AND RELIGIOUS Muslims seeking shelter and supplies, lands at the Viking settlement on the River Volga. After introducing themselves as best they can with no common language, they indicate their wish to trade Arabic coins for some Viking furs.

After the exchange, the Vikings permit the visitors to stay at the settlement for a period to wait out a snowstorm. The devout Muslims partake in meals provided by their hosts, but soon find themselves disgusted by the Vikings' lifestyle of rampant debauchery, filth, and publicly vulgar sexual exploits.

Most shocking of all to the Arabian men are the strange ceremonies they witness surrounding the death and burial of a Viking chieftain—so unlike their own desert custom of a simple white cloth burial within twenty-four hours of a death. As a matter of respect, the visitors attend these rituals, which they are appalled to see will be led by a woman whom the Vikings call "the Angel of Death."

As the proceedings begin, the woman announces that a slave girl has chosen to be sacrificed and buried with the deceased chief she had served. But before that final act, the chief's family digs a shallow hole in the ground, where they lay the dead man's body, and over which a wooden hut is erected to stand for ten days. The Vikings place provisions, including strong drink, fruits, and a harp, beside the chief's body.

Over the next ten days, the community divides up the dead man's belongings, and stitches fine new clothes for him to wear during his cremation. When the outfit is complete, Ibn Fadlan writes of the attire. The chief's blackened body, he says, is dressed in "drawers, leggings, boots, with a kurtak and chaftan cloth of gold, with gold buttons, and a sable-trimmed cap laid on his head." Then the dead chief

is carried to his own longboat and placed upright against a bed of pillows on the deck. The people place his weapons and a variety of dead animals at his side.

The slave girl is then prepared for sacrifice, as Ibn Fadlan watches. (He will later record the ritual in vivid and horrific detail.) She first takes off her two bracelets and hands them to the Angel of Death, who seizes her by the head and drags her into a tent erected on the ship. Six men then enter the tent to have sex with the slave girl, while the other Vikings beat on their shields with staves. Soon afterward, the slave is tied by her arms and feet and stabbed to death by the Angel of Death. Finally, with the girl laid at her master's side and the remaining Vikings assembled onshore, the chief's ship is set on fire and pushed down the Volga River.

Under the rule of the Emperor Zeno in the fifth century, Constantinople claimed Rome's legacy as the "center of the world." It retained Rome's administrative structure, but Greek replaced Latin as the empire's official governmental and military language. Located at the crossroads between Europe and the Near East, Constantinople was a major force for several centuries.

VIKING RAIDS

NORWAY SWEDEN

NORTH SEA

DENMARK

IRELAND

ENGLAND

MORAVIA

London

Paris

CAROLINGIAN EMPIRE

ATLANTIC OCEAN

Bordeaux

GALACIA

DRAGON SHIPS

The dreaded "dragon ships" of the Vikings were swift, narrow-hulled ships with true keels and shallow drafts. Named for the fierce dragon heads carved into the upturned ends of each ship, they could sail long distances in the open sea using either oars or sails. Unlike the wider, deeper-hulled ships of Western Europe, they could land men directly at the mouth of a river or on the beach of a small island. The symmetry of the design, with an identical bow and stern and the mast at the exact center, meant the ship could go in either direction. Being able to withdraw from shore without turning around meant the ships could leave as quickly as they landed, increasing the blitzkrieg feel of a Viking raid.

THE POLYNESIANS

Viking seafaring skills were equaled, if not surpassed, by those of the Polynesians.

The first stage of the Polynesian migration took them from the islands along the northern coast of New Guinea and into the western Pacific, reaching the islands of Tonga and Samoa around 800 BCE.

Around 1100 CE, they set out again, sailing thousands of miles across open sea in large, double-hulled canoes that were about twenty feet smaller than a Viking ship. By 1200 CE they had reached virtually every habitable island in the eastern Pacific, including the Cooks, Hawaii, Australia, Rapa Nui (Easter Island), New Zealand, and the subantarctic islands.

It is the founding and history of Rapa Nui, called Easter Island by the European explorers who came upon it in 1722, that leave baffling questions. The mystery of Easter Island has only been magnified by surviving bits of oral history and the hundreds of *moai*— stone statues—that still stand, averaging 4.05 meters (13.2 feet) in height and 12.5 tons. Why were these statues built? And, how, on an island with no metal, were they carved and transported? Archaeologists and anthropologists have done their best to answer these questions, with speculations that usually combine stone tools, ropes, wooden sledges, and tracks.

Beginning with the first wave of Islamic expansion in the eighth century, Constantinople was under constant attack. Its armies defended themselves against Arabs, Bulgars, and Magyars, against the Viking Rus' in the ninth century, and against the Seljuk Turks in the eleventh century.

Worn out by centuries of fighting, with their capital's wealth and defenses eaten away, the citizens of Constantinople were defenseless against the new power that rose in the fourteen century—the Ottoman Turks. By 1362, the Ottomans had conquered most of the Eastern Empire, and Constantinople was reduced to a city-state. It was finally captured by the Ottomans in 1453. Mehmed II renamed the city Istanbul and made it the capital of the growing Ottoman Empire. The Roman Empire of the East was dead.

Well before the end came, the threatened demise of Constantinople served as a rallying cry for popes and knights seeking treasure and control of the Holy Lands.

NOVEMBER 27, 1095. FRENCH, German, and Italian noblemen had come to the French cathedral city of Clermont to hear an announcement by Pope Urban II. The crowd was far too large to meet in the cathedral itself, so they gathered in a field outside the city's east gate, despite the November chill. Men pulled their cloaks tightly around them and blew on their hands to keep them warm, hoping that whatever the pope had to say was worth the trip.

Urban delivered an unexpected and blistering sermon. Christendom was in danger. The Turks had attacked Constantinople, capital of the Byzantine Empire, which even now trembled in fear. Christianity's holiest shrines were in the hands of the infidel—no, had been *defaced* by the hands of the infidel. It was no longer safe for Christian pilgrims to travel in the Holy Lands. He ended with a call for men of faith to cease shedding the blood of fellow Christians and to instead take up arms to reclaim the Holy Sepulchre in Jerusalem from the Turks.

For a moment the field was silent, and then a huge cry went up, echoing off the city's walls. *"Deus le volt!"* ("God wills it!")

As the last echo quieted, Adhemar, bishop of Le Puy, came forward, knelt at the pontiff's feet, and became the first to "take the cross," the cross-shaped red patch that would become the badge of the crusaders. The First Crusade had begun.

MUSLIMS, JEWS, AND CHRISTIANS had lived amicably under Muslim rule in Jerusalem since 637 CE. No one had called for Christendom to take action before. What changed in the eleventh century?

Christianity had spread more slowly in Europe than it had in the Mediterranean portions of the Roman Empire. Being a missionary to the tribes of Europe was a thankless and dangerous business in the centuries after the fall of Rome, as likely to produce martyrs as converts. As late as 785 CE, Christianity had made so little impact among the Germanic kingdoms that Charlemagne ordered the death penalty for any newly conquered Saxons who refused to be baptized. In 1095, there were still pockets of Europe that worshiped pagan gods. The Scandinavians would not be brought into the fold until the twelfth century. The eastern Slavs were converted even later. The Lithuanians were the last hold-outs, finally converting in 1386. Even with paganism thriving on its fringes, by 1095 Christendom was solidly Christian—and Roman Catholic. Pope Urban II held more political and spiritual power than his predecessors.

Europe was more prosperous than it had been since Rome's fall. Small technological improvements in European farming techniques had combined to trigger the same mechanism that we saw in the Near East in the ninth century BCE. Surplus crops led to the creation of permanent markets, which grew into towns. Some people were released from the land to work as craftsmen. A small middle class began to form in the cities. Over the course of the eleventh century, money reappeared in an economy that had long been driven by barter and reciprocal duties. With coin in hand for the first time in centuries, the wealthiest and most devout Europeans began to go on pilgrimages—to Canterbury, Lourdes, Rome, and most important, to the Holy Lands. Pilgrims returned home with tales of religious experiences, adventure, and Islamic wealth.

It was unfortunate that the beginning of pilgrimage on a larger scale coincided with a change of power in the Near East. In 1071, the Seljuk Turks seized control of Palestine. Newly converted to

Leaders and conquerors throughout Europe had amassed riches and power, but not everyone could win at this game.

Islam, the Seljuks were less tolerant of other religions than the city's previous Islamic rulers. Christian pilgrims found themselves subjected to small indignities and large fees at every turn. They returned home complaining of their treatment at the hands of the infidels.

Leaders and conquerors throughout Europe had amassed riches and power, but not everyone could win at this game. The idea of primogeniture reduced succession battles when a king died, but it also created a group of younger sons with no land among the nobility. Nobles believed that the only legitimate occupations for their landless sons were the upper levels of the church, and war. By the eleventh

On a hot, dusty day, a young European noble-man named Tancred is leading the first charge of crusading knights into Jerusalem. Tancred is as ambitious as he is religious. What is at stake for Tancred and other knights like him fighting "under the cross" in Jerusalem is a singular chance at fame and wealth. Now Tancred has a chance to earn both. As they cross the gates of the city, Tancred's knights immediately meet resistance and begin fighting their way street by street, leaving corpses in their wake.

At a lull in the action, Tancred pulls his horse to a stop and watches as hundreds of Muslim men, women, and children run in search of refuge on top of Al-Aqsa Mosque. Seeing this, Tancred calls an end to the killing, and offers the refugees the protection of his banner.

That night, Tancred prays on his knees, giving thanks for the day's easy victory. Driven by an overwhelming sense of faith, he believes his Christian beliefs to be worth dying for and, if need be, worth killing for.

Morning comes, and Tancred returns to al-Aqsa where he anticipates making a different kind of killing when he trades the hostages he collected the day before for a considerable bounty. When he reaches the mosque, he cannot believe his eyes. Bloodied bodies of hostages lie in every direction. His soldiers have killed every one of the Muslims to whom he had promised safety! His men have gone against his orders. Such wholesale disobedience threatens his authority, and he must take action to punish those responsible. He roots out and rounds up the ringleaders among his warriors and orders them tied to posts. Tancred goes so far as to take the whip in his own hand, infusing the lashings he doles out with the fury he feels about the lost ransom he will no longer collect.

century, the need to fight invading barbarians was coming to an end. Even the Vikings had settled down and become Normans, producing their own cadre of landless nobles. The prospect of a war in the east offered restless young men a chance for glory, plunder, and possibly a landed estate of their own.

Knowing all of that, Pope Urban assumed soldiers would answer his call to arms. In fact, men and women of all social classes took the cross. The first crusaders who headed east in the spring of 1096 were not soldiers, but groups of the poor, known as the People's Crusade. Led by men such as Peter the Hermit, they were poorly equipped and untrained, but they proudly wore the cross-shaped patch of red cloth sewed on their clothing. The first Muslim ruler to encounter the ragged crusaders

didn't even recognize them as an invading force. The Muslim armies wiped them out as if they were bands of brigands.

The second wave of the Crusades was a different story. Groups of knights and archers led by experienced military commanders, men whose only job was war, arrived in Palestine in the summer of 1097. The crusaders moved ruthlessly through Palestine, taking Nicaea, Edessa, and Antioch in turn, pillaging the countryside for both food and plunder. Muslim rulers were too busy fighting among themselves to unite against the European invaders. By the time the crusaders reached Ma'arra (Maarat al-Numaan in modern Syria), the besieging crusaders were almost as desperate for food as the besieged. The crusaders sent word to the city that if they would open the city gates and surrender, no one would be harmed. But when the city surrendered, the crusaders went on a rampage. According to one witness, Albert of Aix, "Not only did our troops not shrink from eating Turks and Saracens, they also ate dogs!"

With word of the horrors of Ma'arra preceding them, the crusaders marched on relatively unopposed. They reached Jerusalem at the beginning of June 1099.

The city did not go down without a fight. At the end of a forty-day siege, the crusaders made the same offer to the people of Jerusalem that they had made to Ma'arra: surrender and no one will be hurt. Amazingly enough, Jerusalem's citizens surrendered. Once again, the crusaders reneged on their promise. They went on a two-day spree of killing and plundering, piling severed heads, hands, and feet on the streets. Virtually none of the city's Muslims survived. The city's Jewish population took shelter in the main synagogue, trusting in its sanctity to protect them; the crusaders blocked the doors and torched the building. Even Jerusalem's Christians were not spared. Because they were members of the various Eastern churches, the crusaders declared them heretics, confiscated their property, and drove them into exile.

Jerusalem had been recovered from the Turks, but the Crusades continued. For two hundred years, crusaders went east to fight for the cross, and to fill their pockets. Some crusaders settled in one of the four small kingdoms that members of the First Crusade founded near Jerusalem. Most fought in the Holy Lands for a few years, and then went home with some exotic trinkets, a little Arab gold, and a papal dispensation for their sins.

The experience had a larger impact on Europe than it did on the Muslim world. Muslim fortifications changed how Europeans built castles. Exposure to Islamic medical care transformed the medieval *hospitalia* from hospice to hospital. Returning knights brought back a taste for Muslim luxuries. The Venetian merchants who had provided transportation for the Crusades established small enclaves in Muslims cities and became the newest players in the East-West trade routes. Over time, the Venetians would import not only silk and spices, but knowledge: Arabic numerals, navigation techniques, and the technologies for creating fine textiles, hard soap, paper, pottery, and glass.

CENTURIES OF CLASHES BETWEEN Europe's Christian conquerors and Palestine's defending Muslims spilled more than blood. The Crusades brought Europeans back into contact with the rest of the world. New ideas flowed between east and west for the first time in centuries. Some were large, like Arabic science, numbers, algebra, and spherical geometry. Others were smaller, like chess, hot baths, and the fork. (Chess was the only one to catch on quickly.)

The West was forever changed by its military, commercial, and cultural contacts with the East during the Middle Ages. The shared human enterprise of learning moved from one culture to another as Arabic learning fueled the birth of the European Renaissance. The Crusades sowed the seeds for future wars over the Holy Lands.

More immediately, though, history introduced a new, unfamiliar conqueror from the steppes of Central Asia. For the Mongol warriors who were about to swarm centers of civilization across Eurasia, religion and learning took a backseat to pure might. Under Genghis Khan, human ingenuity was applied to the tools and methods of conquest—creating human slaughter on an unprecedented scale.

5

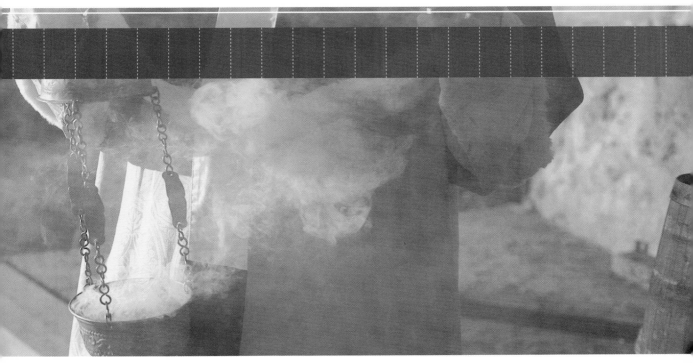

PLAGUE

THE TWELFTH CENTURY IS COMING TO A CLOSE. AS A NEW CENTURY LOOMS JUST AHEAD, THE EAST AND WEST ARE MORE CONNECTED THAN AT ANY PREVIOUS TIME IN HISTORY.

Ideas flow from one continent to the other. Trade between Europe and Asia flourishes, even in the midst of wars both civil and religious.

Meanwhile, an extraordinary young man has risen up through Mongol society. Using a combination of brilliantly calculated strategy, ruthlessness, and charisma, he has pulled together warring tribes and created a confederation of armed horsemen. Now, this "universal leader" emerges from the Central Asian steppes. Leading his army of nomads, he creates the first Eurasian empire.

The life of Genghis Khan, born Temujin, is an example of survival of the fittest in human form—one exceptional person triumphing against hostile natural and human forces to move mankind into a new age. The earth has become hotter. Khan responds by taking his people and livestock into greener pastures to the east. Then, combining nomadic war skills with technology borrowed from sedentary cultures, he crafts a new style of warfare, turning the small Mongol horses into the ultimate weapons of war. Soon his realm—the Mongol Empire—includes every acre and person from China to the Mediterranean Sea. It is the largest empire ever conquered by a single man—and will survive his death by 150 years and live on for another five centuries in empires created by his descendants.

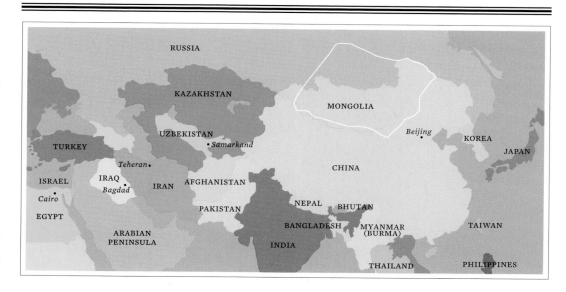

LEFT: *Mongolian ruler Genghis Khan created the largest empire ever conquered by one man.*
ABOVE: *map of the Mongol territory when Genghis Khan came to power*

Under Genghis Khan and his successors, the Mongol Empire links the conquered territories to great effect. The Mongolian Peace allows a new freedom of trade from east to west and back again. Goods, merchants, and ideas travel more freely than ever. Unfortunately, so do rats and fleas.

By now, man assumes he has dominion over all other creatures. But for the generations immediately following Genghis Khan, that assumption will be shaken when a barely visible enemy takes a free ride on the Mongols' cross-continental highways and sea lanes and brings about the near annihilation of the known world. Disease will sweep from Asia into the Middle East and Europe. It is the Black Death, and it will kill nearly half of the human population. Mankind has reached one of its darkest hours.

Meanwhile, isolated from this apocalypse, new civilizations rise in the Americas—continents not yet known to Europe that hold the key to civilization's future.

1206 CE. THE MONGOL LEADER Temujin pitched his camp at the headwaters of the Onon River, near the sacred mountain Burkhan Khaldun in Mongolia's Khentii region. There he called for a *kurultai:* a gathering of the tribes. At forty, he was the most powerful leader in the vast, treeless steppes (semiarid grasslands) of his homeland. His authority reached from the Gobi Desert to the Arctic tundra, from the forests of Manchuria to the Altai Mountains in western China. He had earned his power in battle and killed the blood brother of his youth to defend it. But victory on the

Mongolian felt-walled yurts have changed little from the time of Genghis Khan.

battlefield wasn't enough to make him *khan*—or ruler—of all the "people of the felt walls." He had to be publicly chosen by the kurultai. The tribes would vote with their feet. Those who acknowledged him as their ruler would come at his invitation. Those who rejected his rule, and his protection, would not send a representative.

Tribe after tribe arrived in response to Temujin's call, the largest kurultai in Mongol history. Soon a temporary city of felt huts, called *yurts,* surrounded Temujin's campsite, stretching for miles in all directions. Vast herds of animals grazed nearby to provide milk and meat for the crowds. Young men competed in the traditional Mongol sports of wrestling, horse racing, and archery during the day and got drunk at night on *koumiss,* a powerful beverage made from fermented mare's milk. Shamans drummed. Musicians crooned, the deep reverberation of Mongolian throat singing filled the night.

After days of celebration, the tribes installed Temujin as their ruler. Hundreds of thousands of Mongols watched as Temujin was led to a black felt carpet that his followers had spread on the ground. A spokesman for the tribes pronounced him their leader, giving him a new name—Genghis Khan, "Universal Ruler." His followers then lifted him up on his carpet and carried him to his throne, where the leaders of all the tribes and clans swore their loyalty to him.

His mother had named him Temujin. He was the son of the chieftain of a small clan, the Borjigin, which survived its relationship to a larger clan, the Tayichigud, like a jackal scavenging from a lion's leftovers. When Temujin was nine, his father was poisoned in an intertribal feud. Without a leader who could fight and hunt for the group, the larger clan had little use for Temujin's clan and abandoned them to fend for themselves. For several years, Temujin, his father's wives, and his siblings

Genghis Khan battling with the Khitai and Jurje tribes

lived on small game, such as marmots and field mice, and on the few plants they could forage from the harsh landscape of the steppes.

In the meantime, the leader of the Tayichigud feared the boy Temujin would grow up and take

GENGHIS KHAN AND GLOBAL WARMING

———

We often forget how the climate can shape human history.

Genghis Khan's rise to power took place at the end of a period of relative warmth known as the Medieval Warming Period.

For several centuries, from roughly 800 to 1200 CE, Europeans enjoyed mild winters, long summers, and good harvests. With the luxury of more stable food supplies, Europeans took the first steps out of the Dark Ages, rebuilding trade routes first within Europe and then with Asia. At the northernmost edge of Europe, the Norse took advantage of favorable ice conditions to travel to Iceland, Greenland, and across the northern Atlantic.

Warm centuries in Europe brought problems in other regions. Higher temperatures and changes in rainfall patterns created unpredictable climate swings. Extended periods of drought contributed to the end of the Chaco Canyon culture in New Mexico and Angkor Wat in modern Cambodia, and weakened the Mayan states of Central America. In Mongolia, the Medieval Warming Period meant a hotter, drier climate and reduced grazing land for Mongol horses, prompting Genghis Khan to mobilize his armies to the east to conquer more fertile lands. In this case, global warming actually helped contribute to the expansion of the empire.

Today the Medieval Warming Period is a hot button in global warming discussions. People who don't believe humans have caused global warming point to the medieval experience as an example of a natural rise in temperature with positive effects that was followed by the cooler conditions of the Little Ice Age. In fact, the Medieval Warming Period was several degrees cooler than the recorded mean temperature since 1971.

revenge against the tribe that had turned his family into outcasts. When Temujin committed the unthinkable crime of murdering his older half brother, the official head of the exiled family, the Tayichigud leader used it as an excuse to hunt down and capture the adolescent. The boy was locked into a *cangue*, a device similar to a yoke or pillory, allowing him to walk but making it impossible to use his hands. With help from a family of war captives, Temujin escaped from captivity. When he returned to his own family, he discovered that his escape had made him a hero among the lower-class members of the Mongol tribes.

Over the next two decades, Temujin attracted a small group of followers drawn from several different tribes and clans. This band of devotees became a pseudoclan based on ability and loyalty rather than family relationships. Temujin also made two important allies. He entered into a blood-brother relationship with the ambitious, young Jamukha, a member of a distantly related Mongol clan of higher status than Temujin's Borjigin. He then offered allegiance to a man named Toghrul, a powerful Mongol leader who had been the blood brother to Temujin's father. Toghrul accepted him as a sort of stepson.

Over time Temujin earned a reputation as a skilled war leader. With each success in the field, more tribes acknowledged him as their ruler. He began to systematically eliminate all rivals, including Toghrul and Jamukha. As his following grew, he reorganized Mongol society from tribes into units of a thousand people. By the time the tribes proclaimed him the Universal Ruler, Temujin—now Genghis Khan—had transformed the tribes into what he called the Great Mongol Nation. Under his leadership, the Mongol nation would grow into an empire.

Having unified Mongolia, Genghis Khan turned toward China, which had a long history of

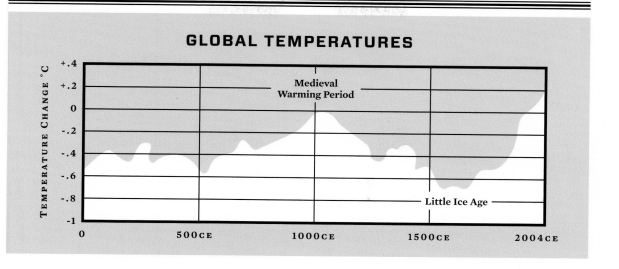

GLOBAL TEMPERATURES

Medieval Warming Period

Little Ice Age

TEMPERATURE CHANGE °C

+.4
+.2
0
-.2
-.4
-.6
-.8
-1

0   500CE   1000CE   1500CE   2004CE

conflict with the Mongol tribes. Like the Xiongnu and other steppe tribes, Mongols had raided the Chinese border for centuries. Previously, the Chinese had dealt with the nomad tribes by manipulating tribal divisions. Now the Mongol tribes were united. China was not.

When Genghis Khan first set his sights on China, it was divided into a number of kingdoms that often fought among themselves. Three were larger and more important than the rest: the Tangut and Jin dynasties in the north, themselves descendants of Central Asian nomadic tribes and the Sung dynasty in the south.

Genghis Khan defeated the Tangut in 1211, leaving the dynasty in control of their own lands in exchange for tribute and their oath of loyalty as vassals of the Mongols. He then marched against the Jin. Mongol forces besieged the Jin capital of Zhongdu (modern Beijing) in 1215. Zhongdu's ruler, Xuanzong, known to his subjects as the Golden King, only lasted a week before reluctantly surrendering at the urging of his councilors. Genghis Khan offered the same treaty terms to the Jin ruler that he had offered to the Tangut. The Golden King

paid the Mongols a handsome tribute of silks, gold, silver, three thousand horses, and five hundred slaves. He became a vassal of Genghis Khan and gave the Mongol one of his daughters as a wife.

The Mongol forces withdrew, leaving the countryside around Zhongdu untouched. As soon as the Mongols were gone, Xuanzong broke the terms of his treaty, fleeing south with his family, his leading generals, and his courtiers.

Though tired of the dirt of city life and longing for the open grasslands of the steppes, Genghis Khan reversed course and marched his army, fifty thousand strong, back into China. The leader of the Great Mongol Nation could not tolerate betrayal by a newly conquered underling, not if his empire was to keep growing—and become the largest in world history.

The Mongols eventually took Zhongdu with the help of Genghis Khan's new Chinese allies, including some of the Jin forces left behind to guard the city. The terms of surrender given to Zhongdu's surviving leaders were brutal. The Mongols got to engage in a twenty-day pillaging. To pay their army, the Mongol leaders permitted the

MONGOL SIEGE

O N AN OPPRESSIVELY HOT SEPTEMBER DAY IN 1214,
Zhongdu's 350,000 inhabitants are in a frenzied panic, running through the streets, balancing small children and prized
possessions—gold, silver, porcelain—in their bare arms. Word has
spread that Genghis Khan and his armies are returning. Because of the
treachery of their Golden King, the people in this walled city know that
Genghis Khan will show them no mercy. The sight of their own Chinese soldiers marching in formation toward the city's barricades does
nothing to reassure them.

Where can they go for safety? Unfortunately, there is nowhere for
them to hide from the barbarians rapidly approaching their gates. Better for them to be on the move, they decide, than to wait at home for an
inevitably brutal end at the hands of the dreaded Mongols.

One teenage girl knows exactly where she is headed as she breaks
away from the sea of people running in every direction through the
streets of Zhongdu. Reaching an unguarded section of stone wall, she
stops to look around before beginning her ascent. Finally, at the top, the

girl grows dizzy as she peers at the ground on the other side of the wall, and the three moats ringing its eighteen-mile length.

When she looks up, the girl sees an even more ominous sight: a long cloud of dust rising from the horizon. She is sure it is the advancing Mongol army on horseback. Seeing the enemy in the near distance makes the girl even more determined to complete the task that brought her here.

A little farther down from where she crouches, two Chinese soldiers take their positions in one of nine hundred guard towers atop the wall. As they prepare their bows and arrows for the Mongol onslaught, the soldiers fail to notice the girl stand up and move her toes to the wall's

edge. Nor do they see her leap forward into the air. Only after her body thuds to the ground do the two men turn and look down. They point at her body but do not scramble down to see if the girl has survived. They know she will not be the last Chinese girl or woman to jump today.

Some sixty thousand young women throw themselves from the bastion of the fortress that day. Meanwhile, the same fear that causes young girls to leap to their deaths is driving Chinese farmers who live outside the walled city to do as they're ordered. The Mongols force them to push a wheeled battering ram into the Zhongdu city gates. They use other Chinese prisoners as human shields against the defending Chinese army, whose arrows fly through the air en masse, only to kill their own people. Still, the Chinese forces will manage to resist the Mongol takeover for ten long months of siege and starvation before they are finally forced to surrender in June 1215.

looting of conquered peoples. When this looting period was up, they torched the city. As a final punishment, the Mongols trampled the surrounding fields, turning plowed farmland into pasturage for their livestock.

Leaving his generals to finish the subjugation of China, Genghis Khan left China and marched his 150,000 warriors more than a thousand miles to the west to defeat the Turkish state of Khwarazm, which had rejected his overtures of peace. In a campaign considered savage even for these brutal times, Mongol horsemen crushed a Turkish force that outnumbered them two to one and sent its leader Muhammad II fleeing for his life.

Genghis Khan pursued the Khwarezmid forces into Afghanistan and Persia, defeating all who opposed him. The Mongols sacked cities, killing everything down to the cats and dogs. They burned fields and destroyed crops. In Persia, they destroyed the *qanat*, the underground canal systems that irrigated the fields, transforming what is now western Iran and northern Afghanistan from a fertile region into the desert it is today.

In the West, Genghis Khan is remembered primarily for the ferocity of his campaign against Khwarazm. Among the Mongols he was known as a liberal ruler and administrator. He was magnanimous to those who surrendered; he slaughtered those who did not. He ordered a scribe to create a written language from the spoken Mongolian tongue. Once a written language was in place, he created a sweeping law code known as the Great Yasa. His legal code made no distinction between conqueror and conquered. He rebuilt selected cities among those he destroyed in the course of conquest, and took care to restore a subjugated region's economy on a sound footing.

Genghis Khan's greatest accomplishment was the Mongolian Peace. For the first time ever, the

trade routes from China through Central Asia to the West were under the control of one power. Genghis Khan and his successors actively promoted trade. Like the Persians before them, they built shelters every twenty to thirty miles along the major highways. These shelters served as relay stations that provided fresh horses to imperial messengers and as rest stops for traveling merchants. They provided provisions, guides through difficult terrain, and armed protection to merchant caravans. The level of service the shelters provided to a traveler was tied to a graded system of passports called *piazzas*. Each piazza was a gold, silver or wooden tablet that allowed its holder to travel throughout the empire under Mongol protection.

With travelers assured of protection, transportation, and accommodations, Asia's highways were safer than they had ever been. The number of caravans increased. For the first time merchants were able to travel from east to west and back again.

Genghis Khan did not get a chance to enjoy his empire. In 1226, at age sixty-four, he led his soldiers once again toward China, where the Tangut had

HORSES AND OTHER WEAPONS OF WAR

Humans have always used their ingenuity to find more deadly ways of waging war. Like other great conquerors, Genghis Khan pushed the limits of available technology to create armed horsemen who were more powerful than either man or horse would be alone.

The Mongols fought on horseback using a double recurve composite bow made of several different types of wood, animal horn, and sinew, held together with strong glue made from boiled fish bladders. The famous English longbow, from the same period, could shoot an arrow an impressive 750 feet; the Mongol bow could shoot an arrow 1,050 feet. Their horses were strong and fast, but small enough that a Mongol warrior could grip his horse with his legs, hang over one side, and fire his arrows beneath the horse's belly. Venetian traveler Marco Polo, who saw Mongol forces in action, said, "Their horses are so well-broken-in to quick-change movements, that upon the signal given, they instantly turn in every direction; and by these rapid

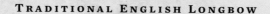

TRADITIONAL ENGLISH LONGBOW

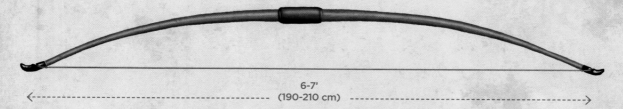

6-7'
(190-210 cm)

The traditional English longbow, made from a single piece of wood, revolutionized warfare in Europe. It had a maximum range of around 250 meters. Because of it's length it was practical only for use by foot soldiers.

MONGOLIAN COMPOSITE BOW

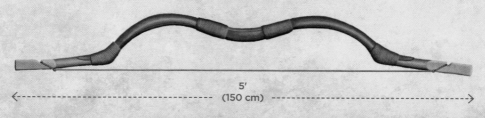

5'
(150 cm)

maneuvers many victories have been obtained."

Under Genghis Khan, the Mongols adapted weapons from other cultures with whom they came in contact, creating a flexible arsenal unmatched by their contemporaries. Instead of carrying siege engines with them, they carried something much more powerful—engineers who could create siege engines on the spot. In addition to hurling rocks and fire, the way besieging armies had done for centuries, the Mongols' siege engines also threw pots of burning liquids, exploding devices, and incendiary materials. They created immense crossbows mounted on wheels and portable towers with retractable ladders from which they could shoot down on defenders of the walls. When confronted by a moated city, they pushed prisoners of war forward to fill the moat, creating living ramps for their siege engines.

Conflict often pushes mankind to make the next leap in innovation. At the end of World War II, America also created new technologies that raised the stakes of war. By pooling the knowledge of the world's leading physicists, America tapped the power of one of the primordial elements that have existed on earth unchanged since the Big Bang: uranium. Scientists used radioactive uranium to break apart the nucleus of the atom, producing an explosion of electromagnetic and kinetic energy capable of unimaginable destruction. Taming the atom was the closest we have yet come to re-creating our own cosmic birth in the Big Bang.

GENGHIS THE GREAT?

"Ruthless conqueror, responsible for the deaths of thousands." The phrase could describe Alexander the Great and Napoleon Bonaparte as easily as it does Genghis Khan. But Alexander the Great is hailed as one of the greatest generals of all time. Depending on your national alliance, Napoleon Bonaparte is either the beloved Little Corporal or the Monster of Corsica, but no one doubts he was a military genius. Genghis Khan, on the other hand, is often depicted as a bloodthirsty barbarian.

When you look at the details, how do these three great conquerors of history stack up?

ALEXANDER THE GREAT
(356–323 BCE)

BORN: Son and heir of the king of Macedonia

EDUCATED: Tutored by Aristotle

COMES TO POWER: Inherited the throne at age 20

SIZE OF ARMY: 32,000 men

AREA CONQUERED: 2 million square miles

DIED: Age 33, after a drunken orgy

LEGACY: Alexander's sons were murdered and his empire divided among his generals.

NAPOLEON BONAPARTE
(1769–1821 CE)

BORN: Son of a Corsican lawyer, who claimed to be descended from Tuscan nobility

EDUCATED: Five years at the French military college at Brienne

COMES TO POWER: Coup d'état

SIZE OF ARMY: 600,000 men

AREA CONQUERED: 720,000 square miles

DIED: Age 52, in exile on Elba Island. Possibly poisoned

LEGACY: Napoleon's empire was dismantled at the Congress of Vienna. His nephew used Bonaparte's prestige to become Emperor Napoleon III.

GENGHIS KHAN
(1162–1227 CE)

BORN: Orphaned son of a tribal chieftain

EDUCATED: Illiterate

COMES TO POWER: Acclaimed the Universal Ruler by the combined Mongol tribes after twenty years of making and breaking alliances

SIZE OF ARMY: 110,000 mounted horsemen

AREA CONQUERED: Between 11 and 12 million contiguous square miles, the largest empire ever conquered by a single man

DIED: Age 65, surrounded by family and soldiers, on his way to new conquests in China

LEGACY: His descendants ruled his empire for 150 years.

risen in rebellion. Early in his march to the east, he fell from his horse and suffered serious internal injuries. His doctors and his generals begged the elderly ruler to stop and rest. Growing steadily weaker, Genghis Khan refused to turn back. In August 1227, the Mongol ruler died as he had begun, in a nomad's felt yurt.

At the time of Genghis Khan's death, his rule stretched from Beijing to the Aral Sea, the largest empire ever conquered by a single commander. His final command to his sons and generals was to keep his death a secret and continue the campaign against the Tangut.

ON APRIL 8, 1241, A NEW GENER-ation of Mongols was traveling towards Europe. A hastily assembled army of twenty-five thousand soldiers—Teutonic Knights, German gold miners, Templars, Hospitallers, and Polish levies of foot soldiers and cavalry—waited for them at Liegnitz in modern Poland. The European troops were battle hardened. They outnumbered the approaching force by some five thousand men. But still they trembled. For two months now, the Mongol horsemen had ravaged the Polish countryside, fighting with a speed and ferocity that bewildered the European troops.

The Mongol commander, Genghis Khan's grandson Batu, was aware that King Wenceslas of Bohemia was only a day's march away with reinforcements. The European commander, Duke Henry II of Silesia, was not. Batu decided to strike before the reinforcements arrived.

The Mongols rode forward. To European eyes, their small, sturdy horses looked like something a child would ride, compared to the horses of the Polish cavalry. Cheered, the Polish cavalry advanced, only to be driven back by volleys of arrows from the powerful Mongol bows. Seeing what he thought was a small army, Duke Henry II ordered his own cavalry and the Teutonic Knights to attack. To their surprise, the Mongols retreated. When the Europeans pursued them, the Mongols broke formation, seeming to flee in disarray. Henry and the remaining knights followed, leaving the infantry behind in their eagerness to take part in the destruction of the fearsome barbarians.

Suddenly, more Mongol cavalry appeared, flanking the attacking knights and separating them from the infantry. The Mongols carried smoking pots that obscured the field with dense clouds. With the knights trapped between two wings of Mongols, the nomads attacked them with a shower

> At the time of Genghis Khan's death, his rule stretched from Beijing to the Aral Sea, the largest empire ever conquered by a single commander.

of arrows. As bewildered and wounded knights rode out of the smoke, the Mongols to their rear turned and attacked the infantry. Duke Henry was killed in the rout.

By day's end, bodies of fallen soldiers were strewn across the battlefield. The duke's head was impaled on a Mongol lance and displayed to the surviving soldiers, a familiar tactic. A conquering European general might well do the same to the fallen commander. As shuddering Europeans watched, Mongol soldiers cut an ear off of each fallen enemy soldier, a practical if gruesome way to count the dead. It had been a bloody battle. His troops presented Batu with nine sacks of the grisly trophies.

Chapter 5: PLAGUE

BEFORE HE DIED, GENGHIS KHAN chose his third son, Ögedei, to be the next Great Khan. With Mongol chieftains scattered across Western Asia and northern China, it took two years to assemble the kurultai needed to acknowledge him as ruler. Ögedei was known to drink too much koumiss, and some of the chieftains raised questions about whether he was fit to rule. But when the time came to vote, the transfer of power went smoothly. The Mongol tribes accepted Ögedei as their ruler.

Ögedei was as ambitious as his father. He believed that the primary Mongolian god, Eternal Blue Sky, had selected the Mongol tribes to rule the earth. To fulfill that destiny, he sent his nephew Batu and the respected general Subutai on a campaign to the west. Batu's troops quickly conquered Kiev and Moscow, then swept into southeastern Europe, the legend of their fierceness preceding them. A group of eastern European dukes and princes formed a coalition to meet the threat. The heavily armored European knights were no match for the mobile nomads. The Mongols destroyed the allied forces at Liegnitz on April 8, 1241. Three days later, Subutai defeated the Hungarian army. The road to Vienna lay open. Batu and Subutai crossed the Danube and advanced on Vienna in mid-December. There seemed to be little hope for Europe.

Suddenly, the Mongol troops retreated without even sending a messenger to the city leaders, asking them to surrender. Europeans thought they had been saved by a miracle. In fact, the Mongols had received news that Ögedei had died, and the kurultai had once more been called to elect a new ruler.

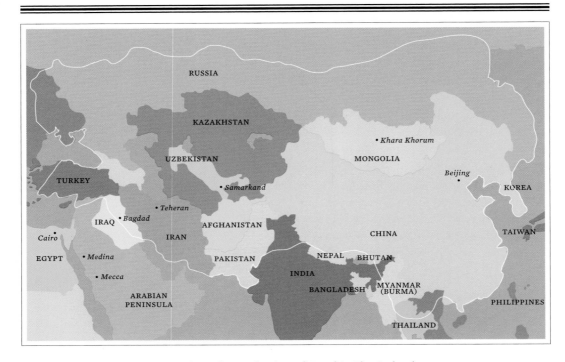

Mongol Empire at the time of Genghis Khan's death

THE DIVINE WIND

In the fall of 1274, Kublai Khan sent a force of forty thousand troops on nine hundred ships to conquer Japan. When they landed in November, the samurai came out prepared to battle the Mongols one on one. Dueling was not part of the Mongol military style. The Mongols fought as a unit, slaughtering the samurai. The Japanese retreated inland. Instead of following them, the Mongols withdrew to their ships. In the night, a fierce storm hit, capsizing much of the fleet and killing more than a quarter of the attackers. Kublai Khan's forces withdrew but did not give up.

In 1281, Kublai Khan assembled a much larger force—140,000 men and more than four thousand ships. The Japanese held their attackers on a narrow strip of beach for fifty-three days. Then a major typhoon struck. The storm raged for two days, smashing the Mongol fleet against the rocks. Few of the ships survived; two-thirds of the Mongol force died. The Mongols retreated again.

Kublai Khan died before he could organize a third invasion fleet.

The Japanese believed the gods had protected them and dubbed the typhoons that saved them *kamikazes*, or divine winds.

Japan remained unconquered until the end of World War II.

Japanese monk Nichiren summoning the divine Shinpu wind to destroy the Mongol-Chinese fleet attacking Japan in the thirteenth century

Chapter 5: PLAGUE

Unlike his father, Ögedei had not chosen a successor. His death triggered a series of succession struggles between Genghis Khan's sons and grandsons. In 1251, ten years after Ögedei's death, Genghis Khan's grandson Möngke became the Great Khan.

Soon after taking power, Möngke headed to China to continue the conquest of the Sung dynasty, which Ögedei had begun. He sent his brother Hulagu to solidify Mongol rule in Persia and expand the empire into modern Iraq. Hulagu's forces laid siege to Baghdad in 1258. The city's defenses crumbled within a week, bringing the Abbasid Caliphate to an end. Under Möngke, the Mongol empire reached its greatest expanse, covering China, most of Russia, Central Asia, Iran, and Iraq.

In 1259, the death of a Great Khan once again brought an end to Mongol military campaigns and unleashed bitter succession struggles. The assembly of Mongol chieftains was unable to agree on the next Great Khan. Rival factions elected two of Möngke's brothers and refused to compromise. The result was a bloody civil war.

It was 1264 before Genghis Khan's ablest grandson, Kublai, succeeded his older brother Möngke as the ruler of the Mongols. Some members of the royal family refused to acknowledge him as the Great Khan; others gave him only symbolic recognition. During his reign, multiple power centers formed throughout the Mongol Empire as Genghis Khan's other grandsons began to treat the regions under their control as semi-independent kingdoms. Kublai himself focused on China, to the detriment of the rest of the empire. He proclaimed himself the emperor of China, taking the reign name Zhenghong, or "Central Rule," a Chinese approximation of Genghis Khan. He unified China for the first time since the Han dynasty and founded the Yuan dynasty, which would rule China for ninety years.

MARCO POLO

In 1271 CE Italian merchants Niccolò and Maffeo Polo set out on a voyage from Venice to the court of Kublai Khan in China. The Polo brothers had been guests of the Chinese court before and were eager to return. Niccolò's seventeen-year-old son, Marco, traveled with them on the four-year voyage across the Near East and Central Asia.

The young Venetian quickly became a favorite of Kublai Khan. During his time at the Mongol court, Marco traveled with diplomatic missions to Persia, India, and Southeast Asia. He served on the emperor's council. He even held the position of tax collector in the city of Yangzhou for three years. He never learned Chinese, but neither did most of the Mongols in the Great Khan's court. Like them, Marco became fluent in the languages of the Mongolian ruling classes: Persian and Mongolian.

Seventeen years after they arrived, the Polos left China, escorting a Mongolian princess who was to marry the Khan of Persia. They sailed to Persia by way of Sumatra and South India, then traveled overland to Constantinople. They finally reached Venice in 1295, carrying a fortune in precious stones.

Marco Polo would probably never have written his account of their travels if he hadn't volunteered to command a galley in the ongoing war between Venice and Genoa. Captured during a skirmish, he spent a year in prison at Genoa, where he amused his fellow prisoners with stories of his travels. His audience included a writer of romance tales, who urged Marco to write down the story of his travels. Popularly known at the time as , Marco Polo's travels was a fourteenth-century best seller.

No Great Khan took Kublai Khan's place at his death. Instead the Mongol Empire was divided into four independent *khanates*: the Great Khan, which ruled over East Asia; the Chagatai Khanate in Central Asia; the Il-Khanate of Persia; and the Kipchak Khanate in southern Russia, known in the West as the Golden Horde.

A descendent of Genghis Khan still ruled in Bukhara when the Soviets took the city in 1920.

In the thirteen century, the world was more stable than it had been for centuries. Trade was flourishing. Empires were growing. Technology was advancing.

No one could have imagined that an invisible enemy would come close to destroying humankind and the civilizations of Eurasia: an emeny that traveled on the trade routes that mankind had created, causing devastation greater than any conquering army had ever inflicted.

IN 1346, MONGOL FORCES UNDER the command of Janibeg, the Khan of the Golden Horde, besieged the Genovese trading city of Caffa in the Crimea. The Italian merchants had built the city as a trading post for their sale of Russian slaves to Egypt. Sometimes the Mongol rulers cooperated with the Italian slave traders; sometimes they tried to suppress the trade and expel the Genovese. Janibeg was trying to close the post. Then the plague broke out among his Mongol troops, killing more men than did the Genovese defenders of Caffa.

They fell by the dozens, dying so quickly they could not be buried. The Mongols were forced to withdraw. But in a final act of aggression, the Mongols loaded their catapults with the bodies of their own plague victims and flung them into the city—in a bid to have the Italians share their sufferings.

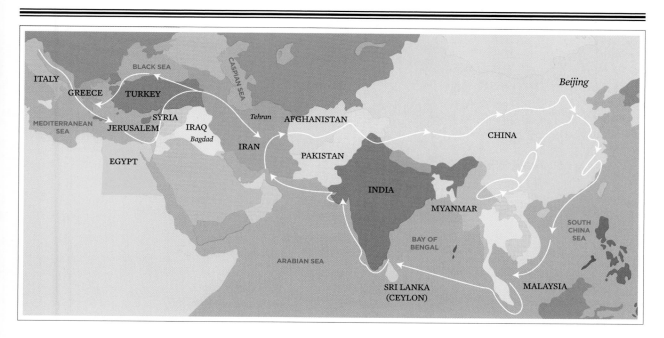

Marco Polo's Travels

BIOWARFARE

The Mongols were not the only people to use biological warfare against an enemy.

The practice of using infectious bacteriological agents as tactical or strategic weapons of war appears again and again in human history. In the eighteenth century, British officers tried to spread smallpox to indigenous tribes who resisted their spread into new territories in North America. The Japanese used plague and cholera against the Chinese in the Second Sino-Japanese War. The Nazis and Soviets were also known to have tested and used biological weapons.

The United States joined the international treaty against the offensive use of biological or chemical weapons in 1975. Today, according to the U.S. Department of Defense, more than ten countries are suspected to have continuing offensive biological warfare programs, including Russia, Israel, China, Iran, Syria, and North Korea. Offensive biological warfare programs in Iraq were dismantled after the first Gulf War (1990–1991). Libya dismantled and disavowed its biological warfare program in 2003. The fate of the old Soviet biological warfare program, including stockpiles of weaponized smallpox and anthrax, remains undocumented.

TOP: *Siege machines such as the trebuchet could be used to launch plague-infested corpses into castles being attacked.* • BOTTOM: *U.S. military personnel training for potential biological warfare.*

The Genovese threw the Mongol bodies into the sea as quickly as they came over the wall, but it made no difference. The besieged city's close quarters provided perfect conditions for the disease to spread. The plague spread through Caffa as rapidly as it had through the Mongol military camp. Panicked Italian merchants abandoned the city, carrying infected rats aboard with them

The Black Death didn't start at Caffa. The first known plague epidemic hit China in 1331, killing 90 percent of the population of Hopei (Hebei) province. The disease traveled from China along the trade routes, black rats infested with disease-laden fleas traveling with caravans in grain wagons and bundles of trade goods.

One place the plague stopped on its travels from China to the West was the tiny trading oasis of Issyk Kul, located on the borders of modern China and Kyrgyzstan. Travelers went from this outpost east to China or west to Caffa, Baghdad, or Tabriz. Records show that in 1338, a man in Issyk Kul was struck down by a mysterious disease. His wife tried all the folk remedies available, to no avail. Within a few days her husband was gone, and so was she. One hundred six more residents of Issyk Kul would fall ill and die suddenly within the next year, 102 more than in an average year, and according to headstones in the village graveyard, the cause of death for all 106 villagers was the same.

Plague, the Black Death that would peak from 1348 to 1350 and decimate between one-third and half of the West's population of 90 million, sailed into Europe through the Italian port of Messina in 1347 on a fleet of twelve Genovese trading ships. Most of their crew was dead or dying from a plague so virulent that if anyone so much as spoke to one of them, he, too, became infected.

After reaching Messina, the plague spread to Genoa and Pisa within months. By year's end, the disease had raged through Italy and then spread north on merchant ships to Paris, the Low Countries, and England. In 1349, the epidemic spread into Germany, Austria, and Scandinavia. In 1350, it crossed the North Atlantic to Iceland and Greenland, where it wiped out the failing Viking settlement. It reached Russia two years later.

Europe's success in reconnecting with the world on the other side of the Mediterranean created the conditions that led to the spread of the Black Death through Europe. Under the Mongolian Peace, trade caravans traveled with greater frequency from east to west. After 1291, when a Genovese admiral defeated the Moroccan fleets that had previously prevented free passage through the Straits of Gibraltar, ship traffic between the Mediterranean to the ports of northern Europe increased.

The disease destroyed its victims with such speed that Italian author Giovanni Boccaccio, who lived through the Black Death in Florence, claimed that some "ate lunch with their friends and dined with their ancestors." Most suffered from the bubonic plague, in which a sudden high fever was followed within days by painful black swellings (buboes) the size of apples in the armpits and groin as the lymph nodes were overwhelmed by the bacteria. The buboes sometimes burst, letting out a mixture of blood and noxious pus. The black blotches for which the plague was named would spread over the victim's arms and legs. Convulsions, vomiting of blood, and delirium followed. The victim was usually dead within five days; the lucky ones died in less than one. A few survived. A second form, the pneumatic plague, was less common but deadlier, and much more contagious. This disease attacked the lungs instead of the lymph nodes, causing the victim to drown in bloody foam. The deadliest of all was the rare septicemic plague, in which the bacteria attacked the bloodstream directly, bringing death before any visible symptoms appeared.

The speed at which the epidemic swept through Europe and the number of its victims were terrifying. Densely populated towns and religious communities were hit harder than rural regions. Some communities, like Milan, seem to have escaped the disease entirely. But many small towns and villages were wiped out. North Africa and Asia suffered similar losses.

turned on local Jewish populations, who were often involved in the eastern trade. Rumors spread that the Jews had caused the plague by poisoning wells. Some Jews were burned in their houses by fearful mobs. Others were tortured until they confessed to crimes they hadn't committed. In July 1348, Pope Clement VI issued a papal bull placing the Jews of Europe under his protection and ordering Christians to stop the violence against them, with no effect. The persecution continued to escalate, reaching its most extreme point in Strasbourg.

Europe's success in reconnecting with the world ... created the conditions that led to the spread of the Black Death.

Those who could fled the cities. Others practiced a reverse quarantine, shutting themselves up in their houses. Some abandoned stricken family members, fearful of catching the disease themselves. Boccaccio reported that parents deserted their own children. Some saw the plague as a sign of God's wrath against a sinful people. Groups of flagellants roamed the cities, whipping their own backs with spike-tipped thongs in an attempt to purge themselves of sin.

Even though people did not understand the causes of the disease, they did recognize the relationship between the disease and the trade routes. Some cities tried to close their gates against outsiders. Frightened citizens blamed foreigners and then

Eyewitnesses later described this day, when paranoid Strasbourg Christians marched their captives to the city's Jewish cemetery. There, in an ad hoc legal proceeding, the Jews were accused and tried for poisoning the city's wells and spreading the plague. After being tortured, some of those prisoners confessed to the charges against them. As a result, thousands of other Jews were killed or expelled from this and other German cities. Some were given a choice between converting to Christianity or burning. A few of those captured in Strasbourg renounced Judaism and converted. Some two thousand others, including Rabbi Meier and his family, did not and were then burned to death.

A FIRSTHAND ACCOUNT OF THE PLAGUE

The plague began in Siena in May, a horrible and cruel event. I do not know where to begin describing its relentless cruelty; almost everyone who witnessed it seemed stupefied by grief. It is not possible for the human tongue to recount such a horrible thing, and those who did not see such horrors can well be called blessed. They died almost immediately; they would swell up under the armpits and in the groin and drop dead while talking. Fathers abandoned their children, wives left their husbands, brothers forsook each other; all fled from each other because it seemed that the disease could be passed on by breath and sight. And so they died, and one could not find people to carry out burials for money or friendship. People brought members of their own household to the ditches as best they could, without priest or holy office or ringing of bells, and in many parts of Siena large deep ditches were dug for the great number of dead; hundreds died day and night, and all were thrown into these pits and covered with layers of earth, so much that the pits were filled and more were dug.

And I, Agnolo di Tura, known as the Fat, buried five of my children with my own hands. And there were those who had been so poorly covered with earth that dogs dragged them from there and through the city and fed on corpses. Nobody wept for the dead, since each was awaiting death and so many died that everyone thought that the end of the world had come.

—Agnolo di Tura del Grasso

ANTI-SEMITISM AND MOB RULE

The massacre of Jews in fourteenth century Strasbourg is a reminder of one of humanity's recurring failures: our tendency to seek scapegoats in times of trouble.

Failed crops, pandemics, and failed economies all make it is easy for a charismatic leader to fan the flames of mass hysteria, inciting fearful people to violence against a persecuted or despised minority. We see variations of the pattern over and over throughout history. Christians persecuted in ancient Rome. Witches burned in sixteenth century Europe. Pogroms against Jews in Russia and Poland in the nineteenth century. The massacre of Armenians in Turkey in the early twentieth century.

Nazi Germany's murder of six million Jews in World War II.

Ethnic hatred, superstition, prejudice, and ignorance are powerful forces, that have divided communities and nations and have caused enormous suffering throughout time.

ABOVE LEFT: *The Massacre of Jews at Strasbourg by Eugene Beyer depicts a scene horribly familiar to modern readers.* • RIGHT: *Buchenwald Concentration Camp, 1945*

BLAMING THE JEWS

STRASBOURG, GERMANY, FEBRUARY 14, 1349.
Outside the city's Jewish quarter, Rabbi Meier walks alone, on his way home with a bundle of fresh food. He is one block from the Jewish ghetto gates when, from the street behind him, he hears commotion. Turning to look, he sees an agitated crowd of people advancing quickly. They're waving sticks and shouting threateningly in his direction. Why, he doesn't know—but he knows enough to run the rest of the way to safety.

With his wife and children assembled at the dinner table, Rabbi Meier is leading the family in prayer. Suddenly, the sounds of footsteps and yelling from outside prompt him to stop and listen. A flaming object comes through the window, and lands on the floor. The fire begins to spread, causing the Meier children to scream and run to the front door—just as it is kicked in. A group of angry men grab the children, the rabbi, and his wife and drag them out of the house onto the street. Turning to look one last time at his burning house, Rabbi Meier sees a man and a woman running through the flames and out the front door, carrying pieces of the family's silver.

Chapter 5: PLAGUE

From one witness to the day's events came this report: "The Jews of Strasbourg were stripped almost naked by the crowd as they were marched to their own cemetery and into a house prepared for burning. At the cemetery gates, the youth and beauty of several females excited some commiseration; and they were snatched from death against their will. But the young and beautiful and the converts were the only ones to see sun set in Strasbourg that Valentine's Day. Marchers who tried to escape were chased down the street and murdered."

The plague did not disappear after the first wave of deaths. Subsequent epidemics hit Europe at irregular intervals in the 1360s and 1370s and continued to flare up as late as the Great Plague of London of 1665. Communities that had escaped the first epidemic were hit badly in later epidemics. Yet none of these later epidemics was as devastating as the first. Those communities that had suffered before experienced lower death rates, since survivors of earlier attacks became immune.

**IT TAKES A CITY
TO MAKE AN EPIDEMIC**

Epidemic diseases are described as "crowd diseases" for a reason. They are the companion of permanent settlement and the growth of cities.

From the plague to swine flu, all epidemic diseases share several characteristics:

• The disease spreads quickly and easily from an infected person to the healthy people around him or her.

• Victims either die or recover completely in a short period of time. (The fact that we describe those who catch epidemic disease as *victims* says a lot. In a very real sense, microbes mug their human hosts.)

• Those who recover develop antibodies that leave them immune to the disease.

It would be almost two hundred years before Europe's population grew back to the levels it had enjoyed before the plague.

Within four years the plague killed two hundred million people, nearly half the population of Europe. Europe suffered a substantial depopulation of rural areas and a labor shortage in both town and countryside. Villages lay empty and abandoned. Fields went unworked. The Roman Catholic Church, which lost a disproportionately high number of clergy, found itself with a list of open appointments and had difficulty training enough new priests to fill them. Governments found it equally difficult to recruit soldiers and were forced to increase wages.

JUNE 1763. FORT PITT WAS surrounded. Chief Pontiac of the Ottawa had organized the Indian nations of the Great Lakes region into a confederation to drive the English back to their settlements along the sea. Eight of the ten British forts west of Niagara had already fallen to Pontiac's forces.

Fort Pitt's commander, Captain Simeon Ecuyer, had received prior notice of the uprising. The stockade was well supplied with food and ammunition. Ecuyer assured his superiors that he would be able to hold out until reinforcements relieved the siege. In the meantime, he was willing to try to break the siege another way. Smallpox had broken out in the fort. Everyone knew the Indians had no stamina where disease was concerned. When two of Pontiac's chiefs came to the fort to urge the English to surrender, Ecuyer gave them two blankets and a handkerchief that had belonged to smallpox victims. He hoped it would have the desired effect.

Three weeks later, Lord Jeffrey Amherst, commanding general of British forces in North America, had the same idea. He wrote to Colonel Henry Bouquet, who had relieved the siege at Fort Pitt, "Could it not be contrived to send the Smallpox among those disaffected tribes of Indians? We must on this occasion use every stratagem in our power to reduce them." Bouquet, like Ecuyer, thought smallpox blankets would do the trick.

The Americas were blessedly free of the terrifying epidemic diseases that repeatedly swept through Europe and Asia. Smallpox, measles, influenza, plague, tuberculosis, typhus, cholera, and malaria traveled from Asia to Europe, leaving the dead and the immune in their wake. Even when they did not rage in epidemic proportions, these diseases lingered in endemic form in the cities of Eurasia, kept alive by the poor sanitation and crowded streets of early (and not-so-early) cities. Exposed to endemic variations of the most dangerous diseases, large portions of the Eurasia population developed immunities. The peoples of the Americas did not suffer from the ravages of epidemics, but neither did they benefit from the creation of an immune population.

Eurasian crowd diseases evolved from Eurasian herd animals. Unlike the peoples of Eurasia, the populations of the Americas had few domestic animals: the turkey in Mexico and the American Southwest; the llama, alpaca, and guinea pig in the Andes; the Muscovy duck in tropical South America; and the dog throughout both continents.

Even if one of the pre-Columbian civilizations had developed an epidemic disease, it had no way to spread across the continent. Alexander the Great, the Romans, and Genghis Khan created huge empires that linked otherwise separate regions of the Eurasian world. Even when Central Asia was divided into smaller, feuding kingdoms, the East-West trade

Smallpox killed an estimated sixty million Europeans, including five reigning European monarchs, in the eighteenth century alone.

of the Silk Roads continued, carrying germs as well as silks, spices, and precious gems. By contrast, vast distances separated the three civilizations of the Americas: the Andes, Mesoamerica, and the American Southeast. Maize cultivation spread across both continents from Mesoamerica, but the cultures that grew up around maize in all its forms were never connected by regular trade. Andean cultures traded with Mesoamerica for the feathers of brilliantly colored tropical birds. Seashells from the Yucatán Peninsula made their way to the Mississippi. But

WORST EPIDEMICS IN HISTORY		
SMALLPOX	300+ million	10,000 BCE to 1979
MEASLES	200 million	7th century BCE to 1963
SPANISH FLU	50–100 million	1918–1919
PLAGUE	75 million	1340–1400
PLAGUE OF JUSTINIAN	25 million	541–750 BCE
HIV/AIDS	25+ million	1981–present

BACTERIA, DNA, SURVIVAL

———

Humans evolved from single-cell bacteria, yet microscopic bacteria cause diseases that continue to kill human beings.

Furthermore, bacteria are everywhere. Our bodies are covered with them; 600,000 on one square inch of skin. We depend on bacteria to live. Only when a new strain arises and comes after us can they threaten our health and lives.

Scientists did not discover the germs that cause diseases until 500 years after the plague ravaged Europe and Asia. It would take another century for human beings to work out how to kill bacteria in our bodies without also killing our bodies' "good" cells.

Much later still, when scientists completed the epic work of cracking the human genome, reasons for the survival of some from the plague and other pandemics became clear. Some descendants of people who lived through the plague and survived had a gene that would protect them from HIV, Ebola, and other infectious diseases. What doesn't kill man makes him stronger.

Today we can cure the plague, and promising new medicines are in development to prevent and slow the advance of HIV/AIDS. Less reassuring is the fact that bacterial "superbugs" such as E. coli, staphylococcus, and streptococcus are mutating to resist some of our best medicines, including old standbys, such as penicillin. The human race continues to fight an evolutionary struggle with deadly bacteria as their resistance to synthetic antibiotics allows these germs to evade our best efforts to kill or contain them.

nothing like the East-West trade of the Silk Routes existed to connect the Andes to the Mississippi.

At the same time the Eurasia population was being ravaged by the plague, the civilized populations of the Americas were growing. On the eve of the Spanish conquest, that number was roughly 100 million, much of it centralized around the three central cultural areas.

Like early Mesopotamia, Mesoamerica was home to a series of cultures with shared characteristics, each building on the earlier cultures it replaced, beginning with the Olmecs in 1200 BCE. In the Yucatán, the process of urbanization and state building culminated in the Mayan civilization, a loose confederation of about five dozen city-states and kingdoms held together by a shared culture and extensive trade routes that linked the larger Mesoamerican world.

In Mexico, the militarized states of the Mixtec, the Zapotec, and the Toltec grew, conquered, fell, and were conquered in turn. Each of the American states was tapped into the same trade routes that supplied the Maya. Their cities were supported by a network of villages and towns that grew crops using irrigation and the raised-field farming known as the *chinapa* system.

When the Aztecs' ancestors moved into the Valley of Mexico from the north, they were foragers and small farmers who settled into the marginal farmlands between the region's major city-states. Like the barbarian tribes who infiltrated Rome in the fourth century, Aztecs aspired to the comforts of the more developed cultures. In the fourteenth century, also like the Germanic tribes, Aztecs began to hire themselves out as mercenaries to the armies of the existing powers. In 1428, they overthrew their masters and created a dynasty of their own, the most aggressive imperial power seen in Mesoamerica prior to the arrival of the Spaniards. In less than a century, their capital city, Tenochtitlán had a population of roughly two million.

Mayan ruins in Central America dating from between the sixth and tenth centuries CE.

Much the same process occurred in the Andes, although the earlier cultures are less well known than those of Mesoamerica. Two city-states developed around 500 CE: Tiwanaku, near Lake Titicaca, by the Peru-Bolivia border; and Wari in southern Peru. Both states built on earlier Andean cultures—the Pukará, Huarpa, Moche, and Nazca. Both developed extensive trade networks throughout the region. The Wari developed a string of colonies that stretched for one thousand miles along the spine of the Andes. At its height, Tiwanaku's population was approaching one hundred thousand in the city, with a quarter million in the surrounding countryside. (It would be another five hundred years before Paris could claim similar numbers.) Both states fell apart soon after 1000 CE, their lands and culture absorbed by other Andean cultures, ending with the Inca Empire in the fifteenth century.

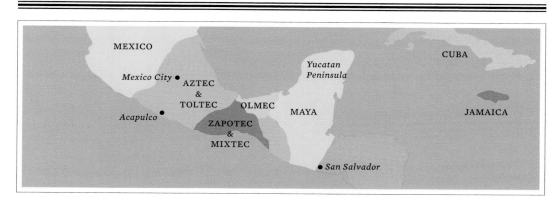

Mezo-American cultures in the first millennium BCE

AROUND 1250 CE, A WARLIKE
people calling themselves the *Incas*, or "lords,"
entered the valley of Cuzco and settled among
the tribes who had lived there for centuries. Their
ruler was known as the *Sapa Inca*, or "sole Lord."
Under the leadership of men with names like
"War Chieftain," "Unforgettable," and "He Who
Weeps Blood," they made and broke alliances with
other tribes, conquering them one by one.

In 1438, with the entire Cuzco valley under
Inca control, the ninth Sapa Inca, Pachacuti
("Earthquake," or "Earth Upside Down"), grew
more ambitious. He conquered a swath of terri-
tory from Lake Titicaca to Ecuador, turning the
Inca state from a regional power into an empire.

Andean cultures, 1250-1450 CE

His son, Topa Inca, the "Unforgettable King," succeeded him. Topa Inca was the Genghis Khan of the Native American world. No Native American ruler before or since conquered so much territory in such a short period of time. Between 1471 and 1483, he expanded the Inca Empire beyond the boundaries of Peru into modern Bolivia, Chile, and Argentina, then moved northward, conquering coastal Ecuador and the mountain kingdom of Quito.

Topa Inca did not always show mercy to those who surrendered. On one occasion, he promised the people of the coastal city of Huarco that they would be treated fairly if they surrendered. When they left the safety of their walls, he attacked. Thousands were killed. Their bleached bones littered the ground around the city for generations.

Topa Inca's successor, Huayna Capac ("Young Man with Many Virtues") was chosen from more than sixty of his father's sons as heir to the throne. The last of the great Inca rulers, he expanded the empire's borders still further, completing the conquest of Ecuador and advancing to what is now southern Colombia. When he died in 1527, the Inca Empire measured nearly three thousand miles from north to south, reaching from "Mother Sea" in the west to the Amazon jungles in the east. The Incas called their empire Tawantinsuyu—the "Land of the Four Quarters."

Led by Pachacuti, the warrior prince of the city of Cuzco, the Incas built their empire in isolation—both the key to their success and the cause of their eventual undoing.

At its peak, the Inca confederation included the lands and tribal peoples of modern Peru, Chile, Bolivia, and Argentina. Expert farmers, they produced a trio of high-energy superfoods: potatoes, maize, and peanuts.

QUIPU

The Inca had no written language, but they had a sophisticated system of keeping records based on knots, known as *quipu*.

The quipu was a rope with colored strings dangling from it. It could be as short as two inches or as long as ten feet. Each color had a different meaning. Yellow stood for gold, white for silver, green for cocao, red for soldiers, etc. Information was recorded on each string using a complicated pattern of knots that formed a binary code similar to modern computer languages. Quipu makers from every quarter, district, and province were charged with recording the details of life at each level of the empire. Each quipu gave a snapshot of the empire, a region, or a village at a given moment. A quipu could tell the emperor how many people had died in a village in a year and how many had been born. Different strings could tell him the ages of his villagers, the number of people working in each occupation, the size of the quinoa crop, and, most important, the number of men available in time of war.

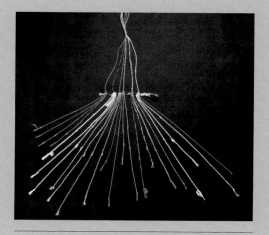

Incan Quipu accounting device

EARLY PAIN RELIEVERS

The Native Americans of the Andeans discovered the results of chewing the leaves of the coca bush long before the Incas came to power. A mouthful of coca leaves would keep a man working through hunger and fatigue or relieve the pain of the wounded.

Under the Incas, coca production became a royal monopoly and coca use a royal prerogative. All plantations belonged to the Sapa Inca. Only royal favorites were allowed to chew the leaves. It was a great honor to receive a mouthful of coca leaves from the jeweled bag the Sapa Inca wore at his side.

When the Spaniards gained control of Peru, they established commercial coca plantations to supply the demand among workers in the silver mines.

They had no writing, so oral history served as the primary glue for their amalgamated culture and religion. Nor did they have access to iron, so most Incan tools were made of stone. Most amazing, given the scale of their engineering feats, the Incas had no large draft animals; it was their manpower and advanced architectural design that gave them a permanent place on the list of the world's most wondrous human-built achievements.

How did the Incas build twenty-five thousand miles of roadway to link their empire through the rugged Andes mountains?

Nobody knows.

More perplexing still, how did they achieve the great pre-Columbian engineering feat that is Machu Picchu? Again, we are left to wonder.

Made up of 140 buildings, 600 terraces, and more than 100 stone stairways, Machu Picchu took an estimated workforce of five thousand to build. Each of its granite stone blocks weighs fifty tons, stacked and arranged with *nothing* to attach one block to the next. Still, these blocks fit together so snugly, not even a knife blade can fit between them. And not even an earthquake (in an active seismic zone) can move them from their assigned places.

Some anthropologists believe the Incas built Machu Picchu as a form of psychological warfare against any potential invaders. Perhaps its sheer size would ward off any human predators. Yet within a hundred years, Machu Picchu was abandoned, as the New and Old Worlds ended their separation and came into lethal contact.

Despite, or perhaps because of, their isolation, the Incas constructed one of the great wonders of the world. The same isolation left the Incas unprepared for more powerful technologies and weapons in the form of European gunpowder and biological warfare.

AMERICAN CULTURES OF THE thirteenth through fifteenth centuries were so heavily populated and energetic that Spanish reformer Bartolomé Las Casas, writing in 1542, described them as "a beehive full of people." By the time Las Casas wrote his history of the Aztecs, Eurasian diseases had emptied the beehive.

The newly discovered American continents—insulated from the plague and possessing vast new resources for mankind—offered unimagined opportunities to Old World colonists brave or desperate enough to travel across the Atlantic.

On the horizon, Africa beckons, tantalizing with its vast deposits of accessible gold. As Africa becomes a trading partner to Europe and Asia, ideas and merchandise are also exchanged and human knowledge is enriched. The search for another precious mineral, salt, becomes a driver for forging global connections; like gold, salt shapes new trade routes, builds up new cities and states, and destroys others.

As human civilization becomes more sophisticated and acquires new foods, ideas, and weapons, man again places himself at a precipice. In front of him lies modernity. The tendency to fall backward into chaos and unchecked violence is the only thing that can stop him from making the next big leap forward for mankind.

Machu Picchu, the center of Inca culture, dates from the fifteenth century CE.

NEW ERA

RISING FROM THE WASTELAND OF PLAGUE-RAVAGED EUROPE, HUMANITY REGAINS ITS FOOTING AND ITS WANDERLUST. IT IS A TIME OF MOVEMENT, REBUILDING, AND REBIRTH.

Italians and Portuguese sail around the Horn of Africa into the Indian Ocean in search of silk and spice. Traders in camel caravans go overland, risking the suffocating heat and sandstorms of the Sahara to exchange salt for gold. New ideas travel the same routes: Hindu mathematics and Greek philosophy are reinterpreted in the course of their passage through the crucible of the Muslim world. Ideas that had been greeted with suspicion in the twelfth century are embraced by the West, leading Europe to its rebirth.

While Europeans are ready to embrace new ideas, the Chinese turn inward, creating a culture defined from the start as *"ming"*—brilliant, founded by a leader armed with the first guns. By forging new global connections, mankind comes back from the brink and scales new heights. Banking is born. The printing press is invented. Mapmaking comes into its own. In the new era, there are winners and losers, conquered and conquerors, great wealth made and lost.

And what drives human progress? Mankind searches tirelessly for the traces of a nugget that fell to earth in a celestial shower some 4 billion years ago. But people of every tribe and nation soon discover that gold shifts the centers of power—and gives them new reasons to spill their neighbors' blood.

LEFT: *The Forbidden City, in the center of Beijing, was the Imperial Palace during the Ming and Qing dynasties.* • ABOVE: *Caravan crossing the desert.*

SILENT TRADE

A true historical oddity, the "silent trade" was a wordless transaction that took place between traders in fourteenth-century West Africa. In this oft-repeated scene, African miners exchanged gold for salt and other merchandise without laying eyes on or saying a single word to their trading partners. Foreign traders would arrive at the marketplace and set their goods on the ground. Next, they would announce their presence by beating a drum. Then they'd leave. Hearing the drum, the local gold miners would return to the marketplace. After examining the merchandise, they would pour out a measure of gold dust next to each pile of goods, beat the drum to signal that a trade had been made, and they, too, would leave. It was then the foreigners' turn. If they returned to find the amount of gold dust acceptable, they would take it and be on their way. If not, they'd beat the drum again so the miners could come back and make a counteroffer. Each group would go back and forth until they reached an agreement or decided against the trade. The locals did not want to give away the sources of their gold. And with no human contact, they made sure there were no slips of the tongue.

1324 CE. MANSA MUSA, THE KING of Mali, left his capital of Niani to make the hajj to Mecca, as all good Muslims should. He set off in great pomp, accompanied by sixty thousand of his subjects, great princes and soldiers among them. Five hundred slaves ran in front of him as he rode, each carrying a four-pound staff of pure gold. Led by a Tuareg guide, his caravan traveled across the invisible trade roads of the Sahara, through the salt mining city of Walata, to the northern oases in Tuar. Many among his entourage stayed behind at Tuar, laid low by a foot ailment. Mansa Musa continued on his pilgrimage.

He arrived in Cairo after eight months. The Muslim chroniclers of the city recorded his visit—and tried to guess how much gold the richest king of Africa carried with him. Each gave a number more outrageous than the last: One hundred camels laden with gold. Three hundred camels, each carrying three hundred pounds of gold. A thousand camels carrying one hundred pounds of gold apiece. So much gold, however you counted it, that the value of the precious metal dropped wherever he traveled. It took twelve years for the Cairo gold market to recover from his visit.

Mansa Musa was a big spender. He built a mosque everywhere he stopped for the Friday prayers. He paid for every service in gold and gave lavish gifts to his hosts. Beggars lined the streets when he passed, hoping to receive a gold nugget that would allow them to never beg again. His generosity and his princely display of wealth were so great that he ran out of money on the trip back to Mali and had to borrow in Cairo. Merchants eagerly lent to the king from the land that produced gold on such a dazzling scale.

On his return from the hajj, Mansa Musa erected a new mosque in Timbuktu, designed by the celebrated Andalusian poet and architect Abu Ishaq as-Sahéli al-Tuadjin al-Granata. The city's first building made from brick and stone, the mosque was designed for learning as well as for prayer, complete with rooms for students and books.

Timbuktu was already a city of learning when Mansa Musa left for Mecca. A quarter of its population was students who had traveled from all corners of the Islamic world to study there. Scholars at Timbuktu wrote commentaries on the Qur'an that were read in Cairo. One scholar traveled with Mansa Musa from Cairo to Timbuktu, expecting to teach. He found the scholarly standards there so high that he was forced to return to North Africa to study further before he could teach in Timbuktu.

Mansa Musa's extravagant spending drew Europe's attention to West Africa for the first time. Venetian and Genoese merchants in Alexandria sent word home about the king of Mali and his immense wealth. Soon trading firms from Granada, Genoa, Venice, and the Flemish markets of the north sent merchants to establish new posts in Maghreb towns such as Marrakech and Fez, trading manufactured goods for gold. Timbuktu became a legend—and a goal.

The West African kingdoms of Ghana, Mali, and Songhay were built on gold. For four centuries the region's merchants had grown rich trading

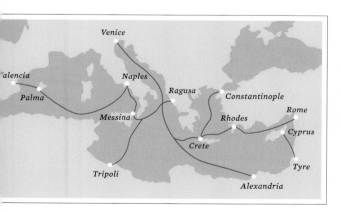

FROM GOLD DUST TO DUCATS

Gold arrived in Mali as gold dust. From there, North African traders carried it on camels from Timbuktu through the Sahara to Alexandria, where it was loaded onto ships bound for Venice.

In the thirteenth century, the city of Venice gained control of trade in gold and held on to it for the next four hundred years. The market was strictly regulated. All imported gold had to be registered at the official assay office in the Rialto, the economic and trade center of Venice, and could not be exported unless it had been refined to at least 23 carats. Beginning in 1266, officials at the gold office tested the weights and scales of all money changers at least once a month.

In 1273 refining imported gold was entrusted to two goldsmiths chosen and paid by the assay office. The price of gold was fixed officially every day on the Rialto. Unlike today's financial markets, Venice had no newspapers to quote prices. The Rialto was the only place to gain information about gold—often by eavesdropping. Insider information was prized.

In 1284 Venice opened its gold mint and the next year struck the first gold ducat of 3.55 grams (0.114 ounces). The ducat soon became Europe's premier currency and the most widely accepted coin since the Romans' solidus.

By 1380 the officials regulating the world's gold trade were no longer just money handlers. When they officially began taking deposits, the Venetians became the first bankers, as we recognize their job description today.

By 1490, one out of every thirty Venetians had bank accounts.

LEFT: *map of Venetian trade routes in the 14th century*

AFRICAN GOLD

———

Long before humans, or even dinosaurs, roamed the planet, millions of tons of rock from outer space struck the earth at tens of thousands of miles per hour, bringing an abundance of gold and burying it deep within the mantle layer. Over the billions of years that followed, volcanoes released this gold from the mantle and carried it up toward Earth's surface.

Since gold is the only metal that can be found in the ground in its pure form, many scientists believe it was the first metal discovered by early Homo sapiens.

In most of the world, gold must be extracted from mines deep underground, with backbreaking work performed by thousands of laborers. But in West Africa, the River Niger does the hard work, washing gold out of the bedrock and depositing it as dust across the flood plain. Gold is so abundant that people can scoop it out of the water and from the topsoil.

SALT

Life originated from a process of chemical transformation in Earth's primeval waters. Today the concentrations of sodium, potassium, and chloride in our bloodstreams still mimic the seas from which life first sprang. In fact, human blood contains roughly the same percentage of salt as the ocean.

The chemical compound *halite*, consisting of sodium and chlorine, is the substance we know as "ordinary" table salt. Yet, there is nothing ordinary about it. Salt is as essential to life as water. No living thing can survive without it. Without salt, our bodies could not digest food, transmit nerve impulses, or move muscles, including the heart.

When we were hunter-gatherers, the salt we needed came from wild game. But as mankind settled and our diet changed, we had to find salt from other sources.

Salt is everywhere on Earth. But common as it is, salt was often difficult to obtain before modern industrial mining and salinization methods. Thus, the demand for salt became one of the driving forces of civilization. In search of salt, humans created new trade routes across the most inhospitable places on Earth. Desert caravans with as many as forty thousand camels carried salt across the Sahara and back again.

Many salt roads, such as the "Via Salaria" in Italy, were in place by the Bronze Age. Today salt is readily available: produced either by evaporating salt water or by mining. We take our salt shakers for granted. But not so long ago, cities and states rose and fell based on their proximity to accessible *salt*.

WHITE GOLD

Salt was so valuable in ancient times that when other currencies were scarce, Roman soldiers were paid with salt. Thus it was said that soldiers who did their job well were "worth their salt."

THE GREAT MOSQUE AT DJENNÉ

The same desert caravans that transported salt and gold also carried Islam south across the Sahara.

In 1240, Djenné's twenty-sixth ruler, Koy Kunboro, converted to Islam. In a grand gesture of devotion, he demolished his palace and built a mosque on its site. According to local legend, the desert *djinns*, or spirits, helped him with the construction, carrying baskets of clay from the desert on their heads so the renowned masons of Djenné could work more quickly. Built from sun-dried bricks the size of a Coke can and plastered with a layer of mud, Koy Kunboro's mosque was a wonder for almost six hundred years.

In 1819, fundamentalist leader Seku Amadu declared jihad against Djenné, swearing to bring the city back to a purer form of Islam. He captured Djenné after a nineteen-month siege. As a first step in purifying the city, he closed the Great Mosque and built another that was less great in every way. Islamic law forbids a Muslim to destroy a mosque, but mud buildings are fragile. Without regular maintenance, Amadu could count on the annual rains to destroy the building for him, especially after he ordered the gutters blocked. When the French captured Djenné in 1898, the mosque was in ruins.

In 1907 local masons, still skilled in the traditional art of mud construction, rebuilt the mosque. Today, the Great Mosque of Djenné is the largest mud building in the world. The city takes no chances on losing its Great Mosque to the rains again. Replastering the building is part of the annual Ramadan celebration, a messy, mud-splashed party that involves the entire community.

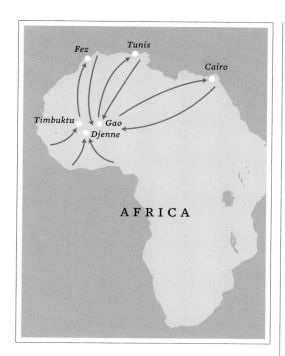

map of west African trade patterns in the 14th century

---

gold, slaves, and ivory for horses and cloth from North Africa, books and other treasures from the larger Islamic world, and salt from the Sahara desert, the dried-out remains of an ancient salty sea. North African Moors, Arabs, and Berbers traveled across the Sahara from Tangier, Tunis, and Tripoli in caravans of tens of thousands of camels, in search of African gold.

In the fourteenth century, Timbuktu in Mali was the commercial center of West Africa. Two-thirds of the world's gold was traded there. The city was home to fifty thousand people, but its numbers could triple with the arrival of trade caravans from the north. Trade created wealth. Wealth attracted scholars and holy men from all over North Africa and the Middle East, from Cordoba, Marrakech, Baghdad, Alexandria—and Mecca.

VENICE WAS ORGANIZED FOR trade from its beginnings in the sixth century CE. The city was built in a malarial marshland, resting on nothing but oak pilings set into the mud. It had no fresh water, no surrounding land to support it, no natural resources, no agriculture, and no industry. It existed on the quality of its ships, the skills of its sailors, and the ability of its merchants to move goods from the place where they were produced to any market that would buy them. At a time when most of Europe was ruled by feudal lords who earned their income at war and from their land, the Venetian nobility were merchant princes.

Technically under Byzantine rule in their early years, the merchants of Venice turned their faces to the East and worked the sea routes that linked Western Christendom to Byzantium and the Muslim lands. Venetian merchants sold the Muslims timber and slaves, literally Slavs from Eastern Europe. With the gold they earned, the Venetians bought silks, jewels, and saints' relics to sell to Frankish kings, princes of Italian city-states, and luxury-loving bishops. They were in constant trouble for selling war materials to Muslim Egypt—first with their Byzantine overlords and later with the pope in Rome. At one point the entire city of Venice was excommunicated for ignoring papal injunctions against trade with the Muslim "infidels."

Venice remained a town of modest size and importance until the eleventh century, when the Crusades catapulted it into prominence. Knights from the north arrived in Venice, prepared to pay for passage to the Holy Lands. Returning crusaders brought home a taste for Muslim luxury. The same ships that carried crusaders back and forth from the Holy Lands brought all the spices of Araby—not to mention glass, silks, soaps, perfumes, paper, and

VENETIAN JUSTICE

TWO NON-NOBLE CAPTAINS OF THE GUARD POLICE the Venetian banking thoroughfare. Each has a squadron of as many as twelve men who patrol the Rialto day and night. They maintain a constant watch over Venetian ship galleys recently arrived from Egypt, laden with African gold. They also guard the benches (*bancos*) where the bankers conduct their business.

Pietro Venier is an employee of the Pruili bank, a large financial enterprise in the Rialto. On his bench he displays his gold coins, as do other bankers.

Along comes small-time thief Cristofo Enrico. He runs up and sweeps the bowl of coins into a sack before Venier can jump to his feet.

Losing this much money will cost Venier his job and could mean the end of the Pruili bank. Fortunately for Venier, Enrico is caught still in possession of his sack. The robber is quickly tried and sentenced, and his left hand is amputated. Then Enrico is paraded around the canals of Venice, tied to the mast of a grand barge. As a final message of warning to the watchful masses, Enrico is hung in the Rialto. (Venice's soaring crime rate is a sign of the city's success.)

Bankers like Venier finance the beautification of their city, investing in public art and architecture. Together they create the Piazza San Marco (St. Mark's Square), the Doge's Palace, and the Rialto—and bring about a new age of learning and art: the Renaissance.

African gold—back to Europe from the bazaars of the Muslim world. By the thirteenth century Venice was the hinge connecting Europe and the East. Its wealth made it the banker of Europe. Every European king was in hock to the merchants and bankers of Venice.

The Venetians suffered crisis after crisis in the fourteenth century. Like the rest of Europe, their city was devastated by the plague. More than half of Venice's population died in barely two years. To make matters worse, the widespread casualties across Europe as a whole hurt Venice in another way. Depopulation meant a drop both in production of and demand for goods. As trade volume decreased, Venice and its ancient sea rival, Genoa, struggled to control the smaller market. The longstanding conflict between the two city-states flared into war in 1350, and again in 1378. For two years, Venice and Genoa were engaged in an all-out war. All trade ceased. The Venetian fleet was ruined. The city's treasury was emptied. Venice won the final victory at the battle of Chioggia in June 1380, but its economy and its foreign trade had been shattered.

The city rose again, more spectacular than before. In the years after the war, the Venetians rebuilt their fleets. They also consolidated Venice's position as the center of East-West trade and reinforced the ranks of the patriciate by ennobling thirty citizen families, all of whom had made major contributions to the war with Genoa. With its ruling oligarchy energized by new blood, Venice experienced a burst of colonial expansion, creating a trading post empire of islands, ports, and fortified bastions strung out along the sea routes to the Levant.

By the fifteenth century, Venice was the bazaar of Europe.

HUMAN THUNDER

In the tenth century CE, Taoist alchemists in China, searching for an elixir of immortality, discovered instead a new and very efficient way to cause explosions using a compound of saltpeter (potassium nitrate), sulfur, and charcoal: gunpowder. At first, gunpowder served as an amusement at the emperor's court—the equivalent of modern fireworks. Four hundred years after its discovery, it began to change the course of history when Jiao Yu fired a lead ball out of a handheld iron tube at three hundred meters a second.

Once ignited, gunpowder's three ingredients go through a tremendous chemical transformation. The sulphur acts as an initiator, much like kindling, setting alight the charcoal. Together they produce large quantities of hot, expanding gas. The potassium nitrate, or saltpeter, provides oxygen, accelerating the burning process at such a fast rate that it results in an explosion. The more saltpeter there is in the mix, the bigger the bang.

When ignited in the open, gunpowder burns with a pop and a burst of flame. Enclose it in a sealed container with a fuse, and the gas creates enough pressure to blow the container apart. The tougher the container, the more violent the explosion; a bomb is essentially a firecracker with a harder shell. Pack the powder into a tube with one open end and the power of the gases rushing from the tube will drive it forward, creating a rocket. Add a hard object to the open end and the expanding gases will push that object out, converting chemical energy into mechanical force: the basic principle behind every gun.

The gun brought radical social change, undermining the role of armored knights and putting power in the hands of ordinary soldiers. In time, the same ancient principles that gave us guns would also give us piston engines and the rockets that would propel us to the moon.

1355 CE. THE PLAGUE IN CHINA has undermined the hated Mongol hordes, giving the Chinese a chance to defeat them. But the key to China's victory is not the plague. It is a secret weapon invented by a monk, who, centuries earlier, christened his handiwork *huo chi:* "human thunder." The Western world will rename it *gunpowder*, but it will be the Chinese people who earn the distinction of using it to bring mankind into the era of modern warfare.

The times in China are troubled. The reigning Yuan emperor's mind has grown tired and muddled. Peasants have formed revolutionary bands. Bandits and warlords have appeared on all sides, like bees from their hives, assuming false titles of king and tearing the empire apart. Taoist scholar

Jiao Yu has long prepared for this day, studying the use of "fire-weapons" in warfare. Now he is ready to share his knowledge with the man he believes to hold the Mandate of Heaven as the next emperor of China: Zhu Yuanzhang.

When Jiao Yu presented his new fire-weapons to Zhu Yuanzhang, the peasant-turned-war leader examined them carefully. Zhu Yuanzhang was familiar with fire-weapons. Chinese armies had used gunpowder weapons since the early eleventh century including perforated metal balls that, when tossed by a catapult, sprayed fire and ignited the structures they hit. The arsenal also included smoke bombs to confuse the enemy and handheld flamethrowers made from bamboo rods that could shoot a six-foot-long tongue of flame, metal splinters, and broken porcelain. They could ignite fire arrows with a handful of gunpowder the size of a pomegranate, sealed to the shaft with pine resin. But this was something different, a three-foot-long tube of cast iron with a wooden stock. If it did what Jiao Yu claimed, it would give Zhu's armies an edge against the Mongol forces.

Zhu Yuanzhang ordered General Xu Da to test the weapons. Xu had his soldiers set up a suit of Mongol armor three hundred paces away. Made of overlapping plates of leather, Mongol armor could turn a shot from a powerful composite bow, but it was no match for Jiao's invention. The stone "bullet" behaved like flying dragons, penetrating several layers of armor before embedding itself in the stone wall.

Zhu Yuanzhang knew the importance of what he had just seen: "With these fire-weapons I will conquer the whole Empire as easily as turning the palms of my hands upside down!"

In the hands of these ragtag rebels, a revolutionary new weapon was about to change how we wage war. With the gun, humans would build and overthrow empires, win wars, tame wildernesses, and create new countries.

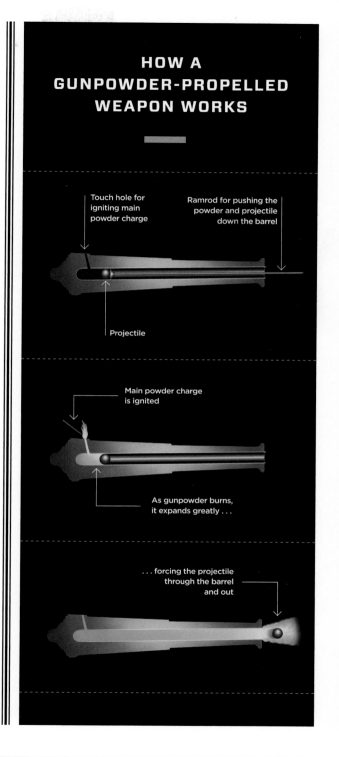

HOW A GUNPOWDER-PROPELLED WEAPON WORKS

Touch hole for igniting main powder charge

Ramrod for pushing the powder and projectile down the barrel

Projectile

Main powder charge is ignited

As gunpowder burns, it expands greatly . . .

. . . forcing the projectile through the barrel and out

BY THE MIDDLE OF THE FOUR-teenth century, conqueror dynasties had ruled China for more than a hundred years: the Tangut, the Jin, and finally, the Mongols. With more than half the population dead from the Black Death, the Yuan dynasty, founded by Kublai Khan, began to fall apart. Peasants revolted. Regional warlords seized power. The Mongol forces, torn by internal dissension and diminished by disease, struggled to retain order.

Zhu Yuanzhang was a peasant who had starved and begged as a boy. His parents often moved to look for work or evade rent collectors; they even had to give away several of their children because they couldn't afford to feed them. In the 1340s, Zhu's home region in Anhui province was hit by flood, drought, famine, and then the plague. When he was only sixteen, his father, older brother, and his brother's wife all died. A neighbor let Zhu bury them in his field, but he had no way to pay for the proper rites for their souls.

With no relatives to turn to, he joined a Buddhist monastery to avoid starving, a common practice for the sons of the poor. Like many Buddhist monks, Zhu was sent out to beg for food in emulation of the Buddha. He traveled through China as a wandering mendicant for the next three to four years before returning to the monastery. But the monastery was his refuge for only a short time.

In 1351, a peasant millenarian sect known as the Red Turbans rose in rebellion and enjoyed considerable success against the Mongol cavalry. In the course of fighting the rebels, the Yuan government troops burned down Zhu Yuanzhang's monastery. Zhu, then twenty-four, joined the rebels. He rose quickly through the ranks, especially after he married the adopted daughter of one of the commanders.

With command over twenty to thirty thousand men, Zhu soon attracted a band of capable soldiers of peasant origin, many of whom later became officials in the Ming dynasty, of which Zhu would be the first emperor. Educated men also joined his movement, including some Confucian scholars who suggested he gradually distance himself from the Red Turbans, whose millenarian beliefs did not appeal to the educated elite. As Zhu's power grew, so did his ambition. In 1367, he sent his troops north against the Yuan capital, located in modern Beijing.

Zhu's armies took the Yuan capital in 1368. The emperor, Toghün Temur, did not even wait for the rebel forces to arrive. He and his closest advisers fled to Mongolia a few days before the troops arrived. Zhu razed the Yuan palaces and, together with his wife, now the Empress Ma, declared the establishment of a new dynasty—the Ming. Its name means "brilliant," and it would last for three hundred years.

TWO DECADES EARLIER, GOLDSMITH Johannes Gutenberg had seen a thirst for knowledge in Europe and a growing demand for books and the written word. The newly founded universities had created a market for more books than

Zhu Yuanzhang

GUTENBERG'S DEBT

NOVEMBER 6, 1455. Mainz, Germany. Johannes Gutenberg paced the floor of his workshop. A chill wind swept over the Rhine and seeped in the windows, causing the large sheets of printed paper that hung from the ceiling to flutter a little. More sheets, already dry, sat in stacks on a nearby worktable. There were thousands of them, ready to be bound into the Bible that would be his masterwork.

Gutenberg and Fust with the first printing press, Germany, 1450s.

He could lose it all. His partner, Johann Fust, was in court at that very moment at the Convent of the Barefoot Friars, pressing charges against Gutenberg for an unpaid debt. Presses, type, molds, inks—and the beautiful printed pages of the Bible, Gutenberg had pledged it all when he borrowed money from Fust to set up the workshop. If Fust would just let him finish his Bible, the profits would allow him to repay the loan. But his partner wasn't willing to wait. He wanted his money now, and, if not his money, he wanted the workshop.

The door to the shop burst open, and Gutenberg's two assistants hurried in with the cold air. He had sent them to court to hear the verdict. As soon as he saw their faces, he knew the news was bad. The judge had ruled in favor of Fust. Gutenberg had lost everything.

Replica of the printing press invented by Johannes Gutenberg around 1440.

Europe had ever seen. A newly literate middle class was eager for secular literature in the vernacular languages. The growth of commerce required records and documents. The church sold thousands of letters of indulgence each year, each one painstakingly written by a clerical scribe.

Except for the block-printed picture book with few words, every book and document made in Europe was printed by hand. Between 600 and 1200 CE, most books made in Europe were copied and illustrated by monks as an act of devotion. Their work was slow, beautiful, and expensive. A fine copy of a Bible took one monastic scribe three years to produce and cost as much as a small house. With the growth of the universities, book production moved out of the monasteries. Booksellers hired nonclerical copyists to produce books on a commercial basis. Scribes organized themselves into guilds in every university town. Manuscripts were prepared and bound in separate sections so that scribes could divide the labor of copying and several people could read the parts at the same time. Thousands of books were being created, instead of dozens.

Gutenberg had been convinced that there was a market for still more books if he could produce them quicker and cheaper.

In 1435, Gutenberg began experimenting with the idea of printing using metal type. For ten years he worked in secret, building his press, creating new metal alloys, casting type, and experimenting with ink. In 1448, he printed a few copies of a popular grammar text, as a demonstration.

His printing press worked, but it still needed refinements, and Gutenberg was out of cash. In 1450, Gutenberg convinced a wealthy local businessman, Johann Fust, to loan him the money he needed to complete his invention. Fust invested eight hundred gulden—$150,000 in today's money—in Gutenberg's printing press. The collateral for the loan was the printing equipment yet to be built.

PAPER COMES WEST

Before Gutenberg could invent printing, he needed paper.

Fine medieval manuscripts were copied on parchment, which is made from the skin of goats, sheep, or lambs. The material lasted indefinitely, and it could be scraped and reused if needed. But it was expensive, and it took a lot of skins to make a book. An elaborate version of the Bible could take as many as two hundred skins to make.

Papermaking reached Europe from China by way of the Islamic world. Buddhist missionaries carried the technology west as far as Samarqand, where Muslims first encountered it in the early eighth century at the beginning of the Muslim golden age. They adopted paper as readily as they adopted Hindu numerals and Greek philosophy. By the eleventh century, Muslims were making paper everywhere from Samarqand to Valencia.

The first European paper mills appeared in Italy in the middle of the thirteenth century and slowly moved west, reaching England by the fifteenth century.

PRINTING IN CHINA

Johannes Gutenberg wasn't the first person to come up with the idea of printing.

Around 868 CE the Chinese began printing sacred Buddhist texts on sheets of paper, using a hand-carved wooden block for every page. The technology left no room for error: if part of a sheet needed to be changed, the entire block had to be carved again.

The next advance came in 1045, when a Chinese printer named Pi Sheng had the idea of pasting separate fired-clay characters, no thicker than a coin, on an iron plate with tree resin and wax. The plate could then be inked like a woodblock. If a character needed to be changed, the plate could be heated to soften the paste.

Over the years, other printers tried making reusable characters from wood, tin, and porcelain. Wood was too uneven; tin was too soft; porcelain cracked. But the real problem was not the material used for the type; it was the nature of the Chinese language. With thousands of separate characters, making movable type was expensive.

By the thirteen century, some printers were producing booklets, calendars, and dictionaries using a combination of woodcuts and movable type, but block printing was cheaper and more common.

Gutenberg ran through the loan in two years. Fust came to the rescue again, but this time the money wasn't a loan. Fust wanted equity in the business, and a share of the profits.

In 1455, Gutenberg and his foreman, Peter Schöffer, had almost completed the first print run of Gutenberg's forty-two-line Bible when Fust took him to court for defaulting on the original loan. The court ordered Gutenberg to repay the loan immediately or forfeit his machinery and type to Fust. With no cash to repay the loan, Gutenberg was forced to turn over the shop. Fust finished the edition of the Bible with the help of his new partner, Peter Schöffer. The new firm of Fust and Schöffer continued as printers for four generations.

Fust could take Gutenberg's machinery, but in the days before patents, he could not claim ownership of Gutenberg's ideas. Gutenberg started a new print shop with financial assistance from another wealthy lawyer, Konrad Humery. He spent the next three years making new type molds, casting type, building presses, and printing another, less-elaborate edition of the Bible.

Soon, several other print shops were operating in Mainz. Pupils of the early printers spread across Europe. Within thirty years of Gutenberg's first press run, there were printing presses in more than 110 towns across Europe, and more than 15 million copies of books had been printed. By 1600 CE, Europe had twenty-five hundred printing houses. Every city and big town had one. Together they produced more than ten million copies of forty thousand different titles: from grammar texts and vernacular Bibles to scientific treatises and manuals on how to conduct religious inquisitions.

Books were cheaper. More people learned to read and write. Ideas spread more quickly and reached more people than ever before: good ideas, bad ideas, old ideas, new ideas—revolutionary ideas.

THE PRINTING PRESS CHANGES HISTORY

The printing press was not a single invention. Gutenberg created a whole series of new materials and techniques to make a working press: a metal alloy strong enough to allow repeated impressions of a piece of type; ink that would actually stick to the metal type; paper of just the right weight and density; and the flat, shallow frame, called a "chase," that locks type together into text. The press itself was based on the screw press used for making wine and olive oil.

Gutenberg's most important innovation was molding and casting movable metal type, an early application of the theory of interchangeable parts, which would become a basic principle of the machine age. He carved each letter of the alphabet onto the end of a steel punch and hammered it into a copper blank. He then put the copper impression into a mold and poured molten metal into it. When the metal cooled, it left a reverse image of the letter attached to a metal base that could set in the type chase. The base varied in width according to the size of the letter.

Before the printing press, it took a scribe three years to produce a copy of the Bible, which then sold for the price of a fifteenth-century home. Gutenberg's invention of movable type—single, reusable, metal letters and characters—that could be mass-produced and reassembled page by page to produce a whole text—was the breakthrough

Page from the Gutenberg Bible, ca. 1455

that enabled us to spread knowledge through the written word.

The printing press forever changed the evolution of mankind, enabling our intellectual progress on a previously unimaginable scale. Printing laid the foundation for the Renaissance and the Protestant Reformation. It also ignited the machine age and set the stage for the industrial revolution. Learning and communication were never the same, with ramifications up to and including the invention of the Internet, and the digitization of every book ever written— a massive undertaking appropriately called "Project Gutenberg."

Alhambra Palace, Granada, Spain

THE FALL OF GRANADA

JANUARY 2, 1492 CE. GRANADA,
Spain. Isabella of Castile and Ferdinand of Aragon walked together up the heavily shaded hill that led to the Alhambra, the palace of the Muslim rulers of Granada. They were dressed in Moorish clothing for the ceremonial occasion. The palace grounds were already in the hands of Spanish troops. Boabdil, the last ruler of Muslim Spain, handed the keys to his ancestral palace to the Catholic monarchs. Moments later, their banner and the Christian cross rose above the highest tower of the Alhambra, signaling the completion of the Reconquista, the Christian reconquest of the Iberian Peninsula.

Boabdil, also known as Muhammad XII, rode away from the city with his family and entourage, their safe passage guaranteed by the Spanish crown. When he reached the last point from which he could see the city, Boabdil turned and wept, a moment known as "the Moor's last sigh."

His mother reproached him, saying, "You may well weep like a woman for what you could not defend like a man."

With "the Moor's last sigh," eight hundred years of Muslim Spain had come to an end.

THE END OF THE MOORS' CONTROL
of the Iberian Peninsula played out over four centuries.

The Umayyad dynasty of Spain crumbled in the early eleventh century. By 1031, the glorious state of al-Andalus had fractured into twenty-three city-states and small principalities, known as the "taifa," or "party kings," from the Spanish word for *faction*. The cultural brilliance of Muslim Spain did not dim with the fall of the Umayyads. The rulers of Seville, Granada, and Toledo competed to attract the artists, scholars, and scientists who had made Córdoba an intellectual and cultural mecca.

The taifa states maintained the cultural legacy of the Umayyads, but they lacked the military and political strength of the earlier dynasty. For the first time in centuries, the states of the Christian north were in a position to reclaim Spain for Christendom.

The most aggressive player in the effort at Reconquista was the state of Castile, which shared a long border with Muslim Spain. Beginning in 1037, Castile attacked one taifa state after another, marking each stretch of conquered territory with a defensive castle. In 1085, Alfonso VI, king of Castile and Navarra, besieged and captured Toledo, the former capital of Spain under the Visigoths who had ruled Spain before the Muslims.

Shocked by the loss of Toledo and unable to stand up to the continued assault by Christian forces, the emirs of the taifa states reluctantly called for help from the Almoravid dynasty of North Africa. The party kings knew it was a risk. The Almoravids were Berber nomads honed by military struggle on Islam's desert frontier, and potentially as great a threat to taifa freedom as was Christian Castile. Muhammad Ibn Abbad Al Mutamid, the emir of Seville, summed up their difficult decision: "I would rather be a camel-driver in Africa than a swineherd in Castile."

In 1086, an Almoravid army routed Alfonso IV at the Battle of Zallaqa (also called Sagrajas). The Almoravids withdrew to North Africa, as they had promised, but they were not gone for long. The taifa states were unable to defend themselves against their Christian neighbors, or each other. The Almoravids found the prosperity and military weakness of al-Andalus irresistible. They returned in 1089, conquered the taifa states, and reunited Muslim Spain.

Unlike the rulers they had deposed, the Almoravids were revivalists who followed a literal interpretation of Islam's core values. They imposed their rigid orthodoxy on a population accustomed to a greater degree of religious tolerance, alienating Christians both inside and outside the borders of Muslim Spain.

The reunification of Muslim Spain under the Almoravids coincided with the beginning of the Crusades. Pope Urban II chose to treat the Reconquista as another crusade. He offered knights who fought against the Muslims in Spain the same indulgences against sin that he gave knights who fought the Muslims in the Holy Lands.

By 1145, the Almoravids' hold on Spain had disintegrated. Another group of party kings called on another puritanical dynasty from North Africa to intervene. Despite initial successes, the Almohads were unable to halt the progress of the Reconquista. A coalition of Christian kings under the leadership of Alfonso VIII of Castile defeated the Almohads at the Battle of Las Navas de Tolosa in 1212 and went on to conquer the great Muslim cities of Valencia, Seville, and Córdoba.

By 1260, Muslim rule had been reduced to a single kingdom: Granada. Precariously balanced between the twin threats of the Christian kings and the Muslim rulers of North Africa, Granada managed not only to survive but to flourish for more than two centuries. Christians and Muslims existed in an uneasy truce marked by low-grade warfare at the borders and increasing religious intolerance on both sides.

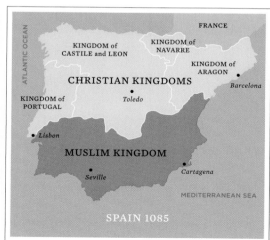

GUNS, WAR AND THE AXIS OF POWER

When the gun arrived in Europe from China, the addition of a trigger turned it into the most powerful weapon on any battlefield.

Previously, guns were held at the waist and set off with an external fuse, a dangerous, clumsy enterprise. The *arquebus*, a hand-held gun crafted by Italians and manufactured by Germans during the fourteenth-century intra-European wars, was a change for the better. It featured a wooden stock to nestle on the shoulder, and a hook with which to fire. A revolutionary "matchlock" device allowed the gunner to concentrate on aiming as he moved a lever to

ARQUEBUS

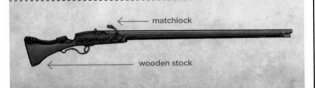

matchlock

wooden stock

mechanically align the lighted match to the touchhole in the bore of the gun. With a refined trigger, the soldier could fire the arquebus faster and farther.

By the time the Spanish declared war on the Moors of Granada, the use of the arquebus as a tactical weapon had been perfected, thanks to revolutionary new battlefield strategies developed by Spanish military leader Gonzalo Fernández de Córdoba. Córdoba invented the *Spanish Square*, a mixed infantry formation of pikemen, swordsmen, and *arquebusiers* or "musketeers" who fought in a mutually supportive formation.

Córdoba's tactic was widely adopted, and it dominated European battlefields in the sixteenth century and the first half of the seventeenth century.

Religious intolerance hardened when Isabella inherited the throne of Castile in 1474. She was determined to complete the Reconquista with the conquest of Granada. By 1480, preparations for the campaign were under way. The pope allowed priests to sell indulgences to finance the costs of the war. Isabella hired French and German engineers to make heavy artillery, ordered Venetian and Genoese ships to blockade Granada's ports, and secured thousands of donkeys to carry supplies. Isabella required all nobles in the kingdom to fight. Knights from France, England, and Ireland flocked to Spain to take part in the war against the Moors.

The Granada War lasted from 1482 to 1492. One by one, Isabella's forces captured the Muslim towns and cities around Granada until the city was surrounded. By the end of 1491, Granada had been under siege for nine months. The sultan, Abu `Abdallah Muhammad XII, known in the West as Boabdil, signed a secret agreement with Ferdinand and Isabella, agreeing to surrender the city in exchange for safe passage out of Spain, ending eight centuries of Muslim rule.

Boabdil tried to provide another form of safe passage to the thousands of Muslims he left behind in Granada. Under the terms of the "Capitulation of Granada," signed and ratified between himself and Spain's Catholic monarchy, Ferdinand and Isabella's new Muslim subjects would be free to practice their own faith. But unlike the Muslim rulers they had followed, the king and queen did not honor their promises of religious freedom. Within a decade, official attempts to convert Muslims sparked a revolt in Granada. Once the revolt was repressed, Isabella issued a decree that all Muslims in Castile must convert or be forced into exile. Many Muslims left for lands under Muslim control. Others accepted baptism and remained in Spain.

These new Christians and their descendants came to be called Moriscos, or "little Moors." Over the years, they endured various forms of persecution and oppression. Beginning in the 1530s, the Spanish Inquisition arrested thousands of Moriscos and confiscated their property. They were subjected to public penances, lashings, torture, and even execution. In 1609, Phillip II ordered the expulsion of the Moriscos from Spain. At least three hundred thousand Moriscos were driven out of the country by 1614. Those going to Muslim countries were forced to leave behind any children younger than seven so they could be raised by Christians and thereby "saved."

1434 CE. GIL EANES, SQUIRE OF Prince Henry of Portugal's own household, stood on the deck of the caravel and prepared to travel to his death.

Cape Bojador was the Cape of No Return. Everyone knew it was as far south as you could safely sail along the coast of West Africa. The tides and shoals around the cape formed a furious surge twenty miles across that forced any sailor foolish enough to try to circle it out into the dark Atlantic Ocean. That was frightening enough, though the prince's sailors now regularly sailed hundreds of miles from the coast to the Azores and Madeira. The mariners' tales of boiling seas and man-eating monsters were worse.

Eanes had made the same voyage the year before without success, returning with excuses that the currents and the south winds had stopped him. Henry had railed at him for believing in childish fables. This time Eanes's instructions from the prince were clear: sail around Cape Bojador and return with an account of the Cape and the seas beyond, or don't return.

Prince Henry the Navigator of Portugal was not a sea captain or a navigator. His only personal seafaring experience included trips along the Portuguese coast and the short voyage from the southern tip of Portugal to Ceuta in Morocco. But for more than forty years he pushed Portuguese sailors to sail farther than they ever had before and to make careful records of what they found.

Henry was the third surviving son of King John I of Portugal. With little hope of inheriting the throne, the ambitious prince created a role for himself in Portuguese politics as a crusader and adventurer. He won his reputation at the age of twenty-one in the Portuguese assault on the Moroccan port of Ceuta in 1415. The Portuguese took the Muslim stronghold in a single day, giving the young prince the moment of glory that he sought. More important, it also gave him his first glimpse of the riches of Islamic Africa. Ceuta was an important commercial city, both as a Mediterranean port and as the northern end of the trans-Saharan caravan trade. Caravans carried European silver and horses to the powerful Muslim kingdoms south of the Sahara; they returned with gold, slaves, ivory, and other luxury goods.

In 1419 Henry was sent back to Ceuta to put down a Muslim uprising. While there, he learned everything he could about the gold-laden caravans that crossed the Sahara from the mines of West Africa. He returned to Portugal determined to find a sea route that would bypass the overland caravans through Islamic lands. It was a bold plan with the potential for a big payoff, half commercial venture and half crusade. Henry wanted to gain direct access to the gold of Guinea, but he also wanted to convert the heathens and form an alliance against the Islamic states of North Africa with Prester John, the legendary Christian king of Ethiopia.

Henry sponsored his first expedition along the largely unknown African coast in 1418. His goal was to find a way around Cape Bojador. Shallow reefs, difficult currents, and changing winds meant the only way to round the cape was to sail into the Sea of Darkness that surrounded the African continent. Sailors said it was impossible to sail around the cape, telling mariners' tales of horrors at sea. Henry refused to believe them.

Henry's first expedition was blown off course, reaching the Atlantic island of Porto Santo Madeira instead of Africa. It was a lucky error, providing useful information about the possibility of sailing west into the Atlantic.

It took twelve years and fifteen expeditions before Henry's ships reached the equator.

Henry's expeditions continued south along the African coast, passing Cape Blanco in 1443 and Cape Verde in 1444. Having passed the southern boundary of the Sahara and successfully circumvented the Islamic caravan routes, the expeditions began to pay for themselves. In addition to knowledge about ocean currents and the topography of the African coast, Henry's ships brought back gold dust and exotic goods, like ostrich eggs. Their most profitable cargo was slaves. By 1448, the slave trade was so large that Henry built a fort and a warehouse on Arguin Island off the coast of Mauritania—the first European trading post overseas.

Portuguese trade with West Africa grew quickly. Soon twenty-five caravels made the voyage down the African coast each year. Although most of the ships were dedicated to trade, exploration continued. Henry's mariners discovered the Cape Verde islands in 1456, traveled sixty miles up the Senegal and Gambia rivers, and sailed as far south as Sierra Leone.

Portuguese explorations continued after Prince Henry's death in 1460, increasingly driven by the desire to find a sea route to the Spice Islands of the Indies and cut out the Arabic and Venetian middlemen.

The stream of trade from Asia had shifted south to the Indian Ocean when the Ming dynasty closed

By the end of the sixteenth century Portugal became Europe's first maritime empire.

Replica of a caravel

its northwest border in 1426, but that hadn't affected the western end of the Silk Roads. Indian dhows shipped the luxury goods of the East to Jeddah on the Arabian shore, where they were ferried across the Red Sea and repacked onto camels that carried them to Damascus, Beirut, and Cairo. At Cairo, the merchandise was floated down the Nile to Alexandria, where Venetian merchants shipped it to the West. That was about to change.

Pope Alexander VI had already drawn a line 360 leagues west of the Azores, giving Spain the maritime rights to everything west of the line and Portugal the maritime rights to everything to the East, including a monopoly on nautical trade with India and the Spice Islands. The sea route would prove to be faster and less expensive than the old Silk Roads.

By the end of the sixteenth century, desert caravans would no longer bring silk and spices from the East, and Portugal would become Europe's first maritime empire, with possessions that ranged from the west coast of Africa to the South China Sea.

AT THE END OF THE FIFTEENTH century, mankind stands poised for change on a worldwide scale. Armed with revolutionary ideas and weapons, hungry for the treasures of the East, and determined to convert Africans to Christianity, Portuguese mariners sail farther and farther east. Eager to compete and flushed with their triumph over the last Islamic kingdom of Spain, Ferdinand and Isabella back a man with the radical idea of sailing west to reach the East. With the firepower of guns, the inspiration of the printed word, and the gold of the Spanish crown behind him, Christopher Columbus will sail across the ocean and discover a New World, launching an age of empire and exploration that would shift the axis of power from East to West.

MAPPING THE SEAS

At Prince Henry's instruction, his mariners kept detailed logbooks and charts, which he used to create maps of the African coast, based on the *portolans*, or coast pilots, used by sailors in the Mediterranean. Henry introduced the use of unfamiliar nautical instruments borrowed from Islamic sailors—compass, astrolabe, and quadrant—and encouraged the design of a new, more maneuverable, type of ship, the caravel.

Using the caravel, Henry's sailors discovered that the easiest way to return home from a southward voyage down the African coast was to sail westward into the Atlantic for several hundred miles to reach a portion of the ocean with favorable winds from the south and west instead of sailing north along the coast against contrary winds.

NEW WORLDS

HUMANS ARE IRREPRESSIBLE EXPLORERS, HAMPERED ONLY BY IMPASS-
ABLE MOUNTAINS AND UNMAPPED OCEANS. ONE THOUSAND YEARS AGO,
A BAND OF SEA-TRAVELING RAIDERS FROM SCANDINAVIA WERE THE
FIRST TO SAIL FROM GREENLAND ACROSS THE NORTHERN ATLANTIC.

Landing at the place we now call Newfoundland, the Vikings encountered a tribe of native people, the Innu, who put up a fierce resistance, driving the Vikings out of their territory. It was a brief encounter. The old and new worlds did not meet again until Columbus made the next attempt five hundred years later.

In Columbus's time, Europeans believed the Atlantic, known as the Ocean Sea, was a great expanse of water that surrounded the landmasses of Eurasia and Africa. Assuming the Earth was round, as most educated people of the time were already aware, it was only logical that if a ship left Europe and sailed west around the globe, it would reach the shores of Asia. Intent on finding new trade routes that would allow them to bypass the middlemen of Venice and Genoa—Spanish and Portuguese explorers discovered lands they only slowly realized were not Asia.

The Americas were a New World only to the Europeans who claimed to have "discovered" them. They were already inhabited by tens of millions of people. Some were still hunter-gathers, who relied on generations of traditions and wisdom for survival. Others belonged to civilizations as sophisticated and advanced as those in Europe. The meeting transformed both cultures. For the conquerors, untold riches awaited; for the Native Americans, devastation.

Christopher Columbus and his men reached Hispaniola after seventy days at sea. He had estimated they would reach the Indies in only four days.

Chapter 7: NEW WORLDS

In the heart of the Old World, the rise of the Ottoman Turks from a tiny principality in the foothills of Anatolia into a major power brought Christendom and Islam into conflict once again. In his fifty-three-day siege of the thousand-year-old walled city of Constantinople, Sultan Mehmet II forever changed the tools of war—and how cities were built.

Once the Old World's desire for natural resources was paired with Portuguese and Spanish advances in shipbuilding, mapmaking, and sea navigation, isolation was no longer an option for native peoples of the Americas. Hostile confrontations between European conquerors and conquered peoples in the New World raged for the next four hundred years. At the beginning, neither side knew anything about the other. Both sides, initially, may have intended to trade. But any such plan soon turned to violence, depopulation, and plunder, with native peoples unable to withstand the deadly combination of European gunfire and European disease.

1 0 0 1   C E .   N O R W E G I A N   L E I F Eriksson "the Lucky," credited as the first European to reach the shores of North America, led the first Viking expedition to the New World. Leif didn't stay long, and after him, only a handful of other expeditions followed before the Vikings concluded that the risks presented by the New World's native peoples outweighed the potential rewards.

With a growing population at home, the Vikings typically undertook vast sea journeys to amass wealth. Viking culture was based on war and fighting prowess; raiding increased a man's stature in society, and both men and women were judged and respected based on their physical abilities. Their modus operandi was to carry out well-planned raids against targets that could be attacked, plundered,

and abandoned quickly. Vikings stayed along the coast or on navigable rivers; they avoided overland marches. Their goal was to grab as much valuable booty as possible before their victims could raise an effective defense. Typical spoils included weapons, tools, clothing, jewelry, precious metals, and people who could be sold as slaves. Their ability to creep up on their opponents silently and without warning was what made the Vikings such successful raiders. However, they were about to meet a people who knew a thing or two about surprise.

The Innu and Beothuk peoples who inhabited Newfoundland and Labrador in the eleventh century were descended from the first Americans who arrived thirteen thousand years ago, when ice sheets connected Asia to the Americas. Their homeland, where they had lived for millennia, was a vast area of subarctic spruce and fir forest, lakes, rivers, and rocky barrens. They called the land Nitassinan. The Vikings called the lands they reached Markland and Vinland; today this territory is called Newfoundland and Nova Scotia.

The Innu lived as nomadic hunters. For most of the year, Nitassinan's waterways were frozen, so the Innu would travel in small groups of two or three families on snowshoes, pulling toboggans. When the ice melted, they would row their canoes to the coast or a large inland lake to fish, trade, and meet friends and relatives. They hunted bear, beaver, and porcupine; caught fish; and gathered berries—but most of all they relied on the herds of caribou that migrated through their land every spring and autumn. The Innu got all they needed—food, clothing, shelter, tools, and weapons—from the caribou. These indigenous people proved to be more than an equal match to their Viking invaders. They were not prepared to give up their home.

DEFENSE OF THE INNU

1003 CE. The Vikings land their dragon boats on the shore of Vinland. Thorvald and his men are unaware that Innu hunters are watching them from the woods.

The Vikings stand between the Inuu and their canoes. When the Vikings turn away and start toward the chill pine forests, the Innu crawl through the brush and then make a run to the canoes. Afraid they will be spotted, they take shelter under one of the canoes, where they crouch motionless and terrified, unsure whether these are men or pale-skinned monsters from the shamans' tales.

Halfway between the forest and the shore, Thorvald and his men stop. One of them has caught a flicker of movement from the corner of his eye. He points to the skin-covered canoes. Thorvald nods and motions the men forward.

The Vikings surround the canoes. They don"t know whether there is something under the canoes, but they have their weapons in hand— just in case. As soon as the Vikings upturn the canoes, the Innu spring to their feet. Ready for a fight.

As fierce as the Vikings are, the Innu hold their own, wearing the trespassers down before escaping into the woods.

That night, as the Vikings sleep in tents around the fire, the Innu rush from the forest and attack the unprepared Vikings with bows and arrows. Thorvald is one of the first killed. Leaderless, the Vikings grab his body and retreat to their boats. They have had enough. The survivors—what is left of them—promptly leave for home.

THE VIKING EXPERIENCE IN North America was brief—and as brutal as any of their raids in the British Isles. The Vikings called the Native Americans they met *skraelings*, a derisive term roughly translated as "barbarian weaklings." According to the Norse sagas, written two hundred years later, attempts at trade failed and were followed by violence. The marauding Norsemen did not hesitate to kill groups of Native Americans without warning. (On one occasion, they killed a group of sleeping Innu where they lay.) The native people fought back, though stone weapons were at a disadvantage against iron. Still, the Vikings were driven out of Vinland in the spring of 1014 and never went back. Vinland, protected by the Innu, was too much effort for too little profit.

AFTER ROME FELL IN THE FIFTH century, the Eastern Roman Empire lived on for several more centuries—as Byzantium. Under the rule of the emperor Zeno, Byzantium's capital, Constantinople, claimed Rome's legacy as the "center of the world." Its rulers kept Rome's administrative structure, but Greek replaced Latin as the official administrative and military language.

Located at the crossroads between Europe and the Near East, Constantinople was a major force for several centuries. As one of Europe's biggest and most important trading centers, it linked the West with the riches of the East. Silks and spices traveled thousands of miles to reach Constantinople, where they would be traded. The most coveted spice was pepper. By the time it reached Constantinople, pepper was worth as much as gold.

Beginning with the first wave of Islamic expansion in the eighth century, Byzantium came under constant attack. The empire defended itself against Arabs, Bulgars, and Magyars. Then Christian Crusaders from the West sacked Constantinople in 1204. Each wave of invaders bit off a portion of the empire.

Worn out by centuries of fighting, their wealth and defenses eaten away, Byzantium's soldiers were not able to defend their empire against the new power that rose in the fourteen century—the Ottoman Turks. By 1361, the Ottomans had conquered most of the former Byzantine Empire and

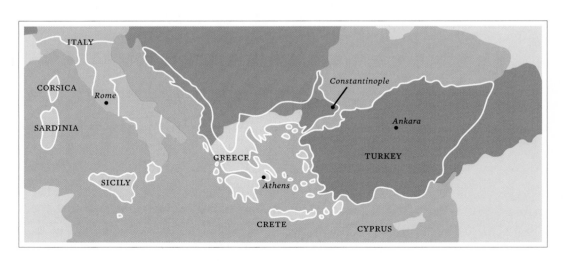

Map of Byzantine Empire, ca. 700 CE

HAGIA SOPHIA

The Byzantine emperor Justinian ordered the construction of Hagia Sophia, the Church of Holy Wisdom, in 532 CE. Two churches had stood on the site previously; both had burned down, the second during an insurrection that almost cost Justinian his throne. With the revolt crushed, Justinian was determined to rebuild the church on an even grander scale. He asked provincial governors to remove the most beautiful parts of ancient monuments and send them to the new capital, along with the most skilled craftsmen and artisans. The emperor then appointed the greatest mathematical physicist of the time as architect, assisted by a renowned geometrician. Together, they devised a revolutionary way to erect a dome on a square base by transferring the weight from the dome to four massive supports using triangular stone pieces called "pendentives."

When the structure was completed five years later, it was topped by a dome more than 100 feet across and 180 feet high that seemed to float above the open space of the interior. The building appeared so miraculous that later generations believed it was built with supernatural help.

After Byzantium's conquest by the Ottomans, Mehmet II, who understood the value of symbolic gestures, transformed Hagia Sophia from the greatest church of Christendom into the foremost mosque of the Ottoman Empire.

How? Simply by having the Friday prayer read there on June 1, 1453. Later sultans would complete the transformation by adding four minarets at the corners, reinforcing the structure with massive buttresses and covering its glorious mosaics with a coat of whitewash.

Hagia Sophia continued to be used as a mosque until 1931, when the Turkish government under Mustafa Atatürk converted it into a museum and a symbol of modern Turkish secularism.

controlled the straits that connected the Black Sea to the Mediterranean. The Byzantine Empire was reduced to the city-state of Constantinople.

When it faced the gravest threat to its security, Constantinople was well past the height of its glory. But it was still a stunning and grand place—full of churches, monasteries, gold, and gilt. It also retained huge importance as a Christian stronghold. The Ottomans had tried before to starve out the city's faithful—and failed. Constantinople's fortifications had held up to everything—until 1453, when Byzantine emperor Constantine XI met the brilliant Ottoman military leader, Sultan Mehmet II.

The Ottoman Empire under Mehmet was already vast but lacked a worthy capital. Ottomans controlled lands surrounding Constantinople, but the Turks had not been able to take the city itself. They pined for Constantinople and gave it the name "Red Apple"—a rich and luscious prize. Five Ottoman sieges had failed to pluck the fruit. Mehmet was determined to succeed. His motive was less religious than imperial. He wanted glory, land, power, and wealth.

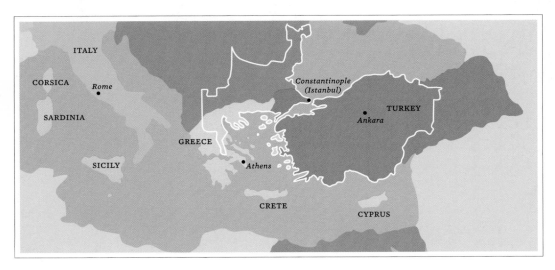

Map of Ottoman Empire, 1453

Mehmet was fascinated by military history. He had the life of Alexander read to him daily. His ambition was to carry Islamic banners into Europe. He wanted nothing less than to be the World Conqueror—Alexander and Caesar rolled into one.

Mehmet was also a genius at logistical arrangements. He studied maps of Europe and Italian manuscripts on siege warfare and was thirsty for the latest technological developments. To prepare for conquest, he organized the manufacture of armor and siege equipment, tents, weapons, food, cannonballs, and gunpowder—and amassed thousands of horses, camels, and pack animals.

On April 14, 1452, Mehmet began his campaign to take Constantinople by building a castle on the European side of the narrowest point of the Bosphorus, on land that was still technically Byzantine. He not only designed the castle himself; he helped the workers build it. His new castle stood opposite an existing Ottoman castle on the Asian side, giving him absolute control over shipping in and out of the Black Sea. Mehmet named his new castle Rumelihisarı, "the Strait Cutter." He proved

the accuracy of the name by sinking a Venetian ship that defied his order to stop and decapitating those crew members that survived. The days of relieving a besieged Constantinople by bringing troops and supplies by sea were over.

When the castle was completed in August 1452, Mehmet camped outside Constantinople's walls for three days, studying the city's fortifications. Heavily fortified walls, treacherous currents, and a massive chain that could be hooked across the mouth of the Golden Horn protected Constantinople from attack by sea. On the landward side, the city was protected by double walls four miles long and fortified with 192 towers and eleven gates. The outer wall was twenty-five feet high; the inner wall was forty feet high. Outside the walls, the city was further protected by a sixty-foot-wide moat that could be flooded in parts. The city's only obvious weakness was a spot where a small river fed into the city through a conduit under the walls.

Aware that the city had successfully held off Ottoman attacks twice before, Mehmet brought the entire force of the Ottoman Empire against the

Byzantine capital. He recruited thousands of irregular forces to fight beside the Anatolian infantry and the elite forces known as "janissaries," from across the empire and beyond its borders: Turks, Slavs, Hungarians, Kurds, Germans, Italians, and Greeks. Turkish craftsmen worked for months to equip the army with weapons and armor, including sixty new guns of various sizes. Engineers built battering rams and catapults. The Turkish fleet, some of it newly built for the purpose, patrolled the Sea of Marmara, keeping Byzantine ships in and reinforcements from the West out.

Most important, Mehmet hired the Hungarian master gunsmith Urban to cast guns. The year before, Urban had offered his services to the Byzantine emperor. Constantine turned him away, unable to afford the smith's salary or the materials he needed. It was a costly mistake. Urban went next to Mehmet, who asked him if he could cast a cannon capable of breaching the walls of Constantinople. Urban replied that he could make a cannon that would bring down the walls of Babylon. Mehmet hired him, for four times more than he had asked in Constantinople.

Within three months, Urban had cast a large-caliber cannon for Rumelihisarı. Impressed, Mehmet ordered Urban to cast a cannon twice as big to take down Constantinople's legendary walls. The finished cannon was twenty-eight feet long. The walls of its bronze barrels were eight inches thick. It was so heavy that it took sixty oxen to haul it from the Ottoman capital of Edirne to Constantinople. When the cannon was first tested, the ball traveled a mile and sank six feet into the ground. City walls would never be safe again.

Rumeli Castle, Istanbul, Turkey

CANNON FIRE BLASTS
THE WALLS OF CONSTANTINOPLE

When the first emperor, Constantine, built his capital city, he put total faith in the city's massive walls. By erecting a triple defense of towers and ditches two hundred feet wide and a hundred feet high, Constantine believed he was providing his descendants on the Byzantine throne a perpetual defense.

Although many had tried before the Ottomans, no attacking army had yet found a way to crack Constantinople's ten-story-high fortifications—until Sultan Mehmet II.

Amassed outside Constantinople, Mehmet had tens of thousands of troops and an array of cannons standing at the ready. He was prepared to use both in a first-of-its-kind coordinated attack that would forever change the art of war. The Turks at Constantinople used cannons—developed in China and perfected in Europe using the metal casting techniques previously used to make church bells—to lethal effect.

For any people or state in proximity to what was left of the Byzantine Empire in the fifteenth century, the fall of its capital city to Ottoman cannon fire was equivalent to the fall of the World Trade Center Towers after the terrorist attack on September 11, 2001. What was once considered impenetrable became shockingly vulnerable.

The fall of Constantinople changed the art of war and the design of cities. Before 1453, people flocked to cities to escape an invading force, counting on the walls to protect them. With adequate food, water, and ammunition, the besieged always had the advantage. Mehmet proved that city walls could no longer hold off armies: with cannons in the equation, the advantage moved from the besieged to the besiegers.

The Turkish Bombard, also known as the Dardanelles Gun, was used by the Ottoman army of Mehmet the Conqueror in 1453 to lay siege to Constantinople. Cast from bronze, it fired stone cannonballs 25" in diameter.

THE FORTY-EIGHT-YEAR-OLD emperor of Byzantium, Constantine XI, waited inside Constantinople's walls as the Ottoman troops encircled the city. He had spent his entire adult life trying to hold off the Ottoman advance. He had no difficulty estimating his forces. He simply counted them—one by one. The total was just under eight thousand. Despite the disparity in numbers, the defenders were hopeful. After all, the city's walls had held off invaders for centuries.

But they had never experienced mass cannon fire before.

On March 5, 1453, Mehmet sent an ultimatum demanding the immediate surrender of the city. Relying on the legendary strength of the city's defenses, the Byzantines refused. Here is how a confident Mehmet described the task ahead to his assembled troops:

> I do not offer you an impregnable wall, but a wide plain fit for cavalry for you to cross with your weapons. And what should I say about our opponents? There are very few of them, and most of these are unarmed and inexperienced in war. For, as I have learned from deserters, they say that there are but two or three men defending a tower, and as many more in the space between towers. Thus it happens that a single man has to fight and defend three or four battlements, and he, too, either altogether unarmed or badly armed.

The Ottomans fired on the city for the first time on April 6. Even with constant attention, the big cannon could only be fired seven times a day. Every day the Ottomans brought down a section of the walls. The city's defenders worked night and day to repair the damage. Serbian sappers from the silver mines of Novo Brdo tunneled under the city's walls.

The Byzantines countered by flooding the tunnels and burning the mine supports. Because the chain across the Golden Horn kept the Ottoman fleet from entering, the sultan ordered the ships hauled overland on rollers for eight miles behind the hills and then down into the Horn.

The Ottomans' attack was groundbreaking not so much for their use of cannons, but for their ability to maintain a sustained artillery bombardment, day after day for fifty-three days, thanks to Mehmet's skill in managing a supply chain. His grasp of the logistics of artillery warfare was as revolutionary as his use of cannon. It was no longer enough to feed your troops. Artillery warfare required adequate supplies of hand-carved stone cannonballs and gunpowder and a corps of founders to repair or recast cannon on site. In a siege that lasted almost two months, Mehmet's guns fired five thousand shots and used fifty-five thousand pounds of gunpowder.

One eyewitness to the bombardment of Constantinople, in describing the cannon fire, wrote, "Sometimes it destroyed a complete portion of wall, sometimes half a portion, sometimes a greater or smaller part of a tower, or a turret, or a parapet, and nowhere was the wall strong enough or sturdy or thick enough to withstand it, or to hold out totally against such a force of the velocity of the stone ball."

For seven weeks, the Ottomans bombarded the city but failed to break through the defensive walls. Diaries of the siege read like the accounts of shelling in the First World War: monotony alternating with terror. Besieged and besiegers were equally weary. Rumors flew that a Venetian fleet would soon arrive to relieve the barraged city.

On May 25, Mehmet offered to raise the siege if Constantine would pay him an annual tribute of one hundred thousand gold bezants or leave the city with a guarantee of safe conduct. Constantine made a counteroffer: he would turn over everything he

The Ottoman Turks capture Constantinople in 1453. Engraving by Matthäus Merian the Elder (1593-1650)

owned except Constantinople itself. The Ottoman vizier, Çandarli Halil Pasha, who was rumored to take bribes from the Byzantines, argued for the immediate end of the siege. The younger beys argued in favor of continuing. Mehmet sent officials through the camp to test the opinion of the men. The troops were eager. The Ottoman camp spent two days preparing to attack and a third day in prayer.

On the morning of May 29, three hours before dawn, the Ottomans began an all-out attack on the city. Sixty-eight cannons. Five thousand cannonballs. Fifty-five thousand pounds of gunpowder—enough to put a rocket into space. The great cannon blasted a hole through the outer wall that had protected Constantinople for more than a thousand years. The Anatolian infantry poured into the city through the gap. They were slaughtered in the narrow space between the inner and outer walls by the city's defenders, led by the emperor himself. The resistance was fierce but short-lived. The Byzantines, in turn, were trapped between the city walls when they were hit by a shower of arrows from Ottoman janissaries who had climbed the outer stockade. The Turks were already climbing the inner wall when they saw their flag flying from one of the inner towers; a small group of Turkish soldiers had found a small side gate that had been left open and entered the city without challenge.

Constantine XI attempted to rally his forces at the breach and died in the final defense. Within hours, the Ottomans had control of Constantinople. Mehmet had employed gunpowder-fired weapons on an unprecedented scale to take his prize.

The last relic of the ancient world was dead.

Western Europeans reacted with a mixture of shock and fear. The news reached Venice first, on June 29, 1453. Constantinople had been home to more than ten thousand Venetian merchants and their families. All the Venetians in Constantinople had been either enslaved or killed. According to an eyewitness, Venetians greeted the news with "great and desperate wailings, cries, and groans, everyone beating the palms of their hands, beating their breasts with their fists, tearing their hair and their faces."

From Venice, the news rippled across Europe within a year and became the subject of widespread lamentation. It was felt to be the end of something. It tilted the world onto an unpredictable axis.

Long-established assumptions and beliefs fell with Constantinople. It was the last remnant of the classical world. It was the buffer against the Islamic world. It was the last Christian foothold in the eastern Mediterranean. It was the best launchpad for the long-cherished hope of recapturing Jerusalem. All these things died in 1453. Christendom was no longer united enough to push back the Turks. The classical world was emphatically dead. The age of the crusades was over. The world of medieval chivalry was being replaced by the era of gunpowder. The Ottomans were permanently established in Europe. They were moving closer.

With this realization came the fear that the Turks might conquer the world. Suddenly Europeans could feel the hot breath of Islam on their collars. "The enemy is at our gates!" wrote an Italian. "The axe is at the root. Unless divine help comes, the doom of the Christian name is sealed." Mehmet

was identified with the Antichrist: implacable and unstoppable. "Mehmet will never lay down arms except in victory or total defeat," wrote Pope Pius II in 1459. "Every victory will be for him a stepping-stone to another, until, after subjecting all the princes of the West, he has destroyed the Gospel of Christ and imposed the law of his false prophet upon the whole world." All his worst fears seemed confirmed when Mehmet landed an invasion force on the coast of Italy in 1481. A titanic two-hundred-year military and ideological contest—the prototype for later contests for supremacy between contrasting world views—had begun.

VENETIANS SUFFERED MORE directly from the fall of Constantinople than anyone else in Europe. They had enjoyed special trading privileges in the Byzantine city since 1082, privileges that helped them dominate trade in the eastern Mediterranean and become one of the wealthiest cities in Europe.

The Venetians sat tight and waited for diplomacy to restore their relationship with Mehmet. Within a year they were trading again in Constantinople, but from then on trading was always more insecure. Merchants in the city and throughout Ottoman lands could be imprisoned or killed at a whim; trading privileges could be withdrawn; taxes could be higher and more arbitrary. The price of commodities traded through the Ottoman world continued to rise. The Venetians were as often at war with the Ottomans as they were at peace.

With their eyes fixed on the Ottoman threat, the Venetians scarcely noticed a threat that would turn the eastern Mediterranean into a cul-de-sac rather than a trade route: the Portuguese search for a direct sea route to the spice markets of the East.

For thousands of years, no seaman had dared sail a ship into the open ocean for fear of never getting home. Using compass and portolan charts, Bartolomeu Dias defied history and sailed south along the African coast for six weeks, heading toward the point where mapmakers' information ended and mariners' imaginations began.

In August 1487, Dias embarked with two caravels and a third ship carrying extra food and supplies bound for the mouth of the Congo River. The small fleet was sailing off the southwest coast of Africa when the ships began to have trouble making headway against stiff winds and strong currents. The small fleet had almost reached the point marked on their maps as "unknown" when the tropical storm hit.

Conflicting currents and violent weather made it dangerous to sail close to the coast. Dias had to make a quick decision. If the ships hugged the coast, they could be dashed on the rocks. If they headed out to sea, they could be lost forever. He made the riskier choice and turned toward the uncharted waters of the open sea. By sailing into the middle of the ocean, Dias moved away from the southerly winds and currents that flowed down Africa's eastern coast and around the cape coast and toward the wind belt called the "westerlies." The crew struggled to keep their balance as the ships rolled beneath their feet. The sky turned black. Mountains of water tossed the ships as if they were toys.

Instead of fighting the storm, Dias had let it carry him south into the middle of the ocean, accidentally discovering the most efficient way for a sailing vessel to round the southern tip of Africa.

Dias's ships were blown east as the storm raged for thirteen days. When it was over, two caravels

OCEAN GYRE

The combination of wind and current that pushed Dias around the southern tip of Africa owes much of its force to a phenomenon called an *ocean gyre*, a circular ocean current formed by the wind patterns and the rotation of the earth. The earth's rotation, in a pattern called the *Coriolis effect*, forces ocean currents into a clockwise motion in the northern hemisphere and a counterclockwise motion in the southern hemisphere. Because the continents that border the oceans restrict the flow of the water, the currents close in on themselves, creating a circular flow of water around a calm center.

There are five major ocean gyres, two in the Atlantic, two in the Pacific, and one in the Indian Ocean. These gyres are responsible for much of the ocean's surface currents.

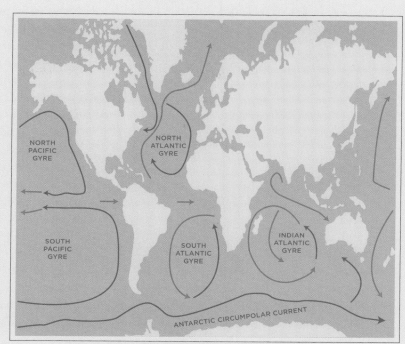

An ocean gyre is a large circular rotating current. This is a map of the five major ocean gyres.

were still afloat, but the store ship was gone. His crew wouldn't need stores if they'd just cut the trip short and sailed home—if they could find home. Dias studied the noonday sun and his navigational charts and ordered the men to sail east. They sailed east for days without seeing land. Dias decided to go north. Finally on February 3, 1488, the crew saw land on the horizon. Then they realized that the coastline was in the wrong place. They had gone past the southern tip of Africa without realizing it and were now sailing in the Indian Ocean.

Once Dias realized he had sailed around the tip of Africa, he dropped anchor and went ashore to put up the first *padrão*—a large, stone cross bearing Portugal's coat of arms—on the eastern coast of the continent, 250 miles east of the tip of Africa. He was ready to sail up the coast and across the Indian Ocean, but his men threatened mutiny and demanded to go back. The officers supported them. Dias reluctantly agreed, but only on the condition that the sailors sign a document stating that Dias was not responsible for turning back. As they sailed away, Dias looked sadly back at his *padrão;* he wrote in his log that he felt as if he were taking "his last leave of a son condemned to exile forever."

On the return voyage, Dias saw the point where Africa ended, which they had passed blindly in the storm. He named the promontory the Cape of Storms.

Chapter 7: NEW WORLDS

THE COMPASS

At its most basic, the compass is a floating magnet.

All magnets have two poles, one north and one south. If you put two magnets together, they will either attract each other or repel each other, depending on how you line up the north and south poles.

The earth is the largest magnet of all. The center of the earth is a ball of iron, created when the earth was formed. As the earth spins on its axis, molten iron swirls around the core, creating an electric current and a magnetic field strong enough to affect all the other magnets on earth, including the magnetized needle in a compass.

When a compass needle points north, it points to "magnetic north," not "true north." This is because the magnet at earth's core is not perfectly lined up with the North and South Poles. The difference between true north and magnetic north is measured in degrees and varies depending where you are.

Dias and his caravels arrived back in Lisbon in December 1488. They had been gone for more than sixteen months and added fourteen hundred new miles to the map of Africa. King John the Perfect was pleased with the new charts of the African coast, but he didn't like the name Dias had given to the cape at the end of Africa. He used a king's prerogative to rename it the Cape of Good Hope.

It was nine years before a new Portuguese king was ready to try again, spurred on by competition with Spain. In 1497, King Manuel appointed Vasco da Gama the leader of a new expedition to follow Dias's route around the Cape of Good Hope, and then go across the Indian Ocean to Calicut. One hundred seventy men signed up for a three-year journey; four ships were outfitted with twenty brass guns each, as well as crossbows, javelins, pikes, and spears in case there was any trouble with the Muslims who controlled the trade at Calicut.

Da Gama was a clever navigator. He decided to avoid the coastal storms that almost wrecked Dias's ships. Instead of hugging the coast, he sailed west from the Cape Verde Islands and then south into the open sea, taking advantage of the circular trade winds that blew there. He returned to land just north of the Cape of Good Hope on November 4.

Arab and Hindu traders and mariners were well familiar with Africa's eastern coast, but it was new to da Gama and his men. As they worked their way up the coast, da Gama soon decided his main task was to find an experienced pilot to guide them across the Indian Ocean to Calicut. At the port of Milinda, in what is now Kenya, da Gama hired a famous Arab navigator, Ahmad ibn Mtjid, known as the Lion of the Sea in Fury.

In one of the great ironies of history, the great Arab navigator ibn Mājid brought da Gama's ships safely across the Indian Ocean to Calicut, laying the foundation for the Portuguese trading empire that would bring an end to Arab control of the Indian Ocean.

Meanwhile, the Atlantic Ocean continued to fire the imaginations of other ambitious Europeans seeking a new route to the same Eastern riches. By setting sail for the western horizon, Europe's best seamen were in for a monumental surprise. Not a route to India, but a vast new world lay in their sights. Would a crew of European adventurers have more success against the mighty Aztec warriors than the Vikings had against the Innu defenders of Newfoundland? At this juncture the odds seemed to be against them.

CHRISTOPHER COLUMBUS WASN'T the first would-be explorer to propose sailing west to Asia. As early as 1474, Florentine mathematician and geographer Paolo dal Pozzo Toscanelli wrote to King Alfonso of Portugal, suggesting it would be easier to reach the gold of the Indies by sailing west across the Atlantic. He included a nautical map of the sea and the lands around it to help make his point.

Ten years after Toscanelli, Columbus tried to convince King John of Portugal to fund his scheme, claiming that China, and its fabulous wealth, lay only 1,100 leagues (roughly 3,300 miles) away. King John submitted the idea to a committee of mapmakers, astronomers, and geographers, who said (correctly) that Asia must be farther away than Columbus thought. No expedition could be fitted with enough supplies to survive the voyage across an empty sea.

Rejected by the Portuguese king, Columbus turned to Spain. He first proposed the expedition to Isabella of Castile in 1486. The Spanish queen was in the fifth year of the costly war with Granada and had no resources to devote to exploration. He laid the proposal before Isabella a second time in 1491,

ALGERINE FISHERMAN

LATEEN SAIL

The triangular lateen sail, borrowed from Arab ships, was a key feature of the Portuguese caravel.

With a square sail, a ship could only sail before the wind. The lateen sail had a crossbar on its diagonal side that was bisected by a vertical mast. With its free corner secured near the stern, it could take the wind on either side, allowing a ship to tack into the wind in a zigzag fashion, creating forward momentum in any direction and allowing faster navigation in all weather conditions.

Because Dias's ship was rigged with lateen sails, he could sail into the wind, push out into the ocean and escape the rugged coastline, and navigate right around the southern tip of Africa. The combination of bravery and technology allowed him to pioneer a sea route to the riches of the East.

when she was camped outside the city of Granada. With victory at hand, the queen was at least willing to listen. She had Columbus present his proposal to an assembled committee of experts. Like their Portuguese counterparts, Isabella's experts advised against the venture, saying Columbus couldn't possibly be right about the distance to China and the ease of sailing there and back.

After the Moors surrendered in 1492, Isabella agreed to sponsor Columbus's voyage. She was willing to pawn her jewels if that was what it took to fund the expedition, but the manager of the royal treasury said public funds could be used. Wealthy Spaniards and Genoese merchants who lived in Spain also put up money for the voyage. In addition, Isabella put pressure on the coastal town of Palos, which owed the crown an as-yet-unpaid fine for smuggling, to provide Columbus with two caravels.

Isabella drew up a contract with Columbus, outlining their agreement. The crown would retain control over all discovered territories. Columbus

Columbus thought he could make the voyage in four days. Instead, it took seventy.

would receive the hereditary title of Admiral of the Ocean Sea, serve as governor over any discovered territories, and would have the right to one-tenth of the riches he brought back.

On August 3, 1492, Columbus set out on his voyage in his three famous ships, the Niña, the Pinta, and the Santa Maria. The ships were well-provisioned with salt cod, bacon, biscuits, flour, wine, olive oil, and plenty of water, far more than needed for the brief voyage Columbus anticipated. He carried a letter of safe conduct from Isabella and Ferdinand, declaring, "We send Christopher Columbus with three caravels

through the Ocean Sea to the Indies, on some business that touches the service of God and especially of the Catholic faith and our own benefit." Since Columbus expected to land in India, he made sure at least one crew member was a native speaker of Arabic, the lingua franca of the Asian trading world.

Columbus thought he could make the voyage in four days. Instead, it took seventy. The discrepancy did nothing to shake his conviction that he had reached Asia. Neither did the differences between Marco Polo's description of the complex cultures of the East and the tribal cultures of the islands on which he landed.

OCTOBER 12, 1492. CHRISTOPHER Columbus had expected to reach China, or at least Japan, by now. His fleet of three small ships had left the Canary Islands five weeks ago, heading west across the uncharted Ocean Sea. There was still no sign of land. Food and water were growing short, too short for turning around to be an option. Worse, his crew was on the verge of mutiny. Some of them whispered that they should just throw the red-haired Italian overboard. Why should they risk their lives listening to a crazy foreigner?

They were hungry, they were tired—and they were afraid. None of them had ever been out of sight of land for so long. The Ocean Sea was sometimes called the Sea of Darkness. Everyone knew dangerous monsters lurked beneath the waves: sea serpents and giant crabs that could crush a ship in its pincers.

Columbus offered a fine silk coat to the first man who sighted land.

The men greeted the announcement with sullen silence. What good would a silk coat do if they were lost at sea?

The caravels that Christopher Columbus set out on his expedition: Pinta, Niña and Santa María

Later that day, Columbus spotted a flock of birds flying toward the southwest. Land had to be close. He ordered the ships to follow the birds.

The next night, the moon rose shortly before midnight. Two hours later, a sailor on watch on the Pinta yelled out, "Land! My God! Land!" He fired a cannon to catch the attention of the other two ships. Sailors crowded the decks to catch a glimpse of land. At dawn, the Niña, the Pinta, and the Santa Maria dropped anchor in calm, blue waters alongside a stretch of white sand. They lowered their boats and rushed to the shore. Instead of the silk-robed Chinese they had expected, the people waiting to greet them on the beach were almost naked and had no weapons other than long wooden fishing spears.

When Christopher Columbus stepped foot in the Bahamas, he thought he was in Japan. In fact, when Columbus veered a thousand miles off course and landed in the Caribbean, he stumbled across an entire hemisphere full of people whose cultures had nothing to do with Europe or Asia. In sharp contrast to the encounter five hundred years earlier between the Vikings and the Innu, Columbus took a peaceful stance toward the native islanders, and the Tainos responded in kind. Columbus was there looking for gold, not conquest. And he was willing to trade for it. Before departing, Columbus exchanged gifts with the Taino people. Then he and his crew boarded their ships for the trip home.

Little did he know that he had left something unintended—and deadly—behind: smallpox.

UNDAUNTED BY THE SURPRISING appearance of the natives and landscape he encountered upon reaching solid ground in the Bahamas, Columbus sailed back to Spain loaded with enthusiasm and souvenirs; monkeys, parrots, cinnamon, chili peppers, ten members of the Taino tribe, and most significantly, several small pieces of gold—setting off a centuries-long gold rush in the Americas.

Columbus helped create his own celebrity by sharing the diary he kept of his exploits. Of his time on the Bahamian island he had named San Salvador, Columbus wrote: "I kept my eyes open and tried to find out if there was any gold, and I saw that some of them had a little piece hanging from a hole in their nose. I gathered from their signs that if one goes south, or around the south side of the island, there is a king with great jars full of it, enormous amounts. I tried to persuade them to go there, but I saw that the idea was not to their liking."

As word spread, people crowded the roads from Lisbon to Seville, hoping to catch a glimpse of the explorer and his exotic finds.

EUROPEAN DISEASES IN THE AMERICAS

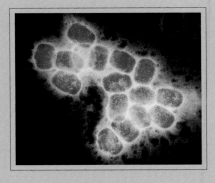

Some of the most influential actors in human history were not great men but microscopic organisms. Diseases such as flu, measles, yellow fever, and smallpox are thought to have originated in the animals that the peoples of the ancient Middle East domesticated thousands of years ago. Centuries of contact with these animals meant Europeans gradually built up resistance that protected them from these diseases.

Native Americans had few domesticated animals, no exposure to their diseases—and no developed immunities. The arrival of Europeans and the diseases they brought with them killed millions.

The Caribbean island of Hispaniola had more than a million inhabitants when Christopher Columbus landed there in 1492. Within twenty years, more than a third of the population was dead, most of them from an epidemic disease they had never seen before—smallpox.

Hernán Cortés and his men wreaked the same havoc on the people of Tenochtitlán, when they unwittingly left behind a time bomb in the form of a dead, smallpox-infected Spanish soldier. Within weeks, the entire capital was under siege by the smallpox virus, which killed one-fourth of the city's inhabitants.

The epidemic spread throughout Mexico and eventually helped the Spaniards defeat the Inca Empire. Without the help of the deadly smallpox virus and other epidemics, Europeans might not have conquered the New World so easily. Within a single century, 90 percent of all Native Americans died from those first contacts with Europeans.

Today, the smallpox virus that once devastated the Americas has been eradicated. Many other diseases are controlled, thanks to mass vaccination. However, our age-old struggle with microscopic enemies is not over. Following the same ground rules—what evolutionary theorist Herbert Spencer dubbed the 'Survival of the Fittest'—as mankind, viruses and bacteria are constantly changing their own immunities to modern medicines in order to survive. More confrontations and challenges to our survival on earth undoubtedly lie ahead.

Columbus made three more trips to America between 1493 and 1504. He visited the Greater and Lesser Antilles, as well as the Caribbean coast of Venezuela and Central America, claiming them for the Spanish Empire. Even after completing four voyages to the New World, Columbus failed to realize he had not discovered a new route to Asia. That honor went to Amerigo Vespucci.

In 1499, Ferdinand and Isabella were growing concerned about the conflicting reports that were coming back from the new colony of Hispaniola. They asked Vespucci, who had been involved in equipping ships for Columbus's second and third voyages, to take part in a new expedition. Two ships would go to Hispaniola; two would sail farther south and explore.

Vespucci was a pilot on one of the ships of exploration. His ship sailed south along the coast of what Vespucci still believed to be India. The almanac he carried with him showed the position of the moon and the planets for each hour of the night for every night of the year.

One night in mid-August, he noticed that the almanac said the moon and the planet Mars would stand at the same place in the sky in the city of Ferrara at midnight on August 23. On the evening of August 23, he noted that at his location those same bodies stood in conjunction at 5:30, not at midnight, a difference of six and one half hours.

Suddenly Vespucci realized he could now figure out his distance from Ferrara in miles. The Greek geographer Ptolemy had calculated that the earth was twenty-four thousand miles in circumference and that it turned all the way around every twenty-four hours. If the earth turned one thousand miles an hour, the time difference meant he was sixty-five hundred miles away from Ferrara. Since he knew the distance from Ferrara and Lisbon, he was now able to calculate his position east

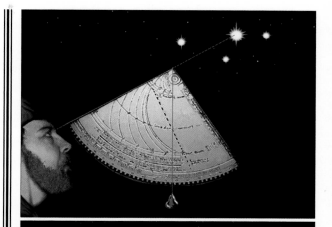

CALCULATING LATITUDE

Columbus used a quadrant to help him navigate.

The quadrant was a quarter circle of metal with two sighting holes on one of its straight sides. A string with a weight on one end was tied on the straight edge. Degrees were marked along the curved edge. The pilot aligned the quadrant so the North Star could be seen through both sighting holes. The weighted string would fall across the curved edge, showing the pilot how many degrees above the equator he was.

The quadrant became useless when sailors went south of the equator and the North Star was no longer visible. Portuguese navigators learned to find their latitude by determining the height and angle of the noonday sun and checking it against astronomical navigation charts.

CALCULATING LONGITUDE

Amerigo Vespucci's method of calculating longitude was too complicated for the average mariner. It required a stable platform for taking observations and an astronomical almanac. It was 1735 before English clockmaker John Harrison invented the marine chronometer that could measure time accurately on a rolling ship, the first step toward establishing longitude.

Chapter 7: NEW WORLDS

AMERIGO GETS HIS NAME ON THE MAP

German mapmaker Martin Waldseemüller was making a world map that showed the new continent as a narrow strip of land that blocked the way to Asia, with the island of Japan just beyond its borders in a hitherto unknown sea. He had recently read accounts of the new continent attributed to Amerigo Vespucci and named the continent America. Spanish mapmakers continued to call the continent either the New World or the Indies. Waldseemüller removed the name America from later maps, but it was too late. As far as Europeans were concerned, the New World was America.

and west as well as north and south. Using this new navigational tool, Vespucci realized that his ship was nowhere near India. Columbus had not found a new route to Asia. He had found a fourth continent that no European knew existed.

THE AZTECS BELIEVED THAT their god, Huitzilopochtli, had given them a sacred duty to conquer the entire world.

The Aztecs migrated to the Valley of Mexico in the early thirteenth century. They believed that the gods had ordered them to leave their homeland and migrate south. At least seven different tribes left on the great migration. Most settled along the way. The Aztecs continued moving south. They would stay in one place for ten or twenty years, clearing land for farms and building temples. But they always moved on, driven by a vision from Huitzilopochtli telling them that they would know they had reached their final homeland when they saw an eagle resting on top of a cactus growing out of a rock.

When the Aztecs reached the Valley of Mexico, they first settled in a desolate region known as Grasshopper Hill. The neighboring peoples drove them away. The king of Culhuacan, a region near the southern shore of Lake Texcoco, allowed them to settle for a short time in a snake-infested swamp near the lakeshore. They soon fought with their neighbors and were driven from their homes once more. For years, they wandered the regions surrounding Lake Texcoco, which filled much of the Valley of Mexico. Finally, in 1325, they encountered a large eagle, sunning itself with extended wings on a cactus growing from a large rock. The Aztecs had found their homeland in the swampy islands at the southern end of Lake Texcoco.

The Aztecs named their new city Tenochtitlán (today's Mexico City), the place of the "cactus on

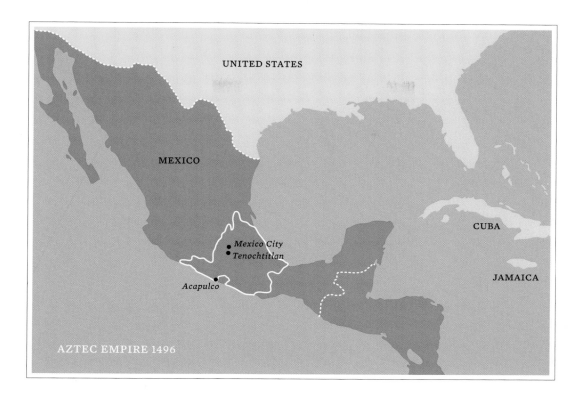

UNITED STATES

MEXICO

CUBA

JAMAICA

● *Mexico City*
● *Tenochtitlan*

● *Acapulco*

AZTEC EMPIRE 1496

the rock." They turned swamp into fertile land by building raised gardens on reclaimed swampland and inventive systems of dikes and canals across the lake. By the end of the fourteenth century, Tenochtitlán's population had quintupled and their uninviting swamp had turned into a garden that produced a stable food supply.

Their political power grew more slowly. For many years, they paid an annual tribute of military service to a powerful city-state ruled by the Tepanec, who had settled on the lake's western shore in the twelfth or early thirteenth century. In 1426, the Aztec ruler, Itzcoatl, organized the local peoples to revolt against the Tepanec. When the revolt was over, the Aztecs, the Tlacopan, and the Acolhua joined together as the Triple Alliance. The control of the Triple Alliance spread throughout the Valley of Mexico and over much of

Mesoamerica, creating an empire based on the payment of tribute rather than direct control. The empire was vast, but control was loose, rebellion was common, and war was almost constant.

Thanks to a succession of strong Aztec leaders, by 1486, the Triple Alliance had effectively become the Aztec Empire, with local kings replaced by Aztec-dominated puppet rulers. Tenochtitlán had a larger population than Paris or London, though it was still smaller than Venice or Istanbul. It was an astonishing city built on artificial islands and canals in the middle of a great mountain lake. Its streets were clean and wide. Its stone palaces and temples were ornately carved. Its markets were full of goods from the far corners of the empire and beyond. Three giant causeways linked the island city to the mainland. Long aqueducts carried fresh water from the mountains and over the lake to the heart of the city.

Chapter 7: NEW WORLDS

THE STONE OF TIZOC

THE GODS NEED NOURISHMENT AGAIN, AND THE
time has come for another sacrifice. The Aztecs have chosen
their victim: the notorious prisoner and onetime warrior Tlachicole. Tlachicole, already intoxicated with a ceremonial drink, is tied
to the Stone of Tizoc.

His opponent, the celebrated warrior Motepopoca, is armed with a flat club of wood set with razor-sharp obsidian blades. Tlachicole is given a similar stick—fairly heavy, but set with feathers instead of obsidian. He knows he can't win with it, but he will try.

The fight begins. It is not a fair contest; a rope restrains the fallen warrior. But Tlachicole is a brave fighter; he will not go down easy.

His opponent attacks, again and again, but with each attack, Motepopoca gets hurt himself! Amazing that Tlachicole can still inflict damage with a weapon such as he has. And even tied to a stone, he wears out the great Motepopoca.

But it is only a matter of time. Minutes in, Tlachicole collapses, exhausted. He is now ready for the gods. His adversary, the mighty Motepopoca, cuts out his heart—and offers it to the sun.

In 1502, a new ruler came to the Aztec throne: thirty-four-year-old Montezuma II.

The Aztecs felt indebted to and dependent on their gods. As the gods had sacrificed themselves to create the world and human beings, then humans needed to give thanks to them with the most precious substance they had, their own blood. The Aztecs believed that spilled human blood nourished and fortified the gods, in particular, the Sun.

The Aztecs feared that everything would cease to exist if the gods did not receive an adequate amount of human blood. This fear compelled the Aztecs to war. The need to pay their debt to the gods was the main reason for war.

OBSIDIAN

Native American cultures never learned to forge iron, but they made good use of obsidian, a naturally occurring volcanic glass. Obsidian is hard and brittle, making it easy to fracture into thin blades with sharp edges that were used for swords, spears, and the ritual knives used to cut the hearts out of sacrificial victims in Aztec religious festivals. Obsidian was so important to the Aztecs that they believed that death by an obsidian blade was a form of life: offering up the hearts and blood of brave humans to the gods was the only thing that could ensure that the universe would not end.

Today obsidian is still used for some surgical scalpel blades.

Sometimes the Aztecs would perform a special type of sacrifice called a gladiatorial sacrifice: a one-on-one battle between a prisoner (normally a noble) and one of the Aztec's best warriors. The prisoner would be given weakened weapons, such as a wooden club covered with feathers. The encounter between prisoner and Aztec warrior was a ceremonial act, carried out on the Tizoc Stone.

The market of Tenochtitlán has arcades all around, where more than sixty thousand people come [to] buy and sell, and where every kind of merchandise produced in these lands is found. Ornaments of gold and silver, lead, brass, copper, tin, stones, shells, bones, and feathers. They also sell lime, hewn and unhewn stone, adobe bricks, tiles, and cut and uncut wood of various kinds. There is a street where they sell game and birds of every species found in the land.

—*Hernán Cortés*

In 1519 Hernán Cortés landed on Mexico's eastern coast with a force of 530 Spanish soldiers, several hundred Cuban Indians and Africans, a few dozen arquebuses, twenty cannons, sixteen horses, and a pack of large dogs trained for warfare. The first reports that reached Montezuma about the strange men from across the sea came from the people on the eastern seashore who had seen fair-skinned, bearded men climb out of "two towers or small mountains floating on the waves of the sea." The emperor sent messengers to meet the strangers, bearing costly gifts that only whetted the Spaniards' greed for gold.

Cortés's small army marched inland, accompanied by thousands of warriors from the city-state of Tlaxcala, on the east of Lake Texcoco, which had

never fallen under the control of the Triple Alliance. When Cortés and his men reached Tenochtitlán, Montezuma welcomed them into the city as honored guests. The city dazzled its would-be invaders; it was bigger and wealthier than any city in Spain. One Spanish observer later described his first impressions of Aztec civilization: "When we saw all those cities and villages built in the water, and other great towns on dry land, and that straight and level causeway leading to [Tenochtitlán], we were astonished. These great towns and buildings rising from the water, all made of stone, seemed like an enchanted vision. . . . Indeed, some of our soldiers asked whether it was not all a dream."

The Aztec capitol of Tenochtitlán dazzled its would-be invaders; it was bigger and wealthier than any city in Spain.

Inside the city without a fight, Cortés was nonetheless aware that Montezuma could "obliterate all memory" of his forces with a single command. So a week after entering the city, Cortés seized the Aztec ruler and held him captive in his own palace. Montezuma cooperated with the Spanish, heaping upon them gold from the Aztec storehouses for Cortés to take back to the Spanish king as tribute from his new vassal—an act that made sense in the context of the Triple Alliance's style of empire building.

Like Venice, Tenochtitlán was a city of canals. Its only roads were three main causeways that met at the center of the city. When under attack, the Aztecs pulled up drawbridges across the causeways, cutting off access to the city.

For seven months, Cortés demanded more and more from his captive, including conversion to the Christian god. Worse, when Cortés briefly left the city, one of his officers attacked an unarmed crowd of singers and dancers at the religious festival Toxcatl, killing thousands of Aztec nobles. The city rose up in response to the massacre.

The Aztecs besieged the Spanish in Montezuma's palace, fewer than fifteen hundred men at the mercy of thousands. Their fate lay in the hands of the captured ruler. Cortés, now back in Tenochtitlán, took a chance and pushed Montezuma onto the roof of his palace to address the crowd. He told the emperor that he must order his people to put down

> Disease not only greatly reduced the population; it destroyed power structures as leaders died and succession processes crumbled.

their weapons. It was a risk. With one wink from the Aztec ruler, his subjects could swarm to his rescue.

The crowd grew silent at the sight of their king. But to their disappointment, Montezuma raised his arms and begged his people to disperse. The crowd roared in anger and pelted the ruler with rocks.

Spanish records say Montezuma was killed by one of those stones; Aztec histories say he was driven back into the palace, where the Spanish killed him. Either way, with Montezuma dead, Tenochtitlán erupted in violence. During what the Spanish called "the sorrowful night," Cortés and his men were driven from the city, more than half of them dead and many of the rest wounded. They retreated to Tlaxcala.

If the Tlaxcalans had repudiated their earlier treaty, Cortés's invasion of Mexico would have ended in failure. Instead, the combined Spanish and Tlaxcalan forces attacked the Aztec imperial capital in 1520. After a fifteen-week siege, Tenochtitlán fell into Spanish hands. Three-quarters of the population was dead. Many were killed in the fighting; more were dead from starvation or the smallpox that swept the city after the expulsion of the Spaniards like a punishment from angry gods.

The Spanish faced even greater odds against the Inca Empire, and it fell even more quickly. By the time Francisco Pizarro and his small band of conquistadores reached Cuzco in 1530, the empire was already on the verge of collapse, weakened by a raging smallpox epidemic. The disease had swept down Mexico from Tenochtitlán, through Central America, and was now raving through the central Andes. With the center weakened, unrest among recently conquered tribes and bitter rivalries between ruling families had erupted into rebellion and civil war. Playing the warring factions against each other, Pizarro was able to smash Incan resistance with only 180 men, sixty-two horses, and one cannon.

But the real conqueror throughout the Americas was disease. Europeans brought with them smallpox, measles, bubonic plague, cholera, typhoid, pleurisy, scarlet fever, diphtheria, mumps, whooping cough, pneumonia, strains of influenza, and possibly typhus. The African slaves the Europeans brought to the New World beginning in 1510 brought malaria and yellow fever.

Smallpox was the greatest early killer of Native Americans. The first epidemic of smallpox hit in 1520, followed by the measles in 1531, influenza in 1559, bubonic plague in 1545, typhus in 1586, and diphtheria in 1601. True epidemics, these diseases did not simply kill a generation of Native Americans and disappear. They came in recurring waves, killing again and again. Disease not only greatly reduced the population; it destroyed power structures as leaders died and succession processes crumbled.

Our clearest picture of how badly diseases devastated Native American cultures comes not from the golden civilizations of the Aztecs and the Incas, but from the smaller Mississippian culture. When Hernando de Soto landed in Tampa Bay in 1539, he found flourishing Mississippian chiefdoms from Florida to the upper Tennessee River Valley, with an estimated population of about one million. De Soto had been with Pizarro in Peru, where he earned a reputation as the most brutal of the brutal. He displayed the same brand of brutality during the four years he spent in the American Southeast, pillaging the countryside in his search for gold. De Soto and his men were personally responsible for thousands of deaths, but the diseases they brought with them were responsible for hundreds of thousands more. When French explorer René-Robert Cavalier, Sieur de la Salle, arrived by canoe in 1682, the area was virtually deserted. De Soto found Mississippian cities packed together; La Salle didn't see a single village for two hundred miles.

OVER THE NEXT CENTURY, American resources would flood across the Old World. Gold and silver poured into Spain, and back out across Eurasia, reaching all the way to China as part of the growing trade with the Indies.

Precious metals were the most dramatic and most glamorous of America's resources to reach Europe, but not the most important in the long term. A cornucopia of new foods changed the European diet forever. Maize, tomatoes, and peppers. Lima beans, kidney beans, pinto beans, and wax beans. Chocolate and vanilla. And most important of all, the miraculous potato, which could be planted in fallow fields, produced more calories per acre than existing grain crops. Potatoes could also be left in the ground until needed, making them difficult for plundering soldiers to take in times of war.

1492 marked a fundamental shift in the axis of power in human history, from East to West. Columbus's voyages across the Atlantic led to the first lasting European contact with America, inaugurating a period of European exploration and colonization of foreign lands that lasted for several centuries. Hereafter, maps would be redrawn, and the story of us would change direction.

The meeting of Old and New Worlds was, of course, inevitable. What was harder to predict was how mankind's future would be shaped by the ingenious inventions, cultural exchanges, and unintended consequences that stemmed from this great age of discovery.

Only time would tell.

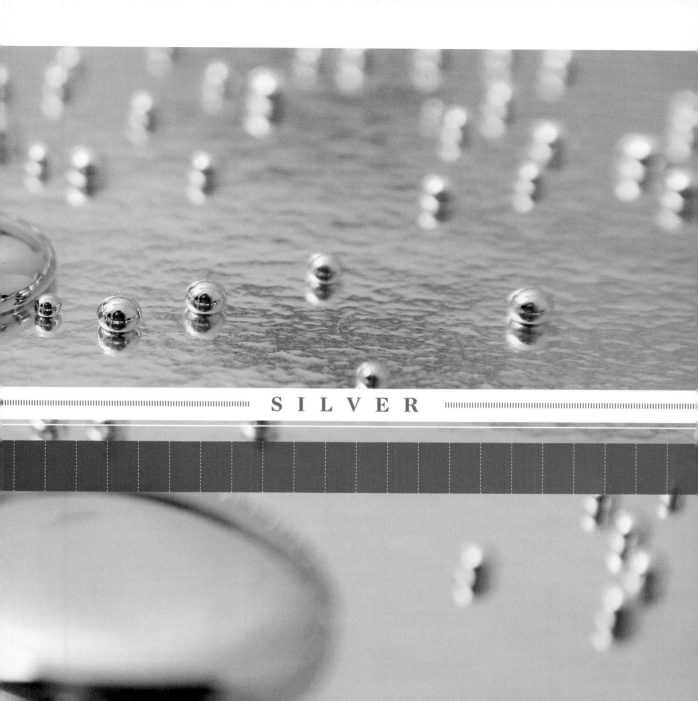

SILVER

Columbus stumbles upon a tropical paradise and encounters, not Asians, but partially clad Tainos wearing gold baubles. Enthralled by exotic new foods, fascinating new materials like rubber, and—above all—gold, he and his men gather samples and tales to excite potential investors back home.

Soon, reports of the place Columbus calls Hispaniola sets off a gold rush to the New World. But instead of stockpiles of gold, the Spanish who follow him find *silver*. Rivers of silver. Mountains of silver.

European explorers and rulers are quick to divvy up the New World's spoils and trading lanes, and then set about amassing raw materials and enlarging the scale of production to enable trade on a global scale. Driven by avarice, they enslave native peoples and force them to refine, harvest, and carry goods to waiting ships. Globalization dawns. The need to share the hazards of global trade will one day lead to the creation of the world's first stock exchange.

But in the meantime, Spanish businessman Bartolomé de Medina discovers a new chemical process for making high-grade silver out of low-grade ore in the Peruvian Andes. One man's ingenuity becomes the world's bounty—until unexpected complications arise.

Moche headdress, Peru 700 AD

MANKIND'S LUST FOR RICHES HAS sent us places we wouldn't otherwise go. And has prodded us to invent things and processes we might not have puzzled through without the drive for wealth of the sort that lies deep within the earth or in the far reaches of a rain forest. Ultimately, the human race is as practical as we are greedy.

The pre-Colombian cultures of Latin America used gold and silver for ornamentation and ritual purposes but did not value them as precious metals for their own sake. As the son of one Panamanian chief told the Spanish, gold ore was no more valuable than a lump of clay—until it was used to make something either beautiful or useful. The Aztecs, the Incas, and even the Tainos, who inhabited the islands where Columbus first landed, used gold and silver ornaments as a sign of rank. The Incas in particular made a lavish display of what they described as the "tears of the moon" and the "sweat of the sun."

Inflamed with greed, the Spanish invaders conquered the existing American civilizations, killed their rulers, melted down their beautifully worked gold and silver ornaments, and went in search of more. They found more—in modern Mexico and across the Andes, from what is now central Chile to modern Colombia, in Taxco, Pahuca, Porco, La Plata, and most of all, at Potosí, in modern Bolivia. "As rich as Peru" became a popular description of something valuable in Spain after Pizarro's conquest of the Inca Empire. Cervantes's Don Quixote changed the saying to "as rich as Potosí."

Potosí in the Andes of modern Bolivia is a conical mountain, dark red in color and nearly fourteen thousand feet above sea level. Sometimes known as *Cerra Rica*, the rich hill, it contained one of the largest, richest silver lodes ever found. We don't know who named the mountain Potosí, what the name means, or even what language it came from. One long-held tradition is that it means "high place." But in the seventeenth century, it meant "silver."

Latin American silver flooded into Spain for 250 years. It not only turned Spain into a global

P ERU. 1544. GUALPA IS LEADING HIS LLAMA train back to Porco from La Plata. Carrying food from the rich farmland of the valleys to the Spanish mining town is profitable business for a man who knows his way around the mountains.

He stops at the foothills of the red mountain to water the llamas. Gualpa has no intention of climbing that mountain today. He has business to do.

But suddenly, one of his beasts breaks free and wanders up the side of the mountain. Gualpa doesn't see it at first, but then . . .

There she is, the wayward llama. Gualpa mutters a curse. He can't afford to lose the animal—or her cargo.

Gualpa takes off after the stray, scrambling up the steep hill through the twisted evergreens. Even though he stays on the narrow trails worn by hoofed feet, the going is rough. The gravel shifts under his feet; he grabs a shrub to steady himself, but he falls as the shrub uproots.

Gualpa scrambles to his feet, brushing dirt and rocks off of his clothing—and instantly forgets all about the roaming llama. He's spent enough of his life around the mines to recognize that the soil on which he now stands is rich with silver.

INCA SMELTING

In the early years of Peruvian silver mining, Native American smelters dominated the industry.

Spanish smelters soon discovered that the ore was too rich for European methods: if heated too quickly, the silver content burned and volatilized instead of melting. Traditional Incan metallurgy allowed a smelter to maintain more precise control over smelting temperatures. The native smelters used portable ceramic ovens that had slits in the walls of the fuel chamber. When the oven was set up on a hill and the charcoal in the chamber was ignited, the slits used the wind to create a blast furnace effect. Smelters controlled the temperature by estimating wind velocity and moving the oven up or down the hill to get the correct draft. Once the silver was extracted from the ore, using the wind oven, it went through two more refining operations, ultimately producing ingots of pure silver. By agreement, Native American smelters delivered a specific amount of refined silver per hundredweight of ore, keeping the remainder for themselves.

Once the methodology of silver extraction changed, the power equation of mining fundamentally shifted—bringing devastation and centuries of misery to the Native American tribes who had built and mastered the first foundries.

RIGHT: *Native Americans Working in Spanish Silver Mine*

power; it created the first global economy, linking Mexico and Peru to India and China by way of Spain, Britain, and the Netherlands. The power of silver fueled Spain's empire and financed its wars. The labor needs of the silver mines drove the Portuguese slave trade and decimated the Native American population of the Andes. Soon, silver decorated Europe's churches and palaces and paid for Europe's maritime trade with Asia.

OVER THE NEXT FEW MONTHS, Gualpa uses the llama train as his cover. He returns to Potosí again and again, gathering and refining the rich ore. It is hard to keep his new and growing wealth a secret, especially from his friend Guanca. Guanca begs to be let in on the secret. Finally Gualpa gives in and takes his friend to the source of the silver.

It is a big mistake. Soon the friends disagree over how to work the lode. Out of spite, Guanca shares Gualpa's secret with his master at the Porco mine, Juan de Villarroel.

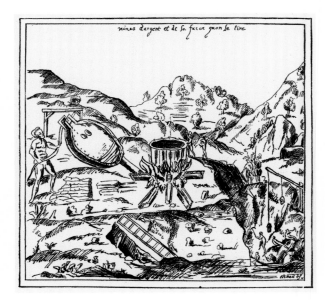

In the sixteenth century, Potosí was the world's largest industrial complex

In April 1545, man and master file a formal claim on one of the richest veins of ore on the mountain—and push Gualpa aside.

When Juan de Villarroel, the principal Spanish mine operator at Porco, investigated the reported deposit at Potosí, he saw a massive outcropping three hundred feet long and thirteen feet wide. It was high-grade ore—50 percent silver. The visible lode, exposed by years of erosion, was just the beginning. Most of the Potosí lode was hidden.

When de Villarroel filed his claim on the exposed outcropping in April 1545, he triggered the silver rush of 1545. One hundred seventy Spaniards, eager to get rich at the new lode, abandoned the newly settled mine town of La Plata and came to Potosí, bringing with them three thousand Indians in their service. The would-be miners barely had time to establish their claims before winter forced them to move down to a less-hostile elevation, displacing the existing Native American population. Within eighteen months, the invaders had built a ramshackle boomtown at the foot of the mountain. Fourteen thousand miners, refiners, merchants, and moneylenders lived in twenty-five hundred hastily constructed, straw-roofed shacks. Concentrating

solely on the silver, the settlers grew no crops, and they manufactured nothing in the town. Every tool, shirt, bed, and morsel had to be brought up from below by mule and llama train. But transporting goods to a town almost fourteen thousand feet above sea level was difficult—and costly. Prices soon got higher, thanks to the profligate spending habits of successful miners.

The Spaniards had already discovered that African slaves did not survive hard labor at high elevations and low temperatures. The local Native American population was too small to provide enough forced labor to work the mines. Mine owners were forced to rely on a free labor market, whether they liked it or not. They had plenty of labor to choose from as Spaniards and free Native Americans hurried to Potosí, hoping to get rich. Some of them did.

The mines at Potosí produced more than 127 million pesos of silver during the first eleven years, but production tapered off as the more accessible veins of high-grade ore became exhausted. There was still a mass of low-grade ore to mine, but no easy way to extract the silver from it. Potosí was on the verge of financial collapse.

IN 1569, PHILLIP II OF SPAIN
sent a special task force headed by Francisco de
Toledo to investigate and reform the administration
of the American empire. His goal was to increase
the production of precious metals and, not inciden-
tally, Crown revenues. Installed in the former Inca
capital of Cuzco in February 1570, Toledo brought
two new ideas that increased silver production at
Potosí: the forced labor system known as the *mita*,
and the *patio process* for extracting silver from low-
grade ore. Both ideas were devastating to the Native
American population of the Andes.

The *mita* required every Native American village, once a year, to send one-seventh of its men
between the ages of eighteen and fifty for a four-
month term of paid labor in the mines or on other
projects. In theory, a given man would work a period

of 121 days once every seven years, under closely
regulated terms. In fact, men were frequently forced
to work for longer periods than their term of service. Often, they were not paid, or they earned less

TOP: *Potosi silver mine* • BOTTOM: *Mining works, Trujillo, Peru 1780s*

than the regulated wage. Soon, villages were forced to send more men, more often.

A summons to labor in the mines was seen as a virtual death sentence, thanks to a combination of excessive labor, dangerous conditions, and inadequate food. Miners worked in semi-darkness, exposed to foul air and toxic dust. Disease and accidents were rampant. The most dangerous job was carrying the ore out of the mines. Laborers climbed hundreds of feet through narrow, steep tunnels with large, heavy baskets of ore on their backs, only to emerge, exhausted and sweating, into freezing winds on the mountainside.

The *mita* remained in place for 250 years. During that time, more than three million Quechua Indians were forced to work in the mines. Hundreds of thousands died, reducing the native population of the Andes by 80 percent. Despite these enormous human costs, the *mita* made it possible to bring tons of low-grade silver ore out of the heart of the mountain. Bartolomé de Medina's patio process made that ore usable by adopting and perfecting an old Roman method of using mercury to amalgamate gold and silver. Under Toledo's direction, the patio process transformed silver production at Potosí. Highly skilled Native American smelters working small wind ovens on the side of the mountain were replaced by a vast refining and processing complex within the city. Toledo built 132 walled and fortified plants, each with a private residence for the owner, a chapel, common kitchens, and living quarters for the workers.

LIKE MUCH OTHER ANCIENT knowledge, the process of using mercury to amalgamate gold and silver was lost after the fall of Rome, though not entirely forgotten. By the 1540s, European silver refiners and alchemists were experimenting with the process, especially in Italy and New Spain.

MERCURY

The only metal element that is liquid at room temperature, mercury has fascinated mankind since ancient times. Egyptians believed it offered eternal life. Ancient Chinese and Hindus added it to elixirs designed to extend life. Alchemists used it to search for the philosopher's stone that would transform other metals into gold. Sixteenth-century physicians prescribed it for syphilis.

Despite its historical associations with medicine and eternal life, mercury is toxic, whether absorbed through the skin or inhaled as a vapor. Mercury poisoning causes both psychological and physical symptoms, often resulting in death.

The Incas knew about mercury, including the toxic effects on those who mined and handled it. Because they had no use for it, they made mining it illegal and ordered the word obliterated from the language.

But later civilizations were slower to learn. For decades, industrialists mined mercury and used it in industries across the globe.

Eventually the poisonous metal found its way into waterways, contaminating both the water and the fish that lived there—the same fish and water supplies that were sustaining mankind. Twentieth-century scientists soon began linking mercury exposure among pregnant women to birth defects and cognitive deficits in children living in contaminated areas, such as the U.S. Great Lakes region. At last, civilization awoke to the dangers of mercury, and thus began a process of cleaning up mercury-contaminated lands and waterways.

That process continues today.

Chapter 8: SILVER

DISCOVERING AMALGAMATION

NEW SPAIN. 1553. IT IS DAWN WHEN BARTOLOMÉ de Medina opens the front door of his home in the mountain village of Pachuca, where he has lived for nearly two years on the banks of the Rio de las Avenidas. He is relieved to not encounter any of the dozen visiting *mineros* who have come to obtain news of his progress in the grand experiment of which word has traveled throughout the New World. Today Medina feels nothing like a messiah of metallurgy. Instead, he senses a black cloud of failure trailing him as he walks out of the gate.

Weary from a night of little sleep and excessive self-doubt, Medina reverses direction and heads, not to his courtyard workshop, but to the small church in the center of Pachuca. Unlike his native Seville, Pachuca has a haphazard look, its main road flanked by hastily erected warehouses, stables, and servants' quarters—all built in recent years to support the silver mining industry that employs the region's able-bodied men and enriches New Spain.

Medina greets friendly passersby with a polite "Buenos días," growing sadder as he remembers the shocked expressions and dire warnings he received from fellow traders, his friends, and business associates in Seville after he announced his intention to quit the mercantile trade and risk everything, at age fifty, to pursue an elusive chemical process in this godforsaken land. He pushes such thoughts out of his head, trying to allay his frustration at his lack of progress in this mission.

He is relieved again, as he opens the heavy wood door, to find the church empty. He makes his way to the altar, then holds on to a railing as he slowly bends two stiff legs to kneel on the stone floor. In front of him, adjacent to a large wooden cross, an aged statue of the Virgin Mary looks down on him with a kindly smile. Medina's gaze rests on the Blessed Mother.

"Our Lady," he prays, "I come to you a broken man. I left my wife and children and traveled here for the purpose of rendering a great service to Our Lord and to his Majesty and all the realm. After spending my life's fortune and years of my life on this task, I'm anguished to admit I am not worthy of this great project. And so, I beg you to enlighten and guide me, so that I might be successful." With that, he crosses himself, rises, and exits the chapel.

Medina feels lighter, his head a bit clearer, after leaving the church. He is ready to return to his work. En route, he recalls the formula his German friend Maestro Lorenzo, the man who inspired this mission, had given him back in Seville. "Grind the ore fine," Lorenzo had said.

"Steep it in strong brine. Add mercury and mix thoroughly. Repeat mixing daily for several weeks. Every day, take a pinch of ore mud and examine the mercury. See? It is bright and glistening. As time passes, it should darken as the salt decomposes the silver minerals and the silver forms an alloy with the mercury. Amalgam is pasty. Wash out the spent ore in water. Retort residual amalgam; when the mercury is driven off, silver remains."

"So why hasn't it worked?" Medina asks himself as he enters the large courtyard patio with the broad, well-grouted flagstones that front formal gardens and provide the staging area for his grand-scale experiments with silver ore.

Today, like every day at the workshop, ground ore is spread out on the flagstones like *tortas*, arranged in pancake-like circles of thick mud. Across the courtyard, Medina sees his assistant, Juan de Plazencia, an experienced local silver miner who shares his curiosity and zeal for making silver extraction easier. Plazencia walks toward him.

For months now, the two men have been putting mercury droplets on pieces of ore in varying amounts, hoping the globules would darken, indicating that the salt strewn on the surface is decomposing the silver ore.

According to Lorenzo, that's the first step in the process of converting ore to metallic silver. So day after day they have mixed, combined, waited, and watched . . . yet nothing has changed. The mercury continues to glisten in the sun, losing none of its sheen—sullying only their reputations.

But today, as he meets Plazencia's glance, a new idea comes to Medina. "What if we add *another* chemical to the mercury?" he asks, placing both hands on his heart as if suddenly breathless.

"What chemical?" Plazencia inquires, raising his eyebrows at Medina's sudden intensity.

"I can't believe I haven't thought of this before," Medina says, looking around the workshop as if searching for something. Plazencia watches as Medina paces and throws his hands up in the air before finally explaining how in Seville, tanneries use vitriol, a highly corrosive sulfuric acid, to darken leather. What if *they* were to mix a corrosive additive into the mercury globules on the silver ore? The same chain reaction might occur!

Wasting no time, Medina and Plazencia spend the next several days trying different acids before they come up with one they christen "magistral," a combination of iron and copper sulfates. At the moment of reckoning, Plazencia pours several drops of magistral onto the globules of mercury covering a pancake of iron ore. In a matter of seconds, the mercury begins to lose its sheen and becomes leady, thick, and pasty.

The two men shout out in excitement, and Medina falls to his knees, exclaiming his gratitude to "Our Lady" for this long-awaited breakthrough.

In his zeal to mine larger quantities of silver for God and Crown, Medina has discovered an important chemical principle: salt and silver ore minerals will only react in the presence of a chemical promoter, or catalyst.

Chapter 8: SILVER

In Medina's process, water, salt, mercury and *magistral* were mixed with crushed silver-bearing ore. The dark, pasty substance was then spread out on a stone patio, where it would sit for weeks. Forced laborers, usually barefoot and up to their knees in the mixture, would tread on it throughout the day for up to a month so the materials would be properly combined and the silver would bond with the mercury. Once samples indicated that the chemical bonding of silver and mercury was complete, Medina would separate the amalgam from the mixture by placing it in water, where the heavy amalgam sank to the bottom. After the amalgam separated, he'd place it in a conical mold and squeeze it dry. The resulting cone, called a *piña* because of its resemblance to a pineapple, was made up of five parts mercury and one part silver. The *piña* was then heated to volatilize the remaining mercury, leaving behind high-grade silver and releasing tons of toxic mercury into the atmosphere.

By the end of 1554, Medina had received a six-year patent on his patio process from the viceroy of New Spain. Applied on a massive scale in sixteenth-century Peruvian silver mines, his patio process would prove to be one of the most lucrative scientific discoveries humans would ever make.

Medina lived to see the king's tax revenue increase by 20 million pesos over a twenty-five-year period, thanks in large part to the patio process. By the end of that period, the rate had jumped to the unprecedented sum of three million pesos a year from patio-process silver alone. Production boomed. Between 1550 and 1800, Peru and New Spain produced at least 136,000 metric tons of silver, 80 percent of the world's silver production during that period.

THE SPANIARDS HAD A WELL-designed system for shipping precious metals back to Spain from their American colonies. Each year a heavily armed fleet sailed from Seville to South America. When it reached the Caribbean, known as the Spanish Main, the fleet split into smaller squadrons that visited the ports where colonial officials gathered gold and silver for shipment. The squadrons reconvened at the Cuban port of Havana and sailed home in convoy. It was a good system, but, like many systems, its weakness was its predictability.

Spain found it hard to defend the monopoly over the Americas that it claimed in the Treaty of Tordesillas. Beginning in the mid-sixteenth century, sea raiders from other European nations smuggled goods into the Spanish colonies, preyed on Spanish ships in the Caribbean, and sacked coastal settlements.

A NEW METHOD

As would be the case with so many important discoveries during the next century's *scientific revolution*, trader-turned-metallurgist Medina went through an elaborate process of trial and error, nearly giving up before the desired result appeared "miraculously" before his eyes.

The "aha" moment that Medina attributed to "Our Lady," whom he believed had enlightened him on the essential combination of ingredients and methodology, would later be described as one step in the process called *the scientific method*. The phrase described an *empirical* investigation of the natural world in which, scientists would observe, explain, and predict real-world phenomena by experiment. Thus, their conclusions would be based on, not magic, alchemy, or miracle, but a large dose of a quality that separates mankind from other inhabitants of planet Earth: reason. In Medina's case, and for many scientists since his time, the resulting discovery was both practical and lucrative—if not for the scientist, then for his patrons.

In the 1620s and 1630s, English and Dutch settlers had a permanent base on the island of Tortuga, off the northwest coast of the large Spanish island of Hispaniola. The channel that lay between Hispaniola and Cuba, known as the Windward Passage, was a major coastal shipping lane, linking the ports of Cuba and the colony of St. Augustine in Florida with the Caribbean ports. Smaller squadrons of the annual treasure fleet used this same channel as they headed for the rendezvous in Havana. By the early 1630s, the Windward Passage was a favorite hunting ground for the pirates and privateers who preyed on Spanish ships.

At first they attacked the Spanish galleons using canoes and light pinnaces, depending on the speed and maneuverability of the smaller boats to provide an element of surprise. Over time, buccaneering settlements attracted runaway indentured servants and slaves and naval deserters as recruits. As their numbers grew, they acquired larger and more powerful ships.

Some of the pirates also acquired a veneer of respectability as French, English, and Dutch settlers established colonies on the islands of the Lesser Antilles, southeast of Cuba. For much of the sixteenth and seventeenth centuries, France, England, and Holland were at war with Spain. During wartime, colonial governors were authorized to issue "letters of marque" (also known as "letters of reprisal"), which made the recipient a privateer rather than a pirate. Pirates operated outside the law; privateers operated on behalf of a government. Issuing letters of marque was an inexpensive way for a government to disrupt enemy shipping in exchange for a secure port and a percentage of the profits. In the Caribbean, where small, non-Spanish colonies seldom had the benefit of warships, privateering became a major element of warfare.

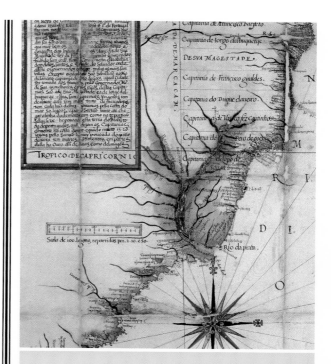

THE TREATY OF TORDESILLAS

The Treaty of Tordesillas, signed on June 7, 1494, drew a new line of demarcation halfway between the Cape Verde Islands, owned by Portugal, and the island of Hispaniola, recently claimed for Spain by Columbus. The line divided the ocean between the two powers. With total disregard for the rights of the peoples already in possession, the treaty gave all lands discovered east of the line to Portugal and all lands west of it to Spain.

The treaty divided the world between Portugal and Spain as neatly as cutting an orange in two, but it didn't stop other European countries from wanting their slice.

Portuguese map showing the boundary line after the Treaty of Tordesillas

SIR FRANCIS DRAKE, PRIVATEER

MARCH 1579. *THE GOLDEN HINDE* SAILS IN THE middle of the Pacific Ocean off North America, the first English vessel to reach these seas. Not on an exploration, Francis Drake, the captain of the *Golden Hinde*, is out for treasure—and revenge.

But first, on the eve of the attack that will make his name synonymous with *privateer*, Drake is having musicians entertain his ship's officers. After that, they will enjoy a fine shipboard meal.

Though renowned as a fearsome buccaneer, Drake is a refined, religious man. With the concert concluded, Drake leads the diners in a prayer. Now the food can be served.

After the meal, Drake pauses dramatically before revealing his daring plan for the following day. He tells his men they will have the honor of helping him exact vengeance against Don Martin Enriquez, the Mexican viceroy who ambushed his friend John Hawkins's fleet last year at San Juan d'Ulloa. They'll do it by taking all the viceroy's riches, which are presently on the Spanish galleon, the *Cagafuego*, en route from Peru to Panama and Spain.

 **MORNING HAS COME, AND FRANCIS** Drake has the Spanish galleon in his sights. He does not want to attack before dark. Knowing that it will raise suspicions on the Spanish ship if he reduces sail, he drags wine pots filled with water in his wake to reduce his speed. That way *the Hinde* can creep up on the *Cagafuego* at dusk, as if it were a merchant ship rather than the *Golden Hinde*.

Soon dusk arrives, and Drake brings his ship up to the rear of the *Cagafuego*. Just as he predicted, the Spanish are surprised and unarmed.

Brandishing his gun, Drake tells them to strike their sail right away or he'll send them to the bottom of the ocean. When they refuse, Drake fires a cannon, knocking down the Spaniards' mizzenmast. His men then board the *Cagafuego* and seize its treasure: an incredible eighty pounds of gold bullion, thirteen chests of gold coins, and twenty-six tons of silver.

Queen Elizabeth's share of Francis Drake's plunder of the *Cagafuego* is larger than her entire royal income. Without question, Drake is the most daring, successful, and rightfully famous privateer ever to sail the world's seas.

Meanwhile, the ill-fated *Cagafuego* never makes land.

PIECES OF EIGHT

Ferdinand and Isabella introduced the Spanish *peso*, literally "weight," in 1497 as part of a currency reform. As the name suggested, it was a heavy silver coin, weighing 26 grams, a little less than the modern ounce. And it could literally be divided like a pie into eight *reales*.

By 1600, the *peso*, known as "pieces of eight" to English speakers, was a global currency. The coin was so readily available that during the American War of Independence, it was the base for the reserves guaranteeing paper money. In 1792, the new American Congress based the weight of the American dollar on the Spanish peso. The parity between the two was so exact that the peso remained legal tender in the United States until the 1850s.

ABOVE: *doubloons and reales*

The notorious Sir Francis Drake, known to the Spanish as The Dragon, was one of the most successful of the English, and Dutch, buccaneers who attacked Spanish ships from nationalist sentiment, religious fervor, and a desire for plunder.

IN CENTRAL ASIA, A DESCENDANT of Genghis Khan, Zahir-ud-din Muhammad Babur, ruler of Afghanistan, asserted his people's claim over the Indian subcontinent. A hundred years later, Babur's descendant would give India and the world one of its greatest man-made wonders: the Taj Mahal.

In 1524, the Indian Daulat Khan Lodi, governor of the Punjab, and Rana Sanga, leader of the powerful Rajput state of Mewar in northeast India, made a serious mistake. They invited Babur to invade northern India and help them dethrone Sultan Ibrahim, who sat on the throne of Delhi. Daulat Khan Lodi and Rana Sangha intended to use Babur to further their own ambitions for Sultan Ibrahim's throne.

The Afghani Babur had his own ambitions. Descended on his father's side from the Turco-Mongolian conqueror Timur (known in the west as Tamerlane) and on his mother's side from Genghis Khan, Babur was a hard drinker, a poet, and a military adventurer. By the time he was twenty-eight, he had conquered and lost Timur's capital of Samarqand—twice. He had seized Kabul and built a home kingdom for himself in Afghanistan. He didn't much like India, but Afghanistan was poor and India was rich.

Babur helped the Indian rulers defeat Sultan Ibrahim, declared himself emperor at Delhi, and set out on a campaign in which he conquered a territory that extended across northern India from Afghanistan to the borders of Bengal and the Rajput desert. He never got a chance to establish real control over his vast new empire.

KHANWA, NORTH INDIA, 1528. Babur's small army was eight hundred miles from their home in Kabul and surrounded by the much larger force of Rana Sanga and the Rajput confederation. Heat steamed from the ground. There was no grain for the men and no straw for their horses. Morale was low. Babur's men longed for the cool mountains of home. Babur did too. India was a pit as far as he was concerned, but it was a rich pit, and with Allah's help, it was going to be his.

Babur called his men together. Before them all, he promised Allah that he would give up drinking if he won the coming battle. Then he called on his men to join him in the pledge. Nearly three hundred men joined him. Together they poured all the wine into the village well and smashed the jugs.

Now they were ready for battle. And with Allah on their side, they would win.

IN DECEMBER 1530, BABUR'S oldest son, Humayan, fell seriously ill. Babur prayed to Allah to take his life instead of his son's. After Humayan recovered, Babur fell ill. On December 26, Babur, the first Moghul emperor died.

For a time it appeared that Babur would be the last Moghul emperor as well as the first. All the enemies he had not had a chance to bring under control threatened his son Humayan's claim to the throne. The new emperor fought for ten years, never completely able to subdue one enemy before another attacked. By April 1540, Humayan's army was so demoralized that they fled in panic from forces led by Afghan Sher Shah Suri, better known as Sher Khan. Sher Khan declared himself the ruler of northern India, and Humayan took refuge with the ruler of Persia.

It looked as though the Moghul Empire was done, but Humayan did not give up. In 1555, he took advantage of a succession struggle between Sher Khan's grandsons and re-captured Delhi on July 23.

Humayan did not enjoy Babur's throne for long. On January 24, 1556, the second Moghul emperor, a drinker like his father, indulged in too much wine and bhang. Inebriated, he fell to his death on the steps of his private observatory, leaving his newly regained empire to his thirteen-year-old son, Akbar.

Akbar lived up to the title by which he became known in Europe, the Great Moghul. Over the course of his fifty-year reign, he expanded the empire's boundaries across north and central India, from Afghanistan to the Deccan. Akbar the Great was more than just a conqueror; he was the true architect of the Moghul Empire. His reign was notable for his policy of religious tolerance toward his non-Muslim subjects. He was succeeded first by Jahangir, and later by his grandson Shah Jahan, whose story involves romance, tragedy—and a work of art.

Shah Jahan fell in love with his wife when he was only sixteen.

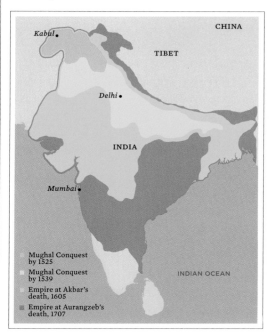

They met at the New Year's Fair at Royal Meena Bazaar, a private marketplace in the palace gardens in Agra, where women of the royal household played at running market stalls. It was a rare chance for the women to meet and talk to men other than their relatives. Shah Jahan, then Prince Khurram, stopped to haggle over gems at a stall run by the prime minister's fifteen-year-old daughter, Arjumand Banu Begum. By all accounts, it was love at first sight.

They were married five years later. The emperor Jahangir was so pleased with his son's choice that he gave her the title Mumtaz Mahal, "Jewel of the Palace."

Shah Jahan had other wives and concubines, but Mumtaz Mahal remained the love of his life. She was the only one of his wives to bear his children, and she traveled with him wherever he went, even on military campaigns.

In 1631, Shah Jahan was once again at war, and Mumtaz Mahal traveled with him, even though she was pregnant for the fourteenth time in nineteen years. She went into labor in the harem of the temporary encampment, 435 miles south of Agra. The baby was healthy, but Mumtaz Mahal did not survive. Shah Jahan sat by his beloved wife's side and watched, helpless, as she died.

After her death, he built a magnificent tomb in her memory: the Taj Mahal.

Shah Jahan brought the best craftsmen to the capital to build the Taj Mahal and insisted on the finest materials: blue-veined marble from Jodhpur, crystal from China, turquoise from Tibet, and lapis lazuli from Afghanistan.

Shah Jahan did not live to see the work completed. Imprisoned by his son Aurangzeb, he died a year before his masterpiece was done.

Aurangzeb would be the last great Moghul emperor.

Mumtaz Mahal and Shah Jahan

THE TAJ MAHAL

The Taj Mahal, inspired by love, was an architectural and engineering tour de force built with rare materials imported from all over Asia.

Persian architect Ustad Ahmad Lahauri is believed to be the principal designer of the Taj Mahal. Construction began in 1632 and was completed in 1653.

The Taj Mahal is located in the city of Agra, near the Yamuna river. Before beginning construction workmen excavated the three acre site, filled it with dirt to reduce seeping, and then leveled the surface fifty meters above the shore of the river.

Next they would build the tomb.

To transport raw materials more quickly and easily, workers made an inclined ramp of tightly pressurized earth. This fifteen-kilometer-long ramp was the lifeline of the whole construction process. To bring marble and other construction materials to the ramp, laborers used bullock carts with special wagons.

Engineers custom designed a pulley system to lift the huge marble pieces into place. They also designed a mechanical bucket system that used ropes pulled by animals to retrieve water needed for the construction from the nearby river. The water was collected in a massive storage tank and was distributed from there to several smaller storage tanks located at various parts of the construction site.

The tomb itself took around twelve years to complete. The surrounding structure, which includes the mosque, minarets, and gateways, took another ten years.

Approximately twenty thousand laborers worked on this building simultaneously. Artisans from different parts of India were hired to carve the marble flowers found throughout the building.

The total cost of the Taj Mahal was roughly thirty-two million rupees, a very large amount at that time.

The Taj Mahal is not only an architectural beauty but also an engineering wonder, inspiring architects and civil engineers around the world—five hundred years later.

Workers used more than 25 different kinds of stones for the exquisite inlay work

MAY 20, 1498. FROM THE PER- spective of Calicut, known as the "City of Spices," the arrival of the Portuguese caravels was nothing new. India was on the way to everywhere. Merchant vessels carrying goods from one Asian market to another landed at the busy trading port every day during the season when the trade winds were favorable. They carried raw cotton, coffee, and attar of roses from the Islamic countries of the Persian Gulf; silks, tea, porcelain, and zinc from China; spices, sandalwood, and ivory from Southeast Asia.

But for Vasco da Gama and his crew, landing at Calicut was nothing short of astonishing. Theirs was the first Western ship to land in India. India was as rich with trade possibilities as they had dreamed. Every crew member had collected money and valuables to trade for silk and spices.

The local Hindu ruler warmly welcomed da Gama, but the welcome did not last long. The time came for da Gama to present his gifts to the king: twelve pieces of striped cloth, four scarlet hoods, six hats, four strings of coral, six pottery basins, a case of sugar, two casks of oil, and two casks of honey. Even da Gama could see that his presents were out of

---

SOMETHING TO TRADE?

As Vasco da Gama learned, the real problem for European trading companies in Asia was finding merchandise to trade for Asian luxury goods. For the most part, Asians did not want what Europeans had to sell. Some products were too expensive. Most, such as the heavy woolen cloth for which England was famous, were not useful or appealing. What interested Asians most were the precious metals from Spanish America. Forty percent of the New World's silver flowed into India and China each year.

---

place in the wealthy and sophisticated Indian court.

The Hindu ruler was insulted. Cheap cloth and trinkets might please the tribal peoples of West Africa, but when merchants came to his court asking for permission to trade, they brought him gold. Da Gama hastily tried to explain that he and his crew were explorers not merchants. That made no sense to the king. There was nothing to discover. The city of Calicut and the kingdoms of Hindustan were where they had always been, at the heart of a complicated trade network that stretched from China to Arabia.

BY 1511, PORTUGAL WAS WELL on its way to replacing Venice and the caravan trade as Europe's primary purveyor of spices and silk.

The new sea route was dangerous. More than a quarter of the ships that sailed from Portugal to the Indian Ocean between 1500 and 1634 were lost at sea, but the potential profits outweighed the risks. Instead of seizing and holding large areas of land, the way the Spanish did in the Americas, the Portuguese created a trading-post empire, controlling the sea routes with a series of armed forts from the Azores to Macao. They seized any foreign ships that tried to sail to the Indian Ocean, and sentenced their crews to work in the galleys of Portuguese ships. Suspected spies were arrested and sent to Lisbon for trial.

The Portuguese spice monopoly was divided into two parts. The "Indian pepper contract" allowed merchants to buy spices in Asia, but required them to sell them to the Portuguese king at a fixed price. The "European contract" allowed merchants to buy pepper from the Portuguese king and resell it. For many years, Portuguese merchants brought the spices from Asia, but the Dutch, who owned the largest merchant fleet in Europe, controlled their distribution.

The illustrations in Linchoten's book Voyages in East Asia *were less accurate than his descriptions of the countryside.*

The Dutch lost their privileged position in the spice trade in 1580 when Phillip II of Spain conquered Portugal. Suddenly Spain's enemies became Portugal's enemies, especially the Protestant regions of the Netherlands, which had revolted against Spanish rule, and Protestant England, which gave the Dutch rebels financial support. No longer able to buy spices from Portugal, Dutch and English privateers captured Portuguese spice ships in the shipping lanes around the Cape Verde islands, the Azores, and the Canaries, just as their Caribbean counterparts captured Spanish galleons laden with American silver.

Dutch merchants knew that piracy was not a permanent solution to their lost access to the Portuguese spice markets. The real answer was establishing direct trade with the Indies. So in 1592, a group of Dutch merchants sent a spy disguised as a trader to acquire information about the Portuguese spice routes.

Before he returned, the Dutch received the information they needed from a source they never expected.

Jan Huyghen van Linschoten was a Dutch Catholic who worked for a merchant in Lisbon. In 1583, he took the job of secretary to the new archbishop of Goa, the Portuguese capital in India. As secretary to the archbishop he had access to information regarding trade routes and market conditions. He also questioned every European traveler who passed through "golden Goa" about the Asian countries further east. When the archbishop died in 1589, Linschoten headed home to the Netherlands. He spent the next four years sailing on Portuguese ships and working for a Portuguese merchant in the Azores.

When he finally reached the Netherlands in 1592, he had all the information the Dutch needed to know to challenge Portugal's control of the spice trade.

Marco Polo had used his experiences in Asia to write the first book for armchair travelers. Three hundred years later Linschoten wrote a travel guide for merchants, *Voyages to the East Indies*. In it, he described the trade routes, including the weather conditions at different times of the year. He noted where ships could resupply with fresh water and vegetables. He reported on the customs in different

SPICES

Pepper, the most prized of all the spices in the sixteenth century and still the mainstay of the international spice trade, is the fruit of a climbing vine *(Piper nigrum)* indigenous to the mountains of Kerala on India's Malabar Coast. It is harvested as unripe berries for green peppercorns or as ripe red berries that are dried to produce black pepper. (The berries sold as pink peppercorns aren't pepper at all, but the berries of an evergreen tree from the Peruvian Andes.) Pepper contains a stimulant, peperine, and is the only spice that can be absorbed through the skin. Once as valuable as gold, today pepper is an inexpensive condiment, grown throughout tropical Asia.

Cloves are the dried flower buds of an evergreen tree *(Syzgium aromaticum)*. The name *clove* comes from the Latin word for the nails that the spice resembles. Cloves originally grew only on a few small volcanic islands in the Indonesian archipelago.

Nutmeg and mace both come from *Myristica fragans*, a bushy tree native to the South Moluccas, islands within Indonesia. The tree produces a yellow, plumlike fruit with a glossy brown seed the size of a marble, covered with a bright-red, lacy covering, the *aril*. The spices come from the seed, which is hulled and left to dry. Once dried, the aril is removed and broken into "blades" of mace. The inner seed is the nutmeg.

Columbus sought a new trade route to India and China to obtain coveted spices, such as cinnamon and black pepper. Of course, Columbus didn't reach the "Indies," but he did bring some exotic new spices back to Spain, including *chili (red) peppers*, and a dried, unripe fruit of the plant *Pimenta dioica* that combined the flavors of cloves, pepper, cinnamon, and nutmeg, and was later called *allspice*.

Asian countries from India and Japan. He even included up-to-date maps. Most important, Linschoten revealed that the feared Portuguese navy had deteriorated so much that it defended the trade routes primarily with its reputation. The sea routes to the east were open.

In 1595, the first Dutch ships sailed east with a copy of Linschoten's *Voyages* on board. Their goal was Java, which Linschoten had identified as a source of spices that was not part of the Portuguese trading network. They returned with a cargo of pepper. Over the next six years, fifteen more Dutch fleets sailed to the Indies in search of pepper.

Linschoten's book did not give the Dutch an advantage in the spice trade for long. In 1598, it was published in German and English. Editions in French and Latin soon followed. Queen Elizabeth signed the charter for "The Company of Merchants of London trading in the East Indies" on December 31, 1600. Other nations quickly chartered their own East India companies. The race for spice had begun.

FEBRUARY 5, 1637. ALKMAAR, Holland. Local tavern owner Wouter Winkel was dead. Normally, his seven orphaned children would become wards of the local orphanage until they were old enough to work for a living and then would be sent to a mill or workshop to learn a trade. But Winkel had a hobby that would give his children a more comfortable life—thanks to what grew in the garden next to his inn.

The Dutchman had gotten involved in buying and growing tulips early, when they were of interest to only a few passionate connoisseurs. At the time of his death, Winkel owned more than seventy rare tulips and about thirty thousand *azen* of less-valuable bulbs. The collection was a fine one, possibly the best in the Netherlands. Winkel had owned bulbs of some of the most valuable tulips in the Netherlands: an Admiral van Enkuizen, two Viceroys, five Brabasons, three bulbs of the Rosen Admiral van der Ejck, an Admiral Liefkens, a Brown and Purple, a Paragon Schilder, and seven bulbs of the increasingly popular Gouda. Most amazing of all, he had owned the bulbs themselves, instead of a future promise of a bulb. They were planted in a garden next to his inn.

The trustees of the local orphanage decided to auction off the collection on behalf of the orphaned children. It had taken months for the bureaucracy of the children's court to approve the sale, but the timing couldn't have been better. In the months since Winkel's death, tulip prices had doubled—twice.

Buyers came from all over the Netherlands to bid on the bulbs. Tulip connoisseurs and wealthy growers crowded the inns of Alkmaar. Bidders were given a chance to inspect a tulip book commissioned by the court: 124 watercolors of Winkel's tulips. Before the auction even began, one wealthy and determined buyer arranged a private purchase of the most valuable bulb in the collection for an astonishing 3,200 guilders. The price seemed to set the tone for the auction itself. Buyers bid fiercely, raising the price of every bulb to the highest ever recorded. By the end of the day, the auctioneers had raised 90,000 guilders for the Winkel orphans, more than one million dollars in today's money. Winkel's children were set for life; if the orphanage trustees had delayed for a week, the children would have had nothing.

THE TULIP CRAZE OF 1636-37 created the world's first economic bubble—and its first crash.

The Netherlands was the heart of the tulip craze: a tiny country that had become a major economic power thanks to American silver and the

Depiction of tulips on Syrian tile from the 17th century

Asian luxury trade. By 1633, five hundred different varieties of tulips were being grown in the Dutch Republic alone.

Tulip bulbs were so valuable that their weight was measured in *azen*, a unit of measurement borrowed from goldsmiths. One *ace* was 1/2000 of an ounce. Fashionable varieties, prized by connoisseurs for their brilliant color and unpredictable flamed, feathered, and striped patterns, were sold by the bulb—the price based on rarity value and the weight of the bulb. More common, single-colored varieties were sold by the basket. If a particular tulip became widely available, it fell out of fashion and dropped in value, so the owners of highly prized varieties guarded the bulbs carefully. The most famous and coveted tulip of the period, the red-and-white-flamed Semper Augustus, was so rare that one man owned the only twelve bulbs in existence. He refused to share them at any price.

At first the sale of bulbs was tied to the growing season. Bulbs were bought between the time when they were "lifted" from the ground in June until they were planted again in October. Around 1634, growers began to sell tulips in the winter for future delivery, adding new instability to the unregulated tulip market. Sales contracts were written for a particular bulb from a particular location, to be delivered and paid for when the bulbs were lifted the following June. Some contracts included conditions that the bulb be a certain weight or contain a specific number of new buds. Some particularly desirable tulips changed hands several times before they bloomed.

The demand for tulips exploded in 1634 and 1635.

The plague had struck the Netherlands between 1633 and 1635, causing a serious labor shortage. Wages were high, and people could afford small luxuries. A skilled tradesman might not be able to afford a fashionable bulb, like a Gouda or a Viceroy,

FUTURES TRADING

Futures trading, sometimes described by the derogatory term "wind trade," was already a familiar practice in the Netherlands in the seventeenth century. High-ranking merchants and stock exchange specialists bought and sold futures contracts on 360 commodities traded at the Amsterdam stock exchange, including Baltic grain, herring, and East Indian spices.

Futures trading in tulips was less formal, without the regulations and safeguards of the stock exchange. Although a few companies were formed to trade in tulips, most people bought or sold bulbs as a hobby or a sideline to another business. Trades often took place in the back rooms of taverns, regulated only by local practice and the community of buyers and sellers—for this reason it can be said the tulip craze created the first "rogue traders."

but he could easily afford a basket of common bulbs or even a single-color breeder bulb. At the same time, tulips came into vogue among the upper classes in France. Women wore clusters of tulips in their bosoms, and wealthy men competed to buy the most dramatic blooms.

The supply of bulbs could not keep up with increased demand from both the top and the bottom of the market. Prices began to rise and rise and rise. By December 1636, prices were going up so quickly that the value of some bulbs doubled in a little more than a week. An Admiral van der Eyck bulb was offered for 1,000 guilders—the price of a modest house in Haarlem or 5,714 pounds of meat. The price for common bulbs rose even more quickly than the price for rare varieties, increasing twenty times over the course of a few weeks.

The Alkmaar auction marked the height of the tulip market. A week later, the market crashed: the end of the world's first known economic bubble.

Bulb prices dropped by the hour. Sellers worried they would not be paid for bulbs they had sold for delivery in June. Buyers feared they would be forced to pay inflated prices for now-worthless bulbs. Conflicts over the sale of bulbs were so common that the High Court of Holland refused to allow tulip-related claims in the courts.

Within a year or two, the tulip market recovered its equilibrium. Connoisseurs continued to buy rare bulbs at high prices. As first the tulip and then the hyacinth became fashionable in other European countries, Dutch growers developed a thriving export trade in flower bulbs. Ironically, Dutch tulip growers shipped tens of thousands of tulip bulbs to the Ottoman court in the 1690s when Istanbul was convulsed by its own version of tulipomania. Today, the Netherlands produces 70 percent of the commercially grown flowers in the world, and tulips are still the most important flower they sell.

WHAT WOULD 3,000 GUILDERS BUY?

A Dutchman writing at the height of tulipmania claimed that the same 3,000 guilders that bought a single rare tulip bulb could have bought:

EIGHT FAT PIGS	240 guilders
FOUR FAT OXEN	480 guilders
TWELVE FAT SHEEP	120 guilders
TWENTY-FOUR TONS OF WHEAT	448 guilders
FORTY-EIGHT TONS OF RYE	558 guilders
TWO HOGSHEADS OF WINE	70 guilders
FOUR BARRELS OF BEER	32 guilders
TWO TONS OF BUTTER	192 guilders
A THOUSAND POUNDS OF CHEESE	120 guilders
A SILVER DRINKING CUP	60 guilders
A PACK OF CLOTHES	80 guilders
A BED WITH MATTRESS AND BEDDING	100 guilders
A SHIP	500 guilders
TOTAL	**3,000 guilders**

1621. LUANDA, ANGOLA. A HUNDRED year long guerrilla war began between an African queen determined to defend her people's independence and a European power hungry for slaves.

Nzinga a Mbande, the eldest sister of King Ngola Mbande, orchestrated her arrival at the audience chamber of the new Portuguese governor at Luanda with care. She was there to negotiate a treaty on behalf of a country that her brother had already abandoned to the Portuguese. It would be fatal if she appeared as the humble messenger of a defeated king. Musicians heralded her approach when she entered the chamber, a royal princess accompanied by her serving women.

The new Portuguese governor, João Correia de Sousa, was just as aware of the power of symbols as Nzinga. He greeted her from the ornate governor's throne and gestured for her to sit on the floor, where a cushion waited for her, as if an African ruler would be unaccustomed to sitting on a chair. Nzinga would have none of it. She was here to negotiate not to grovel at the governor's feet. She looked around the room for a chair of equal magnificence. Finding no chair at all, she summoned one of her waiting woman who came forward and assumed a position on her hands and knees. Nzinga sat on her back as if she were a human chair, one worth more than any piece of carved wood, no matter how ornate. It was time to negotiate.

The first contacts between the Portuguese and Ndongo, the kingdom of the Mbundu tribes, in the early sixteenth century were friendly. The ruler at the time, Ngola Kiluanji, welcomed trade with Europeans, as long as he was able to dispose of criminals and prisoners of war without enslaving his own people. In fact, his kingdom flourished in the early days of the Portuguese slave trade. Over time, Ndongo's growing prosperity led the kingdom into direct

conflict with the Portuguese slave trade on which it was based. By 1581, when the princess Nzinga was born, Ndongo was at war with Portugal, a condition that would last for nearly one hundred years.

In 1618, Nzinga's oldest brother, Mbande, overthrew their father and made himself *ngola*. Because he was illegitimate and his right to the throne was questioned, he killed all potential rivals for the throne, including his younger brother, Nzinga's only son, and all the chiefs who had supported his succession. Nzinga fled the Ndongo capital and settled in the neighboring territory of Matamba with her husband and two sisters.

Mbande was less successful at fighting the Portuguese than he was at fighting his own family. When the Portuguese advanced into Mbundu territory in search of silver, the *ngola* took refuge on the islands of Kindonga in the Cuanza River.

In 1621, João Correia de Sousa relieved Luis Mendes de Vasconcelos as governor of Luanda. Hoping a change of governor offered a chance for peace, Mbande sent word to his sister, asking her to negotiate a treaty with the Portuguese.

At first Nzinga's mission appeared successful. Correia de Sousa agreed to recognize Ngola Mbande as the independent ruler of the kingdom of Ndongo, to withdraw Portuguese forces from the fortress of Ambaca, and to cooperate with the Mbundu in expelling the Imbangala, an ad hoc tribe of escaped slaves and criminals that both sides had used in recent wars and that now posed a threat to both the Portuguese and Ndongo. In return, Nzinga agreed that Ndongo would return Portuguese prisoners of war and resume trade; that Mbande and his court would return to the mainland; and that Mbande would become a Christian. Nzinga herself was baptized immediately, taking the name Ana de Sousa. The Portuguese governor served as her godfather.

The crucial terms of the treaty were never carried out. Portuguese forces and settlers remained at Ambaca. Correia de Sousa raised troops to attack the Imbangala, but never sent them. Ngola Mbande remained in self-imposed exile in the Kindonga Islands. Nzinga returned to Luanda to convince Correia de Sousa to fulfill the terms of their agreement, without success. Soon after Nzinga returned, Ngola Mbande died. (The Portuguese claimed Nzinga murdered him; Angolan oral history claims he took poison in a moment of desperation.)

In 1624, shortly after Mbande's death, the Portuguese Crown replaced Correia de Sousa with a new governor, Fernão de Sousa. De Sousa arrived in Africa with clear instructions to concentrate on trade, not war. His first steps were to establish government markets for the cloth and slave trade at strategic locations in Portuguese-controlled Kongo and to improve relationships with African rulers who were willing to trade with the Portuguese.

Nzinga, serving as the regent of Ndongo, was eager to open negotiations with the new governor. She wrote to de Sousa regarding the treaty she had twice negotiated with the Portuguese on behalf of her dead brother. If the Portuguese withdrew from Ambaca, she would return to the mainland from the Kindonga Islands and reopen the slave market at Kisala, ordering her subjects to take slaves there.

At first Sousa seemed willing to honor the previously negotiated treaty. He soon changed his position as settlers at Ambaca complained that Nzinga encouraged their slaves to run away and enjoy freedom at home rather than remaining as Portuguese captives. De Sousa not only refused to return the free people who had been illegally seized by the settlers at Ambaca, but he demanded that Nzinga return the illegally captured slaves who had fled the Ambaca settlers.

While negotiating with de Sousa, Nzinga seized the throne of Ndongo. Ngola Mbande had left a minor son as his heir. He had carefully divided responsibility for the boy between an Imbangala ally, Kaza, who was given the boy to raise, and Nzinga, who was appointed regent. Sometime between March and September 1625, Nzinga convinced Kaza to turn the boy over to her, using a combination of lavish presents and an offer of marriage. Blinded by her beauty, the Imbangala leader gave her the boy, whom she immediately poisoned.

De Sousa used the boy's death as an excuse to declare war and set up a rival claimant to the throne, Hari a Kiluanji, as a puppet ruler of Ndongo. Factions of the Mbundu who did not accept Nzinga as a legitimate ruler joined forces with the Portuguese to remove her from the throne.

Nzinga and the Portuguese were almost constantly at war for thirty years. Between 1626 and 1655, the queen commanded her own forces against the Portuguese army, using guerrilla warfare tactics for the most part. In 1630, she moved her people to the east and conquered a new kingdom, Matamba, which she used as a base for attacking settlements under the rule of Ngola Hari and the Portuguese. In 1641, she formed an alliance with the Dutch that almost brought Portuguese rule in Angola to an end.

After the Dutch were defeated in 1648, Nzinga retreated to the highlands of Matamba and continued her guerrilla campaign against the Portuguese. She never recovered Ndongo, but Matamba slowly developed into a kingdom in its own right, welcoming runaway slaves and renegades from the Portuguese army.

In 1654, at age seventy-two, Nzinga gave up the battlefield in favor of diplomacy, using the Capuchin missionaries in her court as intermediaries in her peace negotiations with the Portuguese. When she died in 1663, the nation she had created still survived, ruled by her sister, Dona Barbara, and her descendants.

The modern state of Angola got its name as a result of cultural miscommunication. The Portuguese mistook the title of the ruler (*ngola*) of Ndongo for the name of his country. As a result, they called the kingdom Angola.

The Portuguese retained Angola as a colony until 1975.

WHILE THE SPANISH DUG FOR
precious metals in Latin America, other European
powers were beginning to find their own territories
in the New World—and other kinds of treasure.

The first Europeans to cultivate the resources
of North America were the Basque, English,
French, and Portuguese fishing fleets that competed for control of the fishing grounds off the
shores of Newfoundland, which were filled with
schools of North Atlantic cod.

English settlers arrived in Jamestown in 1607
looking for gold. They settled for tobacco. The
Jamestown settlers were followed by radical Protestants looking for religious freedom for themselves, if not for anyone else, in Massachusetts.

Other early American settlers included refugees from British debtors' prisons who made their
way to Georgia and freethinking Quakers who took
up residence in Pennsylvania. The English were not

the only ones to found colonies. In 1608, the French
founded Quebec, the capital of a colony of fur trappers and missionaries. The Dutch, rulers of the sea
in the first half of the seventeenth century, founded
New Amsterdam, now New York, in 1624 and
spread along the Hudson River Valley. Swedish,
Dutch, and German stockholders founded New
Sweden at the site of what is now Wilmington, Del-
aware, fourteen years later.

The riches of the New World had already begun
to change Europe; now European settlers were on the
verge of transforming the New World. Some fled
oppression. Some were sponsored by joint stock companies or venture capitalists who wanted a return on
their investment. Some were groups of single men
looking to wrest wealth from the wilderness. Others
were families looking to build homes. They all found
hard work, abundant resources, and what they incor-
rectly perceived as an almost empty wilderness.

The early settlers still thought of themselves as Englishmen, Frenchmen, Germans, and Dutch, but the seeds of the idea of America as a "land of the free" were already in place. It would be more than 150 years before they transformed themselves into Americans, boldly seeking independence from colonial powers. They created a new nation founded on principles forged in ancient Greece and nurtured in the Roman Republic.

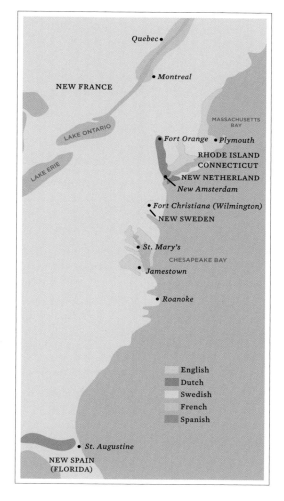

New World settlements 1600 to 1630s

AN ALLIANCE FOR SURVIVAL

The settlers of Plymouth Colony were unprepared for the realities of life in their new home. More than half of them died during the first harsh winter.

When the spring came, they needed help learning to farm the unfamiliar soil of the New World. The Wampanoag showed them how to use freshwater herring as fertilizer to farm a crop they had never seen before. The Wampanoag called it *weachimineash*. Maize became the staple diet for the generations that followed these pioneering American settlers; it remains so in America and around the world today.

After the colonists' first harvest, the survivors organized a celebratory feast. They invited the Native Americans who had helped them to join them. About ninety Wampanoag arrived to share in the celebration; when they saw the inadequacy of the settlers' supplies, they went hunting and returned with three deer they presented as gifts.

In 1863, at the height of the Civil War, President Abraham Lincoln declared Thanksgiving as a national holiday, to be held in November each year in memory of what became known as "the first Thanksgiving."

The Plymouth colonists gave the modern United States more than a national holiday. In their Mayflower Compact, composed on ship during their journey across the Atlantic, the citizens of Plymouth Colony put on paper the principle of voluntary self-government that would form the core of the American republic. Today 10 percent of all Americans can trace their ancestry back to the survivors who arrived on the *Mayflower*.

Chapter 8: SILVER

9

WILDERNESS

FROM THE MOMENT THE FIRST HOMINIDS MIGRATED OUT OF THE RIFT VALLEY, IN SEARCH OF NEW TERRITORY, TO THE MOST RECENT SPACE FLIGHT, HUMANS HAVE ALWAYS EXPLORED NEW FRONTIERS.

We push our boundaries in the hunt for new resources and new knowledge with which to exploit them.

Now it is the seventeenth century, and Europe has entered a period of expansion, exploration, and experimentation that will lay the foundation for the world to come. New frontiers lure mankind to the far reaches of continents and the precipice of modern science. It is a period of stark contrasts: witch burning and the rise of empiricism. The creation both of European states ruled by absolute monarchs and of the political philosophies that will lead to revolution. It is a time of extreme luxury for a few extreme poverty for most. In many places, there is a new sense of possibility in the air.

Tempted by the promise of riches, Spanish, Portuguese, British, Dutch, and French colonists are claiming vast territories in the New World. The wealth of the Americas feeds the royal treasuries of Europe. It also offers unprecedented opportunities to anyone with the courage, imagination, and wherewithal to cross the ocean and settle in an untamed wilderness. With talent and luck, a man can own land, escape the feudal hierarchies of Europe, and create wealth. Russia, too, has begun to expand, across Siberia, through north Asia, and ultimately, drawn by its abundance of natural resources, into the New World.

By the early seventeenth century, fur-bearing mammals in western Europe had become endangered species. The search for new sources of luxury furs drove European expansion into the wildernesses of Siberia and North America.

S IBERIA. 1638. SEMYON DEZHNEV LEADS A SMALL party through the dense pine trees of the Siberian wilderness. Snow crunches under their feet and swirls through the air. It has been a successful trip. Now they are on their way back to the outpost at Yakutsk, carrying the "sable treasury" of furs taken in tribute from the native peoples of the Yana valley region. It's a good haul: 340 prized sable pelts and two of the even more prized black fox skins.

An illiterate Russian peasant, Dezhnev left his family behind to hunt for fur—both for himself and on behalf of the tsar. His primary target is an elusive animal called the sable. This valuable creature is small and weasel-like with luxurious, dark-brown fur. It's the fur of choice for Russian aristocrats and monarchs. Dezhnev is carrying hundreds of pelts belonging to the tsar. Just three sable pelts could buy him fifty acres of land with a good cabin, five horses, ten head of cattle, and twenty sheep. Six would allow him to live in comfort for the rest of his life.

Dezhnev and his three companions are focused totally on the hunt, but they are not alone. This portion of Siberia is the home of the Tungus, a seminomadic tribe. They are dressed entirely in deerskin, from warm boots to close-fitting caps made from the head skin of reindeer, with the animal's ears still in place. Their coats are decorated with goat fur and glass beads. Their leggings and boots are embroidered with reindeer hair. The Tungus hunt with razor-sharp arrows and spears made from animal bone.

The Tungus move quietly through the forest, stalking Dezhnev's hunting party. They have the numeric advantage: more than forty Tungus hunters against Dezhnev's small band.

Suddenly, they attack with a volley of arrows. Dezhnev and his comrades raise their muskets and fire. A few Tungus fall, but the rest continue to shoot arrows at the Russians, able to aim and fire several bone-tipped arrows in the time it takes to reload a musket. Dezhnev is hit in the knee by an arrow. He drags himself behind a rock, reloads, and fires again. More Tungus fall—a few are dead and even more are wounded. The rest flee.

And so ends another day in the wilds.

Chapter 9: WILDERNESS

RUSSIA COLONIZED SIBERIA for one reason: sable, the finest fur in the world.

The influx of gold and silver from the New World and the increase of trade with Asia created a period of prosperity in Europe. More people could indulge in luxuries: pepper, tea, tulips—and fur. Fur became a matter of fashion rather than survival. Once possessed only by aristocrats and the very wealthy, now furs were in the reach of wealthy merchants and even the new and growing middle classes. For a century and a half, the wealthy, aristocratic, and powerful wore fur-lined coats, fur collars, fur capes, fur muffs, and most important of all, beaver hats. No gentleman would appear in public without one. The style of his hat indicated his social status.

The quest for fur linked the planet in new ways, leading Europeans to explore regions known previously only to their nomadic inhabitants. As fur became increasingly rare in Western Europe and Russia, the hunt for "soft gold" led Europeans to explore and conquer the Siberian tundra and the virgin forests of America, taking the first steps toward creating what would become two world superpowers: the United States and Russia.

Sable not only drove Russians to conquer Siberia, it paid the cost of conquest. Like their counterparts in the forests of North America, Russian fur trappers were drawn to the Siberian frontier by a spirit of adventure as well as the prospect of personal gain. Cossacks in the service of the Russian tsar searched for new lands and collected tribute in the form of furs from the native peoples of Siberia. Traders, trappers, and hunters arrived in Siberia, drawn by a "fur fever" comparable to the 1849 California gold rush. By the very nature of their work, they became explorers and conquerors. Some worked on their own. Others were employed by the state or by wealthy merchant agents. The line between the two groups was blurry. Many Cossacks amassed fortunes trading and trapping for themselves, often illegally. Traders and hunters frequently worked for the state at the request of local commanders. Independent fur traders and state employees were equally eager to trap sable. Sables with their feet still intact and untorn across

Siberia's greatest resource was its abundant furs, especially the valuable sable pelts. The best quality sable pelts were not ripped and kept tails, bellies, and paws intact. Here, Canadian furs are shown fully intact.

the midsection sold for ten to twenty rubles; black fox pelts were worth one hundred to three hundred rubles. A single hunting season could make a poor man rich.

Russians did not find an empty wilderness when they first arrived in Siberia in the 1580s. Nomadic reindeer-herding peoples—the Tungus (known today as the Evens), the Yakuts, the Chukchi, and others—lived in the coniferous forests of the Siberia *tiagra*. Seminomadic fishing peoples lived along the rivers and the Pacific shore. Relatives of those who first crossed the Bering Strait into the Americas during the Ice Age, they lived by hunting elk, deer, mountain sheep, and wild reindeer, and fishing in the many Siberian rivers in the summers. Their herds of reindeer were too valuable to slaughter for hides and meat; instead the Tungus and other tribes trained them as saddle and pack animals for long-distance hunting.

Conflict was inevitable. Russians traders were in Siberia to exploit the fur wealth of the hunting and grazing lands of the nomadic tribes. Where Russians saw fur-bearing animals only as a commodity, Siberian nomads combined the necessity of hunting with reverence for the animals they hunted. As Russians exhausted a hunting ground, fur hunters like Dezhnev pushed into new territories, traveling down the rivers in flat-bottomed boats and overland in sledges and horse-drawn carts. It was ultimately easier for Russians, armed with guns, to impose their rule on the indigenous population and force them to pay tribute in furs. With no central political organization and armed only with arrows and spears, the Siberian tribes were no match for Russian Cossacks with guns. Within eighty years, Russians had gained control of Siberia, a region twenty times larger than the state of Texas. Like the Spanish colonies of New Spain and Peru, Siberia was less a place for settlers than a source of material wealth.

THE LITTLE ICE AGE

The Russian and North American fur trades were aided by the fact that between 1500 and 1850 CE, the earth got colder—so cold that glaciers overtook communities in the Alps, and Manhattan Harbor froze over in winter.

We don't know for sure what caused what's known as the Little Ice Age. It has been attributed to changes in the earth's orbital cycles, weakened activity on the sun, and an increase in carbon dioxide due to the return of farmland to forest after the Black Death. Recently, an international team of scientists suggested that the Little Ice Age was the result of a chain of events kicked off by four massive eruptions of tropical volcanoes over a fifty-year period around 1300 CE. The volcanoes sent up enough particles into the atmosphere to blot out sunlight and make summers cooler. According to computer simulations, these years of volcano-cooled summers caused sea ice to expand and send huge glaciers down the relatively temperate Greenland coast. When the sea ice reached the North Atlantic, it melted, disrupting ocean currents. Cooler water made its way back to the Arctic, creating a self-sustaining climate feedback system and proving once again how fragile the earth's climate is. It also provided a stage on which humans could test their ability to adapt, survive, and in some cases, thrive.

Chapter 9: WILDERNESS

FUR

Reptiles have protective scales. Birds have feathers. Most mammals have fur. We humans, on the other hand, are virtually naked from the day we're born until the day we die. Even the hairiest human is bare compared to other mammals. It's not surprising that for thousands of years people in northern climates relied on animal fur to keep them warm.

With up to a million hairs per square inch, fur is the world's best natural insulator: twice as effective as wool and twelve times more effective than human skin. It also resists wind and repels water.

Most fur is made up of two very different layers of hair. The outer coat is made up of long, straight guard hairs. Underneath the guard hairs, most mammals have a dense layer of soft, fine underfur. There are a dozen underfur hairs for every guard hair. The underfur traps air in pockets that help insulate the animal's body against both heat and cold.

The Russians' conquest of Siberia was a world-changing event that almost no one noticed. With the final capture of the "sleeping land," Russia quadrupled in size. The fur trade paid for Peter the Great's transformation of Russia from a backwoods state with one foot in Asia to a great European power. Fur bought arms from Europe for the emperor's Western-style army, funded his wars against Sweden and the Ottoman Empire, and built his new capital of St. Petersburg.

As for Semyon Dezhnev, he earned a place in history as more than just another Russian fur trapper. Dezhnev seems to have shared the restlessness that drove many others to leave their homes in search of adventure and fortune in the seventeenth century. He pressed farther and farther east during his years in Siberia. In 1648, he led an expedition that sailed around the eastern tip of Asia from the point where the Kolymar River empties into the Arctic Ocean all the way to the Pacific, sailing through the Bering Strait eighty years before Russian explorer Vitus Bering made the same voyage and gave the strait its name.

HALFWAY ACROSS THE WORLD from Siberia, western Europeans hunted and traded for furs in the woods of northeastern America. Where the fur trade in Russia was largely driven by the desire for luxury furs, the North American fur trade was based on the insatiable demands of the felting and hat-making industries and the fashion for beaver hats. By the middle of the eighteenth century, the fur trade was the biggest business in North America.

English fishermen traded for furs in Newfoundland as a sideline to cod fishing on the Great Banks from the time of John Cabot at the end of the fifteenth century. For more than a decade after landing in 1620, the Pilgrims depended on beaver

THE BIRCH BARK CANOE

The wilderness of the Great Lakes region was home to many waterways. It was also the perfect habitat for white birch, white cedar, and spruce trees. The Native Americans of the region combined all three to create the ingenious vehicle that became the semi-tractor and trailer of the fur trade: the birch bark canoe.

Canoe makers created a frame of white cedar branches and covered it with the outer bark of the birch tree, lashed together with spruce roots. They caulked the seams between the panels of bark with spruce resin to make them watertight. The result was a tough, lightweight watercraft that could carry three thousand to six thousand pounds of men and gear.

French fur traders knew a good thing when they saw one. They quickly copied Native American construction techniques, making canoes up to thirty-six feet long.

Ojibwa Indians making birch bark canoe.

pelts for the income to buy supplies and pay off their debt to the joint stock company that paid for their passage. The first Dutch settlements were fur trading posts, established by the New Netherlands Company at New Amsterdam (modern Manhattan) and Fort Nassau, near modern Albany, in 1614. But it was the French who dominated the early years of the fur trade in North America.

The French first traded for furs on the St. Lawrence River in the 1530s. The river and its hinterlands became the heart of a fur-trading empire. Unlike the British colonies on the Atlantic coast, the vast French territories of New France (modern Canada) and the Louisiana Territory were thinly settled. No more than three thousand settlers lived there by the middle of the seventeenth century. (The British colonies had a combined population of seventy thousand at the same time.) Most French colonists were hunters, trappers, or missionaries.

Chapter 9: WILDERNESS

"Fur Traders Descending the Missouri," detail of oil on canvas by George Caleb Bingham, 1845

The French traders known as "wood runners" (*couriers de bois*) were the lifeblood of the North American fur trade. Most of the wood runners were born in New France. They spent their summers clearing and farming small homesteads along the St. Lawrence. In the fall, they traveled inland and spent the winter trapping and trading. When the ice on the rivers broke in the spring, they took their furs to Quebec to sell. Born in the colonies, often illiterate, and generally of low social rank, they had three counts against them with the French colonial officials who administered the fur trade from Montreal. Unable to get official trading licenses, they ignored the rules and sought their fortune in the forests. Their unlicensed, illegal trade flourished because no one else had the wilderness or Indian language skills to succeed at supplying furs.

As in Siberia, the trader drove trappers into new territories. From the beginning, French governors of New France supported exploration. The first expeditioners traveled through the Great Lakes and down the Mississippi River. By the beginning of the eighteenth century, French expeditions were traveling west from Lake Superior, hoping to find a river route to the Pacific.

The fur trade continued to drive North American exploration and expansion long after the British seized Canada from the French in 1763. The North American hunters who pushed west in search of beaver pelts and buffalo robes were precursors to Lewis and Clark, exploring the plains drained by the Missouri, Yellowstone, and Platte Rivers and the passes through the Rocky Mountains. Russian hunters crossed the Bering Strait in search of sea otter and seal pelts, founding trading bases in the Aleutian Islands, Alaska, and as far south along the Pacific coast as the Gulf of California. By 1800, fur traders had spread from east and west to embrace all of North America north of the Rio Grande, opening the continent for further expansion of a new nation.

Over time, agricultural settlement and mining displaced the fur trade in the West. By 1890, it was in decline, thanks to a combination of increased settlement and the virtual extermination of the fur-bearing animal population, particularly beaver and buffalo.

The fur trade destroyed more than animal populations. In the United States and Canada, Europeans expanding westward pushed Native America peoples off their lands and into reservations. A similar process occurred when Russians introduced mining, logging, and prisons into Siberia, taking over land that the nomadic tribes used for hunting and grazing. In the 1930s, the Soviets moved the remaining nomadic clans and their reindeer herds into sedentary communities on collectivized farms. After thousands of years, the life of nomadic hunter-gatherers had come to an end.

IN 1602, A HUNDRED YEARS after the Spanish first settled in the New World, Bartholomew Gosnold, a sea captain from Suffolk, England, began exploring New England. His ship, the *Concord,* carried eight sailors and twenty-four passengers, twelve of whom intended to establish a trading post and stay. Gosnold and his crew sailed down the rocky coast of what is now Maine and fished in a cape they named Cape Cod because they caught so many of the fish that they didn't have room to keep them. Ultimately, they decided they did not have enough supplies to last the winter at a new settlement. They had hoped for gold; instead they sailed back to England with a profitable cargo of sassafras bark.

Gosnold returned to America in 1606 as the second in command on one of the ships bringing settlers to Jamestown, Virginia. They hoped to find treasure in North America that would equal that in the Spanish colonies of New Spain and Peru. Instead they found a continent bursting with natural resources: virgin timber, rich furs, plentiful game, lush schools of cod, and an astonishing diversity of plant life.

Thousands of Europeans followed the Jamestown settlers over the course of the next hundred years: fortune hunters, religious refugees, indentured servants, and convicts. They cleared land, built houses, founded towns, created industries.

By the middle of the eighteenth century, England's North American colonies were booming. With a population of two million, the colonies were bursting at the seams. Settlers from Pennsylvania and Virginia began moving west across the Appalachians into territory claimed by the French and their Indian allies: rich lands along the Ohio and Mississippi Rivers and northward along the St. Lawrence River into Canada. To block British expansion, the French built a series of forts along the frontier, triggering a war that spiraled out of North America and into Europe.

When the French and Indian War ended in 1763, the British were the dominant power in North America.

THE FUR TRADE TODAY

Today's fur trade is controversial, though it is still a large and profitable international business. Supporters argue that the fur business is "green": producing natural products that are more effective and sustainable than their petroleum-based substitutes. Animal rights activists argue that wearing fur is cruel, and stage high-profile, often controversial campaigns against those who wear it.

Many furs are expensive luxury goods: a sable coat retails for $150,000 and is just as much a status symbol today as it was in seventeenth-century Russia. In the extreme cold of the far north, however, fur is still seen as a practical item—the best way to protect against the bitter weather. Parkas are often trimmed with wolverine fur because it protects the face from the wind and doesn't become encrusted with ice as water condenses from the breath of the person wearing it.

Chapter 9: WILDERNESS

MUSKETS

In both Siberia and North America, Europeans armed with muskets had an advantage over native peoples armed with arrows and spears.

When the first muskets appeared in the late fifteenth century, it wasn't clear that they were an improvement over the bow. They were less accurate, had a shorter range, and were useless on horseback. A skilled archer could fire six or more arrows in the time it took a musketeer to make one shot. The psychological effect of the noise and the flash was often a greater weapon than the shot itself. Nonetheless, early muskets had two clear advantages over bows. A musket ball could penetrate thick armor, and muskets were easy to learn to use.

Most early muskets were matchlocks, fired using a two- to three-foot-long piece of rope, called the "match," that had been treated with a saltpeter solution so it would burn slowly and steadily. The match was lit at both ends so it would not go out accidentally; musketeers had to be careful to keep it away from their gunpowder. When a matchlock man pulled the trigger, it lowered the match and ignited gunpowder in a priming pan outside the barrel. A spark from the priming powder ignited gunpowder inside the barrel, which propelled the bullet.

The flintlock, adopted in the late 1600s, eliminated the burning "match." Pulling the trigger created a spark by striking flint against steel. The spark ignited the priming powder, which in turn ignited the main charge. Because it was easier to use, a hunter or soldier could fire it more quickly. Accuracy remained a problem. Even the most skilled shooter could not count on hitting a target more than a hundred yards away.

More improvements followed, making the musket safer to use, more reliable in wet or windy weather, and easier to load. By the end of the eighteenth century, when American revolutionaries faced the British army at Lexington and Concord, a marksman working alone could fire his musket five times a minute: the same rate at which a skilled archer could shoot his bow.

MATCHLOCK MECHANISM

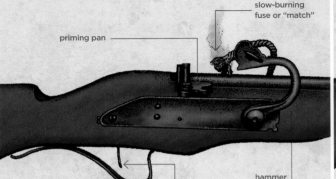

slow-burning fuse or "match"

priming pan

trigger

hammer

FLINTLOCK MECHANISM

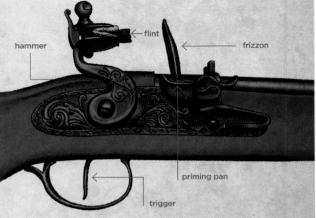

hammer

flint

frizzon

priming pan

trigger

Captain Gosnold trades with the Indians, Virginia, 1634

PEOPLE HAVE ALWAYS TRIED to make sense of the world around them. Science, religion, and magical thinking all begin from the same questions. How did the world begin? What causes rain, thunder, and the sun to rise? What makes crops grow? What causes the plague, the measles, and the common cold? What can we do to make crops grow better and to heal the sick? Sometimes the answers have led us to make sacrifices or offer prayers to the gods—or to a single God. Sometimes they have led us to blame malevolent forces: demons or witches and malicious spirits. At other times, we have sought answers in physical experiments designed to show us how the world works in mechanical terms.

In seventeenth-century Europe, and its American colonies, people did all those things. The 1600s were a time of intellectual and religious ferment. A time marked by witch trials, the scientific revolution, and acrimonious debates between Protestants and Roman Catholics about sacraments, ritual, miracles, and the power of the saints. The vast majority of people, educated and uneducated alike, believed that witches, demons, angels, fairies, and ghosts were real creatures that affected our everyday lives. The Old World view, a mixture of ideas from Ptolemy, Aristotle, and the Bible, tottered and cracked under the barrage of information about new plants, animals, and people, and belief systems that flowed back to Europe from the New World and Asia.

Between 1570 and 1680, roughly 110,000 people were tried for witchcraft in Europe and from 40,000 to 60,000 were executed. Most of the accused were women. Black magic, *maleficum*, was a capital crime, clearly defined by law.

SALEM WITCH TRIALS

MARCH 21, 1692. SALEM, MASSACHUSETTS. The small wooden meetinghouse is packed. In the past, the meetinghouse was used for town meetings and the occasional session of the county court. For the last few months, it has been the scene of dramatic accusations. Salem is in the grip of a witch hunt driven by terror. Its citizens live in fear of God. They fear the devil even more.

A group of young girls take their seats in the front row. Looking around the room, they giggle and whisper to one another. There is a sly, self-satisfied look in their eyes. They have power, and they know it.

Judge John Hathorne takes his seat at the front. He has already sent three people to the gallows for witchcraft.

The room goes silent as the jailers bring in Martha Corey. Her family, friends, and neighbors have branded her a witch. Her primary accusers are three teenage girls: seventeen-year-old Mercy Lewis, eleven-year-old Abigail Williams, and eleven-year-old Ann Putnam. The girls have suffered violent fits. They have been stricken mute or deaf. Strange marks have appeared on their bodies. When the local doctor is unable to cure their symptoms, he diagnoses them as suffering from witchcraft.

Sixty-five-year-old Martha Corey seems more defiant than afraid. Three women have already been accused and found guilty: an African slave, a beggar, and a quarrelsome old woman who had not attended church in over a year. Martha believes her case is different. The devil would have needed little effort to make witches of such idle slothful persons as those already executed. Martha is a well-respected member of the community, the wife of a prosperous farmer, and an avid member of the Salem Village church.

Mistress Corey seldom hesitates to voice her opinion. She does not hesitate now. "We must not believe all that these distracted girls say," she begins, then stops and bites her lip.

The girls scream that they are being bitten.

Hathorne demands, "Why do you hurt these persons?"

Martha grasps her hand. The girls cry out that she is pinching them.

For the first time Martha seems to understand how dire her situation is. Her voice cracks as she defends herself. "I never had to do with witchcraft since I was born. I am an innocent person."

The girls grow increasingly agitated. They writhe and screech over her testimony.

Martha's answers become more confused, but she insists on her innocence. "I am a gospel woman."

Mercy Lewis shrieks and points an accusing finger, "You are a gospel witch!"

In those days, many adverse events lacked an obvious cause. People suddenly sickened and died. Crops failed, and animals stopped giving milk. It was natural to believe that there was a *super*natural cause for these otherwise inexplicable events. Witch hunts began with suspicions, rumors, and fear, then moved into accusations that the suspected witch had consorted with the devil and used witchcraft to harm her neighbors' health, property, children, or livestock. In a culture that believed in witches as firmly as modern society believes in germs, the successful identification and prosecution of a witch in a village could trigger a hysterical search for others.

The Pilgrims sought religious freedom and independence from tyranny in the New World, but brought with them Old World superstitions and scapegoating

In the New World, Pilgrims sought religious freedom and independence from tyranny, but brought with them Old World superstitions and scapegoating.

In January 1692, when the great witch hunts in Europe were almost at an end, the town of Salem was shaken by accusations of witchcraft. Two young girls began to suffer from fits that they and their elders attributed to witchcraft. In the following months, more and more accusers came forward, claiming to have been tortured by the apparitions of witches or to have seen ghosts that accused witches of killing them. Many of the accused were cantankerous older women with dubious reputations who fit the seventeenth-century stereotype of the witch. Others were close relatives of those who had already been charged.

Between February 29, 1692, and late May 1693, when the last suspects were tried, the courts took legal action against at least 144 people, including a four-year-old girl. Fourteen women and five men were hanged, including Martha Corey; a sixth man was pressed to death with heavy stones for refusing to submit to a witchcraft trial.

Some of the most educated colonists were troubled by the proceedings. Minister and scientist Cotton Mather wrote to the court, begging that testimony about dreams and visions not be accepted as evidence. Several months later, as the convictions continued, Increase Mather, then president of Harvard, joined his son in condemning the use of "spectral evidence" in the trials, saying, "It were better that ten suspected witches should escape than one innocent person be condemned." In response, Governor William Phips convened a new court that disallowed spectral evidence and eventually pardoned all those in jail as a result of the trails.

Within five years of the end of the trials, one judge and twelve jurors formally apologized for their roles in the events. Within two decades, the Massachusetts legislature apologized for what were by then viewed as unjust proceedings and voted to compensate the survivors of the trials and the descendants of those who had been executed.

Witch hunts were brutal and dramatic, but they were not the only attempt to control how people behaved and what they thought. Galileo Galilei was put on trial twice, in 1615 and in 1632—not simply for his assertion that the earth moved around the sun, but because he rejected the Catholic Church's literal interpretation of the Christian Bible.

Galileo remained under house arrest from 1633 until his death in 1642, but religious and political

The intention of the Holy Spirit is to teach us how one goes to heaven and not how heaven goes.
—Galileo Galilei (right)

I do not know what I may appear to the world, but to myself I seem to have been only a boy, playing on the seashore . . . diverting myself now and then finding a smoother pebble or prettier shell than ordinary, while the great ocean of truth lay all undiscovered before me.
—Sir Isaac Newton (left)

Galileo explaining his new research at the University of Padua, Italy, painted 1873

authorities were not able to confine mankind's curiosity. Astronomers worked out the motions of the planets and stars in the sky with mathematical precision. Galileo, Kepler, Newton, and others created a new science of mechanics that applied the laws of mathematics to motion. Physicians explored the structure of the human body. Naturalists created new systems for classifying plants and animals that did not fit into existing categories. The development of scientific instruments allowed students to see new worlds in a drop of water and scan the skies with a clarity not possible with the naked eye. Most important, natural philosophers (the name used by scientists at the time) began to perform experiments in a way that could be repeated and verified by others, laying the foundation for modern scientists.

The division between magic, religion, and science was never clear. Sir Isaac Newton, the father of modern physics and possibly the best-known figure of the scientific revolution, spent as much time on alchemy and interpreting biblical prophecies as he did on the scientific theorems for which he is famous. William Harvey, who discovered how blood circulates in the body, carefully dissected one witch's toad familiar, looking for the source of its supernatural power. Johannes Kepler, the great German astronomer, spent six years defending his mother against witchcraft charges after her arrest. Witch hunters and demonologists were for the most part scholars and rationalists. The investigation of witchcraft, magic, and miracles was as much a part of the scientific revolution as was the study of gravity and electricity. The traditional respect for the Bible and ancient texts as absolute authorities was replaced by a new belief in the importance of direct observation and a concern with what constituted reliable evidence. Together, scientists and witch-hunters developed the scientific method and laid the foundation for modern science.

examples of various glass work

THE ABILITY TO MAKE MORE AND more sophisticated tools had been a critical element in our story from the beginning. By transforming one of Earth's most common elements, silicon, into glass, humans unlocked invisible worlds for the first time.

Made by melting silica, a chemical compound of the element silicon, glass is a unique material, with molecules that are arranged randomly, like a liquid, but are locked in a rigid position, like a solid. Long before humans learned to make glass, we created razor-sharp blades from obsidian, a natural glass created when the intense heat of volcanoes melts quartz deep in the earth. Ancient glassmakers added sodium carbonate to lower the melting temperature of sand and calcium oxide, also called lime, to prevent the glass from dissolving in water.

For centuries, artisans made luxury products from glass: beads in ancient Mesopotamia, glass bottles in Egypt, blown glass in Rome, stained glass windows in the Middle Ages, mirrors in the seventeenth century.

Glass was complicated enough. Lenses were even harder.

Tenth-century Arab mathematician Alhazen studied how the refraction of light through water and glass causes images to be magnified. When returning Crusaders brought Alhazen's work to Europe three centuries later, European monks recognized the practical value of his studies. They polished pieces of rock crystal into hemispheres to make "reading stones" that they used to magnify the written word. Italian glassmakers reproduced the expensive reading stones in glass. Near the end of the fourteenth century, someone in Italy applied Islamic optical theory to glassmaking and created the first eyeglasses.

It took another two hundred years before lenses were used for telescopes and microscopes. One story says that the first telescope was invented by accident by two Dutch children who were playing with the lenses in a shop that sold eyeglasses. They put two different-shaped lenses together and looked through them: suddenly the church weather vane was huge! The store owner, Hans Lippershey, looked for himself and discovered the children were right.

Whether the children discovered the effect or Lippershey stumbled across it himself, the shopkeeper quickly realized the invention's potential. At first he set up the lenses in his shop to attract customers. Later he enclosed the lenses in a tube, creating what he called a "look glass." In 1608, he petitioned the Dutch government for a patent, which gave him exclusive rights to sell the new instrument for thirty years. International patent law was nonexistent. Word of the new invention spread across Europe: Galileo made one for himself shortly after Lippershey filed his patent application.

Many denounced the "look glass" as a tool of the devil. Governments and merchants saw practical uses for war and navigation. Scientists saw greater possibilities in the new tool. Galileo, in particular, turned his telescope to the sky, becoming the first man to see that the Milky Way was made up of clusters of stars, that the moon had mountains and craters, and that Jupiter had its own moons. Galileo also used his telescope as a microscope, reportedly telling a visitor, "I have seen flies which look as big as lambs, and have learned that they are covered with hair and have very pointed nails."

Fifty years later, Italian physician Marcello Malpighi turned his microscope to things that were smaller yet. Trying to understand how blood flowed through the body, he used what he called his "flea glass" to examine the exposed lungs of a living frog and became the first man to see blood pulsing through the small capillaries that connect the arteries and the veins.

Using the new tool of the telescope, Galileo looked up into the infinite expanse of space. Malpighi used the telescope's younger brother, the microscope, to look down at the infinitesimally small. Suddenly the universe was a bigger place than we had ever imagined.

SILICON

The chemical element silicon makes up about one-fourth of the earth's crust, more than any other element except oxygen. Silicon is part of almost every form of rock. We use its chemical compound, silica, to make both concrete and glass, materials that seem completely different. The "silicon chips" at the heart of every computer are pure silicon crystals.

REFRACTING AND REFLECTING

Galileo's telescope was a *refracting telescope*. In refracting telescopes, light passes through two lenses—one convex and one concave. The problem with refracting telescopes is that all the colors of light are bent at slightly different angles, creating fuzzy images. Sir Isaac Newton solved the problem by introducing curved mirrors to telescopes, which focused the light. Telescopes with mirrors are called *reflecting telescopes*.

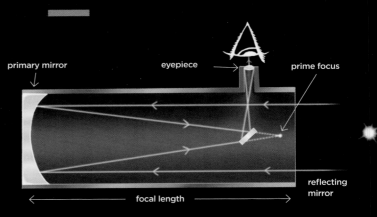

primary mirror   eyepiece   prime focus

focal length

reflecting mirror

REFLECTING TELESCOPE

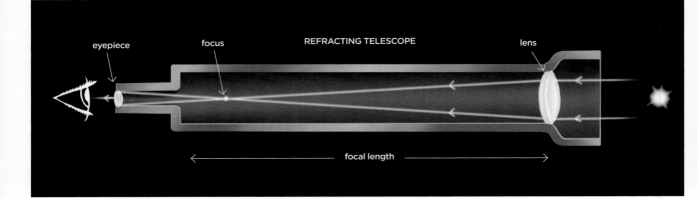

eyepiece   focus   REFRACTING TELESCOPE   lens

focal length

AT THE END OF THE SEVENTEENTH century, shipping was the lifeblood of the new global economy, linking Europe to the Americas, Africa, and Asia in a complicated pattern of export, import, and reexport. Great Britain stood at the heart of it all, with an annual overseas trade worth $800 million in today's money. British merchants brought spices and tea from India, timber and furs from New England, and sugar and tobacco from the Caribbean to the wharfs of London. They carried cloth and metalware to Africa, manufactured goods and beer to send to the British colonists in the Americas, and transported silver to India and China. What had once been luxuries, available only to the rich, were now becoming affordable to the new middle class. Life was becoming a little easier.

Galileo used the new tools of the scientific method to change our understanding of the universe. Other scientists addressed more practical issues, making it possible for merchants to carry goods—and ideas—over longer distances. Since the days of Prince Henry the Navigator, European mariners had relied on maps of the stars for navigation, but those were full of errors and hopelessly incomplete. Sailors and ships were regularly lost at sea. Mistakes cost money and lives. A few days' delay on a ship's arrival could slash a voyage's profit. A shipwreck could bankrupt a man.

One man, John Flamsteed, argued that the solution was obvious: more accurate star charts would allow navigators to determine a ship's longitude at sea.

Impressed by Flamsteed's arguments, King Charles II founded the Royal Observatory at Greenwich in 1675 and named Flamsteed the first Astronomer Royal. In the official warrant of appointment, the king charged the twenty-nine-year-old Flamsteed with the task of "rectifying the tables of the motions of the heavens, and the places of the fixed stars, so as to find the so-much-desired longitude of places for perfecting the art of navigation."

Given a building, a small house, a large title, and an insufficient income, Flamsteed set to work. His first problem was the inadequate instruments available for observation. Flamsteed had already learned to grind lenses and calibrate telescopes for his own use. He now turned his attention to creating accurate instruments for the new observatory. After several false starts, in the fall of 1689 Flamsteed unveiled the device that would allow him to create an accurate map of the stars: the seventeenth-century equivalent of the Hubble Space Telescope. He called it the "mural arc": a finely calibrated instrument with a 140-degree arc that spanned the sky from the horizon to the polestar, and a seven-foot telescopic sight with convex lenses that bent the light and magnified the appearance of the stars. Flamsteed's device was fifteen times more accurate than those of his predecessors and forty times more accurate than the naked eye. It was so powerful that it could measure the diameter of a coin the size of a quarter from more than a mile away.

For the next forty years, Flamsteed quarreled viciously with his scientific contemporaries and plotted the positions of the stars with unprecedented accuracy, taking 28,000 measurements and mapping 2,935 stars. He then created a star catalog that tripled the number of known stars.

Today, sailors still use nautical charts based on Flamsteed's work. But Flamsteed did more than transform navigation; he set new standards for accuracy that shaped the course of astronomy. His star catalog was the standard reference for astronomers for decades; stars are still known by their "Flamsteed numbers." NASA scientists used tools and techniques pioneered by Flamsteed to build the computer programs that guided the first spaceships to the moon.

A ship pilot calculates his position using a star chart.

PHILADELPHIA, PENNSYLVANIA. 1750. Irritated by the widespread view that an angry God caused such wholly *natural* phenomena as thunder and lightning, citizen-scientist Benjamin Franklin published a proposal for an experiment to prove once and for all that lightning had nothing to do with God. Franklin had been experimenting with electricity for several years now and was convinced that lightning, one of nature's most mysterious and deadly forces, was just a flash of electricity discharged from the clouds. He had every intention of proving it as soon as he had the opportunity.

Unfortunately, as a self-made businessman, statesman, inventor, author, and newspaper publisher, Franklin was a very busy man. He just couldn't seem to find himself in the right place at the right time to conduct an experiment. . . .

STARS

Each night, stars, distant as they are, appear to rise and move in an arc across the sky above us as our planet spins on its axis. For thousands of years we have studied the stars and the planets, hoping that knowledge of the heavens will guide both our ships and our destiny. We have used the stars to navigate across seas and deserts. We have built monumental structures to track their movements through the skies, from Stonehenge to the giant astronomical instruments built in the eighteenth century by Maharaja Jai Singh of Jaipur. Ancient Chinese astronomers kept records of eclipses, novas, comets, and sunspots, which could be portents of a failure of the cosmic order. Arab astronomers created accurate star charts to allow Muslims to determine the direction of Mecca.

Today we know the stars are impossibly distant and unimaginably huge: infernos of hydrogen and helium, one hundred times bigger than the Earth. There are more than 200 billion stars in our galaxy alone. After the sun, the nearest star to Earth is more than 4.2 light-years away—24 trillion miles. The light from some of the most distant stars in our galaxy has taken more than 95,000 years to reach Earth.

STEALING GOD'S THUNDER

June 15, 1752. People *still* believe thunder and lightning are the acts of an angry God. Regrettably, Franklin *still* hasn't found the time to conduct an experiment proving them wrong. *Now* he's received a letter saying that a French man has beaten him to it by holding a forty-foot-tall iron rod in the path of a lightning strike.

"Tarnation!" he says, a deep frown creasing his forehead. "The fool is going to get himself killed."

"Father," says his son William, "a storm is approaching. Why don't we do our experiment anyway, right now? The sky is growing darker. And a strong wind has come up."

"All right, then, William," Franklin says, dropping the letter and pulling his rotund torso up quickly from the chair. "This just may be our chance."

Father and son quickly gather the materials they will need for the experiment: a silk kite with a metal wire attached to the top, a ball of twine, an iron key, and a ribbon. Then they hurry outside to the Franklin farm.

With thunder rumbling in the distance, Franklin and his son lay a piece of canvas on the ground and unpack their equipment. Working quickly, glancing alternately at the sky and then back at his work, Franklin attaches the key to the kite, ties an insulating silk ribbon to the kite string to protect his hand, and steps several yards away from his son.

Franklin's lightning rod

Chapter 9: WILDERNESS

With William holding the ball of twine at a distance, Franklin launches the kite into the air. The storm rumbles closer. Franklin scurries to where his son still stands beneath the ominous clouds.

"Come, quick! There's going to be quite a deluge," Franklin says, pulling William with him into the doorway of a cow shed. As they huddle close and wait, William looks down at his father's hand holding the kite string and key.

"Are you sure you won't be burned if the lightning comes down that string?" he asks, a worried look on his face.

"I am almost certain, son," Franklin answers, smiling to reassure William.

"But then, how will we know there's electricity in the sky?"

"If the storm clouds have an electrical charge, the kite string will draw it from the sky down to this key. And I think we'll know it—somehow."

Father and son raise their eyes to the sky again as the storm clouds open, dumping a heavy rain. The dirt beneath their feet quickly turns into a sea of mud.

William jumps involuntarily as a bolt of lightning streaks across the sky, followed by the loudest thunderclap yet. "Look!" he yells, pointing at a flash of light dangerously close to his father's kite.

Franklin arches his neck, straining to see through the deluge.

Just then, lightning meets the wire at the top of the kite. Two pairs of eyes follow the invisible trail of the electrical charge down the kite string.

Sensing a change in the string's temperature, Franklin touches his free hand to the key at its end. Instantly, electrical sparks arc across the back of his hand.

William gasps. Franklin lets out a hoot. "It is proven!" he says with a broad grin.

SCURVY

Navigation wasn't the only problem for long-distance voyages in the Age of Sail.

Scurvy was a bigger bane of the sea than pirates, storms, or shipwreck. More than two million sailors died from scurvy between Columbus's first voyage and the development of steamships in the nineteenth century. An oceangoing ship could lose half its crew or more to the disease known as the "gray killer"—and many did. With larger ships and longer voyages, the problem was getting worse.

Caused by a lack of vitamin C, scurvy attacks the body's connective tissues. Symptoms included aches and pains, exhaustion, dark blotches and bruises, pale skin, loose teeth, bleeding gums, and breath that smelled like rotting meat. Left untreated, it led to a slow, agonizing death.

Working at a hospital for British sailors, Scottish surgeon James Lind was able to observe thousands of cases of scurvy and the conditions aboard ship that caused it. In an early example of a clinical trial, he treated sailors with popular remedies, including vinegar, cider, seawater, and mercury paste. In 1753, he published a paper proving that drinking orange and lemon juice could cure scurvy. Citrus fruits, such as limes, became so common aboard British vessels that the sailors were referred to as "limeys." Without knowing it, Lind had put vitamin C to work to bind the body together like glue—providing the key to long-distance sea travel in the Age of Sail.

The existence of the chemical compounds known as *vitamins* and their role in good health wasn't discovered until 1912. Vitamin C was first identified in 1928.

Franklin was fascinated by unexplained natural phenomena: whirlwinds, waterspouts, storms, the Gulf Stream, and especially lightning and electricity. In his newspaper, the *Pennsylvania Gazette*, Franklin included reports of what he called the "mischief of thunder-gusts" and the devastation caused by lightning.

Electrical experiments were all the rage among educated Europeans in the 1740s. Introduced to electrical experiments at a friend's house in 1747, Franklin began a series of groundbreaking experiments that would lead to his revolutionary, and dangerous, kite experiment. His proof that thunder and lightning were simply a variation of the static electricity experiments performed as parlor tricks, rather than the wrath of God, was not just a major scientific breakthrough. It was as great a shock to devout Christians as Darwin's theory of

A galleon crew reaching for scurvy-fighting fruits

evolution would be one hundred years later, and was greeted with equal resistance.

Franklin's successful experiment was written up in 1767 as *History and Present Status of Electricity*. The author cited evidence that Franklin was insulated from the direct current and not in a conducting path, where he would have been in danger of electrocution as others had been when attempting the same feat.

Franklin himself wrote, "When rain has wet the kite twine so that it can conduct the electric fire freely, you will find it streams out plentifully from the key at the approach of your knuckle, and with this key a phial, or Leiden jar, may be charged . . . and therefore the sameness of the electrical matter with that of lightning completely demonstrated."

Not content with a theoretical finding, Franklin found a practical application for the discovery that lightning was static electricity on an enormous scale: the lightning rod. Lightning rods use the same principle that allowed electricity to flow through the wet string of the kite: a sharp iron pole attached to the top of the building draws lightning to it and then diverts it to the ground through an attached wire. With the design virtually unchanged, the 260-year-old invention still protects buildings all over the world.

EBENEZER MUDGETT WASN'T THE only colonist to grow rich on New England's abundant timber. The colonists used wood to build houses, boats, barrels, and carts; to fence in fields; and to burn as fuel. But it wasn't the colonists' need for wood that made men like Mudgett rich. All across New England, axmen, lumber merchants, and shipbuilders made their living by selling "green gold"—timber—to wood-starved England.

The white pines of New Hampshire and Maine were especially valuable because they grew large

LIGHTNING

——

Beautiful, dramatic and dangerous, lightning strikes the earth about one hundred times every second. It kills approximately two thousand people each year and ignites wildfires that destroy hundreds of acres of forest and grassland.

When lightning strikes, its electrical energy turns into heat—five times hotter than the surface of the sun. This intense heat makes the air alongside the lightning channel expand explosively and contract as it cools, creating the sound waves we call thunder.

Dangerous as it is, some scientists think lightning provided the sparks of energy that made life on Earth possible.

APRIL 13, 1772. SOUTH WEARE, NEW HAMPSHIRE.
It's a busy day in Ebenezer Mudgett's lumberyard. But then,
every day's a busy day in the lumberyard. Mudgett is a powerful timber magnate—one of the largest suppliers of timber to the British shipbuilding industry and a leader among the local mill owners.

County sheriff Benjamin Whiting rides into the lumberyard,
accompanied by his deputy, John Quigly. One by one, Mudgett's men
stop working and watch the sheriff dismount. There's a sense of menace in the way they hold their tools. The way they shift their weight.
They know why he's here. No one looks at the secluded corner of the
lumberyard where a pile of logs marked with a plain white arrow lies
hidden under a piece of canvas.

Whiting reads a warrant for Mudgett's arrest for stealing Crown property: white pine trees claimed for the Royal Navy. Mudgett argues, to no avail. The two officers arrest him and take him away.

Later that day, Whiting releases Mudgett on his own undertaking, agreeing that the mill owner can bring his bail in the morning.

As the news of his arrest spreads, supporters flock to his house. Some offer to help pay his bail, but Mudgett isn't worried about the bail. He wants revenge.

Shortly before dawn, Mudgett and his supporters meet outside the Pine Tree Inn, where Sheriff Whiting and his deputy have spent the night. The lumbermen's faces are blackened with soot and dirt, and they carry freshly cut canes of wood. Mudgett bangs on the door of Whiting's room, saying he has come with his bail. Before the angry Whiting can get dressed, the men burst into his room. The sheriff dives for his pistol, but he's too slow. The mob grabs him and lashes him with their canes: one stroke for every tree the mill owners have been fined for.

Mudgett and his men have taken the first step to separating the American colonies from the burdens of British law. Others will soon follow their lead.

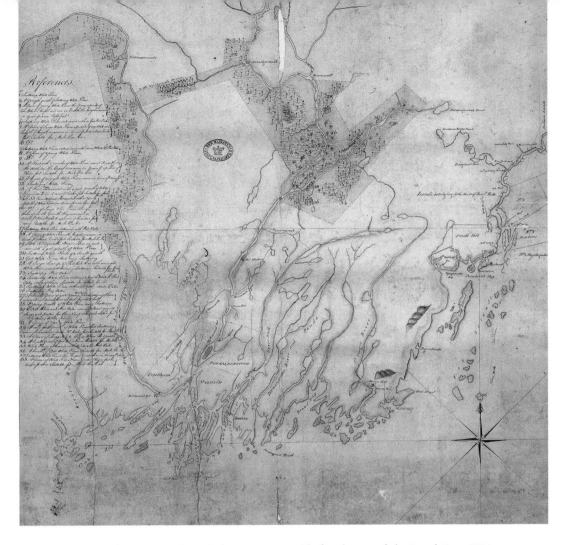

Detail of New Hampshire timber areas set aside for the use of the Royal Navy 1772.

enough that a single trunk could make a ship's mast, unlike European trees, which were smaller and had to be spliced together. Britain was anxious to control a resource that contributed to its naval supremacy. By the end of the seventeenth century, it was a crime to cut any white pine tree with a diameter of twenty-four inches or more without a royal license. Royal surveyors went through the forests, marking the trees as Crown property to be used for masts for the Royal Navy. Anyone who cut down marked trees would be fined five pounds per tree. The best wood in the American colonies was now off-limits to the men who lived there.

For many years, the white pine laws were an irritant. In the years after the end of the French and Indian War, they became one more point of conflict in the growing resentment between the British and the colonists. Anti-British activists began to cut down the trees and use them for floorboards. In response, the British began to crack down on illegal use of Crown timber. In 1771, the deputy surveyor in New Hampshire ordered a search of the sawmills. His men found hundreds of large white pine trees marked with the Crown arrow in six sawmills and began criminal proceedings against the mill owners. Some paid the fines. Sheriff Whiting was ordered to arrest Ebenezer Mudgett, the leader of the recalcitrant mill owners, triggering what became known as the Pine Tree Riot.

The first, often forgotten act of active rebellion against Great Britain's authority over the North American colonies, the Pine Tree Riot was the Boston Tea Party of the forests. Twenty months later, rebels in Boston would lash out against one of the hated new laws and destroy one million dollars' worth of British tea, moving one step closer to a revolution that would inspire the spread of democracy throughout the world.

Throughout history, humans have fought one another ferociously for the rights to consume and control the world's limited natural resources: furs, salt, gold, fishing grounds, grazing fields, and oil fields. Many believe the next large-scale conflicts may be fought over basic human necessities, such as drinkable water and farmable soil. In the meantime, mankind races to synthesize that which we can no longer find in the wild. In addition to creating energy from the wind, the sun, and the warmth of the earth, scientists are experimenting with projects as large as skyscraper farming and as small as providing sustainable access to clean water in African villages. If we can't hunt it, fish it, unearth it, or grow it, we will *make* it.

Or die fighting for what remains.

In both the Pine Tree Riot and the Boston Tea Party, American colonists fought against what they perceived to be oppressive laws.

10

REVOLUTION

THE SEVENTEENTH CENTURY HAS COME AND GONE, AND THE EIGH-
TEENTH CENTURY IS IN FULL SWING. THE 1700S HAVE ALREADY
BROUGHT UNFORESEEN CHANGE: MANKIND HAS UNLEASHED TWO
GREAT REVOLUTIONS THAT WILL TRANSFORM THE WORLD.

In North America, British colonists have risen up against tyranny, creating a powerful vision of liberty and democracy. In Britain, a handful of inspired inventors are using machines and newly harnessed sources of power to enable a few to do the work previously done by many.

Neither revolution is perfect. The American Revolution will be incomplete. Its creators will offer freedom to some, but not to all. In less than a century, unfinished business from America's founding will plunge the new country into its bloodiest war. And the Industrial Revolution is, for now, bringing more suffering than freedom, destroying one way of life to create another. Over the next two centuries, humans will fight again and again to win the liberties promised by the twin revolutions: on the streets of Paris and in the tropical heat of Haiti, on picket lines and in protest marches, with the sword and with the ballot.

But ultimately, democracy and industrialization will prevail—and together they will shape the character not only of the newly created United States but of the modern world.

left: Colonial protests against the so-called "Intolerable Acts", taxing tea, paper and other imports, were often violent. above: storming of the Bastille, Paris, 1789

CORNWALLIS IS TAKEN

OCTOBER 20, 1781. YORKTOWN. LT. COL. TENCH Tilghman rides away from the army camp outside of Yorktown, carrying dispatches from Gen. George Washington to the president of the Continental Congress in Philadelphia. Tilghman is Washington's most trusted aide. He has been with him since the war began in 1776, carrying Washington's messages, writing his letters, and making copies of important documents.

Now Tilghman carries the most important news of all. Cornwallis has surrendered. The war is over.

Tilghman was tired and shaky with fever even before he began the long trip to Philadelphia. It would have been easier to turn the task over to another man, but he is determined to press himself to the limits of his strength and cover the distance as quickly as possible.

Soon Tilghman reaches the York River: for the first two legs of his journey, he will travel by boat.

First, he takes a rowboat downstream on the York River toward Annapolis. The rowboat grounds on the shoals of the York, costing precious time.

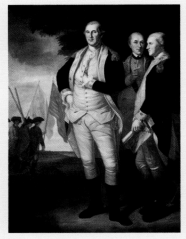

When Tilghman finally reaches the shore, he switches vessels, boarding the regular packet boat. Soon he is sailing toward Rock Hill. But the packet comes to a standstill when the winds fail, and he loses still more time. The delays are agony.

Washington, Lafayette, and Tilghman, who is holding the official dispatches declaring Cornwallis's defeat, at Yorktown, 1781

Philadelphia State House

Eventually, the packet reaches Rock Hill, and Tilghman is first off the boat, eager to make up for lost time. He spurs his horse down the old post road, shouting his message to those he passes on the way. "Cornwallis is taken! The war is over!"

At Chesterton, he stops to change horses and rest at his father's house for a few hours. Then he rides on. The road is little more than a soft-dirt track, a foot deep in mud after the autumn rains. He rides all day and into the night, stopping only to change to a fresh horse wherever he can find one.

Shaking with chills and fever, Tilghman rides into Philadelphia just after three in the morning on October 24. He has traveled almost

Chapter 10: REVOLUTION

Tilghman announcing the surrender of Cornwallis from the steps of the State House in Philadelphia, October 23, 1781

nonstop for four days. He slows his horse to a canter and heads toward the home of his old friend Thomas McKean, now president of the Continental Congress. Before long he arrives at the McKean house.

He dismounts his horse and grabs the letters from his saddlebag. He pauses and leans his forehead against the saddle for a moment to gather his strength. Then he runs up the front steps and hammers at the door.

No one answers. Tilghman steps back and looks up at the windows, hoping to see the glimmer of a lit candle moving through the house. Nothing. He raises his hand to bang on the door again, but before he can, a passing night watchman grabs Tilghman's arm, prepared to arrest him for disturbing the peace. Just then, McKean answers the door.

Relieved, Tilghman presses his letters into his old friend's hand and gives him the news: "Cornwallis is taken."

The watchman calls the hour. "All is well and Cornwallis is taken." Word spreads through the city. Lit lamps appear in every window. People pour into the streets. The State House bell rings out. And Tilghman stumbles into a borrowed bed, exhausted and feverish from his arduous journey.

When the members of the Continental Congress signed the Declaration of Independence in 1776, they did so with sorrow. From their perspective, a long accumulation of grievances had forced them to change from loyal British citizens to Americans.

The problems began with the French and Indian Wars, when British officers treated colonial volunteers like bumpkins. When the wars ended in 1763, the British and the colonists found themselves at odds in very fundamental ways. From the British point of view, the American colonies should help pay for the expensive war recently fought on their behalf and for the increased garrison of British soldiers needed to protect Britain's new possessions in Canada. As far as the American colonists were concerned, they had already paid for the war in blood and sweat. Now the British government had made it illegal to settle in the rich western possessions they had won from France. Parliament assessed new taxes that united almost every class of American against the British government. Americans pushed back, using methods both nonviolent, like boycotting British goods, and violent, such as the Pine Tree Riot.

By 1774, the relationship between the British and the colonists was in a constant state of crisis. When the British closed the port of Boston and occupied the city in response to the Boston Tea Party, towns throughout Massachusetts formed militia companies. By the end of the year, fifty-six delegates from twelve of the thirteen colonies had convened in Philadelphia as the First Continental Congress.

The colonies were a powder keg, needing only a single spark to explode into war. The spark came at Lexington and Concord on April 4, 1775.

At first the American army was no more than a ragtag accumulation of badly equipped local militias, unwilling to accept orders from a central authority and held together by their belief in what George Washington frequently referred to as the "glorious cause" of American freedom. Many of the militiamen had gained some military experience in the French and Indian Wars, but few had served as regular soldiers. Washington had risen to the rank of commander of the Virginia militia, but he did not feel qualified to be commander-in-chief of the new

The colonies were a powder keg, needing only a single spark to explode into war.

Continental Army. He had never led a force of this size, or this complexity.

For the first fourteen months of the war, jubilant American forces enjoyed astonishing successes while the British regrouped: at Lexington and Concord, Charleston, and Fort Ticonderoga. Neither the winning streak nor the jubilation survived the arrival of the British expeditionary force in New York Harbor over the summer of 1776. The scope of the force was enormous: more than five hundred ships, 32,000 British and German troops, and 40 percent of the British navy. Britain would not field a comparable invasion force again for more than 150 years—on D-Day during World War II.

The American forces suffered such crushing defeats at Long Island and Manhattan that many American volunteers assumed the Revolution was over and headed home. Washington learned a different lesson from these defeats: outmanned and outgunned, the American army could not take on the British on their own terms. Washington did not have the resources either to muster sufficient troops or to train them in the European style of fighting in massed ranks. Instead the American army reinvented itself and the art of war, creating a frontier style of warfare based on sharpshooters, long rifles, and guerrilla tactics.

In September 1777, American guerrilla tactics and the American wilderness itself defeated General "Gentleman Johnny" Burgoyne at Saratoga, New York. That victory convinced the French that the Americans had a chance to win. In February 1778 the French entered into a formal alliance with the thirteen colonies.

The French entry into the war changed everything. Suddenly the Americans had access to both a strong navy and a well-equipped army. More important, their enemy was forced to change focus. With the French in the war, the British now had to protect not only their holdings in America, but their valuable sugar colonies in the West Indies as well.

The final, decisive battle came at Yorktown, Virginia in 1781, where a combination of American and French troops surrounded the British forces under General Charles Cornwallis on land and a French fleet blockaded them from the sea. At the end of a three-week siege, Cornwallis surrendered on October 19.

The war was not technically over. The British still held Charleston, New York City, and Savannah. But they had lost the will to continue the war. Back in Britain, the American victory at Yorktown led to the fall of Lord Frederick North's prowar government. Charles Watson Wentworth, Marquis of Rockingham, the leader of the peace faction in

"Surrender of Lord Cornwallis" by John Trumbull, 1820

With the fate of America at stake, I see our job as prolonging the war as much as possible. So unless we are absolutely forced into it, our tactics are to avoid a large battle; in fact, to avoid any risks at all.
—George Washington

I have the mortification to inform Your Excellency that I have been forced to give up the posts of York and Gloucester and to surrender the troops . . . as prisoners of war to the combined forces of America and France.
—General Charles Cornwallis, 1st Marquess

Parliament, replaced North as prime minister. With the Rockingham faction in power, peace negotiations between the British and their former colonists could begin.

The concepts of democracy and national self-determination—and the success of the American rebels—triggered revolution after revolution. The French were the first to follow the American lead in 1789 (and in 1830, and in 1871). In 1791, slaves and free blacks rose up against French rule in Haiti. Revolutions in Spanish America brought independence to Mexico, Venezuela, Colombia, Panama, Ecuador, Peru, and Bolivia in the 1820s. In Europe, Greeks, Belgians, and Poles all fought for national independence in the 1820s and the 1830s.

WHILE REVOLUTION WAS BREWING in the American colonies, a different kind of revolution was under way in Britain.

Britain's population boomed in the mid-eighteenth century, thanks in part to food crops from the New World that improved the diet of the poor—most notably, the potato. A growing populace meant an increased demand for goods of all kinds, including cheap cloth.

Cloth had always been made by human hands: a cottage industry that involved entire rural families during seasons when there was little work to do on the farm. Now it would be made by machine.

The first changes were small. John Kay's flying shuttle, Lewis Paul's carding machine, and James Hargreaves's spinning jenny all increased productivity, but they did not change the basic structure of the industry. Families built additions onto their cottages so they could operate looms and jennies on a larger scale at home.

The real change in the British weaving industry came in 1769, when Richard Arkwright, a small-time wigmaker and barber, patented the water frame. Developed with help from master clockmaker John Kay, the water-powered machine spun perfect cotton—faster, cheaper, better, and more reliable than a human spinner.

Unlike the spinning jenny, the water frame was designed to be a factory machine. More than a century before Henry Ford built his first auto plant, Arkwright combined power, machinery, semiskilled labor, and raw material to generate mass production. Arkwright was soon the world's first industrial tycoon.

The factory system wasn't just a new way to manufacture; it was a new way of life, the biggest change in how humans lived and worked since farming began five thousand years earlier. Both factory and farm workers put in long days of physical

ARKWRIGHT FACTORY UPRISING

O CTOBER 3, 1779. CHORLEY, NORTHERN ENGLAND. A mob is on the hunt, not for a man, but for a machine.

Angry weavers and spinners approach Richard Arkwright's cotton mill, drums beating a march. Arkwright and his neighbors had driven them off two days before. Today they are prepared to fight, wielding axes, firearms, and hatchets. Coal miners and other workers join the displaced textile workers in their march on the mill. They push with ease through the wall of soldiers who block the narrow road to the mill entrance.

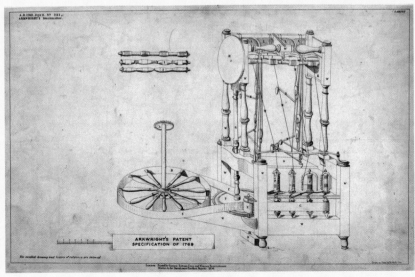

ARKWRIGHT'S PATENT
SPECIFICATION OF 1769

ABOVE: *Richard Arkwright* · BELOW: *Arkwrght's Spinning Machine*

Their target is the Birkacre mill, Richard Arkwright's flagship factory.

Expecting trouble, Arkwright has charged his factory manager, John Chadwick, with protecting the mill. Chadwick is taking no chances. He has called in the army. Sir Richard Clayton is guarding the factory with fifty armed members of the infantry regiment known, paradoxically, as the Invalids.

Two soldiers stand in front of the factory doors, trying to protect the entrance. The crowd pushes them aside. Soldiers on the roof fire warning shots into the air, but they are outnumbered sixty to one. The mob bashes in the doors and pours through. Once inside, they destroy the spinning frames.

The soldiers follow, but they are no match for thousands of enraged workers and are forced to retreat.

At the end of the day, two rioters are dead, eight more are badly wounded, and their leaders are in jail. Ninety spinning frames are destroyed, and the factory is in ruins. But the burned factory is only a temporary setback. Arkwright will rebuild. New owners will erect more factories. Industrialization is here to stay.

LEFT: *Arkwright's water frame* · RIGHT: *Cotton carding machine*

One of the many small children at work in Lancaster Cotton Mills, South Carolina, 1908.

THE NEW URBAN POOR

Just like the change from hunting and gathering to farming, the Industrial Revolution brought society long-term gains at the cost of an immediate fall in the standard of living for many.

Cities couldn't keep up with the influx of new residents. Working-class districts had open sewers and inadequate water supplies. Streets were often nothing more than rutted, muddy paths. Existing houses had to be divided and redivided to create space. New housing was just as cramped and badly built. Many of the new industrial workers could not afford enough of even the cheapest food. They dressed in rags, slept on straw, and worked sixteen-hour days. Disease flourished. Mortality rates were high. And the cities continued to grow.

Today, the same patterns are being repeated in developing countries. Former rural economies are disappearing, to be replaced by manufacturing staffed with cheap urban labor pools. Often housed apart from their families in barracks and working six or seven days a week, these workers are sustaining global manufacturing and sales of everything from toys and sneakers to computers and cell phones.

Roman Ghetto late 19th century

labor. But agricultural work was seasonal and varied. Factory work was monotonous, with few breaks. Supervisors discouraged the song or chatter that made work lighter. As the use of machinery spread, unskilled laborers, many of them women and children, replaced skilled weavers. Cities grew at unprecedented rates as workers migrated from the countryside, in search of employment in the factories.

A second wave of industry followed the first. Textile mills created a demand for new tools, new machinery, and more power. Inventors and engineers created better ways to forge steel and mine coal. They designed faster and more specialized machinery, and found new ways to use machines to extend the productivity of a single laborer. In other words, they learned how to make *more* goods in *less* time.

In the two and a half centuries since Arkwright introduced the water frame, the combination of power and machine has moved beyond the factory and into every aspect of our lives.

THE RAILROAD WAS BORN IN the British mining industry, long before the invention of the steam locomotive. Horses, and sometimes people, pulled wagons full of coal along wooden or iron tracks as early as 1630.

The steam engine also had its roots in coal. First developed to pump water out of mines, it was adapted to run machines in British textile mills. In the early nineteenth century, inventors began to play with ways to adapt the steam engine to a means of transportation. The earliest steam locomotives were simple upgrades on the horse-drawn coal railways.

Steam locomotion moved out of the coal mines and into the public eye in 1825. George Stephenson, a self-taught Northumberland engineer who began his career as the brakeman on a coal pit train, opened the first public railway. The Stockton and

THE LONG RIFLE

Throughout history, changes in weaponry have transformed the art of war. The introduction of iron weapons around 1200 BCE gave soldiers a literal edge over those armed with bronze or stone. The Ottomans' use of cannons at the siege of Constantinople revolutionized siege warfare. The spread of the musket marked the end of the armored knight. In the American Revolution, American troops came to the battlefield with weapons that challenged the traditions of Western warfare.

British troops carried smoothbore flintlock muskets, which were quick to reload and well suited for the close drill of traditional European warfare. They weren't very accurate, but accuracy didn't matter when you were firing at a row of men marching shoulder to shoulder. If you fired, you were bound to hit something. In close combat, the musket's bayonet was often more important than the musket itself.

Accuracy in a weapon was important to American farmers, who relied on hunting for a large portion of their diet. The long rifle, sometimes called the Kentucky rifle, had a rifled barrel up to four feet long, improving the gun's accuracy. In the hands of a skilled marksman, colonial rifles were accurate up to 300 yards: three times the range of a musket. Common practice targets were a turkey's head at 100 yards and the turkey's body at 200 yards. Hitting the body of a horse at 400 yards was no challenge, as British cavalrymen learned to their dismay.

Rifling—spiraled grooves inside the gun's barrel—improved the gun's accuracy, but made it harder to load because ammunition had to fit more tightly in order to engage with the grooves. Loading got even harder under battle conditions because the residue of burnt powder from repeated firing built up in the grooves.

The long rifle was ineffective in European-style battles because it was slow to reload and was not designed to hold a bayonet. But it was perfect for the American style of warfare: raids, wilderness fighting, and sniping at the enemy.

ABOVE: *Minuteman Statue at Lexington Battle Green* • BELOW: *Pennsylvania Kentucky Flintlock Long Rifle*

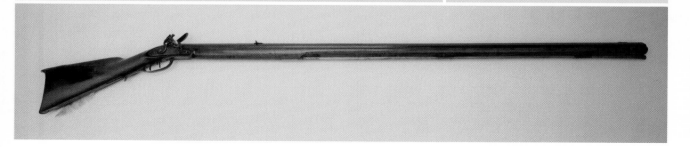

Chapter 10: REVOLUTION

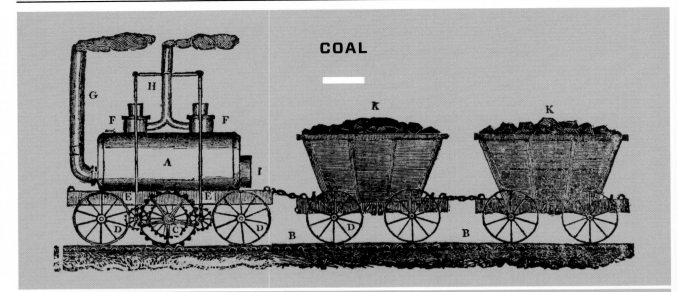

COAL

The nineteenth century was powered by steam—the greatest increase in power since our ancestors learned to control fire. The steam engine drove factories, ships, and trains. It pumped water from mines. Factories no longer had to be built next to water supplies. Transportation no longer depended on draft animals and the wind.

What made it all possible was a miracle material from deep underground—coal.

Three hundred million years ago, Earth was covered by a dense, tropical rain forest. Giant ferns, horsetails, coniferous trees, and mosses grew in vast stretches of boggy land. When they died, the lush, green plants fell and accumulated in the warm, shallow water of the bogs, slowing their decay. Over the millennia, the layers of slowly decaying plants grew deeper. New layers buried the older layers of vegetation and pushed them deeper, turning them

first to peat and then, as they heated up, to coal. The longer the exposure to heat, the harder and darker coal became. The harder and darker the coal, the more efficient it is as fuel.

The steam engine is gone, but coal is still essential to twenty-first-century life. It remains one of our most important energy sources, fueling almost 40 percent of the world's electricity and 64 percent of modern iron and steel production.

Darlington Railway (S&DR) carried six hundred passengers over a twenty-six-mile line in three hours on its first trip; regular passenger service opened a month later. The English went railroad mad. In the 1830s and 1840s, investors formed more than six hundred rail companies that together laid more than ten thousand miles of track.

Steam locomotives caught the American imagination as well. Stephenson had launched the Stockton and Darlington the same year the Erie Canal had

gone into operation. The timing was perfect for introducing the new steam locomotive to America. Baltimore businesspeople, worried that the new canal would give New York a major advantage in trading with the Western states, had already begun to look for faster ways to move people and goods over the Appalachian Mountains into the Ohio River Valley. Wagon shipments to the West took forever. There was no natural East-West river system. And the mountains that outlined Maryland's western border meant that a canal was simply not practical. A railroad appeared to be the perfect solution.

In February 1827 a group of Baltimore businessmen organized themselves to construct the first American railroad. It was a daring leap of faith. The only railroad in operation was the two-year-old Stockton and Darlington: twenty-six miles of straight track on a flat surface. The new Baltimore and Ohio Railroad, or B&O, would travel through almost four hundred miles of rough terrain, requiring engineering marvels in the form of bridges and tunnels.

The transcontinental Union-Pacific Railroad connected the coasts for the first time.

NELLIE BLY

In 1889, American journalist Nellie Bly made headlines by traveling around the world in fewer than eighty days—seventy-two days, six hours, and eleven minutes, to be exact. Without the global rail network, her journey would have taken four times longer.

The new railroad lines would change the face of American—and world—transportation forever. The first mile and a half of track for the Baltimore and Ohio was in place by January 1830; the company offered rides to curious members of the public for a nominal fare. By 1840, America had more miles of track than Great Britain; by 1860, it had more miles of track than the rest of the world combined and was still laying more. The first transcontinental railroad was completed on May 10, 1869, only thirty-nine years after the first excursion ride on the B&O.

The railroads connected town to town, city to city, region to region. Towns on the railroad line grew; those off the line dwindled. Chicago became a major hub for railways from both the East and the West. Western farmers could send their produce east. Southern cotton producers could ship raw material to the textile factories of the North or to the ports, where British ships waited to take it back

J ANUARY 16, 1852. WEST VIRGINIA. THE BALTIMORE and Ohio Railroad is one of the biggest construction projects in North America. Once complete, 379 miles of track will link Baltimore to the Ohio River Valley. The Kingwood Tunnel is the biggest challenge on the B&O: carved forty-one hundred feet through a mountain of slate and limestone. The man in charge is self-taught engineer Benjamin Latrobe Jr., son of the architect who designed the United States Capitol building. To speed up construction, Latrobe has

decided to take a daring risk and dig the tunnel from both ends at once.

For three years now, three hundred men have worked around the clock, shifting two hundred thousand cubic yards of earth and rock using hammers, drills, and black powder. They've worked through labor riots, machinery failures, cave-ins, and bad weather. It is dangerous, highly specialized work. Injuries and death are common. But the workers are almost done.

Teams on opposite sides of the last stretch of rock have a bet on who will get through first. In their hurry to win, one team rushes to blow through the last heading—but fails to give the customary blasting signal. The explosion blows out through the other side, connecting the two ends of the tunnel. One laborer is killed and several others are wounded.

Many more workers will die on the job as the railroads expand across the United States.

CLOCKWISE FROM TOP: *American Express Train, 1854 • locomotive and passenger car in New York City, 1880s • lightning steam press, electric telegraph, locomotive, and steamboat, 1876 • 1882 poster for the Illinois Central Railroad*

to England. Eastern manufacturers, importers, and the new catalog retailers could reach a greater market than ever before. Diets became more diverse as people ate food from other climates. The number of people someone could meet in a lifetime quadrupled as travel, not just to the next town, but to the town beyond that, became easier.

The railroads generated thousands of new jobs, new mines, new steel mills, new towns, new markets. Rails, engines, and cars had to be manufactured. Coal had to be mined. Timetables had to be printed. Whole new classes of workers manned the trains themselves: engineers, firemen, porters, conductors, and stationmasters.

Railroads opened new lands in Canada, Australia, Siberia, and Argentina. They brought rubber out of the Belgian Congo and carried tea from the highland plantations of Assam to ports in western India. In Europe, they leaped across borders, creating connections that had never existed before. By 1889, two hundred thousand miles of track were in operation throughout the world. By 1900, the number of miles of track had doubled again. People could travel farther and faster than ever before.

LIKE THE PLAGUE BEFORE IT, cholera traveled from Asia to Europe along the old trade routes, moving from India, where the disease had been endemic for at least two thousand years, through Afghanistan, Turkey, and Persia to Russia and across Europe. The dirty, overcrowded cities of the Industrial Revolution were the perfect place for cholera to thrive. Drinking water became laced with invisible amounts of human waste carrying the cholera bacteria. Once limited to the South Asian subcontinent, cholera became the first global pandemic.

In 1854, London was the richest city on earth—and one of the most crowded. The city's population

HORSEPOWER

For most of human history, the horse was unmatched as a source of speed and power. A traveler on horseback could travel faster and farther than a traveler on foot. A warrior on horseback was the ultimate fighting machine. Horses were as essential to the spread of civilization as iron. They were used to clear forests, plow fields, and pull wagons.

It's not surprising that when our forefathers built the first mechanical engines, we measured their power against that of nature's locomotion, the horse.

Scottish engineer James Watt coined the term "horsepower" in the eighteenth century. He wanted a way to compare the power of his new steam engine to that of the horses that pulled coal wagons out of the mines. (Coal, steam, and railroads are linked at every point.) He calculated that, on average, a horse could pull 22,000 foot-pounds in a minute. For reasons best known to Watt, he arbitrarily increased that number by 50 percent, making one horsepower the equivalent of 33,000 foot-pounds per minute. That means a horse, or an engine, exerting one horsepower could raise 330 pounds of coal 100 feet in one minute.

In 1808, London crowds happily paid to watch Richard Trevithick's little steam engine, named *Catch Me Who Can* (above), race against a horse.

THE CHOLERA EPIDEMIC

AUGUST 18, 1854. 40 BROAD STREET, LONDON. Two-year-old Frances Lewis is desperately ill. At six that morning, she had begun to vomit. Her stools are green and watery, their smell vile even by the standards of a London neighborhood that reeks of slaughterhouses, manufacturing plants, tripe boilers, and the overflowing cesspools that collect human waste. Her mother, Sarah, has sent for the doctor. As she waits, she changes her daughter's diaper one more time and soaks the morning's dirty diapers in a bucket of water. When the little girl falls asleep, Sarah takes the bucket downstairs and empties it in the cesspool that lies in the basement of the house where they rent a room.

She has no idea that, in the coming weeks, thousands will die because of her actions.

Crevices and breaks in the cesspool leak infected sewage into the Broad Street well that provides the drinking water for Sarah's neighbors and her family. Someone takes the first drink; someone else, the second, and so on.

Another epidemic has begun.

A few hours pass, and to Sarah's sorrow, her baby dies. Thomas Lewis tries to comfort his wife, but he is feverish and has to sit down to rest. Sarah's husband soon shows the same terrifying symptoms that led to their daughter's death: coughing, abdominal pain, and diarrhea. Within a short time, he, too, will be dead.

ORPHAN TRAINS

Orphans have always been among the most vulnerable members of human society. Left without adult protectors, they are dependent on society as a whole to care for them. Cultures have met the challenge with different degrees of humanity. In ancient Middle Eastern cultures, orphans were protected; in other civilizations, such as the Roman Empire or the Mayan cultures, orphans became slaves or were offered as human sacrifices.

In the mid-nineteenth century, the number of orphans in American cities became a social problem of immense proportions as a result of the Civil War and the rise in immigration. Orphanages and aid societies were overwhelmed. One organization used modern technology to address an ancient problem. Between 1854 and 1929, "orphan trains" carried more than one hundred thousand homeless children from the slums of New York to new homes in rural America.

The orphan trains were an ambitious effort by the Children's Aid Society to help the thousands of homeless children who roamed the streets of New York in the 1850s. The program's founder, minister Charles Loring Brace, hoped that farmers in need of labor would welcome the children into their homes and treat them as their own. Many did. Others saw the children only as a source of cheap labor.

Two street boys who found their way west on the orphan trains, Andrew Burke and John Brady, fared better than most. They grew up to be the governors of North Dakota and Alaska, respectively.

had doubled in fifty years. Two and a half million people were crammed into a thirty-mile circle. More than half of them lived in dark, filthy, undrained slums. Sanitation systems consisting of cesspools and "night soil men" (workers employed to remove human excrement from the cesspools and transport it outside of the city), dating from the Elizabethan period, were unable to cope with the human waste of a teeming, modern city.

Broad Street, where the Lewis family lived, was by no means a slum by Victorian standards. A mixture of the working poor and middle-class tradespeople lived there. Unlike many neighborhood water supplies, the Broad Street well had a reputation for clean, pleasant-tasting water.

In the three days after the death of Frances Lewis, 127 people died in the neighborhood of the Broad Street well. Three-quarters of the residents fled the neighborhood. Within two weeks, 616 people were dead.

In the early 1850s, most doctors believed that cholera was spread through the poisoned air, or "miasma" of unsanitary places. One man began to doubt that theory.

John Snow lived and practiced medicine just around the corner, on Firth Street. Snow was one of the new breed of men who believed that measurement and careful scientific inquiry held the keys to understanding not only disease, but the universe. At the time of the Broad Street cholera epidemic, he had already earned a national reputation for his study and practice of anesthesia.

With a new cholera epidemic on the rise, Snow began to make a map of the dead, systematically looking for a link between the victims. He soon came to believe that the water pump on Broad

CHOLERA

Bacteria are the oldest and most successful life form on Earth. Born in the thermal and chemical soup of a still-forming planet, they have evolved into a diversity of single-celled organisms that thrive by the millions in environments that could not support more complex life. Some extract nitrogen from the air. Others live on sulfur or other elements. Still others, like cholera, live in and on the human body.

The only way you can catch cholera is to ingest the bacteria that cause it, usually by drinking water contaminated by the violent diarrhea that is the disease's most noticeable symptom.

At first it seems unlikely that the disease would spread. For the most part, people don't willingly drink water that is obviously tainted by human waste. But in fact, a glass of seemingly clean water can contain two hundred million invisible cholera bacteria—enough to kill you in hours.

The crowded working class districts of nineteenth century London had open sewers, inadequate water supplies and unpaved streets.

Street was the source of the outbreak. But he needed proof if he wanted to persuade the parish council to shut off the water supply.

The proof came from the one death that didn't seem to fit the pattern. An elderly woman had died of cholera in Hampstead, six miles away from Broad Street: the only reported case of the disease in that neighborhood. At first Snow thought her death disproved his carefully drawn conclusions. Then he noticed the victim's name, Susannah Eley. The Eley brothers owned a percussion-cap factory on Broad Street. Seventy of their workers had died of cholera. Snow quickly discovered that Susannah had been the Eley brothers' mother. She had moved to Hampstead several years earlier, but she preferred the taste of the water from her old home. The Eley brothers were good sons and good employers. They took their mother several gallons of water from the Broad Street pump every Sunday. They also made sure their workers had plenty of clean water to drink during the day. Their generosity had been deadly.

Snow had found the link.

ON SEPTEMBER 7, EIGHT DAYS after the first case of cholera on Broad Street, Snow presented his evidence to the parish council. Later that day, they removed the handle from the Broad Street pump and stopped the cholera outbreak.

Twenty years before the medical establishment accepted the germ theory of disease, John Snow's detective work solved the mystery of a deadly threat to the industrialized city—and pioneered the methods that epidemiologists still use today to track outbreaks of disease. Snow's findings led to the creation of one of humanity's greatest engineering marvels, the first modern sewer system. Engineer Joseph Bazalgette designed a system of more than two thousand miles of low-level underground brick tunnels to carry effluent away from people's homes. By 1866, most of London was connected to the new sewer network.

The template would be copied in major cities around the world, virtually eliminating diseases like cholera and typhoid fever from Western cities.

A SHOWDOWN BETWEEN AN illegal drug cartel and a nation attempting to defend its people against the dual threats of addiction and drug violence isn't new. In 1838, in a dark chapter of British and Chinese history, the world's oldest and youngest trading empires went to war over the opium trade.

In the late eighteenth-century, opium was the center of a thriving three-way trade orchestrated by the British East India Company. The British grew opium in India and sold it at auction to specially licensed traders. The traders sold the opium in China, using the proceeds to buy teas, silks, and porcelain to ship back for sale in Britain.

By the 1820s, twelve million Chinese were addicted—fifteen times the number of heroin addicts in the United States today. The growing number of addicts caused problems familiar to anyone who pays attention to the news. Opium smoking destroyed users and their families. The high price of the drug led to violence and corruption. The drain of silver payments to foreign drug merchants threatened the economy.

In 1800, the Chinese emperor ordered a ban on using, importing, and producing the drug that was

CLEAN WATER

People have always known that clean water is better for you than dirty water. As early as 2000 BCE, ancient Sanskrit texts describe boiling and straining water to remove impurities. Around 500 BCE, Greek physician Hippocrates invented the first domestic water filter, known as the "Hippocratic sleeve," for the same purpose. But until Antonie van Leeuwenhoek invented the microscope in 1676, one could only determine whether water was clean by the way it smelled and tasted.

Today, water treatment plants are a standard part of modern cities, but we still haven't conquered the problem of contaminated water supplies:

- One-sixth of the world's population does not have access to safe drinking water.

- In the past ten years, diarrhea has killed more children than all the people lost to armed conflict since World War II.

- Some 6,000 children die every day from diseases associated with lack of safe drinking water and inadequate sanitation.

- Nearly half the world's people lack water and sanitation technology that was available to ancient Romans two thousand years ago.

Chapter 10: REVOLUTION

destroying his country—making opium the world's first illegal drug. The law was no more effective than current laws outlawing marijuana, cocaine, or heroin. Chinese addicts continued to use the drug; British merchants continued to sell it.

In 1838, the emperor appointed the Chinese equivalent of a drug czar, imperial commissioner Lin Zexu. Under Lin's direction, Chinese authorities imprisoned or executed more than two thousand Chinese opium dealers. Like their present-day American counterparts, the Chinese drug enforcement agents soon realized they needed to stop the drug supply at its source.

In theory, controlling the foreign drug merchants should have been easy. The Chinese government maintained tight restrictions over foreign

trade. European merchants could only trade in Canton. They were allowed in the city only between October and March and were restricted to special neighborhoods. They had to deal exclusively with licensed Chinese merchants.

Lin Zexu issued a warning to British dealers who were still bringing the now illegal drug into China. When the merchants continued to trade in opium, Lin had them barricaded in their warehouses until they surrendered their merchandise. Lin Zexu seized and destroyed twenty thousand chests of illegal opium from British warehouses in Canton.

In response, sixteen British warships sailed to China, where they attacked and blockaded Chinese ports, sank Chinese ships, occupied Shanghai, and sailed up the Yangtze River to threaten Nanjing. The nation with the largest population on earth was forced to submit to one of the smallest—thanks to Britain's possession of steam and guns.

ON THE OTHER SIDE OF THE world, north and south in one nation were about to wage war with each other over one side's possession of another "commodity"—the slaves who were the foundation of the southern economy.

Only eighty years after the American Revolution, the United States entered into the first war of the industrial age.

The Northern and Southern states were divided on many issues. The largest and ugliest was the question of slavery. Liberty was incomplete in the country whose ideal of freedom had inspired revolutions around the world. Four million Americans were owned by other humans. Traded as commodities—bought and sold, as if they were animals

rather than human beings, and often treated less humanely than their owners' livestock.

Slavery was an issue in itself, but it was also shorthand for the economic tensions that divided the nation. Even during the colonial period, when 90 percent of the American colonists lived outside of cities, there was a difference between the small farms of the North and the slave-based plantations of the South. In the 1820s and 1830s, cities in the Northeast embraced the Industrial Revolution,

Liberty was incomplete in the country whose ideal of freedom had inspired revolutions around the world.

but the South did not. Northern mill owners bought cotton from Southern plantations at the same time that Northern abolitionists railed against the evils of slavery.

The nation grew closer and closer to war. When Abraham Lincoln was elected president in 1860, Southern states feared that abolition would soon follow. A month after his election, South Carolina seceded from the United States, and the country slid into what would be four years of brutal warfare.

The American Civil War was fought with a combination of up-to-date technology and battle tactics that belonged to a previous era. New, mass-produced weapons created mass-produced death on the battlefield. The Gatling gun, a predecessor of the machine gun, fired an unimaginable two hundred rounds per minute. Rifled muskets loaded with aerodynamic lead bullets changed common soldiers into marksmen. For the first time since the introduction of the gun in Ming China, ordinary soldiers could aim their weapons at a distant target and have a fair chance of hitting it. The day of the infantry charge was over, though officers trained at West Point continued to lead heroic suicidal charges against a line of armed infantrymen. Even troops far from the line of fire learned to protect themselves with trenches and fortifications, foreshadowing the trench warfare of the First World War.

New weapons weren't the only way the Industrial Revolution shaped the Civil War and contributed to the South's eventual defeat. Most of the nation's railroad track, telegraph system, and manufacturing capacity was in the North. Thanks to their extensive rail network, the Union army was able to move men and material to the front more quickly than the South. A newly formed U.S. Military Telegraph Corps strung more than four thousand miles of telegraph wire in the first year of the war and sent more than one million messages flying to and from the battlefield, allowing President Lincoln to monitor battlefield reports and lead real-time strategy sessions with his generals. Weapons, munitions, and uniforms poured out of Northern factories—Samuel Colt's factory alone produced 7,000 rifles, 113,000 muskets, and 387,000 six-shooters over the course of the war.

New York and Pennsylvania each had more industrial capacity than all the seceding states combined. In the end, the South was unable to stand up against the North's manufacturing ability.

"The Fall of Richmond, Va. on the Night of April 2, 1865," detail of lithograph by Currier and Ives.

DEADLY LEAD

In the nineteenth century, weapons manufacturers used Earth's densest and softest common metal to create the deadliest ammunition in history—the minié bullet, known to troops in the American Civil War as "minié balls." Made of soft lead, minié balls had a hollow, cylindrical base and a rounded conical nose. This design made the minié ball faster to load and gave it greater range and accuracy than the traditional ball. Minié balls flatten when they meet human flesh, tearing through muscle and bone. When the ball hits, bones splinter and shatter into hundreds of *spicules*: sharp, bony sticks that the force of the bullet drives through muscle and skin.

Minié balls aren't the only way lead can kill. Lead is a poison. Our bodies don't use it for anything, but they treat it the same way they do calcium: if you are exposed to lead, it accumulates in your body. At low concentrations, lead poisoning causes poor appetites, stomachaches, exhaustion, headaches, and insomnia. Higher levels of lead poisoning can damage the brain and the kidneys.

In the past, lead was man's go-to metal for anything where its malleability and resistance to corrosion were a plus. The Romans used lead for water and sewer pipes. (Roman lead pipe survives today in Roman baths.) For centuries, people added lead to paints, cosmetics, and pottery glazes. In fact, lead paint was used in the United States until 1978. It's amazing anyone survived.

With increasing recognition of lead's hazards, we've reduced the ways lead is used. Today, the primary uses for lead are as radiation shielding, solder for electrical connections, and in lead acid batteries.

APRIL 3, 1865. RICHMOND, VIRGINIA. The war has reached a turning point. General Philip Sheridan's forces have overrun the Confederate defenses at Five Forks. General Robert E. Lee can no longer hold back the advance of the Union army.

Sheridan's troops will reach the Confederate capital by morning. The city is preparing to evacuate. Civilians and soldiers hurry through the streets, carrying as many of their belongings as they can. Some are on horseback. More have loaded their possessions on carts, carriages, and wagons. A few find a place on the last trains to leave the city. Others leave by canal barges, small skiffs, and larger boats.

Two members of the city militia, Captain Herring and Adjutant Linden Kent, are burning official documents in front of the government offices. A man gallops toward them, dust flying up from his horses' hooves. The two soldiers reach for their guns, then relax as they realize it's the man in charge of the evacuation, Provost Marshal Isaac Carrington.

SAMUEL COLT

———

Before Samuel Colt, pistols had to be reloaded after every shot. In the 1830s Colt designed a revolutionary revolving cylinder with six tubes for bullets. Cocking the gun's hammer spun the cylinder so bullets could be fired one after another.

But the invention of the revolver was just one way Colt changed the world of weapons. In the early nineteenth century, guns were made by hand, one gun at a time. Colt introduced the idea of mass production. A machine produced thousands of identical parts, and then the guns were assembled by hand along an assembly line.

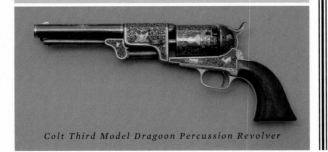

Colt Third Model Dragoon Percussion Revolver

Carrington tells them they have new instructions from General Lee. Evacuation is not enough. Tactical retreat is no longer an option. Kent and Herring are ordered to burn anything of value so it doesn't fall into Union hands. They hurry to follow Lee's orders

Before long, they enter an open warehouse filled with piles of dried tobacco leaves. The leaves are already dry as tinder, but Kent and Herring douse the tobacco and the walls of the warehouse with kerosene. Once outside, they torch the building. Flames lick up the kerosene-soaked walls, then flare into an inferno as they reach the dried tobacco.

All across the city, members of the rear guard are doing the same thing, setting fire to storehouses and arsenals. Soon the flames from burning stores and the embers from smoldering documents begin to spread, fire joining fire until the city is ablaze. When the flames reach the Tredegar Iron Works, the loaded shells that are stored there explode, blowing out windows and tearing doors from their hinges. Soon columns of dense, black smoke hover in the air.

The last members of the army retreat from the city on horseback, leaving a blazing ruin behind them to greet the Union army.

Five hard-fought days later, Lee and the Army of Virginia are surrounded. They have no choice but to surrender to Union general Ulysses S. Grant.

THE AMERICAN CIVIL WAR represented a turning point for the United States—and the world. The weapons and military strategies used, the means of recording what happened, as well as the industrial infrastructure that supported the American Civil War look familiar to us in a way that earlier wars do not. Modern elements had appeared in wars before. The Crimean War (1854–56) saw the first use of the telegraph, the first war

Ironclad warships like the USS Monitor (right) and the CSS Virginia (left) were used for the first time in the American Civil War.

photography, the first true war correspondents, and the birth of modern nursing. (Clara Barton would be the first to acknowledge her debt to the redoubtable Miss Nightingale.) Railroads played a critical role in the Indian Rebellion of 1857. In each of those wars, modern elements played an important role.

In the case of the American Civil War, such innovations shaped the nature of war itself, and by war's end, humanity stood on the edge of a brave, new world—poised for technological revolution on an unprecedented scale.

Chapter 10: REVOLUTION

11

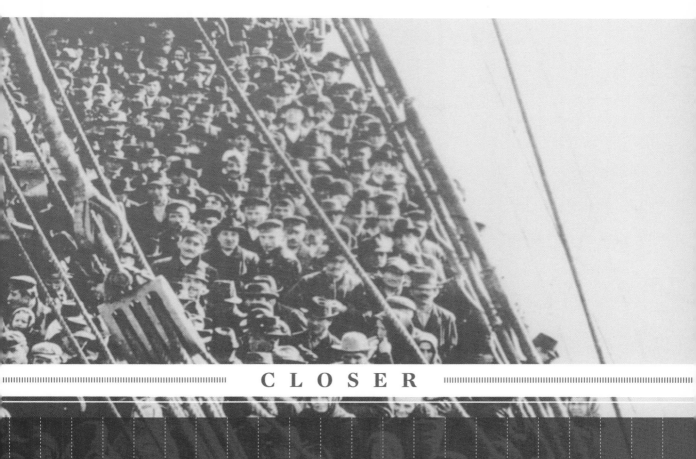

CLOSER

A HALF CENTURY HAS PASSED SINCE THE AMERICAN CIVIL WAR, AND THE YEARS HAVE BEEN MARKED BY INNOVATION AND IMMIGRATION. AMERICA HAS BEGUN A SECOND INDUSTRIAL REVOLUTION THAT IS RAPIDLY USHERING IN A MODERN WORLD.

From the sewing machine to the assembly line, from air-conditioning to the Model T, American ingenuity has created—and is still creating—new technologies that will ultimately contribute to the well-being of all mankind. Businesspeople and visionaries are taking the discoveries of pure science and transforming them into practical innovations. Some new technologies just make everyday life a little easier. Others are completely changing the world.

America's second industrial revolution is fueled by the arrival of millions of newcomers. Ambitious, self-selected risk takers come from all over the world, hoping to share in American prosperity. America transforms them—and they transform America. They work in the factories spawned by new industries. They help build the growing cities. And they are on the front lines of innovation. Yankee tinkerers stand in line at the patent office next to immigrants from Germany, Poland, and Russia. America is a melting pot not only of peoples, but of ideas.

Humans are more closely linked than ever before, by railroad, steamship, telegraph, and radio. People and information travel at speeds unimaginable a hundred years ago. Material progress is changing how we live and profoundly altering our relationships to the earth and to each other. It is also bringing practical challenges and moral dilemmas previously unseen. They will ultimately reveal the best and worst of human nature.

LEFT: *Immigrants awaiting examination at Ellis Island, 1902* • ABOVE: *The Machine Shop at the Phoenix Works Institute*

Chapter 11: CLOSER

LEFT: *Thomas Alva Edison* • MIDDLE: *early 1900s vacuum cleaner* • RIGHT: *Sholes and Glidden typewriter*

IN THE YEARS AFTER THE American Civil War, the world moved from the age of steam and iron to the age of electricity and steel, from the mechanical to the electromechanical. We made massive leaps forward in transportation, communication, manufacturing, and construction.

Ideas were generated, and adopted, at unprecedented speed. In 1863, the United States Patent Office issued fewer than four thousand patents; by the end of the century, it often received a hundred patent applications a week. The feedback loop between scientific discovery and invention accelerated. The growing publishing industry put news of breakthroughs in science into the hands of tinkerers and visionaries who transformed them into useful tools.

Americans were quick to pick up inventions and important ideas from other places and develop them into practical applications with enormous impact. Andrew Carnegie revolutionized the steel industry with English inventor Henry Bessemer's innovative steel-processing technique. Henry Ford combined mass production techniques with the internal combustion engines, independently developed by German engineers Karl Benz and Gottlieb Daimler in 1885, making automobiles part of everyday life. Thomas Edison, a notoriously hard-nosed experimenter, summed up the idea of translating scientific invention into innovation: "We've got to come up with something. We can't be like those German professors who spend their whole lives studying the fuzz on a bee."

Factories flourished. In 1860, manufacturing was responsible for only 12 percent of America's gross national product. By 1894, industrial production had tripled, bypassing agriculture as the main source of America's wealth, and the United States was the world's leading manufacturer.

The immediate effects of the second industrial revolution were not all positive. Between 1870 and 1890, the population in America's three largest cities, New York, Philadelphia, and Chicago, increased by

LEFT: *Ford Model T assembly line, ca. 1913* • RIGHT: *Singer sewing machine, ca 1850*

more than 200 percent due to the growing need for industrial labor. Inner-city neighborhoods were as crowded and dirty as any London slum during the first industrial revolution. Few had paved and lighted streets or sewer and water lines. And 40 percent of America's working class made less than the five hundred dollars per year needed to feed a family of five an adequate diet.

Over time, the benefits of the second industrial revolution trickled down. American inventions, and adaptations of other people's inventions, changed daily life in ways that would have astonished the pioneers of the first industrial revolution. Ordinary people could now enjoy goods and services that had once been available only to the wealthy. Thomas Edison's lightbulb drove the development of a centralized system for generating and distributing inexpensive electricity, eventually bringing light and power to every home. His phonograph allowed rural and working-class people to hear the music of great orchestras for the first time. Isaac Singer's sewing machine, the first home appliance, not only relieved women of the drudgery of hand sewing—it created the clothing industry. The poor were no longer lim-

> We will make electric light so cheap that only the rich will burn candles. —Thomas Edison

ited to clothing they made themselves. Henry Ford's automated production line turned the automobile from a luxury item to a mass-marketed product. The second industrial revolution was bracketed at one end by the completion of the Transcontinental Railroad in 1869, and at the other by the development of aviation and the automobile as practical means of transportation. In the world's newly industrialized countries, people were more mobile than they had ever been before.

THE WRIGHT BROTHERS FIRST FLIGHT

DECEMBER 14, 1903. KITTY HAWK, NORTH CAROLINA. It's a beautiful day for flying. The Wright brothers toss a coin to decide who will get the first shot at testing their newest glider. Wilbur wins.

But the flight doesn't go as planned. The plane rises a few feet in the air, up, up . . . and then plunges straight down into the sand, snapping a skid.

Back to the drawing board. . . .

DECEMBER 17, 1903. THE WRIGHT BROTHERS HAVE SPENT the last three days in the shed they use as a hangar, repairing the damage caused by Wilbur's crash. Now they're ready to try again. And this time, it's Orville's turn.

The weather has changed. Bitter winds blow in from the north at twenty miles an hour. Puddles of water from a recent rain have turned into a layer of ice. Orville thinks the weather is perfect . . . for flying. Nonflyers are less enthusiastic. Only five of the spectators invited to witness today's trial run were willing to brave the cold. But Orville is undeterred.

He runs the engine and propellers for a few minutes to warm them up, unties the anchor ropes, then lies on the lower wing and grasps the lever that controls elevation. The plane moves down the wooden rail the Wrights laid so the craft would have a smooth surface to slide on. It gathers speed. Excited, Wilbur runs alongside, holding one wing to help balance the machine. Orville pushes the elevation lever forward. . . .

Suddenly, the plane rises into the air, soaring over Wilbur's head! Their first flight!

It lasts only twelve seconds and covers just 120 feet. But the persistent Wrights will fly four more times today—eventually covering 852 feet in fifty-nine seconds before a gust of wind catches the engine- propelled glider and sends it rolling, damaging the small craft.

Their airplane may be damaged, but the Wright brothers' sense of elation is not. After years of effort they've succeeded at something no one has done before: heavier-than-air flight. Suddenly, the sky is the limit.

Chapter 11: CLOSER

Leonardo da Vinci made the first systematic study of flight in the 1480s. He left 160 pages of sketches of flying machines and wing mechanisms.

HUMAN BEINGS HAVE ALWAYS yearned for flight. Early on, we studied the earth's winged creatures, effortlessly riding the wind, for clues on how to realize our dream.

In 400 BCE the Chinese applied their understanding of wind and aerodynamics to invent the kite. Its design was a forerunner to manned balloons and gliders.

In the ninth century, Islamic scientist Abbas Ibn Firnas applied his observations of birds in the first known hang-glider flight.

Leonardo da Vinci made a serious study of flight in the 1480s. In his notebooks, da Vinci left insights and hundreds of scaled drawings that led to the modern helicopter.

In 1783, as the French court and a crowd of thousands looked on, Joseph-Michel and Jacques-Étienne Montgolfier demonstrated their hot-air balloon. Filled with smoke from a blazing fire, the silk balloon sailed into the skies above Paris. It carried its passengers—a sheep, a rooster, and a duck—almost two miles before coming safely to earth.

The race to fly in a machine weighing more than air came to an end with the Wright brothers' public experiments of 1908 and 1909. In their early experiments, Orville and Wilbur retraced the history of manned flight—studying the aerodynamics of kites, balloons, and gliders—before christening their 605-pound craft the *Flyer* and launching it in Kitty Hawk.

The Wright brothers' success inspired a generation of experimentation in Europe and America. The French flew airplanes designed by Louis Blériot, the Farman brothers, and Léon Levavasseur that would soon place them at the forefront of aviation. In fact, French airplane design advanced so quickly that planes built in 1913 had more in common with those that would be produced thirty and forty years later than they did with the plane the Wright brothers flew at Kitty Hawk.

In the years between the two world wars, airplanes became increasingly visible. Charles Lindbergh's Atlantic flight from New York to Paris in 1927 and the round of record flights that followed his in the 1930s caught the world's imagination. Races, records, and stunts gave flight an air of glamour.

Airplanes added new horror to warfare and created a new breed of war hero. Sophisticated military aircraft flown by the Allied and Axis powers in World War II carried payloads of bombs that brought Europe's oldest cities to ruin—and wrought devastation beyond mankind's worst nightmares to two heavily populated industrial centers in Japan.

More than any other invention of the time, the airplane separated the past from the future. Planes overturned existing expectations about the speed and cost of long-distance transportation, rapidly bypassing the train and the steamship for commercial uses and successfully competing with the car well into the 1930s. The Wright brothers' basic one-man aircraft design eventually gave birth to jumbo jets with seating for hundreds.

Just forty-four years after the Wright brothers' first flight, Chuck Yeager flew faster than the speed of sound. Following Yeager's feat of advanced engineering and physics, we fulfilled one of our oldest dreams: flying to the moon. Today unmanned rockets are on their way to distant planets. Our hope is that these robotic extensions of us will bring back images and artifacts that may reveal clues to our own origins in the Big Bang.

The number of commercial passengers on airlines more than doubled between 1932 and 1937 •
ABOVE: *During World War II, aviators dropped both bombs and propaganda over enemy territory.*

THE FIRST AUTOMOBILES

From the invention of the first wheeled carts in the third millennium BCE to today's hybrid automobiles, humans have always looked for better ways to travel over land.

In the middle of the eighteenth century, engineers and inventors began playing with the idea of a horseless carriage, inspired by the steam engines of the Industrial Revolution. French engineer Nicholas-Joseph Cugnot created the first successful motorized vehicle in 1769: a three-wheeled gun carriage, powered by a two-cylinder steam engine mounted on the single front wheel. It traveled three miles an hour and could pull up to five tons. It had one major flaw—no braking system. With no brakes it's not surprising that Cugnot's car was not only the first automobile, but the first automobile to have an accident.

Cugnot's car accident didn't deter inventors. Experiments with steam vehicles continued into the 1830s, when the steam locomotive overtook the steam car.

It would be another fifty years before Karl Benz and Gottlieb Daimler created the first practical internal combustion engines and put the search for a motorized vehicle back on the road in 1885. The first automobiles were luxury items. Literally only one American in a million could afford one. The economic gap between car-haves and car-have-nots was so enormous that future president Woodrow Wilson claimed, "Nothing has spread socialistic feeling in this country more than the use of automobiles. . . . They are a picture of [the] arrogance of wealth."

Ford's first ad campaign was practically a call to revolution: "Even You Can Afford a Ford."

LEFT: *Henry Ford with a Model-T in 1921* • RIGHT: *A replica of Cugnot's steam-powered gun carriage.* • BOTTOM: *5th century BCE funerary cart*

STEEL

The traditional samurai sword and Mitsubishi's shipping fleet had one thing in common: high quality steel.

Steel is an alloy of iron and carbon with a very low carbon content. It is cheap, durable, and strong in proportion to its weight. It can be poured into almost any shape, pulled into wire, and rolled flat into sheets.

Before the Industrial Revolution, high-quality steel was expensive because, compared to iron, it required an enormous amount of labor and fuel to create. It was used for small objects that had a high value for their weight, especially razors, surgical tools, and swords. The innovators of the Industrial Revolution developed new processes that enabled manufacturers to make more steel in larger quantities: the *crucible method* and *puddled steel.*

The real leap forward in steel manufacturing came in the 1850s, when Henry Bessemer invented a new process for refining iron. Instead of using heat, the Bessemer converter blew air through

the molten metal to remove carbon impurities. The naturally occurring heat given off by the process of oxidation kept the iron liquid. The new Bessemer process cut the time needed to purify three to five tons of metal from twenty-four hours to between ten and twenty minutes. The savings in labor and fuel made mass steel production affordable for the first time.

The ability to make large quantities of steel changed the face of industry and construction. Miles of steel cable

supported suspension bridges around the world. Steel sheets were transformed into ocean liners and steam boilers. Steel beams made an entirely new kind of building possible: the skyscraper.

Today we use more than eight hundred million tons of steel each year, from pins that hold broken bones together to the rocket booster that launched the space shuttles. Ninety-three percent of the metal we use each year is steel.

were rendered idle, and struggled to live on inadequate stipends.

The samurai were officially abolished as a class under the Meiji Restoration in a series of measures that began in 1871, when all samurais were required to cut off their topknots, and ended with the Haitōrei Edict of March 1876, which took away the samurais' right to carry swords.

The last gasp of the samurai came with the great Satsuma Rebellion of 1877, which pitted the government's new conscript army and the latest weapons against traditionally armed samurai. Many of the rebels believed it was better to die using the traditional weapons of the samurai than to live using modern ones. Not surprisingly, the samurai rebels were defeated.

Manufacturing Bessemer Steel, 1914-1918

THE OTHER MAKERS OF THE MODERN WORLD

Like the Wright brothers and Henry Ford, some of the inventors and industrialists who helped make the modern world saw their names transformed into trademarked symbols of modernity: brand names so common we've almost forgotten that each was once the name of a man with a dream. Birdseye. Goodyear. Singer. Levi Strauss. Westinghouse. Some have achieved hero status: Alexander Graham Bell, Eli Whitney, Thomas Alva Edison, and John Deere.

Other important innovators are now almost forgotten:

- In 1907, Belgian immigrant LEO HENDRIK BAEKELAND developed the first true plastic, which he called Bakelite. Originally used for electrical insulators and billiard balls, easy-to-make Bakelite was as essential to the second industrial revolution as steel. It was inexpensive, would not catch fire or melt, did not conduct electricity, and could be molded into an infinite variety of shapes. Bakelite was used to make everything from toasters and washing machines to subway tracks and automobile ignition systems.

- German immigrant OTTMAR MERGENTHALER invented automatic typesetting in 1886. His Linotype machine was the greatest advance in printing since Gutenberg invented movable type. The new ease in typesetting created an explosion of printed books, magazines, and newspapers, followed by a sharp increase in literacy as the printed word became affordable to the man on the street. Thomas Edison called it the eighth wonder of the world.

- ELISHA OTIS designed the elevator brake in 1853, making practical the tall buildings that completely changed the landscape of the modern city.

- Artist WILLIAM ROSENTHAL and his wife, Ida, invented the modern bra in the early 1920s. Freed from the restrictions of corsetry, women could move and breathe more freely. A simple change in undergarments was almost as important as the vote in terms of giving women more freedom.

- Engineer WILLIAM STANLEY invented the electrical transformer in 1886. The transformer increases the power of an electrical current so it can travel long distances over a wire and then decreases it to the level needed to run household appliances and lights. The Stanley transformer was critical in the development of the modern electrical grid.

BY 1874, YATARO IWASAKI WAS a modern, self-made Japanese man. At twenty-seven, he had gotten a new look—now he had a new investment: thirteen steamships, which he purchased from his government at a cut-rate price.

In 1870, Iwasaki had established a shipping company, called Mitsubishi (from *mitsu,* meaning "three," and *hishi,* meaning "water chestnuts," or "diamonds"; in Japanese, water chestnuts were often used to represent diamonds, and the Iwasaki family crest was made up of three diamonds—it is no surprise that the Mitsubishi logo also has three diamonds). His company began to grow steadily.

His big break came in 1874, when Iwasaki volunteered his ships to deliver troops and supplies for the Japanese government's Taiwan Expedition, Japan's first modern military expedition. Mitsubishi ships made twenty-four round-trips to Taiwan

CLOCKWISE FROM TOP LEFT: *mannequin in an Eva bra ca.1925 • Ottmar Mergenthaler • bakelite radio, late 1940s • early model linotype typesetter ca 1915 • advertisement for Otis Electric Elevator, 1891*

GOODYEAR TRANSFORMS RUBBER

I N A CRAMPED KITCHEN ON THE FOURTH FLOOR OF a filthy New York apartment building, penniless Charles Goodyear experiments with a sticky, almost-black gum derived from the rubber trees of the Amazon rainforest. Goodyear has been experimenting with this substance for ten years, mixing natural rubber with a vast range of chemicals.

The maverick inventor has no training in chemistry, but he does have a clear vision of how rubber could transform peoples' lives. For years he has pursued his obsession with converting raw rubber to practical use. Never staying in one place for long, sometimes landing in debtor's prison, Goodyear has been brewing up smelly experiments in the kitchens and attics of small apartments and cottages from Pennsylvania to Connecticut to Massachusetts.

He's added different chemicals to the raw latex. He's heated it. He's cooled it. But every time he thought he had the formula right, summer proved him wrong, melting each year's crop of rubber-impregnated products.

And yet, Goodyear clearly possesses the two essential qualities of a successful inventor: an unflagging belief in his vision, and an ability to adapt and learn from his mistakes.

Now, in his New York apartment, this self-taught chemist thinks he may have found the magic formula. Marrying intuition with his years of trial and error, he decides to try adding a new combination of chemicals to his latex—with a twist: this time, Goodyear will add sulfur plus magnesium oxide *and* cook them over intense heat.

At first, Goodyear fears he has failed again. He looks more closely and finds that instead of melting like molasses, the rubber chars, and a dry, springy, brown rim forms around the edge.

Charles Goodyear has just discovered how to transform raw rubber into one of the most valuable commodities of the industrial age.

Goodyear names his newfound process "vulcanization," after Vulcan, the Roman god of fire and forges. Soon, Goodyear's "vulcanized rubber"—pliable and heat resistant—will have a myriad of applications in the newly industrialized world.

that summer, carrying men, rice, and munitions. In return, the government sold Mitsubishi thirteen steamships at a low price and gave the company the contract for carrying the mail. Under Iwasaki's leadership, Mitsubishi became the largest shipping company in Japan.

Before long, under his younger brother Yanosuke's direction, Mitsubishi began to diversify. Over the years, Mitsubishi bought coal and copper mines, railroads, insurance companies, and more.

In 1884, Iwasaki leased the Nagasaki Ironworks—renaming it the Nagasaki Shipyard—so his shipping operation could repair its own ships. In 1887, Mitsubishi bought the shipyard and soon expanded into shipbuilding, making the first iron steamship built in Japan in 1895. In World War II, Mitsubishi built Japan's largest battleships and the fearsome Zero fighter planes.

Today Japan is the second-largest ship and car producer and the third-richest nation on earth. All of it was born from the singular vision of a forward-thinking samurai.

THE INVENTORS AND CAPITALISTS who transformed raw materials into usable products and financed the assembly lines of the second industrial revolution created wealth and material progress on an unprecedented scale—ushering in the modern, industrialized world. However, for the men, women, and children who extracted the natural resources that fed these new industries, life was much like that of their predecessors toiling in sixteenth-century silver mines and on first-century Roman roads and aqueducts. That's because the demand for valuable natural resources—and the goods made from them—was relentlessly high.

And it would only grow more intense after an unlikely discovery by a nonscientist working in a New York City tenement in 1839.

Goodyear's recipe made rubber as valuable as silver. And this wonder material made possible huge technological leaps, including one of the greatest inventions of the modern world—the motor car. In Henry Ford's Model T, not only the tires, but *six hundred* other components were made from rubber, preventing the vehicle from shaking to bits.

Today, fifty thousand different products are made from vulcanized rubber—each a treasure mined from Goodyear's discovery during the second industrial revolution. And a glorious revolution it was.

But not for everyone.

FROM THE BEGINNING, THE Industrial Revolution had had its dark side: starvation wages, sweat shops, child labor, the slums of the new industrial cities, diseases caused by exposure to industrial chemicals, and accidents caused by machines with no safety devices. One of the second industrial revolution's ugliest chapters unfolded in Central Africa. Industry's swelling demand for rubber hoses, tubing, gaskets, and insulation created a worldwide rubber boom—and unleashed a reign of terror in the Congo.

At the end of the nineteenth century, the European powers engaged in a desperate race for imperial possessions, known as the Scramble for Africa. Since the fifteenth century, Europeans had been involved to some degree in Africa. They had established trading posts on the coastal fringe of the continent and founded strategic colonies in Algeria and South Africa. But they had left the African interior alone.

Suddenly, in the 1870s, European powers began to carve up the African continent. The nominal causes for the scramble were summed up in missionary and explorer David Livingstone's motto "Christianity, Commerce and Civilization." The true driving

RUBBER

Rubber comes from the milky sap of several hundred varieties of rubber trees that grow in tropical forests. Amazingly versatile, it can be molded to any shape, does not conduct electricity, and is impervious to water.

Unfortunately, rubber is virtually useless in its natural state. It becomes a gooey mess in hot weather and brittle when the weather turns cold. If it is exposed to grease, oil, or acid—all common elements in the manufacturing world—rubber decomposes, giving off a horrible stench in the process.

But mixed with sulfur and heated, a process called *vulcanization*, rubber turns into a wonder material. It stretches when pulled but will snap back to its former shape. It will not melt in the sun or break in the cold.

Our world is shaped by rubber. Without it, the enormous changes brought on by mechanization would not have been possible. Mechanization requires essential natural or man-made rubber components for machines—belts, gaskets, joints, valves, O-rings, washers, tires, seals, and countless others. Mechanized transportation—cars, trucks, ships, trains, and planes—has changed the way we move people and goods. Mechanization of industry has changed the jobs we do and the way we do them. Mechanization of agriculture has allowed the growth of cities and changed our society from rural to urban. Rubber has played an essential part in all these events.

Our exploration of future worlds may be shaped by rubber, as this material—an essential part of space stations, space suits, rockets, and shuttles—is now enabling us to explore horizons beyond our own.

force was rivalry between European nations. England was the biggest player, expanding its South African colonies, occupying Egypt, and claiming Nigeria as part of its sphere of influence. Soon powers new to the imperial game entered the race, looking for what Kaiser Wilhelm II called their "place in the sun."

King Leopold II of Belgium was eager to get his hands on "a slice of this magnificent African cake." Posing as a philanthropist interested only in stopping the slave trade and bringing medical aid to Africans, he carved out a vast private domain in the Congo River basin. Working on behalf of Leopold, explorer Henry Morgan Stanley built a two-hundred-mile road through the jungle, set up hundreds of stations along fifteen hundred miles of the Congo, and signed treaties with two thousand African chiefs. When the European powers met in Berlin in 1884 to decide on the fate of disputed African states, they reluctantly ratified Leopold's hold on a region as large as the United States east of the Mississippi. He called his new kingdom the Congo Free State.

But instead of helping Africans, Leopold's government in the Congo effectively turned them into slaves. At first the entire state was organized around collecting ivory. In the 1890s, Leopold turned his attention to cashing in on rubber from the rain forests. Thousands of Africans were forced into harvesting the valuable crop. Every adult male Congolese was required to produce between six and nine pounds of rubber each week. Men who failed to tap the daily quota were lashed with long whips of twisted hippopotamus hide. (The whips were often wielded by other Africans, who would be flogged themselves if they refused to obey.) Leopold's "army" of mercenary thugs took women and children as hostages from villages that fell behind on their rubber quota.

LEFT: *Congolese rubber slaves* • RIGHT: *victims of King Leopold II's terror regime*

MAY 1904. BARINGA, THE BELGIAN CONGO. The home of Baptist missionaries Reverend John Harris and his wife, Alice, who is also an amateur photographer. The British couple has lived in the Congo Free State since 1898.

The Harrises had moved to Baringa to spread the "Good Word" to their Congolese neighbors. But the urgent message they are about to receive will radically change the nature of their work and put them on the world stage, advocating for a more immediate cause.

Alice Harris hears a knock at the door. *Who on earth can it be?* she wonders. She quickly finishes pinning up her hair, then hurries to open the door.

Over the last six years, Alice and her husband have earned the trust of their neighbors, and she knows many of them by name. But she doesn't recognize the Congolese man who stands before her now, clutching a bundle of leaves to his chest. Still, the obvious exhaustion, despair, and desperation on his face concern her enough to invite him in.

With tears running down his face, he tells her his name is Nsala. He tries to tell her why he has come, but his throat closes on the words. His hands shake as he unwraps the parcel to show Alice the contents: the severed hand and foot of a small child. Alice gasps.

"My daughter," he says, choking back sobs.

Not immediately comprehending, Alice asks, "What happened to her?"

"We did not meet our quota," Nsala replies angrily, then sinks to the floor, still clutching his daughter's bloody appendages. He can no longer hold in his pain. His howls fill the house, bringing Reverend Harris from his study.

"What on earth . . . ?" he begins.

"Why—*why* would they do this?" Alice interrupts, her eyes wide.

Gently, the missionary helps Nsala to his feet and into a chair, then urges the heartbroken father to tell him the whole story. It is simple and horrifying: Nsala had not delivered his weekly six pounds of rubber sap, and Leopold's mercenaries had punished him by maiming his child.

The Harrises decide, then and there, that they must do something.

"I know it is difficult," the missionary says, "but we must let the world see what you and your people are enduring and what you've had the courage to show us tonight."

Immediately, Alice gets her camera. She then convinces Nsala to allow her to take a picture of him with his child's body parts. With shaking hands, she prepares her glass slides, tripod, and camera, then poses Nsala on the porch for a photograph—it is the first of many she will take detailing Belgium's brutality in the Congo.

W EEKS HAVE PASSED, AND THE HARRISES
have been busy. They have traveled five thousand miles
along the Congo and its tributaries, by river steamer, by
canoe, and on foot, visiting village after village. With her camera and his
pen, they have captured stories of brutality by colonial officials and soldiers against the people of the Congo. Alice has taken more than three
hundred photographs documenting conditions in King Leopold's Congo:
a catalog of the terror that reigns in the heart of Africa, unseen by the
wider world. Photographs of Congolese being whipped and chained. Villages burned to the ground. Men, women, and children with missing
hands and feet—cut off as punishment by Leopold's soldiers.

But photos alone, as vivid as they are, will not be enough. The Harrises know they must be the voice of Nsala and the rest of the Congolese people. They have traveled back to England to make their case.

At a church in London, nearly a hundred well-dressed British citizens fill the pews as Reverend Harris goes to the lectern. He thanks the crowd for coming, then pauses, his emotions palpable, before saying, "My good, God-fearing friends, as civilized people, we must speak up and demand an end to horrors being committed on the African continent that put the entire human race to shame."

As he begins to recount the terrible night when Nsala brought his daughter's severed hand and foot to their door, Alice Harris silently displays her photographs, in the form of lantern slides, as illustrative proof.

Gasps and shouts of "No!" fill the church.

And the spark is ignited.

Chapter 11: CLOSER

In Europe, the Harrises' story and Alice's photographs created outrage—and a movement dedicated to ending Belgian atrocities in the Congo. Every week another celebrity joined the Congo Reform Association, bringing renewed publicity to the cause. The Congo became one of the most infamous international scandals of the early twentieth century, and Leopold was ultimately forced to relinquish control of it to the government of Belgium.

His harsh regime had been—directly or indirectly—responsible for the deaths of 10 million people.

King Leopold was shamed and deposed from the throne, but the scars from European colonial rule in Africa lasted well beyond his brutal reign. It would be another sixty years of struggle before much of Africa would regain its independence.

AS AFRICA WAS RESHAPED BY imperialism and struggles for independence, America was enriched by the greatest voluntary migration in human history. Between 1880 and 1923, twenty-one million people streamed to America. By 1912, twenty ships a day landed in New York City. Germans and Irish had dominated earlier waves of immigration. Many of the immigrants at the turn of the twentieth century were from eastern and southern Europe. Like earlier immigrants, some came in search of freedom or to escape persecution. More came hoping to make their fortunes.

Passage from Europe to America was expensive. Often a family could afford only one fare, so the father or oldest son came first. Some traveled on ships specially designed to transport immigrants. Most traveled in steerage class, the lowest part of a passenger liner. In fact, immigrant travel

ABOVE: *European immigrants disembarking at Ellis Island, ca. 1907* • OPPOSITE: *Newly arrived European immigrants at Ellis Island in 1921*

was such big business that many large passenger liners made more profit carrying steerage passengers than they did on the high-paying passengers on the luxury decks.

The Atlantic crossing took about six days. At New York Harbor, the ship docked first at Manhattan, where the first- and second-class passengers disembarked. Then a ferryboat collected the immigrants from steerage and took them to Ellis Island, which was opened in 1892 to process the flood of immigrants.

Many immigrants referred to Ellis Island as the Isle of Tears. Immigrants stood in long lines to find out whether they would be allowed into the United States or sent back to Europe. They were checked for mental illness, contagious diseases, lice, obvious disabilities, and trachoma. Families were sometimes split up if one family member could not pass the medical exam; on occasion, children as young as ten were sent back to Europe alone. An immigrant could also be barred if he had been convicted of a crime involving "moral turpitude," such as anarchism or polygamy. And a few failed the trick question of whether they had a job waiting for them: the correct answer was no. (Coming with a job already arranged was a violation of immigration laws.) Examiners marked the backs of their clothes with chalked symbols indicating whether they had been accepted, rejected, or needed further examination.

Once they successfully navigated their way through Ellis Island's screening process, many immigrants stayed in New York, which soon had the most diverse population on earth. Others scattered across the country, looking for jobs in the growing industrial cities of Pittsburgh, Chicago, and Detroit, where they made the steel that forged modern America and built the new skyscrapers that changed the urban landscape.

Most immigrants spoke little or no English when they arrived. They clustered together in neighborhoods with people from their own countries, turning them into little Italys, little Polands, and little Germanys. They read newspapers in their own languages and shopped at stores that sold familiar foods. The work was hard and wages were low. Most immigrants lived in crowded city tenements with none of the comforts produced by the second industrial revolution.

Even under these conditions, they managed to save. They sent astonishing amounts of money home to pay the cost of a steamship ticket for a relative or friend. With luck and hard work, a person could fulfill the immigrant dream of buying a home and sending his children to school, where they would learn English and become Americans.

BEYOND THE UNITED STATES

In the hundred years between 1830 and 1930, more than sixty million people emigrated from Europe in search of new opportunities and resources. Most went to the United States, but many European immigrants also settled in what they saw as the "empty spaces" of Australia, Canada, Latin America, New Zealand, and South Africa, pushing native populations off the land in the process. French farmers settled in North Africa. British and Dutch planters made homes in India and Indonesia.

A *TITANIC* SURVIVOR

APRIL 14, 1912. THE THIRD-CLASS DECK OF THE RMS *Titanic*. Theodor de Mulder has invited four of his fellow passengers to join him for a card game in his cramped but tidy cabin. The thirty-six-year-old Belgian paid nine pounds ten shillings for his passage to America, a thousand dollars in today's money. He has left his wife and two children at home while he travels in search of new opportunities. He plans to come home a rich man.

De Mulder misses his family, but he has never before had an entire week free of work. A week in which to walk on the decks, listen to his fellow passengers play the accordion or the fiddle, flirt with a pretty girl—and play cards.

He takes a slug of his drink and examines his cards, then allows himself a slow grin. He slams a winning hand down on the table, jumps up from his chair, and crows with delight. His guests shake their heads. De Mulder's been lucky all night. He toasts himself with another glass of whiskey, flushed with excitement and slightly tipsy.

RMS Titanic, *which sank after hitting an iceberg on its maiden voyage, 1912.*

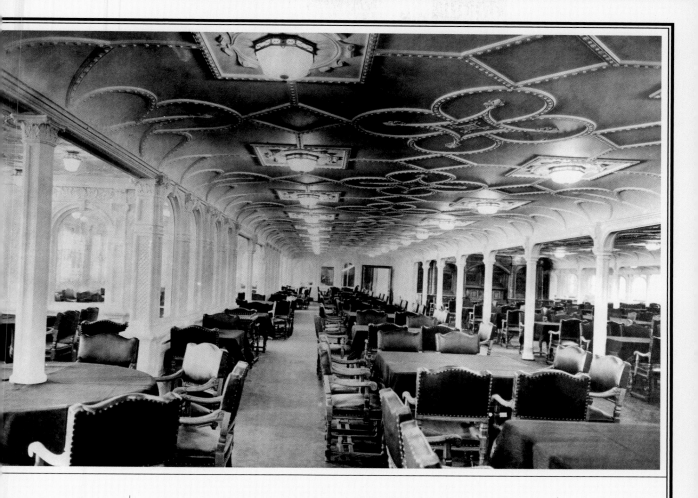

The dining room of the RMS Titanic

Better to quit while he's still ahead. He bids his guests good night, and they stumble off to their own cabins. He falls into bed and is asleep immediately.

But his sleep is short-lived. The electric lights begin to flicker on and off. And *what* is all that racket? De Mulder sits up in bed and tilts his head, as if to listen. What he has heard, ever since he and his fellow passengers first sailed, was the thrum of the ship's engines, so constant that de Mulder has stopped noticing them. Now, he notices, they are silent, replaced by the cacophony of frantic voices in the passageway. *What is happening?*

371

Chapter 11: CLOSER

Three of the Titanic's *lifeboats hanging from the side of the* Carpathia

De Mulder puts his feet on the floor. Water is seeping under the cabin door. He scrambles out of bed and rushes into the corridor.

There is confusion everywhere he looks. Panicked passengers crowd the passageway, all talking at once. "What is going on?" de Mulder asks. The crew has no instructions and no information.

In fifteen minutes, the third-class section is already flooding. De Mulder clambers, along with his shipmates, to get out of the congested passageway. But the flickering lights and the maze of corridors disorient him. He reaches a stairwell, but it is blocked by a locked gate. Turning back, he shoves through a herd of oncoming passengers, takes a hard right down another passageway, and comes to another flight of stairs at the end of the narrow passage.

Also blocked.

De Mulder knows why. US immigration laws. These locked gates are meant to keep third-class passengers separate from the rest of the ship.

The corridor is rapidly filling with water. People are screaming and pushing, separated from their families, desperate.

But de Mulder has found another staircase, and it is *not* blocked. He makes his way up and fights his way to the deck.

The ship is sinking! But people are getting on lifeboats! He tries to reach one, then another, in time, but he doesn't make it; few men from steerage will. Minutes turn to an hour, then two. In the end, de Mulder watches as the last lifeboat is lowered to the water below.

The ship tilts, and desperate hands reach out, struggling to grab for anything they can to break their fall. Some hands make contact with something they hope will save them—pieces of the broken ship, deck furniture—anything that will float. Others only scratch air. De Mulder grabs onto a wooden deck chair. And the ship sinks, along with its passengers, including him.

The night wears on. Debris bobs on the ocean's surface. So do bodies. Hundreds of them, dead within minutes from hypothermia, heart failure, or injuries sustained from the fall.

But de Mulder survives—by clinging to his deck chair in the freezing water.

Serendipitously, he floats close enough to one of the *Titanic*'s twenty lifeboats to cry for help—and be heard. Its passengers pull him to safety.

Four days later, Theodor de Mulder reaches his destination: the promised land of America. He's one of the lucky ones.

The *RMS* Titanic *was more than 880 feet (268m) long and weighed more than 46,000 tons.*

THE *TITANIC* WAS THE LARGEST and most luxurious steamship ever built.

The ship's builders, the Harland and Wolff shipyard in Belfast, Ireland, designed the ship with safety in mind. They divided the hull into fifteen watertight bulkheads, the theory being that if a collision occurred and even two compartments flooded, the ship could still float. Harland and Wolff claimed that the ship's cutting-edge system of watertight bulkheads made it "virtually unsinkable."

For its first-class passengers, its owners marketed the luxury experience more than the journey itself. The ship's promotional materials described its opulent decor, extensive recreational facilities, and modern technology, including ship-wide electric lighting and Marconi wireless communication equipment. First-class passengers had use of a swimming pool, a gymnasium, a squash court, a library, and a Turkish bath, as well as a variety of dining rooms, bars, and restaurants. The most expensive ticket cost $4,246 one way, roughly $92,000 today, for a suite that included a sitting room, two bedrooms, two dressing rooms, a private bath, and a private deck for enjoying the sea air.

Not everyone on the *Titanic* traveled first class. Second-class facilities were still deluxe, surpassing those of the first-class facilities on most rival liners.

More than half of the *Titanic*'s passengers were traveling steerage: 710 people from all over the world, including eight Chinese, on their way to a new life in America. Thanks to the owners' preference for comfort over speed, the *Titanic* offered the highest standard of third-class accommodations of its time. Most of the four decks of steerage were made up of small cabins intended for two to four passengers. Every room had running water—a luxury many of the steerage-class passengers would not have enjoyed at home—though there were only two baths for third class. And the only public rooms for steerage passengers, were a general room, paneled in whitewashed pine and furnished with sturdy teak benches, table, and chairs; a smoking room and bar; and a large dining saloon.

The voyage was scheduled to take just over a week, but the owner and captain hoped to make the ship's maiden voyage from Southampton, England, to New York in record time.

The *Titanic* had been at sea for four days when telegraph operator Jack Phillips received the first of nine messages from other ships, warning them of ice fields ahead. He posted the reports on the message center so Captain Edward Smith and other crew members could see them and take action. Captain Smith decided to continue, adjusting his course to the south—a decision that would sink the world's greatest steamliner and cost hundreds of lives.

The night was clear and bitter cold. The sea was calm. Lookouts in the crow's nests were told to watch for icebergs as a routine precaution. At 11:40 that evening, two hours after the first iceberg warning came through, lookout Frederick Fleet spotted an iceberg. He hit the warning bell three times—the signal for danger ahead—and called an urgent message to the bridge. It was too late. The crew could not turn the massive ship fast enough to avoid the iceberg. The iceberg buckled the hull, ripping open the three forward holds. Two boiler rooms were exposed to the sea. The pumps could expel two thousand tons of water per hour; that amount poured into the *Titanic* every five minutes.

At 12:05, twenty-five minutes after the collision, Captain Smith realized the extent of the damage and ordered the crew to prepare to abandon ship. For the next two hours, the ship was in total confusion. There had been no lifeboat drill since the ship left Southampton. Neither passengers nor crew knew where to go or what to do. Lifeboats were loaded with less than their full passenger load because crew members did not know they could be lowered at full capacity. Some passengers refused to get in lifeboats because they thought they would

lat 42 N to 41.25 N, long 49 W to 50.3 W saw much heavy pack ice and great number of large icebergs also field ice. Weather good, clear.
—Ice report from the SS *Mesaba*

be safer on deck. Many had failed to grab their life jackets from their cabins.

Telegraph officers Harold Bride and Jack Phillips sent out distress calls to all ships: *CQD CQD SOS Titanic Position 41.44N 50.24W Require immediate assistance. Come at once. We struck an iceberg. Sinking.* Bride and Phillips couldn't be sure that anyone would respond. Wireless telegraphy was less than fifteen years old. Few ships carried radios; those that did used them primarily to send personal and business messages. No protocols existed for their use.

One ship was only twenty miles away, but its radio operator had turned off his wireless for the night. The passenger ship *Carpathia*, fifty-eight miles south of the sinking *Titanic*, heard the wireless SOS and responded. It took more than four hours for the ship to rescue some seven hundred people from the scattered lifeboats.

Designed to be unsinkable, the *Titanic* hit the seabed in less than three hours.

MORSE CODE AND SOS

Long before Samuel Morse invented Morse code in 1838, people were sending long-distance messages using code. Their ways and means may have differed—African talking drums, Native American smoke signals, military bugle calls, semaphore—but all broke messages down into coded signals.

Morse code uses the same idea to send messages by telegraph. Each letter of a word is represented by a series of short or long signals. The most frequently used letters use the fewest number of signals.

In the beginning of the twentieth century, operators of the Marconi wireless used Morse code to send the first radio distress signal: CQD—*come quick danger*. In 1906, the International Radio Telegraphic Convention created

a new signal, SOS, which was simpler to transmit in Morse code. But humans are creatures of habit, and radio operators continued to use the old signal. The *Titanic* disaster was the first time SOS was used by an endangered ship.

After the *Titanic*, SOS became the standard international distress signal. Commonly believed to mean "save our ship," the three-letter signal was chosen solely because it is easy to remember and enter.

Wireless operator and survivor, Harold Bride, at work in Marconi Room on RMS Titanic.

FROM THE MOMENT THE FIRST artist painted a bison on a cave wall, humans have sought better ways to communicate. Cuneiform, Gutenberg's movable type, the knotted string of the Incan quipu, signal flags on the mast of a ship, and lamps in a lighthouse all served the same purpose: allowing one person to share information with another.

In the nineteenth century, mankind began to learn more about the energy force called electricity. Samuel Morse was the first to harness it as a means

Titanic distress call received by steamship SS Burma at 11.50 p.m.

Italian inventor Guglielmo Marconi was only thirty-five when he won the Nobel Prize for physics for his work in wireless telegraphy in 1909.

of carrying communication. His telegraph sent messages using electromagnetic currents flowing over a wire. Messages were coded with strokes of a single key. When the key was pressed down, current flowed along a wire: the dots and dashes of Morse code created by the length of time the operator held down the key. At the other end of the wire, the electrical impulses were translated into long and short clicks or printed on a Morse writer as dots and dashes for the operator to decode.

Morse telegraphs spread as quickly as men could string wire. Between 1843, when Congress approved the first telegraph line between Baltimore and Washington, and Morse's death in 1872,

the Western Union Company had strung almost 250,000 miles of telegraph wire across the United States, and the continents were linked by 100,000 miles of undersea cable.

The telephone Alexander Graham Bell introduced to the world in 1876 at the Centennial Exhibition in Philadelphia also used electromagnetic currents to transmit sound. In fact, Bell described the device as a "harmonic telegraph."

The telephone and the telegraph both provided instant communication over long distances, something that was believed to be impossible only fifty years before. Both methods required wires and had a limited range. Ships at sea could not contact people on land. Most experts scoffed at the idea that messages could travel long distances without wires. Some believed that signals would simply disappear into space because electromagnetic waves travel in a straight line and the earth is round. Others argued that it was impossible to generate sufficient power to create electromagnetic waves that were long enough to travel over distances.

Guglielmo Marconi proved them wrong. While still in his twenties, he pioneered a practical method of sending messages at the speed of light across thousands of miles, without wires or other physical connection between sender and receiver.

Marconi began working on wireless telegraphy in 1894 after reading about Heinrich Hertz's work with long wavelength electromagnetic radiation. Hertz had proved that electromagnetism, the combined force of electricity and magnetism, existed as an invisible disturbance in the air, a vibration that moved in waves, like visible light and audible sound. At first known as Hertzian electromagnetic waves, we now know them as "radio waves."

Over the next six years, Marconi built equipment that could transmit electrical signals without wires, beginning with an apparatus similar to that used by Hertz and a Morse signaling key. His first success came when he sent a signal nine yards across the room in his home laboratory. Soon he was sending messages across a mile-wide field, then across the English Channel. On December 12, 1901, he sent the first message across the Atlantic, using an aerial attached to a kite at the end of a six-hundred-foot wire.

By 1909, all the major naval forces in the world and three hundred merchant ships and liners had wireless devices on board, but they were used mainly to carry the news and allow passengers to send personal and business messages. The 1912 *Titanic* disaster illustrated all too clearly the value of the radio when a ship is in trouble. Three months after the *Titanic* sank, new international regulations required every oceangoing ship to carry a working wireless and keep it powered at all times.

THE IONOSPHERE

Like medieval sailors, who thought they would sail off the edge of the earth when they reached the horizon, many scientists at the end of the nineteenth century expected electromagnetic waves to travel straight out to space when they passed the earth's horizon. Obviously that didn't happen. No one knew why until more than twenty years after Marconi's first transatlantic transmission. In 1924, British physicist Edward Appleton discovered the ionosphere, a wave of electrically charged particles produced by the sun's radiation. This electrified layer sixty-two miles above the earth's surface reflects radio waves back to earth, where they then bounce back to the ionosphere. This process continues until the radio wave loses its energy.

THE SAME TECHNOLOGY THAT saved lives on the open seas was adapted for entertainment in the 1920s. Radio broadcasts began with news and music in the 1920s; over the next thirty years, programming expanded to include interviews, speeches, variety shows, and the dramas that took the name "soap operas" from their commercial sponsors. By 1924, 2.5 million radio sets tuned in to more than six hundred broadcast stations in the United States alone.

Today, the effects of Marconi's wireless technology are everywhere: automatic garage door openers, GPS systems, satellite communications, radio telescopes, mobile phones, wireless Internet, and the growing array of tablets, readers, and other devices that depend on wireless communication. The more we unplug, the more plugged in we become.

BY THE BEGINNING OF THE First World War, humans had made giant strides in the battle against our oldest and most deadly enemies—bacteria. English surgeon Joseph Lister had pioneered the use of antiseptics in surgery. French scientist Louis Pasteur and others had identified germs as the cause of diseases like cholera, tetanus, diptheria, and pneumonia. Austrian physician Ignaz Semmelweis had reduced the number of deaths from so-called "childbed fever" by a factor of twenty with the simple—and controversial—suggestion that doctors wash their hands before delivering a baby. Despite these advances, germ theory wasn't universally accepted by doctors—and even those who believed in it had no way to treat bacteria-caused infections. Scientists had identified bacteria as the enemy, but had not yet found a weapon against it.

Dr. Alexander Fleming was one of those who had wholeheartedly accepted germ theory. When the war began, Fleming was a young doctor and researcher in Sir Almroth Wright's inoculation department at St. Mary's Hospital in London. Soon after England entered the war, Wright volunteered the services of his entire staff to vaccinate British soldiers against typhoid and to run a wound treatment and research center in France.

While treating battlefield wounds, Fleming saw thousands of wounded soldiers die from tetanus, blood poisoning, and gangrene—just as they had since humans first went to war. He quickly realized that Lister's antiseptic methods, which worked reasonably well in the controlled conditions of civilian hospitals, had almost no effect at the front. Soldiers arrived at the field hospital with massive wounds that were contaminated with dirt, feces, shreds of clothing, and shrapnel—all prime breeding grounds for the bacteria that caused infections. Fleming demonstrated that the standard method of wrapping wounds with antiseptic-soaked bandages not only failed to kill the bacteria, but damaged both the surrounding tissue and the white blood cells that are the body's natural defense against infection. He developed a new technique for treating wounds: removing as much dead tissue as possible, then flushing the wound with a sterile saline solu-

Scientists had identified bacteria as the enemy, but had not yet found a weapon against it.

tion, which washed away bacteria and encouraged the body to produce new white blood cells.

By the end of the war, Fleming was the leading expert on wound infections. He came home from France determined to find a way to cure them. He later wrote that his experience of being surrounded by men suffering and dying from infected wounds and being powerless to help them left him "consumed by a desire to discover, after all this struggling and waiting, something which would kill those microbes."

After the war Fleming returned to the laboratories at St. Mary's, where he continued his research in fighting bacteria—a life he often described as "playing with microbes." In 1928, he discovered penicillin by chance, thanks to his habit of accumulating unwashed Petri dishes on his worktable. Coming back to his lab after a vacation, he noticed that one dish of *Staphylococcus* bacteria was contaminated by mold. Other researchers had seen

Fleming put his work on penicillin aside because of difficulties in growing and refining the mold from which it was made.

Time *magazine named Fleming one of the hundred most important people in the twentieth century for his discovery of penicillin.*

mold on Petri dishes and thrown it away without a thought. Fleming looked closer; he saw that the area surrounding the mold was free of bacteria. Excited by the possibilities, he started a fresh colony of the mold, a variety of *Penicillium,* in a fresh Petri dish and surrounded it with radiating stripes of bacteria that would allow him to measure the impact of the mold over time. Within a few days he could see that the mold produced liquid that killed several kinds of disease-causing bacteria. Fleming knew he had made a discovery that could change

the world, but when he published his results three months later his fellow researchers ignored them. He convinced a few research chemists to try to extract the active ingredient from what he called "mold juice." They soon gave up when they discovered that penicillin was difficult to produce and deteriorated easily.

World War II and a new generation of infected battlefield wounds revived interest in Fleming's research into penicillin. Two researchers at Oxford, Australian pathologist Howard Florey and German biochemist Ernst Chain, discovered Fleming's 1929 paper on penicillin while studying natural antibacterial substances. Together with biochemist Norman Heatley, they found solutions for the problems of low yield and instability that had caused earlier researchers to abandon penicillin as unworkable.

By 1941, the newspapers had proclaimed penicillin a wonder drug, but production was still a problem in wartime Britain. Florey and Heatley flew to the United States to convince American companies to produce the drug on a large scale.

In 1942, the entire supply of penicillin in the United States totaled only eleven grams. By D-Day, June 6, 1944, American factories were producing enough penicillin to treat all Allied casualties. Unlike Fleming, doctors no longer had to look on hopelessly as suffering soldiers died from infected wounds.

Allied servicemen were the first to benefit from the first antibiotic. After the war, penicillin became available to civilians as well. Fleming's "mold juice" and its younger siblings created a medical revolution. Mankind had a powerful new weapon in the battle against infectious diseases.

AT THE BEGINNING OF THE twentieth century, Americans and western Europeans believe they live in a golden age of progress. The second industrial revolution has transformed every aspect of modern life. Everything is bigger, better, and faster than it had been before. Mass production creates a mass society, making more goods available to more people. Revolutionary processes for creating steel make it possible to build bigger ships, taller buildings, and a network of railroad tracks that circles the globe. Messages fly across continents, carried by the newly tamed forces of electricity and radio waves. People travel faster too: by train, by steamship, and by automobile. For the first

time in history, humans have an effective weapon against infectious disease. Perhaps most amazing of all, the Wright brothers' first flight makes one of mankind's oldest dreams come true. Flight brings with it a new sense of freedom and speed. It seems like the sky is no longer the limit.

But humanity's new sense of progress is not universal. The spread of industry comes at a price. Factory workers are often treated like little more than cogs in society's machine. Traditional crafts are disappearing. Less developed countries are plundered as the source of raw material for Western progress. And with worldwide war on the horizon, mankind prepares to turn its newfound gift of flight into a deadly weapon.

As we move forward, unlocking the secrets of nature will give us our greatest challenges and our greatest opportunities.

Flasks growing penicillin culture, 1943

12

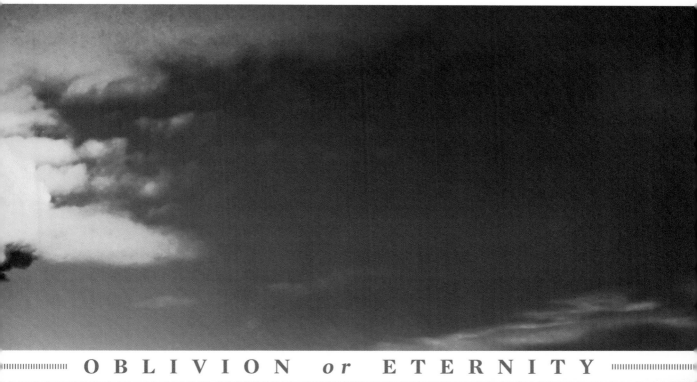

OBLIVION *or* ETERNITY

IT'S THE MIDDLE OF THE TWENTIETH CENTURY. ONCE A RELA-
TIVELY DEFENSELESS MAMMAL AT THE MERCY OF THE PLANET,
OUR SPECIES HAS COME TO DOMINATE IT. EXPLOITING ITS RICHES.

Exploring its farthest corners. Overcoming its geography. For generation after generation, we have overcome problems with engineering marvels, from Stonehenge to the skyscraper. We have found new sources of energy and new ways to communicate.

Now we cross new boundaries as the human race moves from the age of the tinkerer and the independent researcher to the age of Big Science. Humans form focused research teams dedicated to solving clearly defined problems and reaching specific goals. Working together, humans unlock the secrets of the atom, of the stars, and of our own DNA. We find life-changing uses for previously untapped resources, utilize technology to combat the frailties of our bodies, and reach beyond the limits of Earth's atmosphere into space. Breakthroughs in Big Science, from the Manhattan Project to the Human Genome Project, are the modern equivalent of the Egyptian

pyramids and Gothic cathedrals, monumental developments that define their place and time.

For the first time, humans have the knowledge to transform the species and the power to annihilate it.

FOUR THOUSAND YEARS AGO, maize was mankind's first genetically modified crop: a wild grass from Central America that was bred into an adaptable grain. By the middle of the twentieth century, it is the staple diet of a billion people. Dried and ground into flour, it is served as polenta, corn meal mush and hominy grits, as cornbreads, tortillas, and fried cakes. Treated with lye, it becomes posole. Served fresh, it appears in Indian raitas and American succotash. The United States produces more maize than any country on earth. Now, American farmers blend four strains of maize into one superstrong hybrid that will create an agricultural revolution.

LEFT: *Iowa farmer-salesman Roswell Garst championed the adoption of scientific breakthroughs that created an agricultural revolution in mid-twentieth century America.*

Chapter 12: OBLIVION OR ETERNITY

GARST'S HYBRID CORN

IOWA. 1936. ROSWELL GARST TRAVELS ON DUSTY roads from farm to farm in a battered pickup truck loaded with eight-pound sacks of seed corn. In his plaid shirt and suspenders, he looks more like a farmer dressed up for a day in town than the salesman and part owner of Pioneer Hi-Bred Seed Company.

Garst has mortgaged his farm to launch a new company selling a revolutionary product that will transform agriculture around the world—if only anyone could afford to buy it. Garst's hybrid corn sells for five dollars a bag. More than a week's salary for a farm laborer. Four dollars more than a bag of ordinary seed corn. It's a tough sell in hard times. Depression and drought have struck America's heartland. In Iowa, some of the richest farmland in the country, almost half the crops are so damaged by the lack of rain that they aren't worth harvesting. In Oklahoma, Kansas, and Nebraska, the losses are much worse.

Garst has been selling seed corn for six years now. He has spent whole days on the road, selling a bushel or two a day. His sales pitch has been greeted with amusement, resignation, hostility, and, sometimes, with the wrong end of a shotgun held by a farmer who's at the end of his rope.

Now, almost as desperate as the farmers, he has decided to gamble everything and give his seed corn away for free. He persuades farmers to plant half their fields with his hybrid corn and the other half with their usual seed corn. All he asks in return is a share in the increased profit from his hybrid corn. Ten years ago, prosperous farmers would have laughed off such a proposition. But now, crippled by the Great Depression, they have nothing to lose.

Corn and its derivatives play a role in almost every aspect of modern life, from toothpaste to automobile tires.

From the beginning, the size and shape of human society has been limited by our ability to supply ourselves with the food we need to keep us alive. Hunter-gatherers lived in small bands. The advent of farming led to the creation of towns, then cities. Cities grew explosively when the development of the steam locomotive gave merchants the capacity to move food from one region to another.

In the twentieth century, an agricultural revolution that would feed the world began in the heart of the American Midwest. It was led by Roswell Garst, an Iowa farmer turned salesman who became an agricultural evangelist. Not a scientist himself, he grasped the importance of new ideas developed by creative thinkers such as agronomist Henry A. Wallace and demonstrated their value in practical ways that the small farmer could understand and use.

Garst and Wallace met in 1926 in Des Moines, where Garst was selling real estate and Wallace was editing his family's newspapers, *Wallaces'*

Farmer and *Iowa Homestead*. During his free time, Wallace experimented with creating corn hybrids. At the time, farmers saved the best-looking ears of corn from each year's crop for seed, selecting them based on uniformity and size. Wallace, who would later serve as Franklin Roosevelt's secretary of agriculture from 1933 to 1940 and his vice president from 1941 to 1945, had already proven that these factors did not necessarily predict which ears would produce the best crop the following year. Now he was trying to crossbreed plants to produce higher yields.

Garst was so fascinated by the possibilities of hybrid corn that he bought several bushels of the seed from Wallace to use on his home farm. After several years of watching the performance of Wallace's high-yield, strong-stalked hybrid in his own fields, Garst asked Wallace for a franchise to sell the virtually unknown product in northeastern Iowa.

Even in good times it would have been hard to convince farmers to buy expensive, genetically

NITROGEN

Spewed from volcanoes during the birth of our planet, nitrogen makes up 80 percent of Earth's atmosphere. It's invisible. It's odorless. And every living creature on Earth needs it to survive. Plants and animals alike use it to make the amino acids that are the building blocks of protein.

Even though nitrogen makes up more than three-quarters of the air we breathe, we cannot directly use nitrogen from the air. Plants extract soluble nitrogen compounds from the soil. Animals eat the plants (or other animals that eat plants). The bacteria that help decompose animal waste and dead plants and animals release nitrogen and return it to the atmosphere.

Each nitrogen molecule is made up of two nitrogen atoms that are tightly linked together. It takes energy to unlock the bonds of nitrogen molecules in the air so they can bond with other molecules to create nitrogen compounds, a process called *fixing*. Nature provides two ways of "fixing" nitrogen.

One occurs when lightning heats up the air, forcing nitrogen to bond with oxygen. Rain washes the resulting nitrogen oxide out of the air and into the ground, where plants can absorb it. The other natural fixer comes from bacteria that live in the roots of legumes, such as beans, peas, and clover. These bacteria convert nitrogen into soluble compounds that can be absorbed by plants.

When fields are overworked, they exhaust the nitrogen in the soil, making the fields less fertile. For centuries, farmers rotated legumes with nitrogen-hungry grains to protect the fertility of their soil.

At the start of the twentieth century, German scientist Fritz Haber invented a technique for extracting nitrogen from the air. Originally used to make explosives in World War I, synthesized nitrogen compounds became the world's first artificial fertilizer. Once used as a weapon, nitrogen was now a giver of life, making it possible for us to replenish the earth's growing power.

Nitrogen-fixing nodules on soybean roots

modified seed instead of using the open-pollinated kernels from their own fields. During the Depression, it was virtually impossible. Garst had to come up with ways to prove that his advertising slogan, "An Astonishing Product—Produces Astonishing Results," was literally true. His most successful tactic was the "half the increase" technique. Growing both Pioneer hybrid corn and their own seed corn gave farmers a graphic demonstration of the new corn's value. In the worst drought in America's history, Roswell Garst's hybrid corn not only grew; it flourished. Bred to produce a higher yield, the hybrid also proved to be drought resistant. On average, the hybrid corn outperformed the old seed corn by ten bushels an acre. Once convinced, a farmer would sell the idea and the corn to his neighbors. The demand for hybrid seed corn exploded.

THE DUST BOWL

Depression and drought struck the American heartland in the 1930s.

Rainfall was irregular in the 1920s. In 1932, it stopped almost completely. The record drought was accompanied by record heat and unusually strong winds. By 1935, what began as a dry spell had become the worst drought in American history. The Great Plains became a dust bowl.

The seemingly rugged Great Plains are more fragile than they appear. By the 1920s, the native grasses that held the soil in place had been plowed under and stripped by overgrazing. Wheat had exhausted the topsoil. When the drought came, there was nothing to protect the dry soil from the winds. Known as "black blizzards," the dust-laden winds traveled east at sixty miles per hour. The storms came so often that people on the plains could tell where the wind originated based on the color of the dust. In May 1934, a dust storm fifteen hundred miles long, nine hundred miles across and two miles high reached as far east as New York City. The storm deposited a film of dust on President Herbert Hoover's desk in the White House and dropped prairie dirt on ships five hundred miles out in the Atlantic.

With no crops, 2.5 million people, about a quarter of the population of the Dust Bowl region, were forced off their ruined farms when they could not pay their rent or mortgages. Many moved to the nearest city. Others joined the army of migrant farm workers that followed the harvest from Florida to Montana and squatted in shantytowns on the edges of California's cities.

The Great Plains did not begin to recover until regular rainfall came again in 1939.

In fewer than ten years, more than half the fields in America's Corn Belt were planted with Wallace and Garst's high-yield corn.

High-yield corn wasn't Garst's only contribution to America's agricultural revolution. In the 1940s, he began to sell newly developed nitrogen fertilizer with the same passion he had brought to hybrid seed, convinced that the old-fashioned methods of crop rotation limited the output of farmers' fields. Once again using the idea that a demonstration is worth a thousand promises, Garst would mark the letter *N* with nitrogen fertilizer on a hill near the road next to a farmer's land. Dark-green *N*s grew on fields across the countryside; so did the use of synthetic fertilizer.

With the use of hybrid seeds, artificial fertilizer, and other agricultural innovations, farmers eliminated the natural limits on how much food we can grow for the first time in human history. American farm production grew faster than the American population, even with the rise of the post–World War II baby boom.

Beginning in the 1940s, American aid programs encouraged the use of chemical fertilizers, pesticides, and new, high-yielding varieties of grain across the developing world, with the idea that increased crop yields would provide stable food supplies and defeat hunger. Between 1940 and 1944, fertilizer use around the world increased 50 percent, bringing with it amazing increases in production. India in particular was a success story, thanks to high-yield varieties of rice and wheat and government-sponsored improvements in irrigation.

WAR COMES NATURALLY TO humans. Over the course of six thousand years, we have fought more than fourteen thousand wars, costing at least 3.5 billion lives. We have gone to war over land, gold, salt, cattle, and dynastic succession.

THE OTHER SIDE OF THE GREEN REVOLUTION

Concerns about Garst's transformation of American farming appeared as early as 1962, when Rachel Carson's *The Silent Spring* documented the effects of farm chemicals on the environment.

Today environmentalists and food activists are concerned about the loss of biological diversity due to the widespread use of hybrid seeds and the long-term effects of both genetically engineered plants and the use of nitrogen fertilizer.

Hybrid corn (left) compared to non-hybrid corn (right).

We have clashed over eternal principles and small insults. We have fought over a slap in the face with a flyswatter, the severing of a sailor's ear, and the assassination of Archduke Franz Ferdinand. We have battled on land, on sea and—in the last hundred years—in the air.

Humans have been in an arms race from the beginning, using our ingenuity to develop new weapons and different ways of going to war. The atlatl, and later the bow, allowed our ancestors to hurl sharp objects harder and faster than the unaided human arm. We invented gunpowder-propelled projectiles that would stop an armored knight—then destroy a city's fortifications. In the twentieth century, we learned to attack from above, turning the combination of airplane and bomb into the ultimate weapon.

AIRPLANES WERE FIRST USED as weapons in World War I. Less than a decade old, not much more powerful than a modern ultralight, planes transformed warfare. The success of air reconnaissance led to the development of fighter planes and a new breed of military hero, fighter pilots, as armies struggled to keep enemy planes out of their airspace. It was a short step from fighter planes to bombers. By the end of the war, it was clear that future wars would depend on mastery of the skies.

In the 1920s and 1930s, Western governments began to develop long-range bombers, hoping that strategic bombing would force an enemy to surrender quickly. Instead, the new bombers gave warring governments the ability to rain terror from the air. The lesson of modern warfare, first learned in the American Civil War, was that victory hinged on defeating the enemy off the field as well as on. With long-range bombers that could fly hundreds of miles behind enemy lines, it was possible to disrupt production of vital war materials. Destroying

enemy factories and transportation systems became as important as killing enemy soldiers, sailors, and airmen. Weakening civilian morale was as critical as wiping out the factories where civilians worked.

By the time President Truman decided to drop the atomic bomb on Hiroshima, World War II had already raged for six years, from Europe to Africa, from America to Japan and the Pacific. Fifty million people were dead. The combination of devastating new technology and the global scope of the battlefield made World War II the deadliest conflict in human history.

ABOVE: *The Eberhart SE-5E first flew in December 1916* • BELOW: *Corsair fighter unloading its rocket projectiles against a Japanese stronghold on Okinawa, 1945.*

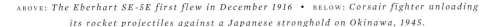

The opposing powers were in a race to make war even deadlier. Conventional explosives depended on chemical reactions. By 1942, Germany, Japan, and the United States were all working to produce a more powerful bomb based on a nuclear reaction.

The United States' bomb program, code-named the Manhattan Project, was under the direction of physicist Robert Oppenheimer and Maj. Gen. Leslie R. Groves of the Army Corps of Engineers. The project was so highly classified that president Harry Truman only learned of its existence when he assumed the office after Roosevelt's death. By the time President Truman took office on April 12, 1945, American scientists predicted an atomic bomb would be ready for testing by midsummer.

The Manhattan Project scientists did not know precisely how much destruction the bomb would cause. Oppenheimer claimed the bomb's effects would be similar to those caused by dropping tons of high-explosive or incendiary bombs on a city, something the United States had already done in Dresden and Tokyo. Manhattan Project physicists knew that, in addition to its powerful blast effects, an atomic bomb would release deadly radiation, which they estimated would extend to a radius of up to two-thirds of a mile. Since anyone within that range would be killed in the blast, they assumed the radiation was irrelevant.

GERMANY SURRENDERED IN May 1945, shifting attention to the war in the Pacific. The outcome of the war was clear; the only question was how long it would take and how many men each side would lose. Determined to avoid the ultimate dishonor of surrendering, the Japanese cabinet developed an official strategy—known as *Ketsugō*, the "decisive" operation—of inflicting casualties so horrific that Americans would lose the will to fight. The number of kamikaze missions multiplied. The Japanese mobilized all men from fifteen to sixty and all women from seventeen to forty into a civilian force prepared to swarm the American invaders. These citizens

LEFT: *Aerial view of "Ground Zero" of the world's first atomic bomb at the Los Alamos site July 16, 1945*
RIGHT: *Scientists in primitive radiation suits prior to inspecting the "Ground Zero" site.*

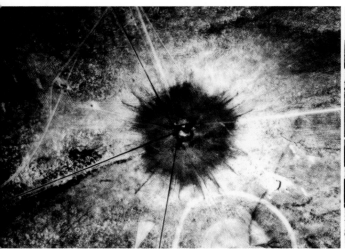

were instructed to kill American soldiers even at the cost of their own lives.

In the most recent American campaigns, at Iwo Jima and Okinawa, the Japanese had inflicted horrendous casualties on U.S. forces in some of the most ferocious fighting of the war. Everyone expected that the Japanese would fight even more ferociously to defend their home islands. Military projections of American casualties for amphibious campaigns against Japan ranged from 193,500, including 43,500 dead, to 1,202,000, with 314,600 dead.

Some scientists and government officials argued that a peaceful demonstration of the atomic bomb before its use on Japan would be enough to make Japan surrender. Others suggested that the Japanese should be given enough warning to allow them to evacuate the city before the bomb was dropped. General Groves and others argued that giving the Japanese advance warning of any kind would defeat the purpose of the bomb, which was to shock the Japanese into submission.

Shortly after he was informed that the first bomb test was successful, President Truman ordered a combat drop on a Japanese city as soon as the army was ready.

HIROSHIMA WAS THE SEVENTH-largest city in Japan and a major port for Japanese troops and supplies. Despite its importance to the imperial war effort, it was one of the few Japanese cities that had not been hit by American firebombs. Residents expected that to change. Tens of thousands had evacuated the city. The army had razed thousands of homes to create firebreaks, hoping to contain the fires caused by Gen. Curtis LeMay's B-29s.

Early on August 6, 1945, a single B-29 appeared over the city, triggering an air raid alert. Citizens took cover. Twenty minutes later, the plane disappeared and the air raid siren wailed again, signaling all clear.

When three more B-29s came into view, residents of Hiroshima watched more in curiosity than fear. Such a small number of planes could not signal a major attack. When parachutes opened beneath two of the planes, a group of soldiers on the outskirts of the city cheered, assuming the planes had been hit and the crew was bailing out. Little did they know that the parachutes carried scientific instruments to measure the blast of the bomb the *Enola Gay* was about to drop.

An atomic blast at an unidentified location. The first successful test of an atomic bomb at Alamogordo, New Mexico, unleashed a force equal to 21 kilotons of TNT and left a bomb crater almost 2,400 feet across.

AUGUST 6, 1945. BOMBER PILOT COL. PAUL TIBBETS, his copilot, Capt. Robert A. Lewis, and bombardier Maj. Thomas Ferebee sit in the pressurized cockpit of the B-29 Superfortress the *Enola Gay*. Their mission will change the world forever. Their destination? Hiroshima, Japan.

The B-29 is a state-of-the-art weapon of war: a strategic bomber designed to fly higher and farther than any plane before it. The greatest technological advance of all rests in the bay behind the flight crew—a four-ton atomic bomb code-named "Little Boy," powered by the most potent force on Earth. Little Boy carries a sphere of uranium the size of a grapefruit, enough to eliminate an entire city.

The bomb commander for the mission, Capt. William Sterling Parsons, climbs through the tunnel into the bomb bay, followed by his assistant, Lt. Morris Jeppson. Parsons knows more about the bomb than

Col. Paul W. Tibbets (center) with the ground crew of the B-29 Enola Gay

anyone else. He helped Oppenheimer design the bomb. He was one of the scientists who constructed it. Now he must arm it for destruction.

Parsons squats down in the cramped bay. Jeppson trains a flashlight over his commander's shoulder, lighting the back end of the bomb. Parsons has practiced this procedure hundreds of times in preparation for this moment. He unscrews the breach plug and removes it. "Unscrewing breach."

"Check."

Parsons picks up the powder charges. His hands and face begin to sweat. One wrong move and the mission will fail. "Inserting charges."

"Check."

Parsons reinserts the breach plug, screwing it back into place.

The bomb is armed. The mission is now in the hands of Colonel Tibbets.

As the *Enola Gay* nears Hiroshima, commanding officer Paul Tibbets is faced with a dangerous decision. The bomb's target is only half a mile wide. Flying into the wind will make the bomb drop more accurate—but it will also slow the plane down, making it harder to escape the blast.

ABOVE: *The* Enola Gay • RIGHT: *Atomic explosion on Hiroshima, Japan, August 6, 1945*

Tibbets chooses the mission's success over safety and heads the plane into the wind.

He switches on a tone broadcast to warn the two escort planes that the bomb drop is about to occur. In sixty seconds the tone ends, and the bomb bay doors open automatically. The bomb drops out.

Tibbets has just forty-five seconds to get away. He takes the plane into a steep dive, accelerating to escape the blast . . . and he and his crew escape.

The people of Hiroshima will not be so lucky.

Chapter 12: OBLIVION OR ETERNITY

Within forty-three seconds of the bomb's release, high explosives inside the bomb fire a uranium bullet into a uranium target at the other end of the bomb at a speed of one thousand feet per second. Together, bullet and target trigger a nuclear chain reaction. In two seconds, the bomb detonates nineteen hundred feet above Hiroshima, generating an explosion equivalent to 16 kilotons of TNT. The temperature at the center of the explosion is ten thousand times hotter than the surface of the sun. A pressure wave of forty-six hundred pounds per square foot ripples out from the blast center, flattening buildings as far as 1.25 miles away.

Hiroshima after the dropping of an atomic bomb, showing the devastation out about 0.4 miles

TENS OF THOUSANDS OF PEOPLE were killed in an instant. Everything directly beneath the bomb vaporized when it exploded, searing grim silhouettes of people who no longer existed into stone and pavement. Half a mile away from ground zero, people were reduced to small piles of smoking charcoal. Another tenth of a mile out, nine of every ten people who were outside when the bomb went off died.

Many who survived the initial blast died in the fires that followed. Near the hypocenter, the extreme temperatures of the explosion caused anything that could burn to ignite. Farther away, the

ABOVE: *Survivors of the explosion of the atom bomb at Hiroshima* • BELOW: *Commercial Exhibition Hall, Hiroshima, Japan, 1945*

BUSHIDO

The samurai class was officially disbanded in 1876, but the samurai code known as *Bushido,* the way of the warrior, played an important role in World War II.

At its simplest, the code boils down to two basic tenets: loyalty and honor. Loyalty demanded that a warrior be willing to kill—or be killed—on behalf of his master. Death was preferable to the dishonor of surrender.

In the "total war" culture of World War II, the tenets of Bushido shaped the actions of the Japanese people in ways that were incomprehensible to the West. From the Japanese perspective, prisoners of war had dishonored themselves by choosing surrender over death and deserved nothing but contempt. This attitude contributed to the brutal treatment of captives in Japanese camps. Kamikaze pilots crashed their explosive-laden planes directly into American ships, committing suicide at the order of their officers. Entire Japanese families, including children, threw themselves off cliffs or blew themselves up rather than suffer capture by American forces.

Japanese Zero, 1939

URANIUM

Born in a stellar explosion six billion years ago and embedded in Earth's crust, uranium lay dormant for millennia until scientists learned to split its atoms and unleash its apocalyptic power.

The nucleus of every atom is made up of positively charged particles called *protons*, and particles without a charge, called *neutrons*. Because like charges repel each other, the protons create a force that attempts to push them apart. If the ratio of protons to neutrons is not too high, other forces within the atom hold the protons together. When there are too many protons, they are not held firmly together and the nucleus becomes unstable, or radioactive.

Uranium is the heaviest naturally occurring element. With 92 protons in its nucleus, the uranium atom can barely hold itself together, making it the easiest atom to split. Once split, it sets off a chain reaction that can shatter a trillion trillion atoms in one second. The energy released by a kilogram of uranium through nuclear fission is about 2.5 million times the amount of energy released by burning one kilogram of coal.

Luckily, uranium isn't as common as coal—and it isn't dangerous until it has been processed down to one single form: U-235, which makes up about 0.7 percent of naturally occurring uranium.

Uranium is not found in a concentrated form. Many tons of ore have to be processed to obtain even one gram of the element. Once processed, uranium has to be further refined before it can be used to create a bomb.

Uranium occurs in three different forms: U-234, U-235, and U-238. Typically all three are mixed together in the ore from which uranium is extracted. Only when the ore has been processed to the point where it has a concentration of 20 percent of U-235 is it capable of generating a dangerous chain reaction.

Washington, D. C.

IMMEDIATE RELEASE

STATEMENT BY THE PRESIDENT
OF THE UNITED STATES

Sixteen hours ago an American airplane dropped one bomb on Hiroshima and destroyed its usefulness to the enemy. That bomb had more power than 20,000 tons of T.N.T. It had more than two thousand times the blast of the British "Grand Slam" which is the largest bomb ever yet used in the history of warfare. . . . With this bomb we have now added a new and revolutionary increase in destruction to supplement the growing power of our armed forces. . . . It is an atomic bomb. It is a harnessing of the basic power of the universe. The force from which the sun draws its power has been loosed against those who brought war to the Far East.

—Press release issued by President Harry S Truman

"We are carrying the world's first atomic bomb. When the bomb is dropped, Lieutenant Beser will record our reactions to what we see. This recording is being made for history. Watch your language and don't clutter up the intercom."
—Colonel Paul Tibbets's instructions to the crew of the *Enola Gay* shortly after takeoff

HOW "LITTLE BOY" WORKED

The development of the nuclear bomb began with the discovery by German scientists Otto Hahn and Fritz Strassman that bombarding the radioactive element uranium with neutrons split the nuclei of uranium atoms in two, creating two new elements. These elements, called *barium* and *krypton*, added up to less mass than the original uranium, raising the question, what happened to the rest of the mass?

Additional experiments proved that the missing mass was transformed into energy. The two fragments of a split element repel each other with one hundred million times more force than is released in a comparable chemical reaction. In addition, each fissioned atom releases several neutrons that can cause more atoms to fission, producing a chain reaction. Spontaneous fissions may occur in a small amount of purified U-235, but after a few fissions the process will stop. With a large enough piece of U-235—called a critical mass—the number of new fissions increases exponentially until the accumulated force blows the uranium apart and stops the reaction.

Little Boy's steel housing contained a tube with subcritical pieces of U-235 at either end. One piece looked like a rounded bullet; the other consisted of rings. High explosives fired the bullet at high speed down the tube and into the rings. Together, the U-235 reached critical mass, causing a chain reaction and, within a fraction of a second, producing the massive explosion that destroyed Hiroshima.

Replica of Little Boy, ca. 1945

Chapter 12: OBLIVION OR ETERNITY

HIROSHIMA TODAY

———

In the years following the bombing of Hiroshima, instead of simply rebuilding the city, the survivors turned the city into an exhibit for peace. The Hiroshima Peace Memorial Park and its Peace Memorial Museum, built on the open field created by the bomb, were designed not only as memorials to those who died but as monuments to peace itself.

The Peace Memorial Museum receives more than a million visitors each year, but physical monuments and museums are only a small part of Hiroshima's efforts to promote peace. Peace education is taught in every school. The city hosts summer programs for children and seminars and conferences for adults. And the mayor issues a formal protest every time a country tests a nuclear weapon.

Each year, on August 6, at 8:15 a.m., tens of thousands gather at Hiroshima Peace Memorial Park to make a declaration for peace. At dusk, they gather on the banks of the Motoyasu River, with paper lanterns bearing the names of the dead. Attendees light the candles inside the lanterns, then send the lanterns floating downriver to the Inland Sea.

shock waves spread kitchen fires and knocked down utility poles, causing live wires to snap and spark. Built largely of wood and paper, the city became an inferno as thousands of individual fires grew and merged.

The devastation caused by the explosion itself was only the beginning of the horror. The bomb dropped on Hiroshima continued to kill long after the war was over. The fireball had released radiation waves that spread far beyond the range predicted by Manhattan Project scientists, poisoning those who survived the blast. The radioactive fallout, known as the "ashes of death," destroyed its victims' ability to create new blood cells. In the decade after the war, thousands died each year from the long-term effects of radiation poisoning.

With the atomic bomb, we crossed a new threshold, creating a device more lethal than the

"Let all the souls here rest in peace; for we shall not repeat the evil."—Inscription on the Memorial Cenotaph, a monument for the atomic bomb victims, Hiroshima

plague and more destructive than TNT. The development of atomic bombs with the power to end the human species and destroy the planet has had profound implications for mankind, sparking intense fear and debate about the ethics of their use.

Floating lanterns on the Motoyasugawa River during the Peace Memorial Ceremony in Hiroshima, Japan, and the Atomic Bomb Dome, an exhibition hall built in 1915 and one of the few buildings to survive the blast.

DAWSON

CHAMPAGNE

EP IN THE HEART OF TEXAS 3600 MI.

WR-821

BORN IN A REMOTE CORNER OF Africa, humans have spent millennia battling Earth's geography. Two of our most basic instincts—the drive to explore and the need to communicate—have led us to build roads across the most inhospitable places on Earth: the silk roads across Central Asia, the invisible routes of the Saharan salt trade, the high mountain roads of Incan Peru. Thousands of miles of road linked the imperial centers of Persia, China, India and Rome to their frontiers.

The Alaskan Highway, like many earlier roads, demonstrates mankind's ability to overcome obstacles with an engineering marvel. The highway was created in the wake of Pearl Harbor. Americans feared that the Japanese would continue across the Pacific and attack the West Coast. Alaska, not yet a state and isolated from the American mainland, seemed particularly vulnerable to Japanese attack. The Aleutian Islands were only 750 miles from the nearest Japanese military base. Alaska's military resources were scant: only twenty thousand troops stationed across the enormous territory, twelve bombers, and twenty fighter planes. The officer in charge of the Alaska Defense Command made the point sharply in a telegram to Washington: "If the Japanese come here, I can't defend Alaska. I don't have the resources."

American strategists had considered the possibility of a road through Canada to Alaska on and off since 1865, but no one had taken the necessary action. With the memory of Pearl Harbor fresh in everyone's minds, President Roosevelt pushed the project through.

The task fell to Gen. William M. Hoge, expert engineer and decorated war hero. His orders were deceptively simple. Build fourteen hundred miles of highway from Dawson Creek, British Columbia, to Delta Junction in Alaska.

Historically, roads are built over existing paths. The Alaskan Highway was created where no natural road had evolved, cut across a heavily wooded, often swampy wilderness. Because of the difficult terrain, the plan was that the army would build a rough road through the wilderness in 1942 to open the way for trucks. Civilian contractors would come behind them the following year to create a permanent highway.

In late spring of 1942, the army dispatched 10,670 American troops to Alaska to build an engineering marvel: a road carved out of the wilderness to provide a military supply line to bring troops, food, and supplies to strategic points in the Alaskan high-country. Men pulled from all walks of life

The Alaskan Highway was created where no natural road had evolved. . . . Their biggest obstacle was time.

were put behind the wheels of bulldozers and supply trucks with little or no training and told to clear their way through a frozen wasteland.

Their biggest obstacle was time. The work crews needed to complete the highway in eight months, before the deadly Alaskan winter made construction impossible. Construction began simultaneously in three locations, with crews building separate sections of the road hundreds of miles apart. Seven regiments worked on the highway, three of them African-American. At first the African-American regiments were given menial jobs supporting the white regiments. It soon became clear that if the road were going to be finished on time, every soldier would have to work

The population of Dawson Creek, British Columbia, where the Alaska Highway began, tripled overnight with the arrival of one regiment of army engineers.

Chapter 12: OBLIVION OR ETERNITY

A pile driver pounding bridge supports into the riverbed, completing another link in the Alaskan highway, 1942.

on construction. For the first time, black and white regiments performed identical tasks, though not with identical equipment. Black regiments were provided with fewer bulldozers and more wheelbarrows and shovels than their white counterparts.

The Army Corps of Engineers knew how to build infrastructure quickly under wartime conditions, but they didn't know how to build in Alaska's subarctic environment. Transportation to all three construction locations was difficult. Supplies, workers, and machinery were often stuck in transit—some of them for the duration of the project. The army often parachuted emergency supplies to their troops. Equipment breakdowns occurred hourly. Engineers

waded chest-deep in freezing lakes to build bridge trestles. They battled with mosquitoes, mud, and the moss-laden arctic bog land known as muskeg. Frostbite was a permanent enemy.

The northernmost construction teams encountered special problems with permafrost, which thawed when bulldozers exposed it to sunlight, creating a deadly layer of muddy quicksand under seemingly stable roadbed. This brought the project to a halt for six weeks—time Hoge and his team couldn't afford to lose.

That's when Hoge borrowed an idea from America's past: George Washington had built log roads through the wilderness. Why couldn't his men?

Engineers became lumberjacks, cutting trees down by hand to create a roadbed paved with logs. The technique, called *corduroying,* had been used as early as the Roman Empire and as late as the American Civil War. Hoge employed it on a new, epic scale. The wooden road insulated the ground, keeping it frozen; but constructing it was slow. Progress on the road slowed from fourteen miles a day to just one. With the arctic winter approaching fast, Hoge and his crews were running out of time.

At the beginning of October, temperatures dropped sharply. One of the coldest Alaskan winters on record had arrived, with temperatures approaching minus fifty degrees Fahrenheit. It was cold enough to kill a man in minutes. Metal machines froze and cracked. Men cut holes in their sleeping bags to turn them into coats. With only 166 miles left to go, two regiments—one white, one black—struggled to finish the road before conditions worsened from horrific to impossible.

In less than eight months, working through extreme weather with inadequate training and supplies, Hoge's men laid fourteen hundred miles of rough highway through the wilderness. A year later, civilian contractors followed to upgrade the surface to a true highway. Although it was never used for military traffic, the Alaskan Highway helped unite a nation and connect a continent. Now part of the world's longest drivable route, stretching three thousand miles from Alaska to Argentina, the Alaskan Highway led to a demand for more roads. Today's network of roads, built across all terrains, is long enough to travel to the moon and back twenty times.

Corporal Refines Sims Jr. was one of the 10,670 troops the army sent to Alaska in spring of 1942. The Philadelphia native was a member of the Ninety-seventh Engineer Regiment, an African-American unit assigned to build the northern section of the new Alaskan-Canadian highway. Like many members of his unit, he enlisted in the army straight from college, eager to help defend his country. He had no experience with construction, road building—or the arctic climate of northern Alaska.

But Sims would make history for more than helping to build an intercontinental highway.

> Lord, it was bitter cold. Your breath would turn to ice inside your blankets at night. If you touched anything metal with your bare hands, you could tear your skin loose. We'd have to keep fires burning underneath our trucks all night, or they wouldn't move in the morning.
> —Sergeant Clifton Monk, Ninety-seventh Engineers

OCTOBER 25, 1942. PRIVATE SIMS IS DRIVING through the forest on a newly constructed stretch of log-lined road. Around him, other members of the Ninety-seventh Regiment are clearing debris. Suddenly, he hears a thundering sound from inside the forest. Trees topple toward him. He frantically slams his bulldozer into reverse. The other men stop and unconsciously take a few steps closer together, preparing to defend themselves from whatever new menace the wilderness is about to throw at them.

Seemingly from nowhere, a second bulldozer breaks through the underbrush, driven by Private Alfred Jalufka, of the Eighteenth Engineers. His face is bloodied with scrapes from the undergrowth. The two ends of the road have met. Sims, a black soldier from Philadelphia, and Jalufka, a white soldier from Texas, jump from their bulldozers, shake hands, and embrace. One of their fellow soldiers takes a photograph of the embrace, and it sweeps across America—a picture that records not only mankind's triumph over the wilderness, but the possibility of triumphing over our own prejudices.

Within five years, the United States Army will be integrated for the first time.

Integration of the country as a whole will not come so easily. African-Americans fought bravely during World War II in what became known as a campaign for "Double Victory"; they aimed to defeat fascism abroad and defeat racism and segregation on the homefront. Many African-American soldiers returned from duty only to find that inequality and racism persisted. They translated their disappointment into action, and by the middle of the twentieth century, the civil rights movement was in full swing. The seeds of this movement were planted as far back as the nineteenth century, but the struggle to achieve equality and full citizenship rights for African-Americans gained powerful momentum in the 1950s and 1960s.

Corporal Sims (left) and Private Jalufka (right) helped hold the ceremonial ribbon when the Alaskan Highway was dedicated in November, 1942.

Chapter 12: OBLIVION OR ETERNITY

MARCH 7, 1965. SELMA, ALABAMA. SIX HUNDRED African-Americans march two by two through the otherwise empty city streets. Their destination is the state capital in Montgomery, fifty-four miles away. Their goal is an end to segregation.

The crowd is quiet and orderly. They don't sing or clap. No one even talks. The only sound is the scuffle of their feet on the pavement. One of the marchers is fifty-four-year-old home economics teacher Amelia Boynton. For two years now, Boynton has volunteered at the county courthouse as a "voucher," helping other African-Americans complete their voter registration forms. Despite Boynton's efforts, in two years the number of African-Americans registered to vote has only increased from 150 to 335. Frustrated by the lack of progress, Boynton is ready to make a bigger, more visible gesture.

The protestors march across the Alabama River over the Edmund Pettus Bridge. When they reach the crest of the bridge, they stop.

On the other side of the river, a wall of blue-shirted state troopers stretches across the road, blocking their path. The officers are aided by a posse of khaki-clad county deputies commanded by Sheriff Jim Clark, a racist bully with a history of physical abuse toward civil rights activists. At six foot two and 220 pounds, Clark is an imposing figure, made larger by the menace of the billy club dangling from his belt. White spectators waving Confederate flags stand beside the road, as if gathered to watch a parade.

The marchers freeze.

Chapter 12: OBLIVION OR ETERNITY

Troopers and posse pull on their gas masks and take out their night-sticks. A trooper calls through a bullhorn. "This is an illegal march. You have two minutes to turn around."

No one moves.

The trooper with the bullhorn gives the order. "Charge."

At first the state troopers hold their clubs at both ends and use them to shove the marchers back. Soon they begin beating the crowd with their nightsticks. Some marchers back away from the police attack. Others try to hold their ground. Tear gas canisters hit the bridge, emitting thick clouds of gas. Eyes and throats burning, the marchers scatter across the bridge. Then the mounted troopers charge.

The troopers are dangerously out of control. The crowd is confused and panicked. People run, screaming. Some fall.

Amelia Boynton freezes in the middle of the crowd, stunned by the sudden violence and confused by the gas and the noise. A trooper hits her on the back of the head. She half turns. He hits her again on the back of the neck. She falls forward under the feet of the crowd. The troopers move on, leaving Boynton for dead. She will remain unconscious for two days.

ACROSS THE AGES, COMMUNICATION breakthroughs, from Gutenberg's printing press to Marconi's wireless, have allowed us to communicate more quickly with more people. Every new technology has allowed changes in society. Reporters in the Crimean War telegraphed stories home about inadequate facilities for treating wounded soldiers, leading to the creation of modern nursing. John and Alice Harris used the new medium photography to expose abuses that were taking place in the Congo to a horrified world. And in 1965, television would broadcast the message of the civil rights movement across the planet.

In 1965, racial segregation still reigned supreme in the American South. The Civil Rights Act of 1964, which outlawed segregation in schools, workplaces, and public facilities, had little effect in

The Selma march marked a turning point in the American civil rights movement—and for social change worldwide.

towns like Selma, Alabama. Blacks and whites were still segregated in restaurants, buses, and movies theaters. Worse, though the 1964 law dealt with segregation, it did not guarantee the right to vote. Black activists, like female suffragettes before them, knew that people without the vote had no power to make changes.

Selma, Alabama, was the perfect place to stage a voting rights campaign. More than half of its population of roughly thirty thousand was African-American; 99 percent of its registered voters were white.

The registration process was intentionally difficult. The courthouse only accepted applications two days a month. Black applications were subjected to unfairly administered literacy tests and unreasonable poll taxes. Applications were denied for the smallest errors. Those who tried to register faced intimidation and scare tactics from Sheriff Jim Clark and his deputies. Despite the difficulties, month after month, year after year, people tried to register and were turned down.

Frustrated by their lack of progress, Boynton and other local activists asked for help from Dr. Martin Luther King Jr. and the Southern Christian Leadership Conference.

King's Selma campaign began on January 2, 1965. For weeks, peaceful demonstrators marched to the Selma County courthouse to register, only to be met with violence and arrest at the hands of Sheriff Clark and his men.

Things come to a head on February 25, when twenty-seven-year-old protestor Jimmie Lee Jackson died after being shot twice in the stomach by a state trooper. Preaching the following Sunday, Rev. James Bevel stormed that he would like to take Jackson's body to Montgomery and lay it on the steps of the state capitol for Governor George Wallace to see.

The idea of a march on Montgomery took hold. At Jackson's funeral, Dr. King announced that a march from Selma to Montgomery would take place four days later.

Governor Wallace denounced the march as a threat to public safety and ordered the state police to put a stop to it. In Selma, Sheriff Clark called for all white males over the age of twenty-one to be deputized. The march ended less than a mile from where it started, stopped by a violent attack by state troopers and county police.

Amelia Boynton wanted to be heard. She accomplished her goal. News cameraman Laurens Pierce captured the trooper's attack on her. That night ABC News interrupted the network's Sunday night movie, *Judgment at Nuremberg,* to screen

THE GENEALOGY OF NONVIOLENT NONCOOPERATION

Dr. Martin Luther King Jr. made masterful use of the tactic of nonviolent noncooperation, but he didn't invent it. Here's how he fits on the nonviolence family tree.

In 1846, American writer Henry David Thoreau refused to pay his poll tax, even though he knew he would be sent to jail. His refusal was an act of civil disobedience intended to demonstrate his disapproval of slavery and America's war with Mexico. He explained his action in his essay *Civil Disobedience*, written three years later: "Under a government that imprisons unjustly, the true place for a just man is in prison."

In 1907, a friend sent Mohandas Gandhi a copy of Thoreau's *Civil Disobedience* at the time when Gandhi was formulating his first civil disobedience campaign in South Africa. Gandhi called his technique of nonviolent noncooperation *satyagraha*, a Sanskrit term meaning "the force of truth." Thoreau's book gave Gandhi an English name for the technique that made sense.

Dr. King gave Gandhi full credit for influencing his ideas about nonviolence, claiming, "From my background I gained my regulating Christian ideals. From Gandhi I learned my operational technique." While still a young theology

student in the early 1950s, King became fascinated by Gandhi. The more he read about Gandhi's use of passive resistance in his campaign for Indian independence, the more convinced he became that Gandhi's philosophy of nonviolence was "the only logical approach to the solution of the race problem in the United States." King applied Gandhi's tactics for the first time in the Montgomery bus boycott in 1955.

Nelson Mandela also acknowledged Gandhi's influence on the nonviolent political tactics used by the African National Congress prior to 1962.

LEFT: *Mohandas Gandhi visits textile workers in Lancashire, England* • RIGHT: *Martin Luther King Jr.*

fifteen minutes of raw footage of what quickly became known as "Bloody Sunday." Forty-eight million viewers, including President Lyndon B. Johnson, watched in disbelief and horror as scenes of police violence in Selma replaced those of Nazi violence in Germany.

Selma's "Bloody Sunday" was a turning point in the civil rights movement. Within days, President Johnson introduced the bill that would become the Voting Rights Act, outlawing discriminatory voting practices.

Two weeks later, Dr. Martin Luther King Jr. led a second march from Selma to Montgomery, this time sanctioned by a federal judge and protected by federal troops. At the end of the march, King spoke to a crowd of twenty-five thousand from the steps of the state capitol. "We are on the move now, and no wave of racism can stop us!"

THE SELMA MARCH MARKED a turning point in the American civil rights movement—and for social change worldwide. The civil rights movement was not the first popular campaign for individual freedoms. But it was the first such campaign to be exposed to public scrutiny through real-time media coverage. The same dynamic of protest, repression, and public outrage has played out again and again in our time—in South Africa, in Tiananmen Square, and most recently, in the Arab Spring. Individual rights are fragile; free speech and media for the masses help protect them.

CHRISTIAAN BARNARD AND HIS eighteen-member team completed the first successful human heart transplant in 1967: five hours of delicate surgery that built on six decades of research by scientists around the world. Although Louis Washkansky succumbed to pneumonia eighteen days later, his heart beat steadily to the end.

Since Barnard's breakthrough operation, heart transplant surgery has extended more than one hundred thousand lives around the world. Today, more than twenty-five hundred heart transplants are carried out each year in America alone.

Eclipsing anything that had come before, Barnard's achievement opened the door to new surgical techniques. For the first time, doctors saw the body as a collection of parts that can be interchanged and improved. Doctors can now repair damaged organs, reconstruct mangled bodies, and transplant many different organs, from hearts and livers to skin grafts and corneas. Scientists are working on growing new organs and building artificial ones. They have created artificial skin from spider silk, used pig proteins to regrow human skeletal muscles, and implanted electrodes to stimulate the neural networks in paraplegics.

Dr. Christiaan Barnard, 1967

THE FIRST HUMAN HEART TRANSPLANT

DECEMBER 3, 1967. GROOTE SCHUUR HOSPITAL. Cape Town, South Africa. Louis Washkansky, fifty-three-year-old former athlete and amateur boxer, is wheeled toward the operating theater. He has already suffered three massive heart attacks, and his heart is failing fast. He has waited three weeks for a suitable donor heart, becoming weaker by the day.

Dr. Christiaan Barnard scrubs his arms and hands in preparation for surgery. He is relatively unknown, but he is already a pioneer in cardiac surgery. Barnard has performed heart transplants on more than fifty dogs, but he has never performed the operation on a human being. No one has.

The operation is a massive gamble. The odds that Washkansky will survive the operation are completely unknown. Without it, he will live only a few weeks.

Washkansky is still awake when Barnard walks into the operating theater. "Where you been? I kept telling them I didn't want any Mickey Finns until you came to say good-bye."

"Good-bye?"

"Aren't you giving me a new heart?"

"Yes."

"So it's out with the old and in with the new."

The team gives Washkansky oxygen. His eyes remain fixed on Barnard. Suddenly he motions that he wants to say something. Barnard leans over so he can hear.

"Did you tell my wife it's in the bag?"

The surgeon nods and smiles. "I told her."

Washkansky nods back. He blinks his thanks. Slowly, his eyes close.

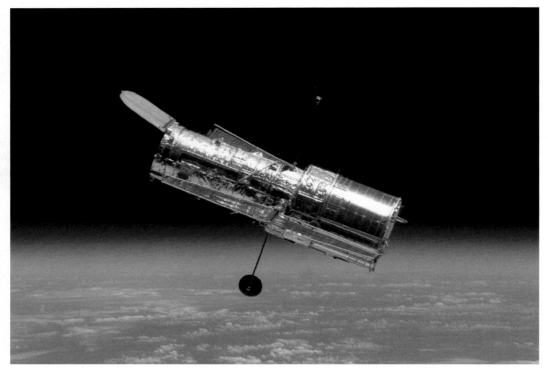

The Hubble Space Telescope works on the same principle as the first reflecting telescope, built in the seventeenth century by Sir Isaac Newton.

Today's medical miracles are poised to go beyond pioneering surgical techniques. Scientists have begun to understand the building blocks of life itself. In 2001, scientists assembled the first complete map of the human genome—the three billion base pairs of DNA that tell our bodies how to be a human. Our new ability to read and manipulate not only our own genetic code but that of disease-causing organisms is allowing medical science to re-invent itself. Researchers are taking the first steps toward fighting disease at the genetic level, with the potential for new solutions to old problems. Some believe that with greater understanding of DNA we will be able to shape the future evolution of our species.

HUMANS HAVE ALWAYS BEEN travelers and explorers, venturing over the next horizon in search of resources, knowledge, and adventure. Today we still explore the depths of the ocean, the frigid wastes of the Arctic, and the challenging peaks of mountains.

In the middle of the twentieth century, humans ventured for the first time beyond the boundaries of the earth's atmosphere, beginning with the Russian launch of the Sputnik satellites in 1957. For thirty years, space programs concentrated on exploring our own solar system. That changed with the development of the Hubble Space Telescope.

In April 1990, the space shuttle *Discovery* launched the Hubble Space Telescope into orbit

370 miles above the earth, free from the distortions of Earth's atmosphere. Astronomers expected that the telescope would be able to see the far corners of the universe and provide the answers to big questions: How old is the universe? How big is the universe? Do black holes really exist?

Astronomers were quickly disappointed. Two months after Hubble was launched, it was obvious that the telescope was in trouble. The mirror at the heart of the telescope was faulty. The solar panels and gyroscopes were failing. It took two years for NASA to design a solution.

On December 2, 1993, the space shuttle *Endeavor* took off, carrying the seven astronauts who repaired the telescope in a series of complicated and dangerous space walks. Once the crew returned to earth, astronomers held their breath, waiting to see the first images from the repaired telescope. They came through just after midnight on December 18, 1993. Repairs to the telescope succeeded beyond anyone's expectations.

In the years since 1993, Hubble has changed the way we look at the universe. In our own galaxy, it has furnished us pictures of the weather on Mars, shown us new moons around Saturn and, given us front row seats when a comet slammed into Jupiter. It has shown us stars being born and dying in distant galaxies, matter rotating around the edge of a

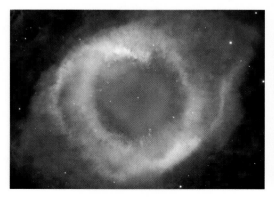

EDWIN POWELL HUBBLE

The Hubble Space Telescope is named after American astronomer Edwin Powell Hubble. Before Hubble's pioneering work at the Mount Wilson Observatory in Pasadena, California, in the 1920s, astronomers believed that our galaxy, the Milky Way, was the only one in the universe. Hubble proved that there is more than one galaxy in the universe. He also discovered that galaxies are moving away from each other. Hubble's Law, which provides the foundation for the Big Bang theory, suggests that everything in the universe is expanding outward from an initial explosion.

Thanks to Hubble's work, we know that the universe contains hundreds of billions of galaxies, each filled with hundreds of millions of stars.

LEFT: *Helix Nebula* • BELOW: *Edwin P. Hubble*

Chapter 12: OBLIVION OR ETERNITY

Astronaut Steve Smith repairing the Hubble Space Telescope, 1997

A barred spiral galaxy has a bar shape in the center, which is possibly a "stellar nursery." Recent studies suggest that the bar shape is a sign that the galaxy is nearing full maturity

suspected black hole, and the first proof that other solar systems may exist. Hubble has revealed that a single dot of light in the night sky is the light from ten thousand galaxies. The telescope has given us new questions to replace the old ones, including those surrounding the existence of a mysterious force, "dark energy," that appears to counteract the gravitational pull of the equally mysterious "dark matter." Most amazing of all, Hubble looks back in time, capturing light that began its journey towards earth billions of years ago, from a star that was formed in the earliest days of the universe and is still moving out and away through time and space.

Looked at together, the scientific studies done using the Hubble telescope help us understand that our planet is a rare gift, the result of thousands of Goldilocks moments needed to create a planet that would support life.

The Hubble Space Telescope is expected to come to the end of its useful life around 2020. Another great telescope is in the planning stages, with a project launch in 2018. The James Webb Space Telescope, named after a former NASA director, is designed to see farther into space than Hubble—so far that scientists will be able to look back in time to study the first light in the universe—the Big Bang itself.

An artist's rendition of NASA's Mars Science Laboratory Curiosity *rover*

MEDICAL MIRACLES AND SPACE exploration were both made possible by another technological revolution—the rise of the computer. The first fully electronic computer was built in 1946 at the University of Pennsylvania. Known as the Electronic Numerical Integrator and Computer (ENIAC) the computer operated on vacuum tubes, filled a large room, and required a full-time team of engineers to keep it running. Only fifty years later, several hundred million people had access to the Internet through personal computers, and more computing power than the operators of ENIAC could imagine. Today computers, cell phones, and satellite navigation systems connect people in a way we have never been connected before.

ONE HUNDRED FIFTY THOUSAND years ago, the first true humans stood on their own two feet in Africa's Rift Valley. Since then, our journey has been nothing less than incredible. From a small area in Africa, we have spread across the planet, making our homes everywhere from the tundra of Siberia to the Sahara desert. Always changing, always adapting, we have developed new technologies at each stage of history: crossbow to cannon, cuneiform to movable type, and sailing ship to jumbo jet. We have continuously sought to improve and innovate. We have reengineered landscapes, rerouting rivers and moving mountains. We have built pyramids, castles, cities, and skyscrapers and connected the world in a web of roads, highways, shipping lanes, flight paths, and fiber-optic cables. We are even on the verge of being able to reengineer ourselves.

For 150,000 years, humans have adapted, improvised, and invented. Today we stand poised to explore both the far reaches of space and the most basic building blocks of life. We now have the power to transform our planet and ourselves in ways that our ancestors would never have imagined possible.

We are exploring new sources of energy, the shape of the human mind, and the possibility of life in space. At the same time, our future depends on the outcomes of millions of tiny uncertainties coming together in ways that we cannot predict to create the Goldilocks moments of the future.

WHAT HAPPENS NEXT IN THE

IT'S ALL

STORY OF THE HUMAN RACE?

UP TO US.

ACKNOWLEDGMENTS

NO BOOK IS WRITTEN IN A VACUUM, AND THIS ONE IS NO EXCEPTION.
I owe a debt of gratitude to many people involved in the project, both officially and unofficially. First, to Kate Winn, SVP Consumer Products at A+E Networks, Kim Gilmore, Senior Historian & Director, Corporate Outreach, and David Wilk, Publishing Consultant to HISTORY, who believed in my work. To my editor, Geoff Stone of Running Press, who kept all the balls in the air. To designers Bill Jones and Frances Soo Ping Chow at Running Press and Paul Kepple and Ralph Geroni at Headcase Design for creating such a beautiful book. To photo researcher Susan Oyama for her tireless research. To Chris Navratil and Craig Herman for their publishing vision. To my agent, Jason Ashlock, who provided a voice of sanity whenever one was needed. To my friend, historian Karin Wetmore, who generously shared her knowledge about the history of science. And most of all to my husband, Sandy Wilson, who read many drafts, demanded explanations, cheered me on, dragged me away from my desk—and was always happy to pick up a pizza when the deadline was tight.

—Pamela D. Toler

TO TACKLE A PROJECT OF THIS SCOPE IS CERTAINLY BOLD, AND BY ITS
very nature there are bound to be omissions and oversights. However, we would be remiss not to thank some of the key players involved in HISTORY's documentary series *Mankind The Story of All of Us*, without whom this book would not be possible. First to our series consultant Ian Morris, Professor of Classics and History at Stanford University, whose works inspire us and thoughtful feedback kept us on track. And to those listed below from Nutopia, the production company who brought this vision to life, and to those at HISTORY for their ambitious programming that continues to highlight and celebrate our collective history.

—Julian P. Hobbs
Executive Producer, *Mankind The Story of All of Us*, HISTORY

NUTOPIA
Jane Root and Ben Goold, Executive Producers
Tim Lambert, Series Producer
Helen Docherty, Assistant Producer

HISTORY®
Nancy Dubuc, President and General Manager, HISTORY and Lifetime®
Dirk Hoogstra, Senior Vice President, Development and Programming, HISTORY
Paul Cabana, Executive Producer, *Mankind The Story of All of Us*, HISTORY
Ian Luce, Director of Photography, A+E Networks
Brandy Crawford, Programming Coordinator, HISTORY